**Delirious Naples**

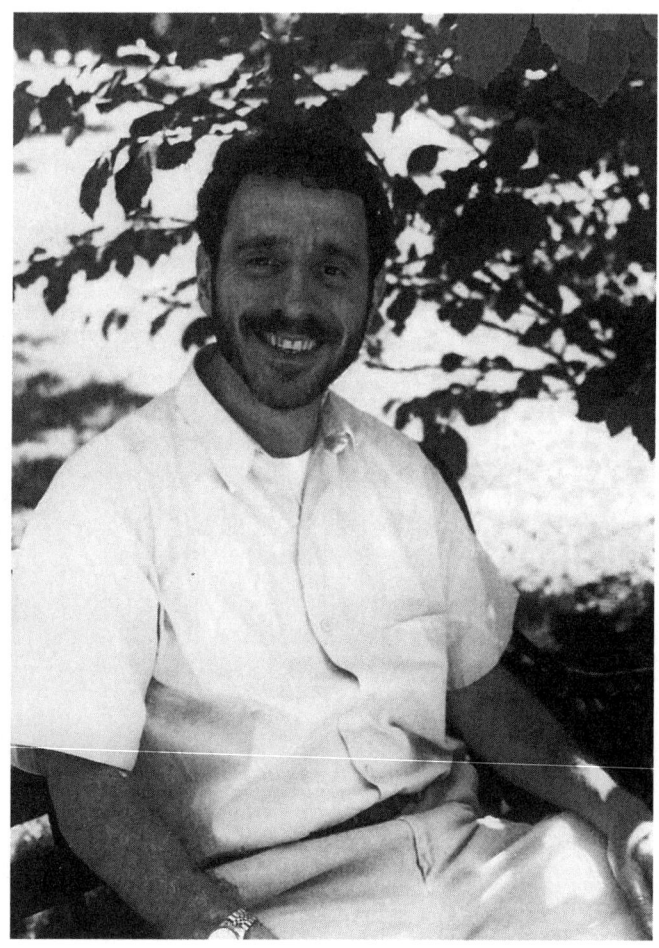

In memoriam, Thomas V. Belmonte (1946–95), author of *The Broken Fountain*. (Christina Belmonte Wexler)

# Delirious Naples

**A Cultural History of the City of the Sun**

*Pellegrino D'Acierno and*
*Stanislao G. Pugliese, Editors*

FORDHAM UNIVERSITY PRESS
NEW YORK 2019

Copyright © 2019 Fordham University Press

All rights reserved. No part of this publication may be reproduced, stored in a retrieval system, or transmitted in any form or by any means—electronic, mechanical, photocopy, recording, or any other—except for brief quotations in printed reviews, without the prior permission of the publisher.

Fordham University Press has no responsibility for the persistence or accuracy of URLs for external or third-party Internet websites referred to in this publication and does not guarantee that any content on such websites is, or will remain, accurate or appropriate.

Fordham University Press also publishes its books in a variety of electronic formats. Some content that appears in print may not be available in electronic books.

Visit us online at www.fordhampress.com.

Library of Congress Control Number: 2018942661

Printed in the United States of America

21  20  19  5  4  3  2  1

First edition

CONTENTS

*Foreword.* Returning to *The Broken Fountain:*
*Omaggio a* Thomas Belmonte
Theresa Aiello                                                                                  ix

*Preface.* The Irresolvable Paradox: Essaying Naples
Pellegrino D'Acierno and Stanislao G. Pugliese                  xiii

Introduction: Naples as Chaosmos or, The City
That Makes You Repeat Its Discourse
Pellegrino D'Acierno                                                                    1

## Learning from Contemporary Naples/Writing as a Neapolitan

1. Napòlide: A Man without Naples
   Erri De Luca                                                                               35
2. Scuorno (Vergogna)
   Francesco Durante                                                                  54

## The View from America

3. *Naples/New York:* Across the Watery Divide
   B. Amore                                                                                   71
4. Auratic Detritus/Sublime Trash: "Rough Magic";
   or, The Art of Transfiguration in B. Amore's *Naples/
   New York* Installation
   Pellegrino D'Acierno                                                                77

5. One Early Twenty-First Century Summer in Naples
   *John Domini*                                                                97

6. Investigating Gilda Mignonette as a "Newpolitan" Approach
   to Popular Culture
   *Simona Frasca*                                                             120

7. Go Make Naples: New Perspectives from Italian
   American Artists
   *Fred Gardaphé*                                                             133

8. You Want to Be Americano?
   *Robert Zweig*                                                              141

## History, Memory, and Mercy

9. Words in Journey: Echoes from Pompeii
   *Angelo Cannavacciuolo*                                                     151

10. One of These Days
    *Ilaria Marchesi and Simone Marchesi*                                      157

11. Mediterranean Crossroads: Naples as a Model
    of Southcentric Cosmopolitanism
    *Patrizia La Trecchia*                                                     172

12. The Delirium of the Neapolitan Baroque
    *J. Nicholas Napoli*                                                       190

13. The Sansevero Chapel: A Case Study
    of the Neapolitan Enlightenment
    *Salvatore Napolitano*                                                     204

14. Caravaggio's Mercy in Naples
    *Terence Ward*                                                             224

## Malanapoli: From the Lazaronitum to Gomorrah/Camorra

15. The Contact Zone: Where Organized Crime
    and Everyday Life Meet
    *Jason Pine*                                                               243

| 16. | *Gomorrah*: The Rest of the Story<br>*Valerio Caprara* | 269 |

## Writing and Singing Naples

| 17. | Anna Maria Ortese: Breaking the Spell of Naples?<br>*Andrea Baldi* | 283 |
| 18. | Filumena Marturano: Eduardo De Filippo's Beloved Whore<br>*Rose De Angelis* | 301 |
| 19. | Matilde Serao's Art of Numbers: Naples and the Game of Lotto<br>*Gabriella Romani* | 322 |
| 20. | Opera and the Classical Tradition in Naples<br>*Joseph Rescigno* | 339 |
| 21. | Poetry<br>*Charles Sant'Elia* | 347 |
| 22. | Evoking Naples in a Story and a Story about Stories<br>*Gioia Timpanelli* | 351 |

## Omaggi, or Parole d'Ammore

| 23. | Tributes to Shirley Hazzard<br>*Joseph Connors and Jonathan Galassi* | 367 |
| 24. | A Tribute to John Turturro's *Passione*<br>*Stanislao G. Pugliese* | 370 |
| 25. | A Celluloid Tribute to Thomas Belmonte<br>*Pellegrino D'Acierno* | 376 |
|  | *Acknowledgments* | *381* |
|  | *List of Contributors* | *385* |
|  | *Color photographs follow pages 114 and 274* | |

FOREWORD

Returning to *The Broken Fountain*:
*Omaggio a* Thomas Belmonte

*Theresa Aiello*

*Thomas Vito Belmonte (1946–95) was professor of anthropology at Hofstra University and the author of* The Broken Fountain *(New York: Columbia University Press, 1979/2005).*

In 1995, after Tom's death, I had the privilege of traveling to Naples with Tom's daughter, Christina, to the quarter and site of the "Broken Fountain" in Naples. All these years later, I find myself still thinking of that visit and of a twenty-four-year-old Tom at the beginning of his fieldwork in anthropology.

I first met Tom in 1991. I had just moved to the West Village and met him at a very volatile first meeting at my home, of the Italian American Writers Group, a group that has since grown and evolved and continues to this day. The meeting took place after the death of Yusef Hawkins and the Italianists had come together to deconstruct this hideous episode in Italian American history. Tom and I formed a bond then and became friends and, later on, lovers in the four years that I had to know him.

Before I met Tom I had already heard of him as the author of an extraordinary book, one that has become a classic in cultural studies in anthropology to this day. People seemed to discuss Tom in whispers with awe and even reverence; this from academics and writers who give praise grudgingly. Finally meeting him, I was struck by his face, striking in chiaroscuro. After his death, at his memorial at Columbia University, I described how his face easily reminded of one of the Byzantine mystery portraits found at Fayum.

The extraordinary quality of his book *The Broken Fountain* lay in his ability, rare in academia, to turn the sometimes arid quality of research into literature, a gift I used to beg him for. His opening chapter, "Paean to the City," had the beauty and magic of entering a great and romantic realm characterized by the carnival of Bakhtin, and written by a great stylist. After its first publication, *The Broken Fountain* was subsequently saluted by no less than Anatole Broyard, Ashley Montagu, and Herbert Gans. I have a memory of reading the review of his work in the *New York Times Book Review* years before I actually was to meet him.

When Christina Belmonte and I went to Naples I think we were both conscious of a very young anthropologist at the beginning of a journey, both scholarly and very much *in vivo*; a dancer within the dance that he set out to study. We were fortunate in being able to meet his Neapolitan friends, in particular Tom's former roomate, Pietro Radice, and one who became our guide and mentor in all things Neapolitan, his close friend Dr. Pasquale Matera. On that first night in Naples, Pasquale showed us Tom's favorite places in the old city. Tom wrote about walking along the bay and it was to this area that Tom returned first on subsequent trips to Naples. When in residence he went there daily to look out over the waters toward America, where his daughter Christina lived. It was there that Christina decided to release his ashes. Chris was also committed to telling his friends in person about his death. Some of them remembered her with great affection as a child, from previous visits. I suspect we both felt a sense of closure by returning to his beloved world.

We were able to enter the courtyard of the broken fountain only with the help of several of Tom's Neapolitan friend, who in turn, contacted the cast of players described in *The Broken Fountain*. Christina was greeted by Gennaro, the head of the family described in the book and by another figure known to the neighbors as "professore" (because he knew everything that was going on). Tom might be pleased to know that Gennaro now has work and owns a lemonade stand. One of Gennaro's sons was, sadly, in prison. We showed them Tom's *New York Times* obituary and Pasquale explained to them that this was the most important newspaper in America. As they read and wept and looked at his photograph, I think they recognized more of the significance of that "young stranger" who once lived among them. We entered a dark, narrow vicoletto into the courtyard, which is guarded by a shrine of one of the Black Madonnas of southern Italy. The fountain was still broken. We saw the steps leading to Tom's first apartment, where "Pepe the Top," so-called by Tom, came in through the windows to observe him writing and where "Leah" threw open her shutters at noon to call down to the *scugnizzi* for a caffè. I think Tom had to be conscious of carnivalic Naples. He was himself attracted to the mythology of "The Trickster" and had written about this figure who appears in so many cultures. He was identified with the archetype of the trickster. I often greeted him by calling him "Shapeshifter" because he was something of a changeling child himself. (He loved Ovid's tale of Vertumnus, another shape shifter, and Pomona.) Afterward we went to a café in Pozzuoli and Pasquale told us that Tom and his friends often would go from café to restaurant to café for most of the night. One favorite haunt was a bar where sailors and young women went. Wherever he was, Tom always gravitated to the jukebox. His favorite songs were "Take Me Home, Country Roads" and, of course, "Light My Fire," that national anthem of the 1970s. Chris and I had the pleasure of hearing his friends, three Neapolitan tenors, sing these to us in broken English.

When Christina decided to release Tom's ashes, Pasquale and I joined her and we climbed out onto the rocks overlooking the Bay of Naples. As the white ash drifted over the water, a whirlpool suddenly formed and a wave and lick of water leapt up to take him. Even the cynical Neapolitan sea just had to be beguiled by a trickster. Fra noi, Tomasso.

PREFACE

## The Irresolvable Paradox: Essaying Naples

This book is intended to stage an encounter—at once critical and celebratory—with historic and contemporary Naples, with a particular emphasis on the so-called tragic centuries (1799 to the present) in which Naples presents itself as an irresolvable paradox: a city in economic and political decline, despite its revival under Antonio Bassolino in the 1990s, that, nonetheless, produces a vital and profound intellectual life and a brilliant and exuberant artistic, literary, and urban culture that approaches the condition of the "national-popular culture" that Antonio Gramsci so ardently prescribed. Neapolitan thought and cultural/artistic creation are, to a great degree, concerned with coming to grips with the paradox constituted by Naples and with all of the aporias that are embedded in the state of emergency informing its history and everyday life. These aporias have come to define the Neapolitan conception of the world: "Napoletanità," to refer to the term used by Raffaele La Capria to derive a psychological history of the city that he finds obsessed with "l'armonia perduta" ("the lost harmony" of the Naples emblematic of the Golden Age), thereby accounting for the Neapolitan "Janus complex"—its radical self-consciousness, its obsession with its history, its sterile nostalgia for the glories of the past. But this formulation is not paradoxical enough and is in need of radical rethinking to account for the ability of Naples to renew itself and to remain culturally and intellectual vibrant and "delirious." As Regis Debray writes, "the ricorsi of Vico have merely sanded down the face of Naples, as if each spiral of time renewed its vitality. In that politically dethroned metropolis, victim of Rome, the clocks are nimble and the word 'decadence,' comical."

Therefore, this book is addressed to "lovers of paradoxes," and we have done our utmost to assemble a stellar cast of Neapolitan and American scholars, intellectuals, and artists/writers who are strong and open-minded enough to wrestle with and illuminate the paradoxes through which Naples presents itself. Naples is a mysterious metropolis. Difficult to understand, it is an enigma to outsiders, and also to the Neapolitans themselves. Its very impenetrableness is what makes it so deliriously and irresistibly attractive. The essays attempt to give some hints to the answer of the enigma, without parsing it into neat scholastic formulas. In doing this, the book will be an important means of opening Naples to students, scholars, and members of the community at large who are engaged in "identity-work." Our primary goal is to establish a dialogue with leading Neapolitan intellectuals and artists, and, ultimately, ensure that the "deliriously Neapolitan" dance continues.

PELLEGRINO D'ACIERNO
STANISLAO G. PUGLIESE

INTRODUCTION

## Naples as Chaosmos or, The City That Makes You Repeat Its Discourse

*Pellegrino D'Acierno*

> Your gaze scans the streets as if they were written pages: the city says everything you must think. Makes you repeat her discourse . . .
>
> No one, wise Kublai, knows better than you that the city must never be confused with the words that describe it. And yet between the one and the other there is a connection.
>
> —ITALO CALVINO, *Invisible Cities*

*To the Reader: An Aside*

This volume was generated by a wildly ambitious and exuberant four-day-long mega-conference held in 2011 that was co-sponsored by the Hofstra Cultural Center and the Casa Italiana Zerilli-Marimò at New York University. The conference sought to create a counter-requiem for contemporary Naples, a metropolis that is too often—automatically and apocalyptically—seen as being in the process of committing a "city-cide" by dint of its failed Renaissances and its continuous *sventramento*, its gutting as an urban space by the ruling class and its official and unofficial accomplices.

Naples has always been a city in crisis, a "panic city," as a result of its vulnerability both to acute shocks (eruptions of Vesuvius, earthquakes, cholera outbreaks, the aerial bombings in 1943–44 by the Allies during World War II as supplemented by the ground-level devastation inflicted by the German occupation) and chronic stresses (its endemic poverty, its congestion and traffic jams, its garbage crises and illegal toxic waste dumping, and, above all, its culture of violence that has come to be organized into a system by the Camorra as documented by Roberto Saviano in *Gomorrah* [2006], his best-selling and prize-winning (im)personal book that embeds within its investigative reportage a howl of protest against the Neapolitan mafia). Consequently, requiems for Naples have been constantly proclaimed, often by rephrasing its canonic proverb—See Naples and Die. Typical are such headlines as "See Naples before It Dies" (1970) and, more vituperatively, "See Naples and Die (of the Stench)" (2008). They have in turn generated counter-requiems, the most effective being: "See Naples and Live" (often repeated, but most effectively by Alberto Arbasino in the 1990s) and, most recently, "See Naples and . . . You'll Find a City on the Rise" (2014), the title of an article by Ondine Cohane published in the *Guardian* that, among other things, praises the turnaround effected by Mayor Luigi de Magistris, first elected in 2011.

However superficial and sensationalistic this contrapuntal branding of Naples may be, it positions us within the dialectic that has perennially informed the narrative of Naples, a city always in the grip of a slow apocalypse that elicits at once jeremiads and paeans, objurgations and panegyrics, denunciations and exaltations. This agon between requiems and counter-requiems reminds us that Naples requires both a critical reading that exposes its colonization through stigmatizing and banalizing stereotypes and a contrapuntal reading that confronts its unresolvable contradictions and paradoxes by integrating them within a master narrative of resilience. Indeed, the most memorable demonstration of its resilience as a city remains the counter-requiem enacted by the people during the Four Days of Naples, the rebellion against the German forces occupying the city during World War II, a Vesuvian explosion of agency on the part of the Neapolitan populace that has all too often been stigmatized as passive and hegemonized subjects inscribed within regimes of power. A motto for its resilience can be found in the concluding line of Eduardo De Filippo's *Napoli milionaria*, a comedy first performed in 1945: "Adda passà 'a nuttata" ("We must see the night through").

The first urbanistic form of its *sventramento* was proposed in the name of the Italian government by Minister Agostino Depretis in response to the cholera epidemic of 1884 and was immediately and polemically denounced as a brutal evisceration of the "belly"—the heart and soul—of the people's city by Matilde Serao in *Il ventre di Napoli* (The Belly of Naples). Its updated installments in the 1950s and 1960s through the 1990s were similarly and perhaps even more polemically attacked by the filmmaker Francesco Rosi in *Le mani sulla città* (Hands over the City; 1963) and *Diario napoletano* (Neapolitan Diary; 1992), exposés of highly flawed urban renewal schemes determined by the politics of self-interest and self-empowerment on the part of corrupt politicians colluding with unscrupulous real-estate speculators. The *sventramento* has culminated in the Scampìa disaster in which the dreamed-for architectural renewal of a zone on the periphery has resulted in a ghetto territorialized by the Camorra, as documented by Matteo Garrone's 2008 crime film *Gomorra*. Furthermore, the *sventramento* seems to have assumed the form of a self-evisceration involving not only architectural and environmental crimes but also all aspects of Neapolitan life. Indeed, it has imposed a "double consciousness" upon Neapolitan self-identity and inflicted a wound upon the Neapolitan collective consciousness, what Francesco Durante has termed *scuorno* ("shame" in English, although the translation does not convey the distress and anguish of self-denial at work in the original Neapolitan word). This stigmatization as epitomized in the figure of Naples as Gomorrah/Camorra has troubled and made defensive Neapolitan identity politics and even infiltrated the discourse on Naples as epitomized by Saviano's militant book—at once a requiem for criminalized Naples and a counter-requiem for Naples that calls for a civil and cultural revolution. How then in writing Naples is one to avoid perpetuating its *sventramento* through the soft lacerations of discourse?

The conference was concerned with confronting this negative narrative of Naples not by erasing or deleting it but rather by incorporating it within a counternarrative that encountered head-on the tangle of contradictions and aporias that Naples presents to those who wish to understand it. Here I resort to a difficult philosophical concept: aporia (logical contradiction, impasse, difficulty of passing, puzzlement), but it is through these aporias or blind spots that Naples reveals itself to us. Therefore, the conference and this volume as a forwarding of the conference attempts to "learn from Naples" by celebrating it as a delirious and aporetic city and by staging a collision between rigorous analysis of the city and its cultural production and more informal approaches that practice the immersive city by essaying it through drift work and flânerie. Performance—musical, dramatic, cinematic—was crucial to the celebratory aspect of the conference, as I shall commemorate below. Although this performative element cannot be presented in the printed format of a book, its brio tinges the essays of our contributors.

Having mentioned Matilde Serao, to whose literary work one of our authors, Gabriella Romani, has dedicated a probing analysis, I should like to cite the following cry from Serao's soul as a motto for reading this volume and its counter-requiem: "Do not abandon Naples again, when you are caught up in politics or business; do not leave this place—which we all must love—once more to its death throes. Of all the beautiful and good cities of Italy, Naples is the most graciously beautiful and the most profoundly good. Do not leave Naples in poverty, filth, and ignorance, without work and without help: do not destroy, in her, the poetry of Italy." I take this as a motto not simply because it is a plangent expression of Serao's love for Naples but because, as the conclusion of her essay, objectively written from a journalistic and editorial position, it embodies the dialogue between the impersonal and the personal that informs the essays in this volume and announces the sort of soul-work necessary for the reading and writing of Naples. The personal voice has a rigor of its own.

## *Why Naples?*

> Qui rido io. (Here I laugh.)
>
> *Eduardo Scarpetta, the comedy writer who inscribed this saying on the façade of his home, Villa Santarella, in Naples*

Although American-born, I am of Neapolitan origins and thus incapable of remaining indifferent or neutral toward Naples, a city that remains a fantasia and an obsession for those who are exiled from it, regardless of whether that exile be voluntary or involuntary. Even though I have attempted to write an impersonal essay—or at best an (im)personal essay—to serve as the formal introduction to *Delirious Naples*, I find myself constantly lapsing into a personal voice as if the porosity that Walter Benjamin famously ascribed to the city of Naples also applies to "writing Naples." This lapse into affection/infection, of course, is a direct result of the deliriousness of Naples.

Here I shall risk being personal by citing my response to the inevitable question—"Why Naples?"—posed to me in an interview conducted by Liliana Rossano, a journalist for a Neapolitan newspaper:

> Why Naples and its culture? Why not ask Mount Vesuvius or the Cumaean Sybil? They would give you cryptic answers that embody the enigmatic nature of Naples through which it casts its spell on those who wish to penetrate its mysteries.
>
> Or just ask Goethe, Nietzsche, and Walter Benjamin, all of whom as outsiders were rendered delirious by and for Naples, albeit for different reasons and at different historical moments. And the deliriousness awakened in them by the experience of Naples generated extraordinary literary, philosophical and aesthetic encounters that went much deeper into the exceptionalism of Naples than the ecstatic cliché: "Vedi Napoli e poi mori." Or just ask Pucinella or Totò, his modern avatar, or any contemporary Neapolitan in the street, all of whom possess the delirious body and facial language, gestural codes, and language games in dialect that epitomize the performance culture of Naples. Or just ask all those revolutionaries who were delirious about creating a Neapolitan Republic only to find themselves hanged like *caciocavalli* in the Piazza Mercato by the Bourbons and spat upon by the *lazzaroni* in the Revolution of 1799, the revolution assassinated by the people. Pardon the eccentricity of these disparate examples—my way of being "delirious" in summoning up the complexity of Naples.
>
> So we chose Naples—or to be exact, it chose us—because of its "deliriousness" both as a metropolis and cultural space and as a subject or topos of intellectual and cultural inquiry whose contradictions and aporias require a "delirious" interpretive approach (the etymology of "delirious" derives from a plowing metaphor, "to be off the furrow," and thus to be out of line or to deviate).

## Learning from Naples

*Delirious Naples: A Cultural History of the City of the Sun* is an interdisciplinary and highly diverse collection of twenty-two (im)personal essays dedicated to writing Naples by thinking/feeling it in ways that respect its complexity as a sublime problem—a city that at once demands to be written and resists being written; a city of difference, of Otherness, that at once demands and resists interpretation. What sort of master-narrative must be elaborated to confront the fractured and multilayered history of Naples both as a place—a solar labyrinth that has a long and difficult history embedded within it; a liminal city at once European and Mediterranean, a Third Space or the geopolitical Other with respect to Europe as well as to Italy that now has become a crossroads of globalization—and as a vibrant and polyphonic cultural space whose artistic creations and philosophic thought have transited throughout Italy and the world? How is Naples to be written and read most effectively/affectively without lapsing into those banalizing readings—carousels of stereotypes and clichés spinning under the shadow of Vesuvius to the pulsating tune of "Funiculì, Funiculà"—that have, ever since the siren Parthenope and Virgil's Golden Great Egg, rendered Naples into an imaginary or (in)visible city? Is there such a thing as a proper (i.e., objective) reading/writing of Naples or is it best encountered through an improper reading—a "delirious" reading, as our title suggests?

We asked our authors—a mix of Neapolitan and American writers, artists, intellectuals, and scholars from various disciplines—to confront the aporias that Naples presents by assuming new and creative reading positions that celebrate the experience of these wicked aporias without, however, lapsing into the down—the blockages, stoppages, impasses—that results from grappling with unanswerable and irresolvable questions. In other words, we challenged our authors to engage in interminable analysis, a task that requires risking one's disciplinary identity as well as one's own cultural identity. Such an analysis enables its practitioners to affirm their methodological identity by constantly risking it, and as a corollary, to bypass the operative or ideological criticism that has conventionalized our view of Naples in terms of what Freud calls "the narcissism of minor differences" (local, ethnic, territorial) and, to rewrite Freud, the narcissism of "major" differences (national, European, Mediterranean, and global as determined by the conflictive geopolitical compass of North versus South and East versus West).

## See Naples and Write

> For decades, I have preoccupied myself with my city. I have read hundreds of books on it, I have written twenty about it, but I have not yet understood anything about it! Without fail things go in this way, Naples is a fleeting city, it is impossible to contain in an image, in a discourse. It is for this reason that it is beautiful and alive.
>
> Domenico Rea

> Writing the city (Naples) is also to be written by the city, suspended in a narration without pretense to finality.
>
> Ian Chambers, "Naples: A Porous Modernity"

> Every person, place, and thing in the chaosmos of the Alle anyway connected with the gobblydumped.
>
> James Joyce, Finnegans Wake

> See Sophia Loren and die.
>
> (A popular version of the old proverb)

Interminable analysis requires an impersonal and (self-)critical stance, but Naples also demands the personal and the affective. Therefore we also asked our authors: "To see Naples and write," a palimpsest and pro memoria that summons up the archetypal phrase: "Vedi Napoli e poi mori" (See Naples and die) that is traditionally invoked by Neapolitans in response to the rare experiences and sacred and profane illuminations bestowed by Naples and through which Kant's distinction between the sublime and the beautiful is demolished. As Goethe famously wrote: "I won't say another word about the beauties of the city and its situation, which have been described and praised often. As they say here, 'Vedi Napoli e poi muori!—See Naples and die!' One can't blame the Neapolitan for never wanting to leave his city, nor its poets singing its praises in lofty hyperboles: it would be wonderful even if a few more Vesuviuses were to rise in the neighborhood." Walter Benjamin and Asja Lacis, in their brilliant essay on Naples (1925) and its porosity, describe the "specialized eroticism" of the Neapolitan language of gestures: "Helping gestures and impatient touches attract the stranger's attention through a regularity that excludes chance. Yes, here his cause would be hopelessly lost, but the Neapolitan benevolently sends him away, sends him a few kilometers father on to Mori. 'Vedere Napoli e poi Mori,' he says, repeating an old pun. 'See Naples and die,' says the foreigner after him" (173).

In the pun on "Mori" ("die" as well as a place name of a small town outside of Naples; in other words, "See Naples and then hit the road"), Benjamin ironizes and deconstructs the accepted ecstatic meaning of the proverb, while the foreigner remains riveted to the literal meaning of the term that expresses the wonder of Naples. The proverb has become fixed in the imaginary of the Neapolitans who use it as a proclamation of their politics of recognition as well as in the global imaginary where it now serves as the slogan, roughly equivalent to "I love New York," by which honeymooners, pizza fetishists, mass tourists, and "tourons" unplug and colonize Naples. But it, too, like everything Neapolitan, is aporetic. It can be translated or paraphrased in a number of ways. "See Naples and then die," that is, once you have experienced the incomparable beauty of Naples, you may then feel free to die because you have already had a peak experience that is unsurpassable. "See Naples and die metaphorically" as a result of the spectacular and excessive beauty of its setting. These are both positive interpretations of the Naples effect. They link the ecstatic and extreme beauty of Naples to death and, like a sexual encounter, that experience of convulsive beauty climaxes in death. But there is also a negative reading. The experiencing of the city of Naples involves danger—the real danger of Vesuvius, of the street violence of slums, the stilettos (and now the Kalasnikovs) of the Camorra, and the spiritual and psychological danger of losing yourself in the labyrinth. Recent films such as the documentaries *Vedi Napoli e poi muori* (2006), directed by Enrico Caria, and Lina Wertmüller's *Munnezza e bellezza* (Garbage and Beauty, 2008) and literary texts such as Saviano's *Gomorrah* and *La bellezza e l'inferno* (Beauty and Inferno) have rewritten the proverb— "See Naples and be killed," in effect (or at least, "be traumatized")—and thus reinforced the dangerous implications, often, as in Wertmüller's and other films, using montage to articulate the shocks and blows imposed by the discrepancy between the two Naples—*bella e mala Napoli*.

So it is important to indicate, as did Benjamin, that the proverb's meaning changes when uttered by an outsider and a Neapolitan. For an outsider it summons up all the stereotypes and clichés associated with spectacular and delirious Naples. For Neapolitans it summons into play their problematic and ambivalent relation with the city. A historian once described Naples as a "città odiosamata," a city that is hated and loved at the same time. So our injunction "To see Naples and write" carries with it the risk of a metaphorical death but also the incitement to write Naples deliriously and fearlessly by confronting it as sublime and dangerous enigma.

To put it another way, we asked our authors to write love letters to Naples not about love, or to be at once impersonal and personal in their methodological approaches and writing styles: "Say, tell or paint whatever you want but here every wait is overcome.... May all those who lose their minds in Naples be forgiven!" (Goethe).

Our challenge has resulted in a passionate and thought-felt (dare I say, "delirious"?) collective attempt—necessarily modest and provisional, however—to contribute to the boundless and contradictory discourse on Naples and its rich artistic and cultural creation, including the cultural identity/identities that it has imposed upon its citizens over time, regardless of whether they remain confined to the city or exiled or self-exiled from or within it. The essays, although employing various methodological and critical approaches and diverse writing styles and registers, share in common the desire to "learn from Naples"—its past, present, and future—and to (re-)read Naples as a real and imaginary city and as a cultural text.

This is no easy task because Naples, the city of obstructed meaning par excellence, presents itself to those who wish to comprehend it as a "Chaosmos," as a collision between Cosmos and Chaos, order and disorder, law and freedom, harmony and dissonance, beauty and ugliness, the euphoric and the dysphoric, the Apollonian and the Dionysian. Here I allude to James Joyce's glorious pun in the form of a portmanteau or blend word—"Every person, place, and thing in the chaosmos of the Alle anyway connected with the gobblydumped."—in *Finnegans Wake*, a "Neapolitan text" in effect by dint of its rewriting of Vico's *Scienza nuova*. Embedded within Joyce's pun is another pun—chiasmus or arch—and perhaps it points the way to a passage beyond the impasses and out of the blind spots imposed by experiencing the aporias of Naples, what Derrida has called putting the experience of aporia to a test.

Confronting the Chaosmos of Naples may necessarily force those who wish to read and write it to employ a paradigm that renders the city "readable." As a rule, that paradigm is governed by binary opposites as epitomized by the infamous sixteenth-century proverb describing Naples as "il Paradiso abitato da diavoli" (the Paradise inhabited by devils; the devils are the plebes). This proverb, which over time has been depleted of its original oxymoronic force, has governed the discourse on Naples, reducing its contradictions to the regime of stigmatizing stereotypes and hyperbolic figures through which Naples is either frantically celebrated or frantically denigrated and ultimately reduced to the opposition between a euphoric and a dysphoric city. Over the years it has been continuously rewritten, with the devils qua plebes being replaced by the *lazzaroni* and their sons, the pickpocketing *scugnizzi*, who, in turn, are displaced by corrupt politicians and unscrupulous real-estate speculators as depicted so accurately by Francesco Rosi in *Le mani sulla città* (Hands over the City), the great jeremiad that exposes the avatars of the devils in the Naples of the 1960s. And of course, the eternal and primary devils need to be mentioned: the daemonic *camorristi* and their operatives, drug pushers. As a result, the City of the Sun becomes "the heart of darkness" or Gomorrah; Paradise is territorialized by Inferno, with Purgatorio available only to the *signori*. Clearly this paradigm and its binary oppositions need to be deconstructed. Nonetheless, it is an inevitable starting point—a necessary fiction—for those who wish to confront Naples as a sublime problem whether as outsiders or insiders. Whether this paradigm can be superseded by assuming what Roland Barthes has called the Neutral—namely, "that which outplays the paradigm, or rather . . . everything that baffles paradigm"—remains a formidable challenge to those who wish to learn from Naples and to comprehend its workings as a Chaosmos.

How then is one to read and write Naples? Certainly, one must resort to tactics rather than strategies for the performance and carnivalizing culture of Naples subverts strategies just as its urban space deranges our psychogeography and our mental mapping. Here I immediately think of the character played by Totò (Antonio De Curtis) in Eduardo De Filippo's 1950 film *Napoli milionario*, a groupography of sorts that treats the communal life of "i bassi" (the lower class) in an impoverished neighborhood in Naples during World War II. Totò plays a wretched poor man forced to practice "the art of making do" in order to get by. To do this he makes a profession out of playing a "morto finto," a fake dead man; a family hires him to outfox a police official who wishes to impose a "strategy" upon him that will lead to his arrest. Totò bamboozles the inspector, thereby providing a parable of the tactical Neapolitan self as it expresses itself through trickery, character masks, and frame-breaking performances: Naples turns everything on its head, including death.

Perhaps thinking of Naples not as a "text of pleasure" that reconfirms our cultural coding but rather as a "text of bliss" that places us into a crisis, to use Roland Barthes's cogent distinction, is a more effective way of encountering it. Or perhaps establishing a dialogue between pleasure and bliss is even more effective/affective. And what critical methodology can best confront its aporias and its double binds and blind spots? Certainly, these obstacles call for a multiplication of approaches that pluralize and dialogize our understanding of Naples. And what form of writing can best comprehend its Chaosmos? Here I think of certain texts through which I have learned from Naples in a plenary way. All of them are written otherwise: the fragments and aphorisms that Fabrizio Ramondino and Friedrich Müller, in *Dadapolis: Caleidoscopio napoletano*, have assembled into a collage or broken text that captures Naples as a collision-city; the letters written by Pier Paolo Pasolini in *Lettere luterane* that are addressed to Genariello, an imaginary interlocutor in the form of a Neapolitan young man, and provide him with a little instructional treatise for navigating the labyrinth of Naples—the letters are a consummate exercise in the affective; Régis Debray in *Against Venice* uses Naples to counterpoint his scolding of Venice for its stylish moribundity and produces a celebratory reading of Naples as a City of Extravagances that is positively delirious in its interactions with Naples—writing Naples in a prose that bursts into laughter while writing Venice in a prose that at best smiles; the lyrics written in Neapolitan dialect by Aniello Califan to the song "'O surdato 'nnammurato" ("Soldier in Love" or "A Soldier's Love Song" [1915]), the most hyperbolic and expressive love song in the world that defies the conventional ballad by being sung to the rhythm of a march.

I shall explore the questions of writing Naples otherwise more deliberately below in order to present the essays in this volume. But here I want to discuss the two tropes or figures that I find most effective in approaching Naples and that a number of our authors employ in their essays, as do I in this introduction.

The first is "porosity" (its etymology derives from "passage"), a term coined by Walter Benjamin and Asja Lācis in "Naples," an essay they coauthored in 1925. "Porosity" as an interpretative figure has generated numerous texts that describes the breaking of borders—sometimes violent—that define or de-define Neapolitan city life and by extension its cultural and artistic practices. Benjamin described Naples's porosity to imply not a classical but a Baroque interplay between private and public space; a psychogeography that lacks boundaries, but that is nonetheless bound together; as an urban space in which the soft or imaginary city and the hard or real city perpetually collide. Following Benjamin, diverse writers such as Ernst Bloch, Massimo Cacciari, and Ian Chambers have used porosity to generate powerful readings of Naples, and following in their footsteps is the anthology *La città porosa: Conversazioni su Napoli* (1993).

It needs, however, to be applied to Neapolitan cinema, especially those films that deconstruct the panoramic or touristic view that privileges monumental and historical space and, instead, position the spectator in a tactile and kinaesthetic ground-level experience that involves moving through space. For example, there is a "moving" (in both the physical and emotional sense) demonstration of porosity in the funeral procession in "Il funeralino," one of the episodes in Vittorio De Sica's anthology film *L'oro di Napoli* (1954), based on Giuseppe Marotta's novel by the same title. As the mourners pass from the rooftop of a tenement to street level, the grief-stricken mother insists on helping the professional casket bearer carry down the narrow staircase the coffin that holds her young son's body, pressing it fervently to maintain contact with her departed one. Once in the alleyway, she helps insert the coffin within one of those elegant Neapolitan white horse-drawn funeral carriages and then assumes the role of directing the procession, making sure that everything (above all, the bouquets of flowers) and every one of the mourners (particularly those in the group of her son's classmates) are in their proper place. She directs the procession as if she were a filmmaker—a stand-in for De Sica—creating a mise-en-scène with the power of her gaze that honors her dead son and expresses her love for him. The funeral procession becomes a carefully ordered spectacle, an exercise in the bella figura. As the procession moves down an alleyway, the first flagrant instance of porosity occurs as an argument between a husband and wife within their apartment penetrates the window and breaks the silence of the procession. Upon seeing the mourners, they make the sign of the cross and break off their argument but then immediately resume it, thereby once again intruding upon the silence. As the procession enters the light of Piazza della Repubblica and then proceeds down Via Caracciolo, we are made to focus on the mother's restrained face and her gaze, her mourning-work executed through elegance and reserve. Her face overrides the architectural spectacle of monumental Naples. But then she unexpectedly performs a supreme act of carnivalization, casting *confetti* into the streets—*confetti* in the Italian sense of the word, those sugar-coated almonds usually associated with weddings and other celebrations. The *confetti* cause another flagrant instance of porosity as the *scugnizzi* rambunctiously hustle to retrieve them, once again breaking the silence with the chaos of the streets. The episode concludes with the *scugnizzi* walking away, with the impressive statue of the Fontana del Gigante to their side and Vesuvius hovering as usual in the distant background. As they walk oblivious to the funeral procession and the spectacularization of death they have just witnessed, they compare the number of their candy gains, thereby proclaiming their right to porosity.

Another film permeated by instances of porosity is Roberto Rossellini's *Viaggio in Italia* (Voyage to Italy, 1954), which stages one of the most profound cultural encounters with Naples by refiguring the conventional tourist film. The film is punctuated by all sorts of profane and sacred epiphanies that are experienced by the female protagonist Katherine Joyce (Ingrid Bergman), whose marriage to an Englishman is on the rocks. The film concludes with a supreme moment of porosity when the couple, after agreeing to a divorce, experience a Being-toward-Death moment: the excavation at Pompei of the embracing corpses of a couple who had been buried alive by the eruption of Vesuvius. As they flee to Naples in their car—throughout the film their car serves as an involvement shield for them—they find themselves caught up in a crowded procession for Saint Gennaro. Exiting their car, they experience the event of porosity—miraculous in their case for it resurrects their love for each other and reestablishes their marriage.

The figure of porosity can also be extended to describe novelistic and other forms of writing. I know of no more powerful example than the writing of Elena Ferrante—the Jane Austen of contemporary Italy—who, in her four "Neapolitan Novels," stages a probing encounter with Naples as a hard city, elaborating a "thick description" of the cultural self and the cultural practices of the Neapolitan *bassi* and a sociological anatomy of the groupographies and clans through which the neighborhood determines the identities of its poor inhabitants. The narrative of the long friendship between Lila and Elena begins in the 1950s when they are childhood friends and classmates who grow up in a poor Neapolitan neighborhood and who, as they mature, manage to express their agency and interiority as strong women—albeit in quite different ways—by resisting the patriarchal system and by unfolding the local, regardless of whether that unfolding is executed from the Neapolitan inside or the outside. Ferrante's account of the two women's attempts to express their conflicted autonomy by unfolding their Neapolitan selves together with her exploration of the intimate politics of their friendship mark her work as feminist and defy those readings that see her writing as chick lit and cosmic chit-chat.

The four-volume narrative culminates in the disappearance of Lila in 2005. Her disappearance into the void is the ultimate version of what Lila as a young woman called the sensation of "dissolving margins" and her way of "writing" herself through invisibility. The tetralogy, often described as a bildungsroman is, in fact, a *Künstlerroman* ("artist novel") that narrates the artistic development not simply of Elena, who becomes a celebrated writer and makes it out of Naples only to return, but of both women, even though Lila does not write or, more exactly, writes by not writing, serving as Elena's interior double—the alter ego of her writing self—who infiltrates and determines Elena's spectral writing. Although the novels constantly portray the porosity imposed by the poor Neapolitan neighborhood and by Naples itself upon both women—Lila who remains (and then becomes a missing person as did her daughter); Elena who leaves or, to be more exact, attempts to leave, for the Neapolitan connection as embodied in their friendship can never be severed. What Ferrante presents is an interior or psychic form of porosity by which the two women infiltrate each other's consciousness and subconsciousness and through which their identities are forever constituted as intersectional selves. As Rimbaud wrote, "Je est un autre," and as Elena might write to describe her internal conversation, "I can think and write myself as and through the other," meaning Lila.

The second figure or trope is the philosophical concept aporia—its meaning as "impasse" connects and disconnects it to the "passage" implicit to porosity—which has just begun to be applied to Naples: see, for example, *Aporie napoletane: Sei posizioni filosofiche* (2005) and, at least in my mind, it is the most effective way of articulating the entanglements and contradictions dictated by Naples, as I hope this introduction demonstrates. Crucial to Jacques Derrida's project of deconstruction that placed the concept on the radar screen, it places the reader/writer in a double bind that challenges him or her to live aporias as creation. Naples as an aporetic experience always defers or postpones its meaning(s) like Mount Vesuvius (currently) postpones its eruptions. Or, to put it in Neapolitan terms, Naples as the supreme aporetic city gives the *pernacchio* (as deliriously demonstrated by Eduardo De Filippo in "Il professore," an episode in the film *L'oro di Napoli*), to those who wish to finalize and objectify its openness and to bypass its difference. Naples cannot be programmed.

Unavailable to Benedetto Croce, the figure of aporia might have helped the philosopher in his attempt to write a monumental history of Naples almost a century ago. I say this because he struggles with the contradictions of Naples in a way that attempts to suppress the emergence of the personal. Nonetheless, Croce locates the supreme aporia embedded within the history of Naples—the history that is no history.

*Naples as a Sublime Problem: The History That Is No History*

> Hence the history of the Kingdom of Naples cannot bear comparison with that of Florence, Genoa, or the communes and seigniories of Lombardy. If it appeals to the feelings of those who choose to narrate it, it is because it arouses, in some, consideration for its uninterrupted disasters, in others severe criticism and, indeed, disesteem, of its population. We have here a *history that is no history*, a development that does not develop. Its notorious characteristic is to be at every step upset and interrupted, whereas the history of other parts of Italy is characterized by the impetus of their political bodies, their struggles for liberty and power, their trade and industries, their seafaring prowess and colonies, their poetry and art. (My emphasis)

Benedetto Croce, the most Olympian of Neapolitan intellectuals and second only to Vico in the universalism of his philosophical interests, writes this disclaimer in his *History of the Kingdom of Naples* (1925), a classic—albeit flawed—of idealist historicism. Writing from an emic position, that is, as an insider not only with respect to Neapolitan "cose" (Vico's term for institutions or practices) but also with respect to the Neapolitan *forma mentis*, for which the historiographic mindset is determinative (to think as a Neapolitan is to historicize), Croce formulates Naples as a site of contradictions, as an obscure object whose "history" refuses both history and the historian—or at least the historian who, like Croce, attempts to think its history as unilinear and teleological. However, Croce's assessment may be symptomatic of his own ambivalence (as well as that of those other unnamed historians who either show "consideration" or "disesteem" in treating it) toward his beloved Naples, a Naples then in the process of being stigmatized as part of the Southern Question, it remains instructive for it designates Naples as an exception, as a space of difference and irregularity that confounds the heuristic rule that would impose cohesion as a principle of its historicity.

But Croce's experience is in no way unique: Naples has always presented itself to those who desire to master it through discourse as a labyrinth whose secret resists being uncovered, as a chaos of contradictions that refuses to be overcome. How is one to capture the difference, the Otherness of Naples, a social and cultural text that almost by definition refuses the discourses that seek to render it intelligible? It has been subjected to innumerable readings and descriptions, many of which, especially those written by outsiders, are written in a hyperbolic and excessive register, as if to write about Naples requires a shift into a language of exorbitance and a slippage from a critical methodology into a "gay science." To write Naples is necessarily to desire it and therefore either to submit to or reject its fascination.

Croce's history of Naples is instructive because it provides us with a parable about the difficulty of assuming the neutral for Croce lapses at times into a politics of recognition as well as into a politics of friendship with his mentor Enrico Cenni, whose glorious and decidedly noble and ennobling history of Naples preceded Croce's. Croce both rejected it and accepted it by rejecting it—a perfect example of an aporia. Croce writes on Cenni's history:

> In this fashion I mulled over, analyzed, and discussed with myself the historic glory of the old Kingdom of Naples, so industriously built up by Cenni. In the course of this examination, my discovery of fanciful transferences of facts and theories, sophisms, exaggerations, and ingenious argumentation did not arouse my contempt for such an outrage to truth; it only awakened respect for the author of such an ill-founded and shaky construction. In him and others of his

ilk, honorable and noble-hearted men, attached by affection to their native places, I sensed—just as in myself, when in the course of my reading I was moved by optimism and concurrence—a legitimate yearning and effort to bolster sentiment with the strength of tradition. Neither individuals nor peoples can live without a myth of their past, present and future potentialities.

So here and elsewhere in his *History of the Kingdom of Naples*, especially in the concluding paragraph in which he blesses the teachers and philosophers of Naples, we can find a strong lesson in learning from Naples, one that reiterates our argument: the impossibility of maintaining the neutral or the objective when encountering Naples. Even the rigorous Croce lapses into the affective and the politics of the personal. Naples demands an interminable analysis that respects the world of aporias into which it plunges those who wish to read and write it, whether by confronting its history, practicing it as an urban space, contacting its people, encountering its art, music, literature, and intellectual production. Croce violates the impersonal by slipping into the personal without accepting the need to dialogize both voices. This leads me to an overview of the pieces in this volume for which I have coined the term "(im)personal essays." (Pace, Croce!)

## *Writing Naples Otherwise: The (Im)Personal Essay*

The city . . . can be comprehended only in the essay form.

*Massimo Cacciari*

E so' napulitano, e si nun canto i' moro!
(I am Neapolitan, and if I don't sing, I die.)

*Libero Bovio*

Here I wish to provide a frame for reading this volume without presenting too many spoilers that will interfere with the pleasure of reading it and encountering the surprises that its montage of essays presents.

Writing Naples is as difficult as writing the sea and the sun. Its difference—its Chaosmos, its extravagance, its exorbitance—requires it to be written Otherwise. The essays in this volume are best described as (im)personal essays, and as such they point the way to writing Naples Otherwise, thereby registering the effects/affects of its deliriousness. Although a number of our authors manage to write impersonal essays by observing the protocols of their academic disciplines, the majority of the pieces oscillate between impersonal and personal voices, something that involves much more than the slippage between the first and third person and, in fact, this intermingling—or contamination—of scriptural voices bears witness to the porosity, which Walter Benjamin famously diagnosed as the determining factor in our street-level encounters with Naples, and its retroactive power to bear upon writing/thinking Naples.

Six of our authors are Neapolitans—Angelo Cannavacciuolo, Valerio Caprara, Simona Frasca, Salvatore Napolitano, Erri De Luca and Francesco Durante (problematically Neapolitan in the case of the latter two, as their essays will make clear). All of them are prominent figures on the Neapolitan literary and intellectual scene, and we are greatly indebted to them for sharing their insider's perspectives with us and for contributing to our attempt to open a dialogue between Naples and America.

The other fourteen contributors constitute a band of outsiders or Neapolitans manqués—Americans of Neapolitan descent, self-exiled Italians who teach at American universities, and Americans Neapolitanized by the agony and the ecstasy of desiring Naples. Here I wish to acknowledge their exquisite contributions to our attempt to learn from Naples. Although I shall describe them in terms of their disciplines, it is their engagement with interdisciplinarity that is most praiseworthy—with interdisciplinarity understood as the last form of humanism.

The volume informally begins and ends with tributes to Thomas Belmonte, whose *The Broken Fountain* (1979; rev. ed., 2005) is a perfect example of writing in the (im)personal register. Indeed, *The Broken Fountain* is a dialogized text in the Bakhtinian sense, an anthropological "novel" that embodies an agon between Tom's anthropological persona—that of the "professional stranger," as he liked to say—and his experiential persona—that of the friend or guest who must be more than a "professional friend" or intimate poacher. In other words, the agon inscribed within Tom's writing involves the conflict between his disciplinary and monological voice as an anthropologist, with its demand to be rigorously theoretical, and his personal and dialogic voice, with its writerly and "novelistic" demands to be personal, "to stick to life," to peg itself to reality (D. H. Lawrence's incantation to experience that Tom takes as a touchstone for his own anthropological writing).

Jason Pine's attempt as an anthropologist and ethnographer to come to grips with contemporary Naples and its *neomelodica* music scene by practicing "the art of making do" can by regarded as an updated version of Belmonte's encountering of Naples. I say updated because, even though Pine is equipped with contemporary theory, particularly affect theory, which sanctions subjectivity and intuition, he too must risk his anthropological persona as well as his personal self in the contact zone ruled over by the Camorra. His contribution to this volume, "The Contact Zone: Where Organized Crime and Everyday Life Meet," is a riveting example of an (im)personal essay that not only confronts the aporias of Naples without undoing them but also by embedding them within his writing, which as a result also becomes a contact zone. As he writes, "In this story, I dispose myself to affective-aesthetic atmospheres. I yield to events of the senses that flare up like 'profane illuminations,' as Benjamin described the productive disorientations that puncture the seamless sameness of bourgeois ('formal') capitalist experience. By performing these dis-positions in writing, I want to conjure a contact zone charged with seductive vitalities and uncertain threats, leaving you to make your way among Camorristi, people who behave like Camorristi, and people (including me) who perform the art of making do."

The volume formally begins with extraordinary pieces by Erri De Luca, one of Italy's most celebrated novelists of this moment, and Francesco Durante, a dominant literary figure on the contemporary Neapolitan scene. Both pieces stage profound existential and cultural attempts to locate the self both outside and within the Neapolitan context and to define the politics of identity at work in contemporary Naples. Both are consummate examples of the writing of the (im)personal essay.

De Luca, in his book *Napòlide* (Naples-less) (2014), the first chapter of which appears in this collection, has limned the effects of his voluntary exile from Naples in terms of memory and through what might be called "palimpsestic writing," which traces the specters of Naples that haunt those who exile themselves from it. You can take the man out of Naples, but you cannot take Naples out of the man, to resort to an Americanism. As he describes the condition of being "Naples-less" in terms of the conflict between the otherness/estrangement it confers upon him as a self-exile and the derailing desire it bestows upon him, with Naples as a "dead object" that, nonetheless, persists in his body and linguistic conscious: his sense of smell—the nose of exile—his acoustics, his rhythms remaining indelibly Neapolitan:

> In Naples, when I get off the train, I don't feel back home. Instead I feel alone, with a more intimate right than I feel elsewhere. A city does not forgive separation, which is always a desertion. I agree with her, with the city: whoever wasn't there, whoever went missing, is no longer there, and his right to citizenship forfeited. Now, he is just another passerby that she takes in, without offering resistance, the glassy-eyed foreigner whom no one drives away, even as he is eyed like ill-gotten goods. I respect a city's exercising its right to scold whoever drifts from her. If I speak on her behalf, I do so as a guest, not as a citizen. And if I have no right to call myself stateless, I can call myself Naples-less, someone who has scraped his origins from his body, to deliver himself to the world.
> 
> I never again took root elsewhere.
> 
> Whoever has detached himself from Naples, detaches himself from everything; nor does he have the spittle to paste himself to something, to someone.

On the other hand, Francesco Durante, who has written two books—*Scuorno (Vergogna)* (Shame) (2008) and *I napolitani* (2001)—that have altered the discourse on Naples, wrestles with the exile and estrangement he experiences as a Neapolitan, always struggling with the issue of whether he should leave or remain, always mindful of De Filippo's howl—an explosive directive—that he addressed in 1972 to the young Neapolitans: "Fuijtevenne!" ("Run for it!"). He describes what he calls the "ridiculous tragedy" of the contemporary Neapolitan condition and delivers an ambivalent tribute to former Mayor Antonio Bassolino—"a great, tragic, and painful figure"—that takes at once the form of an elegy for his failed mayorship and a eulogy for the hope his Renaissance promised. He then presents a cautionary history of the revolution of 1799, the revolution assassinated by the people, and all the other Neapolitan revolutions manqués.

Durante defines impersonally the double consciousness of the Neapolitan identity that takes the form of *scuorno* (or shame) that masks ironically a will to crisis or, at best, tragicomedy in the form of a perpetual identity crisis. He writes: "Our disaster is slow, silent, crawling, common. Like many things Neapolitan, it has no beginning or end, and for that reason it is more difficult to control. Moreover, appearing to be a direct confirmation of deeply ingrained prejudices and stereotypes—about the lack of city sanitation, sloppiness, breathtaking incivility, and Neapolitans' incorrigible attitude to chaos—this dilemma leads to irony, to sarcasm, and even to laughter. A ridiculous tragedy, all told, and as such typically homegrown." At the same time, he defines personally his own divided self and its conflicted *napoletanità*: "Why don't I leave?"

The volume resounds with the voices of American artists and writers who describe their encounters with Neapolitan culture in which they necessarily assume a personal voice. As instances of writing, their essays embody the porosity that Naples engenders in those who wish to write it. In the section titled "The View from America," the installation artist B. Amore, and the writers John Domini, Fred Gardaphé, and Robert Zweig confront their intricate entanglements with Naples and the city's bearing upon their art and self-construction, describing the ways in which Naples has traveled to them and they have traveled to Naples.

In the penultimate section of the volume, two other artists—a conductor and storyteller—encounter the acoustics and rhythms at work respectively in Neapolitan classical music and opera and in its oral narratives, creating a duet that reminds us to "hear Naples and die." Joseph Rescigno, artistic advisor and principal conductor of the Florentine Opera Company of Milwaukee, Wisconsin, who has been described as "a conductor to treasure" and "the conductor's conductor," elaborates an authoritative history of Naples as a center of opera that is punctuated by anecdotes, those anecdotes confirming the notion of the personal. Naples is a city that grants unforgettable anecdotes, such as the one passed onto Maestro Rescigno by his grandfather: "And I said, 'Grandpa, with a trumpet?' Well, he one-upped me, admitting that some instruments were more obviously 'naturals,' but the strangest of all was the tuba player. Yes, out in front of the window of his girlfriend, his serenade was, 'Buona sera, Terè,' followed by a solo tuba's boom, boom, boom. So, I took from this a moral: Whether or not you are a guitarist or mandolinist—even if you are a tuba player—you are expected to serenade your sweetheart. At least in Naples. Now there's something that should never change."

Here I should mention that a perfect counterpoint to Maestro Rescigno's treatment of opera can be found in the musicologist Simona Frasca's compelling tribute to Gilda Mignonette, supreme diva, "Queen of Immigrants," and "Carusiana," who played a crucial role in the transiting of Neapolitan popular music to America during the Great Immigration. Frasca's sensitive reading of Mignonette's vocal style—framed by an exegesis of her counterpath back and forth between New York and Naples—does "a tango, foxtrot, and shimmy," to allude to one of her songs, with both Rescigno's essay and B. Amore's *Napoli/New York* installation that applies the figure of *rondini di passaggio* (birds of passage) as inspired by Frasca's book, *Italian Birds of Passage: The Diaspora of Neapolitan Musicians in New York*.

Hailed as the "Dean of American Storytellers," Gioia Timpanelli is one of the master practitioners of the art of storytelling of our time. As the last of the *cantastorie* and the first of the new storytellers, she has served as a living archive for the repertory of Italian and Sicilian stories and as the animated voice through which the enchantments of the oral tradition have been transmitted to Italian America and introduced to the American public at large. After introducing us to the "delirious Dionysian spirit"—"the spontaneous part of life exhibits a *showing*, a *playing out* where the body meets its soul, its old mate, its partner and lover, where passion may possibly show spirit"—that defines the Neapolitan spirit and her own aesthetics as a storyteller, she presents an enchanting retelling of Giambattista Basile's "The Cockroach, the Mouse, and the Cricket." She finds in this coming-of-age story of Nardiello who learns the art of living ("Ok, Father, I can do it") through the high jinks of his Improbable mentors—the cockroach, the mouse, and the cricket—a parable of *napoletanità*: "People who give themselves over to some natural awe, who unite with plenty and scarcity, with suffering and joyous engagement, at times, are found culturally, socially, psychologically, statistically, physically, naturally, in abundance in Naples."

In the section "History, Memory, and Mercy," our contributors stage passionate encounters with monumental and iconic Naples, including the ruins of Pompei, the metonym for Neapolitan collective memory, that register the shimmers, shadows, and echoes of Naples as a historical and archaeological space at once sublime and beautiful. The section begins with a profound meditation by Angelo Cannavacciuolo, actor, director, and novelist, who proclaims his "visceral" love for Pompei. He initiates his piece by distinguishing between small memory and historical memory and then proceeds to describe the genesis of his project to celebrate Pompei by "putting words on a journey," thereby creating a contemporary installment of the grand tour involving such writers as Gore Vidal, Ethan Canin, Jim Nisbet, and Jay Parini, along with the brilliant photographer Mimmo Jodice, a collaboration that resulted in *Parole in viaggio* (Traveling Words).

Ilaria and Simone Marchesi present a second encounter with Pompeii, also written in the informal style of a memoir, in "One of These Days," an excerpt from their recently published book, *Live in Pompeii* (2016). Whereas Cannavacciuolo is concerned with resurrecting Pompeii by restaging a grand tour, Ilaria and her husband, Simone, present a memoir of a "small tour," in which they guide a group of elementary schoolchildren through the ruins of Pompeii and Herculaneum. Once again we find a cogent example of writing the (im)personal as their dialogue recounts their adventures in the dead city of Pompeii with children whose enthusiasm and curiosity reanimate the ruins. Their enthusiasm is seconded by Ilaria's voicing of her fervent hope as a classicist that the excavations now underway will yield a more complete version of Petronius's *Satyricon*.

Our two art and architectural historians, Nick Napoli and Salvatore Napolitano, stage rigorous encounters with definitive Neapolitan monuments: the Certosa di San Martino, the most conspicuous landmark of the city, perched atop the Vomero hill that commands the gulf, and whose ultimate design was executed under the direction of the sculptor and architect Cosimo Fanzago, the "soul of the Neapolitan Baroque"; and the Sansevero Chapel, the enigmatic "alchemical chapel" whose iconography was created by Raimondo di Sangro, VII Prince of Sansevero. Both of their essays historicize these iconic structures in terms of the late-Baroque and early-Enlightenment aesthetic and cultural contexts from which they respectively emerge. Although both essays are necessarily written in the impersonal register, they experience the call to the personal. Napoli, who attempts to come to grips with the implications of Fanzago's four-decade-long lawsuit against the Carthusians for underpayment, finds the "delirious" at play in the boundary-breaking lawsuit: "Given that the Latin roots of the modern English word, *de*—from, and *lira*—furrow, signifies 'that which goes outside of the furrow,' the lawsuit between Fanzago and the Carthusians goes beyond the furrow in many different ways. This essay explores how the case reveals idiosyncrasies of Neapolitan sculpture and architecture as a language of form, as a sophisticated collaborative practice, and as a significant moment in the social and economic life of the city and its kingdom."

Similarly, Napolitano, as he carefully documents Raimondo's intricate iconography and its attempts to conflate reason and religion, is drawn into the personal when discussing the "Veiled Christ," Giuseppe Sanmartino's ecstatic sculpture. Indeed, he lapses into the first person, thereby underlining the politics of perception demanded by the sculpture as the viewer is made to focus on the physical condition of the life of the spirit embodied by Christ as his flesh is doubled by the veil: "Sanmartino's art is solved here in a dramatic evocation, which finds in Christ's suffering the symbol of the redemption of all the humanity. I find it very significant, finally, that in this work Raimondo and his artist give more emphasis to the direct communication, to the evidence, rather than the codes, or the inextricable intellectual iconography."

In the penultimate section, "Writing and Singing Naples," two of our three literary critics, Gabriella Romani and Andrea Baldi, stage profound, intriguing encounters with the work of Matilde Serao and Anna Maria Ortese, respectively, while the third, Rose De Angelis, explores the representation of the woman protagonist in Eduardo De Filippo's play *Filumena Marturano*. As a set, these essays emphasize the central role that strong women play in writing Naples and in defining its literary tradition— the genealogy that begins with Serao (1856–1927), is redefined by Ortese (1914–98), and then extends from Fabrizia Ramondino (1936–2008) to Elena Ferrante (1943–). What is so compelling about the three essays is their worrying of the contradictions at work in the texts under analysis: Serao's ambiguous treatment of the Neapolitan obsession with Lotto and gambling in general with her writing intended as an antidote; Ortese's frustrated attempt to "break the spell of Naples," a project that will take the form of the so-called "la fuga da Napoli" (the flight from Naples) and the estrangement from *napoletanità* that will govern much of the contemporary discourse on Naples; and Filumena Marturano's struggle as a mother/whore figure to "rescript" herself and to express her agency as a woman in a way that reestablishes her motherhood, wifehood, loverhood, and personhood, an agon that concludes, as De Angelis empathetically notes, with the ambivalence of bittersweet tears that result from the joy of identity recovered and the sadness of time lost. The essays by Romani, Baldi, and De Angelis in different ways bear witness to the interaction between the personal and impersonal in the texts under analysis as they attempt to locate the agency expressed in writing and performing as Neapolitan women. Their readings present Serao, Ortese, and De Filippo's Filumena as madonnas of the Neapolitan politics of identity.

I should like to conclude this overview by foregrounding two essays that egregiously confirm the premise that writing/reading/thinking Naples elicits the personal and calls for an affective response that embeds porosity within one's acts of interpretation and writing. A cogent example of the (im)personal essay can be found in the conclusion to Patrizia La Trecchia's "Mediterranean Crossroads: Naples as a Model of Southcentric Cosmopolitanism." After elaborating an extensive and "thought-felt" critique of the geopolitical discourse that has come to define contemporary Naples during this era of globalization and has stigmatized it in terms of southernness, La Trecchia concludes her piece with a turn to the personal:

> As a concluding personal remark, I will say that Naples is not my city, it is not the city where I was born, but it is the city that has become a symbol of my "southern" roots. When I chose to navigate the space of Naples, I realized that its familiar space encountered the terrain of affects. My narrative of this city is inspired by my own origins and by the memories of the years I spent in Naples. From the distance of my current life in the United States, I have realized that over the years I have been listening for voices and stories that have eventually made their way into my writing. I have tried to engage myself with these stories of places and people I know deeply without losing myself in the process. It is a story of marginality, a story of a people who, although part of an industrialized nation, had and have to endure an existence of marginalization and exclusion.

This turn to the personal is particularly resonant because she begins her essay with an analysis of Francesco Rosi's documentary *Diario napoletano* [Neapolitan Diary] (1992), which confronts the interpenetration between the impersonal and the personal by which Rosi represents Naples as both a hard city whose urban dysfunctions demand a critical reading and a soft city whose magic is to be rediscovered through memory.

## Caravaggio as Necessary Angel: "The Seven Acts of Mercy" as a Figure for Learning from Naples

> Remember that Naples, the Pio Monte and Caravaggio are one.
>
> Count Leonetti, director of Pio Monte della Miseracordia

Terrence Ward, who has graced us with excerpts from his recently published book, *The Guardian of Mercy*, provides in this volume the most explicit instance of dialogized writing or a doubled text. Its theme is set out in his book's subtitle: *How an Extraordinary Painting by Caravaggio Changed an Ordinary Life Today*. The ordinary life is that of a humble Neapolitan named Angelo Esposito, who serves as the guardian of Caravaggio's *The Seven Acts of Mercy*, the altarpiece for the church of Pio Monte della Misericordia in Naples and perhaps the artist's greatest and most astonishing and dramatic painting. Angelo will also serve as Terry's ad hoc mentor in comprehending both the extraordinary enigmas Caravaggio has embedded within his masterpiece and those other ordinary enigmas—be they merciful or unmerciful—that life in contemporary Naples obliges one to confront.

His narrative impels us to read Otherwise, that is, to read through "sliding doors," the metaphor that Terry uses to describes his bold experiment in doubling his narrative. The reader is presented alternately with a first-person and present-tense narrative dedicated to Terry's and his wife Idanna's encounters with Naples, the guardian, and Caravaggio's altarpiece, and a third-person and past-tense narrative of Caravaggio's flight from Rome after killing a man and his sojourn in Naples, where he found protection from the bounty on his head and earned the commission for what would become one of his most definitive and gaze-boggling works. But Caravaggio finds much more in Naples, creating his masterpiece by incorporating into it the spectacles and bodies that sixteenth-century Naples presented him with. Although essentially a biographical narrative, Terry places the reader in Caravaggio's head and gaze, and presents the process not only by which the masterpiece was generated but also by which Caravaggio turns himself into a work of art.

Ward stages a profound cultural encounter with Naples—the Naples experienced by Caravaggio and the contemporary Naples of the guardian—by which Caravaggio's *Seven Acts of Mercy* becomes an icon of *napoletanità*, a sacred emblem of the major forms of grace the city bestows and a call to "remember that Naples, the Pio Monte and Caravaggio are one." (The minor and profane version of that grace, as Terry points out, is the expression of generosity in the practice of the *caffè sospeso*, a secular act of mercy.)

Caravaggio as a painter is an angel of violence, and in the painting that violence is expressed formally by the folding of the vertical into the horizontal, by the folding of light into darkness to create the infinity of chiaroscuro, by the folding of the chaos of sixteen figures into the order of the seven acts of mercy, by the folding of the sacred into the profane by which the ordinariness and materiality of the profane is sacralized. Caravaggio's religious paintings—above all, *The Seven Acts of Mercy*—require their viewers to be necessary angels in the sense elaborated by Wallace Stevens: "Yet I am the necessary angel of earth, / Since, in my sight, you see the earth again." In *The Seven Acts of Mercy*, we see the earth in the faces, gazes, and bodies of the Neapolitan street people that Caravaggio used as models and transformed into compassionate auratic figures.

And Terry's doubled text also requires its readers to be necessary angels through which we bear witness to acts of mercy in both the painting and present-day reality and by which we experience through our empathy as viewers/readers the grace that Caravaggio embedded in his painting and requested for himself by painting it. Within the main narrative of the ordinary but troubled life of the guardian or keeper of Caravaggio's masterpiece, Terry folds the counternarrative of the Neapolitan episode of Caravaggio's extraordinary and troubled life and his creation of the painting that was grounded in his experience of Neapolitan street life, the *lazzaroni* and *scugnizzi* of Spaccanapoli, serving as models for the sixteen figures that collide in an astonishing montage that not only defined the Baroque and its spectacle culture but also would open the way to the aesthetics of shock that comes to define modernism.

Similarly, Naples requires those who wish to comprehend it to be "necessary angels," and Caravaggio's masterpiece can serve as a model for confronting Naples through gaze-work and face-to-face work by which the epiphany of a face is recognized as a visitation. Terry describes the Naples experienced by Caravaggio in which he finds mercy. Terry writes: "Caravaggio will reenact the shocking tumult that confronts each new arrival to this metropolis. In his eye, Naples is a place with no center, a place where words fail. Brimming with life and death. In this city of cities, he will create a universal humanscape of our world." Angelo's vision of contemporary Naples corresponds: "In Naples, we live in chiaroscuro . . . between the sun and moon, life and death. That's what I think Caravaggio found here: life's true face."[1]

The double narrative provides the reader with a engaging reading experience that is rendered dynamic by the counterpointing of the italicized chapters dedicated to flashbacks of Caravaggio and the flash-forwards centered on Angelo, whose troubled life mirrors Caravaggio's. What results is a shifting narrative, a temporal montage by which the reader assumes perspective by incongruity, thereby mirroring the incongruity imposed by the viewing of Caravaggio's altarpiece and the congruity requisite for performing acts of mercy. By writing Naples Otherwise, Ward stages a powerful encounter with the city that dialogizes its history and present reality and in which impersonal and personal voices constantly collide in ways that epitomize this volume's attempt to encounter Naples deliriously as a Chaosmos and a contact zone, as the city that makes you repeat its discourse.

## *Dadapolis: A Manifesto for Reading/Writing/Viewing/Hearing/Performing Naples*

> The traveling citizen who gropes his way as far as Rome from one work of art to the next, as along a stockade, loses his nerve in Naples.
>
> *Walter Benjamin*

I borrow "Dadapolis" from Fabrizia Ramondino and Friedrich Müller, an epithet for Naples coined by them in their book, *Dadapolis: Caleidoscopio napoletano* (1989), a montage of aphorisms, fragments, and excerpts from the vast and multifarious body of writings that constitute the discourse on Naples. The book—canonic as an instance of writing/reading the city Otherwise—needs to be read as a daring work of montage/bricolage/collage that defies the safe haven of the anthology and travel diary, as a broken text that stages through cutting and juxtaposition an encounter with Naples that approximates the shocks and collisions conferred by the actual experience of Naples. As such it carries out the imperative declared by the Dadaist Walter Mehring in his disruptive poem "???What is DADAyama???" (1919;

originally in German), which is cited by Raimondino and is clearly the inspiration for the coinage of a new name for Naples, a city eternally, continuously subjected to renaming and the game of place names—Neapolis, Partenopea, Althenopolis, Neapocalisse, Gommora, and others.

Mehring concludes his poem with this challenge in the form of an incendiary slogan that deconstructs the proverb of proverbs—"Vedi Napoli e poi mori"—that governs much of the discourse on iconic Naples:

<<DADAyama Napoli e
    *Mori*>>

Here Mehring is calling for a delirious encounter with Naples, one that requires the madness of poetry and a kaleidoscopic gaze that turns the soul of the city topsy-turvy and inside out, one that confronts the chaos and contradictions of Naples by entering into communion with the city and its people, thereby fulfilling Naples's Dionysian qua Dadaist imperative— "To-die-in-order-to live." To experience Naples is to perform its surprises and to accept its rhythms, shocks, blows, and fragmentary moments; to see and feel Naples is to be shocked as in viewing Caravaggio's *The Seven Acts of Mercy*. Intrinsic to this DADAyama challenge is the refusal of the panorama, the unbroken and continuous view of the City of the Sun by which it has been auraticized and rendered a *carte postale* in the world's urban imaginary. Instead, one must see/read/write it as a broken or fragmented text that is located on the ground and in the play of surfaces. Naples discloses itself in the collisions of the vicoli and the congestion of the Lazaronitum; in the constant montage between Napoli *nobilissima* and *mala* Napoli, between sacred and profane Naples, between the euphoric and dysphoric city, that "disturbia" in which the sublime violence of Vesuvius is counterpointed by the beauty and ugliness of everyday life, including the ugliness of its culture of violence. In other words, Raimondino and Müller's book provides such an effective model for encountering Naples precisely because it takes the form of a montage and thus through the mediation of writing reproduces a soft version of the shocks and fragmentation governing the experience of Naples.

As a broken text it raises the question of what literary or visual form is most effective in representing Naples: the aphorism or fragment; the essay, long regarded as the most efficacious way of writing the city; the novel; the travel diary; poetry, particularly those poems in Neapolitan dialect—the corporeal language of the skin, the passionate language of the soul—that are converted into Neapolitan songs; and, dominating the twentieth-century and current discourse on Naples, cinema. And what genre of cinema is best suited to capture Naples: the panoramic cinema of the tourist film that enshrines the spectacle culture of Naples; the cinema of continuity epitomized by neorealism and its avatars; or "the cinema of poetry," to allude to Pasolini, in which montage or editing with effect is in force? This is, of course, a rhetorical question for each of these textual forms have their own particular strengths and weaknesses. What is more important is to delineate those specific texts that encounter Naples in profound ways and are strong enough to treat Naples as an aporetic or contradictory experience without resorting to the mask of stereotypes or a lapsing into the stigmatization of Napoli-phobia or the uncritical mystifications of Napoli-philia.

We fondly hope that our volume and its montage of (im)personal essays will lead you to learn from Naples and challenge you to:

<<DADAyama Napoli e
    *Mori*>>

## *Dangerous Supplement: The Parable of the Marinella Tie*

Here I want to express our gratitude to Valerio Caprara, supreme cineaste and film critic for *Il Mattino*, the daily newspaper of Naples, for his piece "Gomorrah: The Rest of the Story," which begins with a "filmosophical"— at once formalist and contextualizing—reading of Matteo Garrone's *Gomorra* (Gomorrah, 2008), a film based on Roberto Saviano's true-crime "novel"[2] and then concludes with an overview of Neapolitan cinema in the new millennium. Caprara gets Garrone's dialogue with Saviano right. As he writes: "Garrone transposes Saviano's descent into the abyss of an underworld entity with a non-formalist's devotion and, instead, has the strength and courage to confer on the writer a renewed expressive register with a particularly cinematic design."

Our view of contemporary Naples has been defined by the feminist politics of friendship represented in Elena Ferrante's tetralogy of Neapolitan novels[3] and by the anti-Camorra politics—the politics of rage and outrage—of the *Gomorra*-phenomenon. That phenomenon initiates in 2006 with the publication of Saviano's apocalyptic "anti-novel," a double-voiced text that involves an interplay between investigative reportage that exposes the Camorra's insidious hold on Naples and a howl of protest against the System. It is then extended by Garrone's equally polemical filmic adaptation (*Gomorra*, 2008), a counter-hegemonic film that disrupts both the content and narrative of the conventional Mafia movie and the formal language of traditional cinema, thereby creating a critical spectatorship that transposes the "Saviano effect/affect" into cinematic terms. It has been labeled as the "anti-*Godfather*" in recognition of its rejection of the fascinating gangsterism and Mafia cool and the patterns of identification with the gangster as "tragic hero" in play in Hollywood crime films. The phenomenon then culminates in the 2014 TV series *Gomorra* (three seasons so far, with a fourth in production), which is only loosely based on Saviano's and Garrone's works; and as a popular TV hit in the form of a Neapolitan version of *The Sopranos*, its politicizing Saviano-effect has been weakened.

Re the Saviano effect: How is the reader to respond to the sound and fury of Saviano's writing? What are the responsibilities of the ordinary ("legal") reader in engaging the text? How does the book position the Neapolitan reader differently from the outsider? Clearly, the neutral or non-Neapolitan and non-Italian reader is politicized at a distance: We affirm as imaginary Neapolitans the book's lesson—"It is time we stopped being a Gomorrah." Ideally, the book should revolutionize the "typical" Neapolitan reader, if such a typical reader capable of a gratuitous reading exists. Does the reading of the book incite the Neapolitan reader to take the leap of becoming an activist? These questions have deranged my own consciousness/conscience as a reader whom Saviano has expelled from the comfort zone of the "imaginary" politics of literature.

Saviano's writing of his "I know"—an allusion to Pasolini—is perhaps the most incendiary part of the book, an attack on the "rhyming lullabies of power" and a diatribe against cement that takes the form of a savage litany reminiscent of Gunter Grass's "There was once . . . ," the cross rhythm that informs the anti-Nazi drumming in *The Tin Drum*. Saviano concludes with a risky blast: "I know and I can prove it. I take no prisoners" (219).

With this "I know" Saviano elaborates an existential epistemology for survival in the land of the Camorra where one is folded into the System and where, consequently, the only form of opposition is to unfold the System by seeing through one's inscription within it.

The mention of folds reminds me of the parable of the narcissistic perfection of those signature Neapolitan ties made with the magic of seven folds. At the Rome airport, I recently encountered an elegant Neapolitan businessman who was "dressed to kill" in one of those elegant bespoke suits characteristic of Neapolitan dandyism and sartorial expertise. The gentleman wore no tie. As our conversation proceeded, I asked him why he was not wearing a tie. He told me about his long addiction to and love for Marinella ties and how his friends at the shop on Via Riviera di Chiaia had always catered to him by rehabilitating and refashioning his time-worn ties. But one day he witnessed a dressed-to-kill Camorrista, who was wearing an ultra-elegant and typically blue Marinella tie, shoot a man to death on the streets of Naples. From that day forward he refused to sport a Marinella tie. What would Saviano and Garrone make of this misplaced and futile act of protest? Can culture wars be waged without ties?

After hearing this story, I found myself in need of a chaser for my Neapolitan blues. If I had been in Naples, I would have purchased ten *caffè sospesi* and then proposed a toast to Saviano's informant and friend Pasquale—"the greatest tailor in the world"—who also appears as a character in Garrone's film in which, after almost being rubbed out by the mob and having lost his job as an haute couture tailor, he catches a glimpse of Scarlett Johansson on TV wearing one of his exquisite dresses.

NOTES

1. Terence Ward, *The Guardian of Mercy: How an Extraordinary Painting by Caravaggio Changed an Ordinary Life Today* (New York: Arcade, 2016), 100.
2. Robert Saviano, *Gomorrah*, translated by Virginia Jewiss (New York: Picador, 2007).
3. Elena Ferrante, known as the Neapolitan Quartet, translated by Anne Goldstein and published by Europa editions: *My Brilliant Friend* (2012); *The Story of a New Name* (2013); *Those Who Leave and Those Who Stay* (2014); *The Story of the Lost Child* (2015).

**Learning from Contemporary Naples/
Writing as a Neapolitan**

ONE

**Napòlide: A Man without Naples**

*Erri De Luca*

Pages, drops, hair, leaves break off that way.

I left home in the year 1968, my eighteenth, after a childhood burned through like a quarantine.

I chose the train and the schedule, not staking my fate on a ride: I wanted to control my departure. I took a window seat and remained rapt looking out at the procession bidding me farewell. While I was breaking away, the city was getting under my skin like one of those fishhooks that, having entered a wound, travel throughout the body, entrenched.

In the din of many slammed doors, I closed mine softly. My father was crying with regular sobs whose rhythm, piercing the ears like a nail, I repeated on the worksite when, whacking the hammer onto the chisel, it rang through my hands. He let me go without so much as a curse word.

His remains are on the hill near a local train station, with a view overlooking a lake.

If the word "return" has any meaning or orientation for me, if I even have a place to return to, it is that hill. "Return" for me is a word to be murmured, not a geographical one.

In Naples, when I get off the train, I don't feel back home. Instead I feel alone, with a more intimate right than I feel elsewhere. A city does not forgive separation, which is always a desertion. I agree with her, with the city: whoever wasn't there, whoever went missing, is no longer there, and his right to citizenship forfeited. Now, he is just another passerby that she takes in, without offering resistance, the glassy-eyed foreigner whom no one drives away, even as he is eyed like ill-gotten goods. I respect a city's exercising its right to scold whoever drifts from her. If I speak on her behalf, I do so as a guest, not as a citizen. And if I have no right to call myself stateless, I can call myself Naples-less, someone who has scraped his origins from his body, to deliver himself to the world.

I never again took root elsewhere.

Whoever has detached himself from Naples detaches himself from everything; nor does he have the spittle to paste himself to something, to someone.

I never spit again; I have only endured, endured.

The punch on my train ticket had the violent sound of a door slammed on one's back. I, not the ticket, was perforated.

There is an Ischian vine, *pér 'e palummo*, or the pigeon foot, that produces a somber, dark red, extracted more from some sort of wine tar than from the squeezing of grapes. Once in the mouth it tightens up the tongue, without relenting. It's a wine that softens voices and makes eyes ever deeper. There at the train window I was drunk on it.

Rome was a good sorting point. I climbed up a long set of stairs and at the top, on the fifth floor, I knocked on the door: furnished rooms. An old man full of wine and tobacco stains assigned me one of the three cots in the room. A communal armoire was the entirety of the furnishings. The room was near the university where I would have soon learned to run, to breath teargas, to pull up *sampietrini* [basalt cobblestones], to keep calm in the midst of a clash.

In the public gardens, the fall of '68 showed off its peace, its warmth, its ambling young women.

In the squares, fall was thick with the gray of antiriot units. I was from a city that had taught me about dense crowds, the agility to slip away from them, in fits and dashes. I could adapt easily to a crowd that incited rushes, charges, getaways in an empty space. Nothingness would open up, the wide open between the irregulars and the troops.

We were lucky that fall; the wind blew over our shoulders and would bring smoke into the troops' eyes.

Naples disappeared behind that curtain of chemical tears. I no longer belonged to her, to any place, nor to any "before." I was part of a revolt that rubbed away the past of each one of us, a revolt that was founding day one of a new city.

I reflect on the gas, on the smoke clouds behind which I saw the city disappear. Each generation of this century has dealt with its different gasses. Our European grandparents suffocated on Yperite, mustard gas for whoever has tasted it, a sulfur that would kill, leaving blistered corpses. Our fathers witnessed the use of Zyklon B in the extermination camps, but no one returned to tell of its odor. Our emigrants learned of firedamp in the coalmines, a highly flammable methane gas.

We were better off. We sampled teargas, we squeaked by with a chemical disturbance to our glands, assuaging them with lemon as an antidote. Perhaps the next generation will be dispersed by laughing gas. For now it is kept quiet by a music that, in heavy doses, acts like a nerve gas.

My gasses: when in the middle of a factory shift the milling machine's gear box would let out a mechanical scream and particle clouds of lubricating oil, when the lathe smoked from the milky, white cooling liquid, at that moment the balcony of my house in Naples was under my feet. The platform of the machine that was assigned to me was narrow and long like a balcony. As a boy, I would walk on it, rapt in my thoughts, closemouthed against the band of horizon that contained me. The factory platform was my eight-hour stroll, up and down with the hoist that held up the 180 kilogram motor axle. In which gas was freedom to be found? In those of the factory or in those that burned off at dawn on the terrace with a view of the sea, where one could hear the muffled sound of diesel engines in the fishing boats of Mergellina, even before the gas of those traveling by car?

The motion with which I would unload the piece from the hoist in order to clamp it into the milling cutter: I would try to do it, imitating with exertion the gestures of a barista who would release the coffee machine lever and who had before him the window and the sea. When I would place the piece under the old American press for straightening, the blow of thousands of kilograms that I would lower through the middle would make a sound on the steel counter like that of the docking drawbridge for the island ferry. And when the first piece might initiate the virgin cutters that I had mounted and throughout the workshop one could hear, on the first cut, the grim whistling of nails on steel, I could only hear the horn of the *Andrea Doria* entering the gulf. My body would respond with physical rhymes.

My hands were full of oil and iron filings; I never wore gloves because the fishermen had never worn them—neither did the bricklayers who were the workers I would encounter in my youth. I did not want to protect my hands. My workmates would laugh, telling me that if I were to pass near a magnet my fingers would get stuck on it.

Other gasses piled one on the other: I no longer recognize those of my birth city, the one that trafficked in waste materials and was covered from road to roof in grease and ash. The only thing that could outdo them was the autumnal southwest wind playing out its crucial scene on the waterfront, leaping over the reef and splashing like a "dead sea" between via Caracciolo and the Villa Comunale.

Napoli has never been satisfied with breathing just oxygen and nitrogen. She added to the blend a fermentation of tobacco, coffee, suet, a never-ending slow-cooking over murmuring flames.

Ragù, more than merely a Sunday sauce, was a need to produce an aroma, a soft smoke, a kitchen incense in action. It was about more than quickly biting into a piece of *maccheroni* bathed in it; it was, above all and even from the day before, the news of the ragù that mattered: a proliferation throughout the apartment building and into the streets. The air itself wore attire, even if rags, so as not to go about naked. In the dry winters with the windows always shut, the flow of air was dependent on the drafts in the broken window fixtures and the domestic asphyxia would thicken, producing a different smell in each room.

Now I sniff the Neapolitan air which has been cleansed of chimneys, coal-burning stoves, pots encrusted with black tomato, and clothes washed in the street. I only take in the insipid hydrocarbon of exhaust pipes that renders all city air the same. The new noses that fill themselves up, the new little lungs out and about under a few trees, they grow up with a homogenized asphyxiation.

There are no longer odors and my senses have been deadened elsewhere, by perils fallen to me far away from the city. I can't detect the sulfur foam that rose up from Pozzuoli with the northwest wind and that mixed with the blowhole of the blast furnaces. And the smokestacks of the ships that unloaded scrap iron, that mineral that did not belong to us, was not to be found in the lodes of our excavations. It came from far off and far off it would go, after being cleaned on the shores of Bagnoli, that coast of cloth bleachers in the South that flung onto the sand the world's dross.

The taste of roasted pitch refined by sea brine—that can still be savored, courtesy of the sea breeze. And the salted oxygen of the port, the rope soaked in the rainbow of furnace oil before passing around the docking bollard. And the hydrous calcium sulfate of the plaster used to shape the populace taken right out of some Nativity scene, on the shepherd's footpaths: the plaster that is the only work dust that never consumes our skin and that can be left in our wrinkles.

If Naples is baroque, my life and my body are not; they have adorned themselves differently: but the nose, upon returning, that sniffs inert materials, of closed workshops, the nose that presides over memories, that is baroque. It seeks out waste products, the stench, the enamel of things consumed, the boat that each spring is sunken so that its wood, soaked through, can be used again.

The nose knows only one love and controls the eyes. One does not cry because onions irritate the eyes but because they attack the nose: if one cannot breath, one cannot cry.

Even if mine has been broken by a fall in the mountains and discerns little, it is a baroque mucosa and makes me tear up when I breathe that cut.

I stop here, I will not go, will not see, beyond the surface, the sense of touch—*tactus* in Latin: that which has touched us, which is, in turn, much of what has been touched.

Goose pimples are a superficial reaction. Naples is a city that goes against the grain, the likes of those that drag nails over chalkboards and knife blades over marble. In its residents it arouses rashlike symptoms.

Whoever comes down to Naples knows this immediately: the experience of being touched many times. Cities that end at the sea gladly slope toward the waves by way of narrow passageways. Perhaps for defense, so that an enemy might awkwardly insinuate themselves into them through funnels, bottlenecks, narrow creases.

In Naples one's ease of motion has been banned. The passerby penetrates the blind labyrinth of touch and adjustment, of the invasion by others of his own person. Shuffling, avoidance, recoiling, and impact are the primary techniques of carrying on. It's really a vain simulation of haste; elsewhere an efficient pantomime for making one's way through a crowd. Haste here is considered a manifestation of a nervous condition. One is part of a general stickiness that cannot be avoided, in which detaching oneself is better left to those who wriggle through by capitalizing on the musclings of others, rather than pushing through on their own. One can easily be immersed in the fluid dynamics of the street. No formula has been transcribed to illustrate this phenomenon: for Naples's streets are flow regulated by crisis. At the point of maximum obstruction one notices a fluidity that suspends in part the weight of bodies, offering them lightness and oil-pressure dynamics. It's the effect that can be seen in a tub full of eels.

It is only in this second half of the century—for the first time in their history—that the well-to-do of the city have distanced themselves from the residential density of the downtown. In districts that are more relatively spacious, they manage to resemble the well-to-do of other cities, and their children share the uncertain honor of being taken for the well-bred youth of Rome or of Milan.

Once upon a time, it was one crammed multitude. The entire restlessness of movement underneath words was useful for pushing one's voice through the crowd, to give space to one's words, to make them heard. The gestures would rise from the termite mound, and they would rally behind a dialect, behind a shorthand of insults, transactions, notices, exclamations, predicaments.

But where Naples preserves still its density, the precious blend of promiscuity saves it from resembling anything but itself. Touching, speaking, never leaving its body inert: the same treatment that we provide to those in a coma. In Naples it is considered thoughtful that one citizen gratuitously sees to this on behalf of the other.

It was good for me, not morally but healthwise, to have passed my youth in this intensive-care city. There was so much of that plagued, but invincible, life in the city of youth to allow any youngster who grew up in a barrel of books to become good at a trade.

It trained my senses, such that I was able to keep my job in the acoustic mess of the workshop, in the perpetual dust of the jobsites. The constriction of the pores that I learned at a ripe age provided me with the indifference to the mice that would frolic at my feet during certain jobs in cellars and in attics; the resistance to vomiting at the unclogging of sewers, at the bats thicker than swarms of mosquitos in the African evenings.

The city skimmed, jostled, swayed, and never stopped rapping at your ears. In the time during which I was her raw material, Naples tattooed onto me dread, diseases, happiness. She traced them atop the rug of my goose-pimpled skin, a rash caused by mistaken squeamishness, repugnance.

I learned what disgust was at an early age. When an adult would chide me, I would get nauseous: if one struck me, the entirety of the repercussion found its way into my gut. The feeling of regurgitation rose in me so that I could have vomited from my mouth the words that had entered my ears. The interaction with adults was pointless for me. The scoldings were merely an attempt to blind me. I would not react externally; instead, I took it all quietly. But I have never been as rebellious as I was as a child, reacting with physical insurrection, vomiting, and fever against the adults' battlefield. Some of them I admired, but I met all of them underneath this sort of repulsion. I would shatter their chidings, repeating them to myself and rebutting them word for word. The better I knew Italian the more I would indifferently disarticulate many of their expressions declared in a moment of correction. Books had a salutary effect on my accusatory argumentations. I had a docile appearance and a court of law within me.

As time passed I resolved the distance between within and without: now it would seem I have a face that emits my seclusion.

I had as a consolation a fantasy that in a child is usually a nightmare: to not be my parents' child; to have been adopted and to have within me rebellious ancestors unknown to them. I never sought out a different identity, I did not daydream about another family; it was enough to think I was someone else's. I retreated into my outsider status, becoming impregnable. To hush in the face of reprimands was for me the utmost form of extraneousness. I was another; they would always take me for another child. Oh, my two poor parents: what sort of mushroom had arisen under their tree? Today my mother says: "I can no longer recall you as a child." It is her quiet, involuntary curse, to have begotten an outsider.

There are some constituent revulsions of one's character that form it and deform it more than pleasures and desires. For that reason I learned little from established experience and more from the opposite realm, my imagination. I would arrange innumerable sorts of difficulties or perils and outfit myself with a reaction. I would thus force myself to acquire such a reaction for my repertory as if it were a real experience. I then acted the part. The instances were many, but the time for reviewing them in my head was even more extensive. "What are you thinking about?," "about nothing," and it was true, it was the nothing of future gestures that was being archived. I would substitute the experience with a variety of different reactions. It was fake life, perfectly rehearsed, more vast and risky than real life. From here, and from the surrounding city, came the beginnings of my story writing.

When I was among them, her citizens had closed the market off to experiences: they were already in possession of them. They possessed all social demeanors, a repertoire of automatic reflexes, whose perfection I re-experienced only in some animal species. The street children knew all that there was to do, to survive, to play, to sidestep, to take a beating, to absorb quick blows. They could really take the punishment, as one might say of certain boxers. All experts, nothing could surprise them; "Ccà, nisciuno è fesso" [ain't nobody here a fool] either out of gullibility or because of some defect. The fools had died young.

In the city there was a tree of the knowledge of good and evil—larger the foliage of evil, being exposed to sun on the south side. It was a local tree and it had not been forbidden. Therefore everyone had taken a bite. Each one knew what to do and how.

The city had its own experience related to its kind, and it did not welcome anything that did not belong. So a child rebelling against its parents' experience would find itself in an expert city, thick with physical tests of membership in which to demonstrate one's quickness in learning, agility in reacting, gestures and vocal tones, flights and cliques of local Camorra bosses.

The more I learned, the more I would dissuade myself from belonging. The city affixed its motto to my skin: "T'aggia 'mparà e t'aggia perdere"

[I gotz ta learn ya, then I gotz ta lose ya], or, I must teach you and then I want to lose you.

Never maternal, never indulgent: I have no memory of her forgiving her own, nor her own forgiving each other.

At home nothing was pardoned in children who hadn't made amends, atoned with public apologies, promises to never fail again. Through a primer full of corrections we would learn to conduct ourselves, to not bang into certain corners in the house, in the city, and execute perfect itineraries, without knocking over the hurdles.

Naples conditioned me to other people. I was able to live for over a year in two rooms in Catania with five other workers; six cots and three work shifts tossed among us night and day. Each of us would sleep, cook, wash clothes, and write home according to different timetables. If I can give an example of the word "civilization," it is our tiptoed steps as we returned at dawn from the night shift, while outside there raged quite an uproar, and our undressing in the entryway in order to not wake up the others in the rooms.

As a result I wrote in confined spaces, with little comfort, an apt condition for stories. Whoever writes must not occupy too much space and neither too much of the surrounding silence. I have written from confined spaces, with little comfort, because I come from the thick of humanity in an overcrowded city: no doorway nor barred window could save us from the sonorous broth of arguments, lunches, toilet flushes, parties, mourning, and the insomnia of others. There was just no standing in opposition, no blocking one's senses to it: the density overflowed, consumed the air. Dialect was the lingo of the suffocated, concise so as to consume less air.

From here I took on my love of the wind, even for the one in the mountains that shakes a consortium of climbers and threatens to blow them from the sheer face of the mountain.

Wind, the *rùah* that suffocates and torments Kohèlet[1] seems like a song to me, fills my nostrils, my lungs and vocal chords, even my ears and all that which makes the body into a sail. It cleanses the air even if it's a scirocco and it makes sand rain down on geraniums. At the work sites, when it would pick up more strongly and where it made currents in empty rooms and everyone shut tight eyes and lips, my throat instead would open into an upwind song: I would swallow dust until it would cease, work or the wind. And when

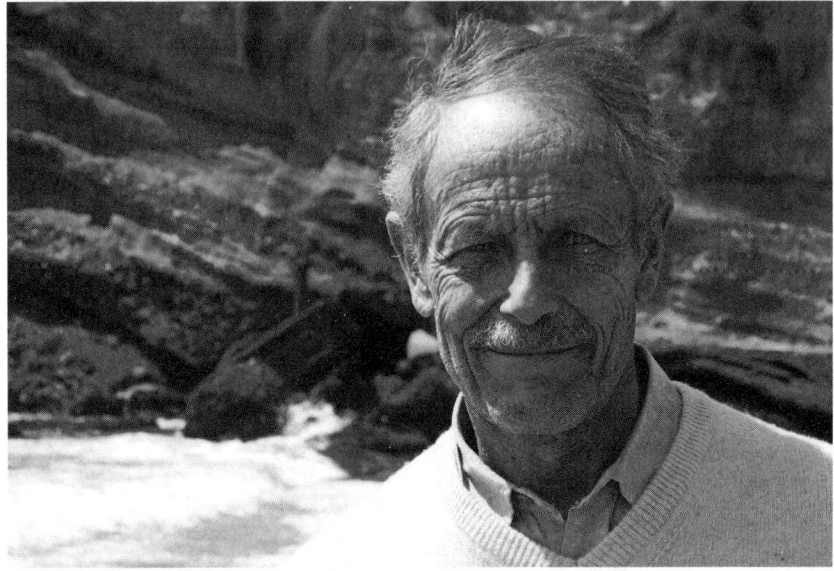

Figure 1-1. Erri De Luca. (Fondazione Erri De Luca)

I growled into fists raised against the north wind that would cleave the blood vessels in my face, then the wind was all right, even as it flayed the sky and killed old folks in the night with a chant made by drafts.

Where we are from, the old used to die at home, drawing up into their noses with the last bit of nitrogen the sleeping breath of grandchildren.

My father spoke again in Neapolitan, with great agony. His tone had a gravitas that only dialect can accommodate. "I'm still here," he told me one morning, having spent the night within a hair's breadth of the end without quite reaching it. "I'm still here"—he was fatigued by finding himself nailed to another day; so ungrateful to still be living. If there are silences in Neapolitan, I hushed just so, lowering my lids over my eyes, imperceptibly nodding my head backwards. The subtitles for those who don't know voiceless Neapolitan: "You're still here."

Dialect is like a sport: it has to be acquired at a tender age. It includes muscular dexterity, capability, moves, and shortcuts that are inadmissible off the field. I use it out of habit with my mother and this is how it goes in many communities. The Jews of Eastern Europe call Yiddish *mamelòshn*, mother's tongue. I use it with aggression toward those I don't know, for concision at work, for merriment at dinner parties, out of a need for precision when I handle a deck of Neapolitan cards, for identification when outsiders speak about the South.

Those who have quit using dialect have renounced a level of intimacy with their own world and have created distances. I have marked out many as well, but I preserve for my salvation a remnant of those abrupt thrusts of meaning and contact that are only possible in a *mamelòshn* . . . Neapolitan for me.

Naples in odd-numbered books and the Old Testament in the even ones; this pendulum of writing oscillates in my body. I stand aside from both; I write from elsewhere, not from my birth city, not out of faith.

In relating my small discoveries as a reader of sacred Scriptures, I considered Naples a counterweight to, right before, the name places of holy tales: the Neapolitan dialect of my birth would cross paths with the unexceptionable Hebrew of the divine. As a nonbeliever I allowed myself to be bedazzled by it. If I were devout, I would consider Hebrew a wonderful conduit, but without faith I've loved it for its perfection, not for its eternity. I never sought refuge in that language nor belonging.

"Who gives himself hath given and takes not back," writes Jacopone da Todi[2] in one of his love verses. I have given, entrusted, myself. I remain without a Naples, as someone who has used up his ration of membership, so little, being born in a place and then forcing his own separation from it: no new alliance could substitute for the destiny of birth. I would come to the Hebrew of the Scriptures out of the need to keep away from that place.

Naples comes from the East; the Tyrrhenian Sea was the furrow of Aegean sails. The mariners of the northeast wind came to found a polis all *nea* and they gave it a girl's name: Parthenope. Since then for whoever is born there, Naples is a rib. Whoever loses this place is perforce disoriented. I chanced to see Naples beneath other cities. Beneath Jerusalem, not the geographic one, but the one written in holy tales, the city atop ascents: the Hebrew language, when not cursing it, recalls it with an affection, even if it is superior, comparable to that of Neapolitan songs dedicated to Naples.

There is in that sacred tongue a pronominal particle of encouragement that one usually adds to a verb and can be taken as "come on!," "if you please!," with the goal of softening a command. This particle is *na*. The most terrible request by Iod/God, the one telling Abraham to sacrifice his son, is accompanied by a *na* that transforms an order into a request, into a top-down prayer, moving in against the flow with regard to the traffic direction of supplications. I like the thought of *na*: even in Naples orders are toned down into requests. The real difference between Germans and Neapolitans comes through in the handling of orders. Germans are used to placing a lot of creativity and much zeal in carrying out orders that might seem otherwise generic. Neapolitans invest much intelligence in hindering and skirting meticulous orders and procedures. For us a command has to be administered with the apparatus of discretion and suggestion; only this way can it arouse the feeling of collaboration and obtain a response. Even if an asking deity employs a *na* of incitement, we are authorized to consider the order an invitation.

I redirect onto Naples a phrase by Ezekiel the prophet about the besieged Jerusalem: "She [the city] is the stewpot and we are the meat." I was a child in a stewpot city, but it took my reading the Old Testament in order to see it.

Therefore, through reading, Naples has become a stand-in for Jerusalem. A second, yet more faded, rainbow forms at times next to the first; Naples is that second rainbow in light of the verses written for Jerusalem. Behind the holy city, and a bit tardier, rises the city of my origins and of the East, my *tabbùr haàretz*, navel of the earth. The navel is not the center; it is only a knot, a point of separation. From it I broke away with a chomp—the cord went to the cats but the knot is mine, sewn tight onto me. From it I extracted myself like a tooth from a jaw.

And if I no longer know how to see the city as it is, occasionally I feel it beneath other places and names. At times I run into the face of my father under the features of some old gentleman and one time in those of a young convict in Rome's Regina Coeli prison. When I notice this, I don't disclose it, in order to preserve the presence just for a bit longer. Because I am convinced that in that instant it's really him come back to brush his greeting past me, out of nostalgia.

I read Naples underneath Jerusalem and I saw it at Mostar among the crushed houses, on the magnificently miserable faces of Moslem slaves on the east shore, men from another time in the middle of incurable ruins and the dead buried in gardens. In the swarms of children I saw again those of my youth. Neapolitan children in eastern Mostar were teaming into the streets during the uncertain truce of May 1994, across from our vans. Scampering along under the sun of a war that had obliged them to remain months on end in the darkness of numbingly cold cellars.

The most alien on the ground were the elderly. Over them hung the offense of having survived children dead and buried, blown-up grandchildren or those taken by hunger. They would skim past the stone walls, looking at the ground with the pretext of not tripping. For them living itself was a sin and each meal a theft that deprived a child or grandchild of weight. In eastern Mostar Moslem grandparents would come forth from the slums across from our vans marked by red crosses, the first crosses that did not bring slaughter from the West. I saw on them the faces of my parents who would come forth to meet the Americans at the end of the summer of 1943, to meet those who had bombarded them a hundred times.

Beneath other flesh and another alphabet I saw Naples. I believe I recognized it even in its disguise.

One might want the city to belong to the South, even if it is at the center of the Mediterranean, the continent and container of the peninsula. We are European only in our rooster's crest called the Alps; as for the rest of our body, we are of the sea. For those born here, in this midpoint, being southern is a recent geographical error that owes to the unity of Italy.

If you were to trace a line from Marseilles to Beirut, from Trieste to Tripoli, from the Nile delta to that of the Rhone, from the Voissa River to the Rio Ebro, you would find the city there, the bisecting angle of the sea that renders Africa and the East, slaves, Arabs and Latins, the populace of a single riviera, all one coastal people. That sea is the room onto which our doors all open—this includes the waters of the Black Sea and the city of Odessa, full of vines and figs, of southern pages written by its very own Isaac Babel.

America came to Naples; here it chose to establish the center of the Mediterranean war. In the postwar period, the city became the brothel stop for American sailors. Elsewhere in Italy the allies were, in still occupied cities, the standing liberators with their encampments, bases, merchandise, cars, parties, courts. Each crime committed by sailors was adjudicated in their tribunal. Italian law was suspended in Naples; no longer the capital of the "Southern Question," it was a military question to be resolved by far-off powers. It had become Saigon, Manila, a strategic port-of-call, a naval station behind enemy lines.

I recall a mixture of two odors: the shoe polish and the torrential urinals overturned, face against the wall, by an off-duty patrol. Shiny black at the feet of white uniforms and beer drained from kidneys passed onto the alleyways, like giants they staggered, staying upright with one hand on a wall, the other hand on their thing.

America was in our house; not the one of those dollars sent back by emigrants who had left like so much cargo in a ship's hold, not the dollars of pain. They were the easy money of military ports from around the world.

A gathering of the Shore Patrol saw in my face the quarter American blood entrusted to me by my grandmother, Ruby De Luca, née Hammond. I cannot say as an inheritance because I never saw a dime, allowing it to wither, I denied that quarter blood in the years of the revolts against the many tyrants of the world, yelling our "go home!" anywhere we saw American soldiers on a tour of duty who dreamt of nothing else. And while I yelled this, one quarter of that scream was a revolt against myself, against my share of heritage that could well have served as an explanation: if I did not feel Neapolitan in a possessive sense, I owed it to the seed of those without a country, founders of cardboard cities, barroom customers, good enough to render to an overseas whore the earnings of a family, ready to vomit into the streets beers of the middle country and have their pockets lightened by those children.

Instead nothing: that American blood had been lost. But not on account of those guys from the Shore Patrol that met up with me in the alleyway during a police roundup. I was sixteen years old with a swimmer's body. They squashed me against a wall, together with a boisterous group of American boys in handcuffs. I said nothing. I admit wanting them to take me away, it mattered little where: if you're not able to do it yourself, you need someone else to snatch you up and sweep you far from home. One time, wars would take care of such things. Only when they emptied my pockets and took out my identification card did one of them, a black man as imposing as a king in Piazza Plebiscito, say to me: "Sorry Mister De Luca," and removed the nightstick from behind my neck.

I had already learned how to be American in Naples, how many times on the street had they asked me about, or offered me, any sundry things with that razzing accent, because when need be Neapolitans could also speak excellent American. They were mistaken with me, out of necessity, out of the habit of chatting up strangers. I did not believe that even the Americans could make a mistake with me. I chalked that up as an homage to my grandmother.

The whole time I was in Naples my body was that of a boy. Far away from there, in the manual labors of the adult age my contours became simpler. Each adjustment contains a loss. I could feel in my filling out a lack of alacrity, the tensing of my neck muscles, struggled to flatten out my hands, even when empty they would stay half closed, as if they always had a stone to hold. I had no desire to stiffen up like the workers. After eight hours I would return to my room and would add another hour of exercise. I would loosen the inflexibility under the weight of another fatigue. It would take a dose of violence to keep me focused.

Under the load of the workaday my body developed, resisted, changed its ways. I made it sweat, hurt it, exhausted it, and it never left me, never took ill. I was twenty-six years old—so many years—when I began to make of my body a worker. And the years then were rings that broadened shoulders, breath, hands: rings, those found in trees that you can count after cutting them down. I would learn to study my body and to understand that it was not mine. It had come from a crowd of masculine and feminine skeletons, struggles, afflictions. It was not mine; it came before me and I came to occupy it, I forced it toward the limits that it would reposition, without ever getting caught between me and some boundary. It wouldn't let himself be caught; I was never able to acquaint myself with it while I was agitated by love atop woman's body, nor on the light emptiness of a mountain wall. There it would shut itself in, absorbed in the task at hand and each triumph was all mine.

Naples was this body shaped by the multitudes, by the substratum, tried and retried and discovered to be greater than the attempt. Her patience is the fruit of a volcano that is there to plunge her into ashes. *Pacienza* [a regional variation of *pazienza*, or patience]: a local word that conflates *patire* [to suffer, perhaps "patiently"(?)] with that of consoling oneself with *pace* ["peace"; thus, *pacienza* would sound like "peacience" in English]; the virtue of a nervous system capable of supporting impossible lives. This is not resignation but the highest civilized state of experience, the sanctity of sailors on dry ground who know how to sleep through a storm. *Pacienza* to eyes, dry like bait [*comm'all'esca*]—that is, like a squid, a *totano* [European flying squid] that was cut into pieces and set to dry on the wood of a boat while one fished. *Pacienza* to live *accussì* [just '*atta way*] which is not just *cosí* [thus] but trammeling over *cosí*, to live *al cosí* [thusly], out of loyalty to a place. Whoever leaves or dies has lost *la pacienza* and *l'accussí* [thus and so].[3]

Other cities have workmen's bodies, fatigued, battle-worn bodies, defeated bodies, stiff, bloated. In the work sites I kept apart from the others, I didn't fit in with those bent backs. My leftover soup from the previous evening did not fit in at noontime with their robust sandwiches and with the liter they would insanely gulp down and then pay for in one breath and their bulging veins during the hours of work that would follow.

Today similar practices have disappeared and at the jobsites the workers follow diets prescribed by doctors and wives. Once upon a time they were men mollified by exhaustion, from their pores rivers of water and salt had gushed, the equivalent of a jetty. They were a mineral extracted each day before sun-up. They never dreamed and neither did I. As a boy I sleep lightly, the night was a fragile shell and it used to crack regularly. My dreams were akin to an egg. Then I would dream, I would take part in the chorus of the night, in brooding over eggs, who knows how much of the city could have fit in the shell. Far from there I learned the fossil sleep of rocks. My dreams were closed drawers; they were, as the Talmud says, unopened letters. The night was only a deposition of the body, a refueling process. After a torrent of years I have lost cognizance of my dreaming.

None of what I have become physically recalls my origins. Only the blow of a nightstick, still of wood then, that sought out my head and which out of instinct I blocked, sacrificing my shoulder as an offering: only that lump taken downtown was a foreshadow of future assaults. I reacted along with the crowd, kicking like a bunch of wild jackasses, braying curtly in the brief fray of the impact. It was an electric strike on the nerves that made bells ring in my head, the kind of bells one would hear at the end of school. Time seemed to indicate a charging pace; the years beat a tarantella tachycardia on the wrist and it all came down to one thing: us or them. From then onward I never felt shame for the skirmishes, because I know not how to judge them; I know only that I've been lucky, far away from my origins.

So it was with kisses as well: I never loved a Neapolitan girl the whole time in which I lived there—my whole adolescence until the age of eighteen. Only as an outsider, many years later, just passing through the city did

I meet one, the kind with open arms. In those belated kisses I was swallowing a saliva that cured all imperfections, even the dry leprosy of my adolescent desires. I tasted the kisses of consolation, prizes for the last one to arrive. They were lips without a future, but they brought peace.

After eighteen years, one: I returned in the seismic year of 1980. Thus a decade of empty rooms for scattered men seemed to begin with evacuations, rubble, and dust. Many of my relatives were residing in a prison, with me on the outside. My domicile then was an adverb of place: outside. Naples was shabby and shaken, as shivers and hordes were discharged onto slabs of tuff [*tufo*] stone.

In my childhood years I was stifled by the tuff-stone dust, by the moss of north-facing façades, the Lichworts, the creeks, the narrow slots in which pigeons would make homes, the birds that used no nests. Hills of volcanic tuff passed through my hands as blocks for walls, ones we had shaped with chisel, with saw; blocks to wet before spreading on the lime. I learned to like tuff stone outside of Naples and it never bothered me the way it did back then even without touching it.

In that roofless winter, no one could trust the stones of Naples any longer: crutches, bulwarks, logs, tubes, clamps, metal grates raised to the heavens, obstruction on top of obstruction and the crowds of people who left others behind to grab for the aid money that they would pour over themselves like rain.

I was there again but without adding a single year to those eighteen. The earlier ones were the whole tree; the last one was but a stick fallen out of that wood. Not for rescue assistance, not for a call of duty to country, for none of those intentions was I there again, but for love, the voice of happenstance that disguises itself as necessity. I had fallen in love one winter evening, in a pizzeria in Fuorigrotta, with a girl who was seated next to me. Would I have ever left if I hadn't met her? A whole other life was passing before me and draping over the former, canceling out the thirteen years of difference. I never left: I stayed here, you are my city; this is what I would tell her.

I used to confuse her name with the places of Naples, her body laying along the gulf, my perspiration and her scent of burned grass. The trill of mirth in her voice sang in my mind all day long, on the job site it continued to caress me deep down, dumbfounded me. I would await it in the evening while preparing dinner in the home we shared. On Sundays we would go back and forth on the curves of the Amalfi coast to munch on fried fish, to then digest them in some bed. I had sandpaper hands; she had delicate skin. No woman ever had opened up herself, bared herself, and squandered herself as much as she with me. A meager life is all I gave her in return for her complete sacrifice. She would end up depleting herself for me, slowly losing her light, becoming sullen. When the year ended, she asked that I no longer touch her. She was leaving with her red skin and the voice that died out at the bottom of the staircase, while from that point the city rose, with the raucous cry of a child. I positioned city and girl together; a life faded away, I was not a citizen of either.

It was late. It was not the girl to ask me not to touch her but the city: because cities coincide with loves, one is a citizen by virtue of embraces and I was one for a year. And after, nothing else to touch.

My father was no longer disappointed in me—his dry eyes would gladly observe me from the balcony, but they could not discern the wide expanse of dazzling blue. He could no longer distinguish sky from sea. Thus Napoli shut herself inside of me, awning upon awning collecting light, just as in the torn retina of my dear blind man leaning out from the balcony.

*Translated by Gregory M. Pell*

*Translator's Notes*

Some thoughts on the title: Though English includes the word "apolid," or stateless, it is of rare usage, and not particularly euphonic. There is very little in the way of directly and accurately translating "Napòlide" for different reasons. Napoli (Naples), comes from the Greek meaning "New City" (Neapolis). Yet, if we examined the word "Neapolis," it contains at once a newness (*Nea*) and the sense of lacking (*apolis*), depending on how we play with the syllabation. The ending of the title (-ide) contains, almost contradictorily within it, a sense of belonging, from the Greek—*ís* or—*ídos*. Furthermore, in a subconscious way, the phonetics of "Napòlide" makes an Italian think of the Latin *Eneide* (Virgil's epic poem about Aeneas, and precisely about his leaving Troy, his migrancy, and his settling in Italy). Thus, we have a number of levels of historic-linguistic tension and wordplay here—not to mention that, if read in a certain light, we could see Neapolis as *Ne* (not) and *apolis* (stateless), almost as if the word itself were a talismanic guard against statelessness and being there is linguistic manifestation of being *in* the state itself: to be Neapolitan is to be quintessentially of *the* city. Last, if we see *polide* (citizen) in opposition to *apolide* (stateless), then even as "Napòlide" seeks to speak of he who lives without an affiliation to Naples, because of the prefix "Nap-," we could read the title as citizen of the new (*nea*) and a reinforcement of being a citizen of Naples, though he no longer truly resides there—as if to say, only by being Naples-less after beginning life as Naples's citizen, can one reexamine what truly makes one a citizen of this mysterious and storied city. Just one word conjured all of this in my mind as I attempted to translate it.

NOTES

1. Kohèlet is the "Teacher," son of David, in Ecclesiastes; the *rùah* is the vital principle or animating force within living beings.
2. Franciscan friar from Umbria, 1230–1306.
3. De Luca's "*al cosí*" is his own invention. It is simply not used in Italian; rather, the author employs it to bridge the standard Italian *cosí* with the Neapolitan *accussí*, which phonetically and prepositionally adds a poetic emphasis and an air of conviction—not just "this" or "that way" but "in this very manner." While *cosí* disambiguates, *accussí* invites the interlocutor with a combination of open hospitality and non-negotiable exhortation for which Neapolitans are famous—sort of like the invitation to a coffee that is a sign of generosity, but one to which you cannot say "no."

TWO

## Scuorno (Vergogna)

*Francesco Durante*

People say: situation critical. It's the suitcase expression into which we stuff the persistence of our problems, the full effort to forget about them and their sudden rising to intensity. We were the city of the last European cholera epidemic in 1973. The earthquake city of 1980. The city of the recurring feuds among the Camorra: Cutolo clan against the New Family (during the 1980s), Secondigliano Alliance against all the others (1990s), the Di Lauro clan against the secessionists (the "aughts" of the twenty-first century). Now, we're the city of trash. The Futurists used to sing that "even after being bombed, Naples sings." Even the garbage crisis arouses our musical disposition. Tony "the Hick" was almost prophetic in 2005, when he cut the song "The Dark Side of the Moonezz."[1] Now many imitators have come out of the works. One of them yielded the impetuous "Toda joia toda monnezza,"[2] as danceable as it is irresponsible. And some evenings ago, down by Via Tribunali, at the "Impermanent Theatre"—whose name reflects its reality—I heard the legendary Virtuosi di San Martino beat any self-critique record by showing off with a number full of chilling dark humor: "Adolf's Great Mistake," where the piece talks of a "slightly inept dictator" and of an "amateurish racist," who, in attempting his genocide plan, had chosen the wrong people. For why have it in for the Jews when there were already the Neapolitans who were, and still are, "really quite annoying?"

Surely a misfortune more devastating than this, even on a symbolic level, could not have befallen us. Buried in trash, as if drowning in a sea of shit, which, by the way, we ourselves produced. Yeah, perhaps an issue for rich people, but perhaps also the most absolutely ignominious fate that could befall a city, its image, its credibility. A tragedy more colossal though less dramatic than [Katrina's] flooding of New Orleans. Our disaster is slow, silent, crawling, common. Like many things Neapolitan, it has no beginning or end, and for that reason it is more difficult to control. Moreover, appearing to be a direct confirmation of deeply ingrained prejudices and stereotypes—about the lack of city sanitation, sloppiness, breathtaking incivility, and Neapolitans' incorrigible attitude to chaos—this dilemma leads to irony, to sarcasm, and even to laughter. A ridiculous tragedy, all told, and as such typically homegrown.

I was thinking about this today, January 7, 2008, while aboard an old streetcar and keeping silent, and as if in a trance amid the shoving of the crowd, which was equally taciturn and engrossed. It seemed that degradation was gripping us all, that it was rendering our gestures mechanical and excluding any wonder. That even if it had quietly established, in that desultory resignation, unprecedented and oblique forms of sociopolitical activism, by which those who needed to step off did so by queuing up in order at the entrance, and those who needed to climb aboard did so with equal discipline, through the exit door: just so, without incident, without the usual jam at each stop. I noticed this curious phenomenon a moment before my gaze fixed on one of the stickers with which the Transportation Agency of Naples has always decorated many of its vehicles. They are none other than notices, like those that one finds on any bus in any place around the world, except that these are written in dialect, and I presume that function like an eye-wink to tourists, offering them a little splash of local color. On the one I was spying at the moment was written: "A lietto stritto, cocchete 'mmiezo" (that is: "If the bed is narrow, sleep in the middle"), an idiomatic motto that in the specific case must have meant, as the sign clarified: "Step off by using the central doors." And the fact that on that old tram there was simply no central door to be found, and that therefore that notice made absolutely no sense, caused me to grow sullen, adding frustration to frustration, like the umpteenth demonstration of our invincible sloppiness, the sort that manifests itself in its gross inadequacy especially when it comes to operating a complex system, as, for example, that of traffic.

Here everything is a bit broken down and improbable, to the point that when something works we are always pleasantly surprised, and even more filled with wonder are other Italians, as accustomed as we are to imagine Naples as some sort of Kobarid[3] in the shared perception, a squandered and immutable reality.

I found strong evidence of this sense of surprise in 1996. Then I was living in the gray Milan of the Northern League mayor, Marco Formentini. In Naples, though, the mayor for just over two years, was Antonio Bassolino, and the whole of Italy witnessed with perplexity the miracles, not those of San Gennaro but the ones the municipality was performing below the volcano. "Lucky you!" I heard some of my Milanese colleagues say in a state of pre-depression, humbled by the idea that their hospitable city might have become the encampment of Po Valley warriors, and I won't deny the shiver of pride, never truly experienced before in as much as I was Neapolitan, that ran up my spine. In that period, by the way, in the same Naples it was possible to happen upon the unprecedented: a pedestrian was reading the riot act to a driver who had passed through the crosswalk just before the light turned green; finger-wagging ladies grilling not very attentive citizens guilty of having thrown rubbish sacks into the dumpster in advance of the actual collection day; or, they scolded dog owners who had not expediently removed the dejections of their little puppies. And the best part was that the scolded did not counter—as one might have expected—with a typical "mind your freaking business," but obliging and contrite under a light of modest embarrassment, head down, they were accepting the criticisms without so much as a shoulder shrug, and at most turning up their arms in a silent request for forgiveness.

In actuality all of this lasted but a moment, and maybe a bit longer, as is always the case, in its media perception. For me today Antonio Bassolino is, as Toni Servillo and Mario Martone had already portrayed him in an episode of the film *The Vesuvians* (1997), a great, tragic, and painful figure, the living emblem of hope transformed into disappointment at the end of a trajectory that might have garnered the loser honor, laurels, and arms, but he didn't even get that. Bassolino has been a classic sinner of hubris, one who could invoke the envy of the gods. He had given it a shot; he had tried, with the meager finances at the disposal of an indebted municipality, and even more by playing on the energy of the charisma that was left from his popular election, to reawaken Neapolitan pride. He had succeeded in convincing them that it was a good and honorable thing to be citizens of this city; that it was right to feel part of it, to contribute to its recovery, to make known to the whole world that Naples is all right, one can find joy and live happily here. "Oui, je suis napolitain," proclaimed at the time the top-selling T-shirt in the city; and when, in Christmas of 1995, under the patronage of Naples, Mimmo Paladino completed in Piazza del Plebiscito the famous *Mountain of Salt*, it seemed it might become a civic masterpiece: in the oldest and most traditionalist city, at the center of that great square once liberated with revolutionary action from the parking lot of cars that used to cover it—contemporary art was becoming the celebration of a new relationship between residents and institutions, a cordial and profoundly democratic relationship. As if that art had always been amid the people, the people would use it, children would scale the mountain and come down from its slope with improvised sleds.

The sensational photo of Bill Clinton in the back alleys of the Spanish Quarter circulated the world showing him engaged in devouring the most classic of all pizzas that one eats on the street, that is "folded like a book," exactly as in all the other cities of the universal brotherhood of bread and fillings one might eat any sort of junk food: a falafel, a pastrami on rye, a gyro. There was at that time a municipal office of Normalcy, and I ended up almost worried that Naples, "step by step, a bit at a time"—as Bassolino kept repeating in his characteristic Afragola inflection—might become for me a truly "normal" city, losing, together with many negative aspects, also part of its soul, and in short that which, for better or for worse, makes it unique. I truly feared this, and nothing could reassure me, not even the fact that, at the time, the old council office of Culture had changed its title and had become the municipal office of Identity.

I've said it and I'll repeat it: for me Bassolino, perhaps also by virtue of certain features of his countenance, is this great tragic figure who today, right when revolting against him are part of those who for years had in great numbers quietly courted him, played the silent praetorian, contributing to the crystallization of his solitude and consequently his inclination toward a government control that comes from the outside, and that stands out ever more alone against the pointlessly blue sky of the Campania region. At a certain point he was pulled into the national government, first by being named minister of labor [or welfare?] and then with his appointment as governor of the region of Campania. The game became tougher, and he needed to play the game with equal toughness. He played and he lost. The defeat assumed the proportions of a spectacular fiasco, so grandiose as to outdo anything one could have predicted. In the end, in the exultant confusion of four hands-down election victories won with public acclaim, at the penultimate and ultimate hour growing ranks of infuriated Madame DeFarges ["tricoteuses" in the original] were able to infiltrate his camp. In the final analysis, it is rather logical that it went as it did: to a certain extent, that of Bassolino had seemed to be almost a revolution, and revolutions, even failed ones, very often end in the worst of ways. From a certain point of view, however, the gallows of [17]99 are way preferable to death by garbage: they were speedy, a clean and decisive bit of work, completely different from this disarray of rubbish taken from one spot and carried hither and thither that—in keeping with the gallows and to use the words of Lichtenberg—is like placing a lighting rod . . . atop the scaffold.

With revolutions, indeed, Naples maintains a quite difficult and tormented relationship. In the course of history she has had many, and at least two have clung to our memory: that of Masaniello, in 1647, and that of the [Republican] Jacobins, in 1799. Both are recalled by posterity, as with many things of this city, in an inextricable weave of tragedy and farce. With Masaniello there is the improvised reawakening of a populace/masses that from that moment onward becomes, for all of Europe, the sinister epitome of ever more vile peasant uprisings, a horrible riff-raff from which to guard oneself by any means. An impression confirmed, with even more vicious evidence, in the moment in which foundering went the republican hopes of 1799, hopes that were, moreover, reawakened by an aristocratic elite that in oh so an enlightened way had taken up the notion of cultivating that same riffraff from which it ought to have guarded itself, and that for this purpose considered enlisting them in a system of duties more ceremonious than substantial, such that they foreshadowed a Khmer Rouge mentality (though if not quite as violent), and even foisting on them wall newspapers in dialect, forgetting that they were illiterate. (And history repeats itself: in the political elections of April 2008, a minister from the outgoing Prodi administration revolted against the populace of Naples with posters that read with a wink: "I share Nicolais."[4] So clear then that of those revolutionaries, Cardinal Ruffo's sans-culottes,[5] that is to say, the most conspicuous part of that same riffraff resistant to its own edification, and a provincial version of it that was ever more brutal and irredentist, they might have eaten their enemies alive. They devoured them in the streets, with the same savage rapture with which, in 1982, Pasquale Barra, aka *'o nimale* [the animal] might have gnawed on the entrails of Francis Turatello in the special penitentiary of Bad'e Carros [in Nuoro, Sardegna]. The lifeless body of Eleonora Pimentel Fonseca dangled from the gallows of Piazza Mercato and the people danced around it, obscenely peeking under her robes, launching cheers of rejoicing in the direction of the executioner, "mastro Donato," and singing improvised rhymes to the rhythm of a demonic jig:

> Oh where has Lady Eleonora gone
> The one who used to dance atop the stage
> And who now dances in the middle of a square
> Together with Master Donato.

From that bloodbath was born the Italian Risorgimento, which then would carry along with it the seeds of a possible failure, united to the profound conviction of the impossibility of bringing the true light of civilization to dark and treacherous districts, if not by making use of brutal force: the same force that was used to repress the post-Unification brigands. The line "If you see a wolf and a Piemontese, shoot first at the Piemontese" has been etched in the memory of many a peoples from the southern Apennines.

I used the word "revolutions" and I realize that it, alongside the Neapolitan temperament, so disinclined to the strategic mobilization of the masses, sounds almost like a paradox. One might do better to call them "revolts" or, in the old-fashioned parlance, "tumults," "uprisings," "upheavals." Sudden storms that unleash themselves on the sea, and raise astounding waves, and gobble up splendid sea vessels. Then the sea subsides, loses any remnant of a ripple, and appears to have never even moved. In its depth remains the wreck of what has passed, deposited atop all of the other wrecks bitten by time's decay, even if still recognizable, always with some Colapesce[6] who might descend to visit them and to meet with their ghosts of blame and rancor who inhabit them and who from far off murmur incomprehensible and irritating dirges. History embeds itself into memory and demands to stay current; and in retrospect it changes into a role-playing game in which the actors themselves might suddenly lose the story line. Just so in 1799: were the actions of the Jacobins barricaded in the Castel Sant'Elmo and already aware of their imminent defeat, or the actions of the hordes of Sanfedisti[7] who, reconciled in a makeshift way by mountains and by countryside, remounted from the far away Calabrias in a single victorious march that led them to the capital, more "revolutionary?" And the Sanfedisti, if one truly wanted to see in them the seeds of an authentic energy, the same ones who sung of wanting to defend king and religion, how were they just able to be the great grandchildren of the same ones who only a century and a half earlier had not hesitated to take to the streets to oppose the arrival in Naples of the Inquisition tribunal?

In Naples there is not one reason to count on the wisdom of the vast majority of a populace that only in this city continues to earn its adjective "low." It is fickle and capricious like a spoiled child. Even today it is a populace that is couched on a pre-modern perspective of life. It is a populace that, unlike the rest of the world, which travels, moves about, chooses to go beyond the garden walls searching for those places in which to make the destiny that they feel they deserve, opts to complain of what a terrible catastrophe is even the idea of migrating, of leaving behind its eternal habits, its family, its neighborhood, the detestable panorama of its poverty. It is a populace that, in large part, prefers to adapt to the city's precariousness, trusting that from its large table some little crumb of food always has a chance of falling. How else to explain the residential density of a metropolis that by now, in one fell swoop, goes from Caserta to Mount Vesuvius, and detouring around it even pushes into the Sorrentine Peninsula on the one side, while on the other it goes toward the fields of Nocera almost right up to the doorways of Salerno? How else to explain that all of them are still here; here where nothing remains, no manufacturing, no office district; here where the factories are illegal and the pay is under the table; here where the only true welfare is political influence—graduated from the managerial role to that of the last socially useful worker—or criminal syndicates?

Only by updating it to this perspective of ruins am I able to appreciate the famous cry of 1972 by Eduardo De Filippo that he addressed to the young Neapolitans: *Fuijtevenne!* [Run for it!]. And I hope that De Filippo's invitation originated from considerations similar to those that I have expounded here; that above all it might help, that is, to put our youth on the alert against the risk of ending up trapped in the spiderweb of familism,[8] of neighborhoods, of bondage through which one can nevertheless eke out an existence, but by paying the horrible price that for far too long we Neapolitans have been paying, and that is to be foreigners in a land of which the world has some notion almost exclusively owing to our inventions and our calamities. Rubbish, or the "hard work" of the Camorra, occupies almost the entirety of our visual field. One might easily forget that so many people, despite all of this, continue to live, to work, and to attempt to construct their own future with dignity. And it is hard to fathom, even if one can do so in a distracted or peevish way, the paradox of Naples's enormous precariousness despite which the city is able to force the importance and value of its frenetic creativity onto an international community. There is its cinema and its theater, and so much contemporary art, and a thriving music scene. And perhaps in Italy there is no other city that produces so many writers. And if all this were to go away?

The other day, Dirk Schümer, a journalist for the *Frankfurter Allgemeine Zeitung*, who, among other things, lives in Venice, Italy, told me candidly, as if it were the most obvious thing in the world: "I would leave." And I, who have left already two times, and returned as many times, and who each time had to start from scratch, without, I would fittingly say, anyone caring the slightest about what I had accomplished, for the simple reason that I hadn't done any of it here, because I had not had the patience to wait for the slow and drawn-out Neapolitan carousel of chance to bestow on me sooner or later some form of recognition; I who know something about comings and goings, nonetheless, had nothing to say to him and, in fact, I was unable to do anything but ask myself: those two daughters of mine, what doctor ordered me to raise them here?

The truth is that I have no answer. I could even leave right now. I could go off to America, perhaps Omaha, Nebraska, or Flagstaff, Arizona. And in

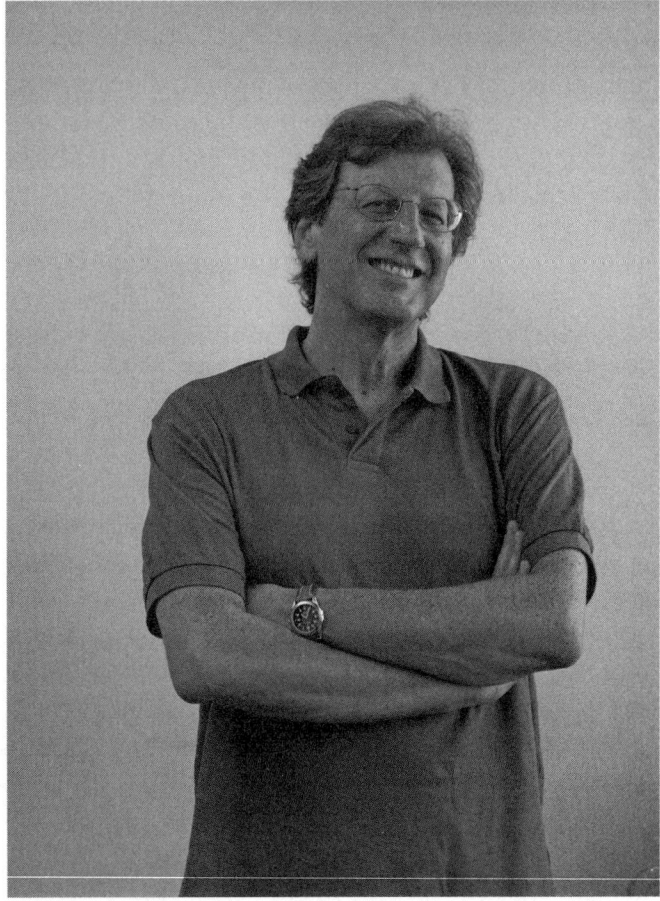

Figure 2-1. Francesco Durante. (Stefano Piedimonte)

my next life I plan on being reborn in the suburbs of a village on the Lofoten islands, and to undertake an honest career in the *baccalà* business; to work conscientiously each day from nine to five, to go to bed early, and to pop off to Oslo every two to three weeks, taking the ferry and getting plastered drunk during the weekend in sprawling Copenhagen. The thought of Norway, considerably more vast than Italy and less populated than the Neapolitan provinces, stays in my dreams, where a pasture of reindeer takes the place of the sacred cows of Chiaia, meaning the large, lazy, temperamental stray dogs that move around undisturbed in the streets of the so-called living room of Naples, gnawing on bones and entrails that a kind butcher throws to them on the sidewalk as if scattering rose petals among the bustle of fake blonds and young kids with drop-crotch jeans. Then I awaken and, aw' hell!, I am still here: I want to dehumanize myself among my peers, also get my shot at languishing on that single bone and the privations around which everyone gathers; I want to pretend nothing is happening each time this goes on, and go off to Capri instead of to the lake district; I want to fill my eyes with a dazzling blue, to drink my gin and tonic in the setting sun. These are modest luxuries, I know, but for now I'll take them. And then I want to also see how it all ends, if chance calls to lend a hand.

They ought to give a medal to those like me, or else make them a laughingstock. Those who one day long ago found themselves in the city of Diomira,[9] and it was a September evening, and from a balcony a woman's voice was yelling: Oh!, and they were happy. Those who also believe that they have returned, to Diomira, and instead have only reached Isidora.[10] The city of which they dreamed was the one that had already contained them, and their desires, since their youth. As Calvino writes, they are by now just memories.

On TV, the writer Valeria Parrella, with brilliant argumentation, has responded to the question that they have asked her, and that is: "why do you stay in Naples?"

Now I am waiting for her here, at the corner of via Duomo and via Foria: absolutely one of the noisiest spots in an already noisy Naples.

"Sant'Anna dei Lombardi beats it," however, I am assured by Valeria, who has made it to our appointment, and who then leads me into the tearoom of a bar in via Foria, the "great street" of Anna Maria Ortese, the one punctuated by heaps of garbage.

"Why don't I leave? Hmmm, why? I could say: I have a particularly advantageous rental agreement so why should I bother moving away?"

"How much do you pay?"

"Four-hundred-fifty Euros a month for 1,250 square feet on the sixth floor. On one side I see the sea, on the other Capodimonte."

"Tough life."

"But I realize that this, this alone, is not enough. And then I say that I am able to enjoy an existential microclimate that I find particularly charming.

Perhaps I am privileged, or rather, I know that I am. And I don't even want to mask my remaining in Naples as if it were the sign of my own special activism. I do not count myself among those who say: you know, if even we were to leave . . . No, that's not how it is—militant activism, if at all, is the next step, when you have decided to stay and you stay. The truth is that I don't have a coherent answer; I've yet to find one. But to those who ask me why I don't up and leave, for now moreover, I feel like responding: well, then why don't you leave?"

"Perhaps you stay because you need Naples in order to write the stories that you do write."

"But it's not even true that Naples is this great producer of stories. And even if it were, you can take Naples with you anywhere, as Ortese or Erri De Luca and many others have done. I have a husband from Perugia, Lorenzo: he has the gait and the close-mindedness of his city. When we got married, and then when we had Andrea, I believe my mother and my mother-in-law were convinced that we would have ended up living in Umbria. That it would have been easier to raise a child strolling through Corso Vannucci[11] or going on outings in the meadows of the Umbria Jazz Festival. But I never thought of leaving. Not only that: when one of my friends leaves Naples, I feel like holding a sort of funeral service. Even if one of them only goes to Rome, which is only about an hour and twenty minutes away by train."

"What is that 'existential microclimate' of which you just spoke?"

"All people experience their city in a different way. Here I feel welcomed, even if perhaps that's not the case. I know that this is an odd sentiment, but that's all I need to reconcile myself to the reality. Naples has this power over me: if you go out and you move about the historic center, it's difficult to spend your days alone. I've told you: it's an odd sentiment, and I guess it's not much different elsewhere, I can't imagine that here there is a network of support more integral than anywhere else. But it's the perceptions that we have."

"How come?"

"From my mother I believe I inherited the ability to succeed in talking with anyone as if it were the most natural thing in the world. One time Lorenzo and I were waiting an hour on line for the funicular and we met this guy who narrated in great detail all about some very private and complicated issue in his life. Lorenzo took me aside and in a soft voice asked me:

'Do you even know this guy?' You understand what I'm saying? In another city, if you keep in mind life in a neighborhood, perhaps the same thing might happen. In small little hamlets it definitely happens. But here this type of thing happens even outside of the neighborhood. Could we then think of Naples as the only big city that is at heart really a small village? I don't know. I do know however that as a little girl I had the opportunity to live in a small town, in Nocera Inferiore.[12] It happened after the earthquake [of 1980]. My father was teaching high school in Nocera and we went to live there for a period of time because the house in Naples needed much restoration and fixing up. I still recall the oppressiveness of the small town, and, mind you, I was really little, like seven or eight years old. I would go back to Naples to visit some relatives, and it would seem like something incredible to me. By myself, I would cross through the Vomero [a wealthy neighborhood], from San Martino all the way to via Luca Giordano, and it was like breathing in a kind of new freedom. I could feel the city embrace me, but the embrace was not like that of the small town. The big city would hug you and then discard you. That's it: perhaps this is my point."

"The embrace and the alienation. But even this can be found in all cities."

"I don't know. In the collection of stories *L'infanta sepolta*[13] by Anna Maria Ortese there is a tale, titled "The Prince's Friend," in which one speaks of a group of friends that was formed around the magazine *Sud* [South]. She says who they are: students, budding journalists, teachers, and even workers, and says that all of them stay together being that at least two are *truly* friends, and around them, around their gathering that is 'detached and radiant like that of some stars,' all the rest get together as soon as they recognize the 'humanity of a [common] accent.' You know what happens when you take a taxi? When right away you start talking to let the driver know that you're from Naples, and he can't take advantage of you? Perhaps this is more than just a preventive strategy; perhaps it helps to emphasize that you are part of the same community. In Milan this never happens."

"There all the taxi drivers are from Puglia. From Puglia and in the Northern League."

"Right. But all in all, here it's different. Below my apartment there are two business owners. Since I moved in, one of them began getting my mail for me—even those things for which a signature or a proxy is needed. I let him do it because it's quite convenient. He just simply does it, like so, without even asking anything in return—not even the postman would do that, just for the record. Then there is another one who is particularly content to know that I live here—imagine that, a woman who writes books right in our building!—and so, with utter casualness, but even with a certain amount of true kindness, if we go on vacation he advises the security guards that check on the store to have a look into our apartment building, and even to come up to our floor to make sure that all is in place."

"You have a job that does not impose a schedule on you. You are a successful writer. In brief, you are in the ideal situation for living in a city where, for those who have yet to make it, everything is much more difficult and tiring."

"I know I'm privileged, I've already said that. And I know quite well how much one needs to struggle here in Naples just to gain some recognition for something. But this is part of what I like about living here. I mean: here, if you are able to accomplish something, it ends up being a political gesture. You can't imagine the satisfaction!"

"It's like having overcome a long obstacle course."

"A lot of hard work, and a lot of losing one's temper. The worst in Naples is to work for an institution. We are not used to straightforwardness or transparency. We end up getting to the point through rather oblique byways. Then there are the institutes of culture, the newspapers, the Teatro Stabile . . . and there is a sort of balancing act between institutional character and private character. Even there one needs some adjustment, but that's okay. And there is the beauty of working exclusively with other people, of finding the same energy, the same enthusiasm. It is as if one were beginning a friendship based on a fact. It is true, you have to bust your hump, but it is also true that whatever you do, even something small, has a greater value. Perhaps it is not even fair: the worth of things should be intrinsic, but in the meantime, that's how it is."

"And so goes work. But there are those everyday things, those banal things that render life more difficult: rubbish, violent crime . . . you who live these things, how do you manage?"

"I have my own arrogance that I know how to employ. After all, I was born here, and I'm not doing too badly. When my mother was pregnant with me, there was still cholera in Naples. I'm not sure that things are much more tragic than they were twenty, thirty years ago. It is the rerun of a tragedy that in some ways is able to find its equilibrium; otherwise the city would already have self-combusted some time ago. At any event, before perhaps people might have stabbed you out of hunger; now they do it to take your cell-phone."

"Do you notice how dangerous Naples is?"

"I notice it sometimes. I'm used to not carrying my bag on the street side, but I have not replaced my bag with a backpack. And I keep on my person original documents, not photocopies. Then, as I have already said, I have my sense of arrogance. A while ago I was in line at the pharmacy and in walks a group of *ianare* [vulgar, trashy "witches"], interrupting everyone to ask something as soon as they enter. I turn around and say to them: Look! I was here first. And they start to screw with me: sure, whatever, our little fragile doll. So I turn around and would have loved to give them the classic head-butt in the face, and instead I come up with this: uh, excuse me, are you talking about me? Can't you see that one should be a bit more respectful here? And then one kept on at it, but with an ever more submissive tone. I said to myself: now I'll go outside and they'll jump me, that much is certain. However, they did no such thing."

"You are young. You have a little boy. Can you see yourself here in the long term?"

"I can, yes. I tell myself that by now I've done okay. As for Andrea, well, I don't know. But if in the end I had to leave, I would up and go to Barcelona. Each time I go there I tell myself: ah, this place could be as beautiful as Naples. Or perhaps I'd go to Genoa, which above all is able to speak to me with familial sentiment: you see that friggin' superelevated highway above the port and you are overcome by a rage that you already know."

*Translated by Gregory M. Pell*

*Translator's Notes*

The title is translated as "Abash (Shame)." In standard Italian, the word for shame is *vergogna*, which is the parenthetical subtitle of the original. But *scuorno* is somehow more than a mere synonym of *vergogna*: it is the shame of someone who has been caught in the act and relieved of his "horns" (*corna*). In other words, he who suffers *scuorno* is one who lives the frustration and humiliation of losing his potency. Though the horns (*le corna*) in Italian can be associated with the horns of the cuckold, in this instance the etymology traces back to the sense of the horns to be found in a military helmet or crown. However, in the case of the title, when considered in the context of Durante's reportage, there is an ironic implication: the problem is not that certain people feel this shame and have to live with it; on the contrary, they have no self-awareness of it in the first place, as in the Neapolitan expression "nun cunosce o' scuorno" (to know no shame).

NOTES

1. "The Barf Side of the Moon" (clearly a play on Pink Floyd's song, "The Dark Side of the Moon," and the Neapolitan word for garbage, *monnezza*, which, in turn, is the dialectic form of *immondizia*).
2. "So much joy, so much garbage" (a play on the Roy Paci song "Toda joia toda beleza," or "So much joy, so much beauty," in Portuguese).
3. City on the border, site of the World War I battle of Caporetto in which Italy almost lost the war.
4. A cross between Veltroni's "I care" and Obama's "Yes, we can."
5. That is, left-wing populist antirepublican masses.
6. Legendary half-man, half-fish, from Messina, Sicily.
7. Cardinal Ruffo's peasant antirepublican movement.
8. On the concept of "amoral familism," see Edward C. Banfield, *The Moral Basis of a Backward Society* (New York: Free Press, 1967); for a critique of "amoral familism," see Sydel Silverman, "Agricultural Organization, Social Structure and Values in Italy: Amoral Familism Reconsidered," *American Anthropologist* 70, no. 1 (February 1968): 1–20.
9. The fictitious city of cupolas from Italo Calvino's *Invisible Cities*.
10. The city of spiral staircases from Calvino's same book.
11. The main drag of Perugia.
12. In the province of Salerno.
13. *The Buried Princess*; borrowing the Spanish word for it refers to the daughter of a Spanish ruler.

**The View from America**

THREE

*Naples/New York:* **Across the Watery Divide**

B. Amore

The origins of the *Naples/New York* series of art assemblages exhibited at the Hofstra University Museum in the fall of 2011 stem from a book tour in Italy during which I picked up intriguing objects from iconic Neapolitan streets: Spaccanapoli, Via della Stazione, Via del Duomo. They became counterparts to what I was already finding in New York City in Soho, Chelsea, on Broadway, 2nd Avenue, and 14th Street. All of these objects were *custodito*—conserved; each "find" in one city finding its complement in the other; some delicate, some crude. The gloves were preserved in bronze, reaching across the distance of the Atlantic's watery divide to clasp hands with one another.[1]

When Pellegrino D'Acierno shared his vision for a conference, "Delirious Naples," and invited me to participate, I continued on the series with an even keener sense of purpose. Working in my studio in Vermont throughout a white winter, sifting through my finds, reliving my own experiences of Naples, waiting anxiously for my friend Stefania Rinaldi's box of "findings" to join with my own, I lived many questions before the actual works of art coalesced. Although I had already collected quite a few bits and pieces from Neapolitan and New York streets, the question of the integrating link was still an open one. I was immersed in an inner debate regarding images, graphic representations, people's faces, places, text.

It was a casual conversation with another friend, Bob Oppedisano, who proffered that Neapolitan music was one of the important links between Naples and New York, that sparked a flash of deeper interest in the possibility that music could be the integrating source that I was seeking. I had grown up in a family steeped in Neapolitan song. Those poetic melodies were the lullabies that preceded sleep, echoing from the circular grooves of my mother's old 78 and 33 rpm records. They were the songs played and sung at all of the family weddings.

After considerable deliberation, primarily because I had originally discounted the music as "too familiar," perhaps even clichéd, there ensued a search for exactly which music might work in the context of both the visual and textual information that I sought. I recalled a show I'd seen at the John D. Calandra Institute organized by Joseph Sciorra that featured the Mark Pezzano collection of historic Neapolitan music, some with ornate cover sheets.[2] Mary Brown, the archivist at the Center for Migration Studies, provided quite a trove of *Farfariello* pieces. A chance meeting with Charles Sant'Elia at an Italian American Writers group gave me another rich source of visual material, drawn from his own family collections and from E. Rossi and Company publications. Stefania Rinaldi, from the San Carlo Opera House in Naples, an old family friend, sent more recent and better known *canzoni*. Simona Frasca's book, *Rondini di passaggio*,[3] further strengthened my interest. What began as a personal studio interest blossomed into a collaborative cross-cultural aesthetic project.

Each of the resultant assemblages is really like a mini-sociological study, particularly if you are able to read the Italian texts. The words and the music traversing three, four generations are, even today, passing on key aspects of culture and history along with the notes of familiar airs. The amount of information contained within each "mini-drama" is continuously revelatory, belying the popular notion that Neapolitan songs merely celebrate or bemoan the throes of love. The pieces that I chose, many of which were written by immigrant songwriters in New York, such as *Holding the Street in My Hands/Sti Mmane* (plate 3-1), reveal the desperation felt in America, tedious work in dark basements, serenades on Mulberry Street, love "American style" where one of the first questions is "Do you have a jobba?"

Thus, Neapolitan song, known all over the world, became the aesthetic leitmotif linking the artwork that was created for the *Naples/New York*. The lyrics and melodies were written by poets and composers both in Italy and in America at a time of flourishing interchange between the two countries. The found pieces, flotsam and jetsam of city life, are juxtaposed with the elegantly designed music covers or actual scores. As an artist, I feel that I am using a contemporary idiom to collaborate with artists from the past. There is interplay between high and low culture, which finds its integration in the finished work of art.

All of my art integrates image, text, and sculptural elements. Experimentation and work with found materials is an essential key to my working process in which accident and innovation are in constant interplay. Each decision to use an image or an object calls for subsequent adjustments, sensitive recalibrations of forms, of colors. The completed pieces become complex mini-installations in relief. The form or gesture of the artifact is never altered. I use archival preservatives and may enhance the given materials in subtle ways by sometimes adding a patina, but always respecting its innate nature and history. The work of integrating the visual music covers, the texts of the songs and the bits and pieces of found objects from the streets of both Naples and New York presented a unique and complex creative challenge.

The songs tell stories in the words of the people who lived the dichotomy of belonging to disparate worlds. In ways sometimes poignant, always expressive, and often ironic, Eduardo Migliaccio "Farfariello," a Neapolitan writer and entertainer who performed in New York, commented on the plight of the immigrant as only an insider could. Using coded Neapolitan dialect words and Italian-English hybrids, he expressed the contradictions and everyday dilemmas best when he wrote "Lu cafone che ragiona" (The Peasant Who Reasons), exposing the seeming naïveté of the protagonist and his insightful observations of his new countrymen.

In the words of "Portame a casa" from the Center for Migration Studies Archives, the immigrant greenhorn is lost on Broadway. He's had one glass of wine too many, and encountered a painted woman of the streets, but all he wants to do is find his way home. Of course, there is always the deeper longing for the mother place, the *luogo del cuore*. These songs written on both sides of the silver ocean give us particular insights into the complex situations of Italian immigrants in the early twentieth century; the stressful work and living conditions, the ability to make money, the strangeness of a new culture and, always, the longing for home.

Each piece of found detritus, the veritable cast-offs of New York and Neapolitan daily life, tells a story, or a part of a story in combination with the Neapolitan sheet music. A glove covered with sparkles, contributed by Mary Brown, excites the imagination. Even when she mailed it to me, she began "telling a story" about it. Many of the elements in the assemblage *Piedigrotta Passione* were found in one winter evening's walk in Chelsea with Pellegrino D'Acierno. (see plate 3-2). The larger fragment of cardboard in the piece actually has "*vetro*—made it Italy" printed on the reverse, but the side chosen to be seen in the finished work was selected, after much deliberation, as a stronger aesthetic contribution to the whole. Fragments of tar roofing from the original Ellis Island Immigration Station are interspersed throughout the *Naples/New York* series and speak to the puzzle pieces of the immigrant experience.

The pairing of the two cities, Naples and New York, seemed natural to me. In the piece *Floating between Liberty and Vesuvius* (plate 3-3), the "islands" of soaked and matted newspaper were found near Union Square in New York and combine with an old hand-forged piece from my grandmother's home village of Lapio in Campania, Italy, to create a story of back and forth, *'nnanza e 'rrete*, between Naples and New York. Each was a locus of tremendous immigrant activity.

The installation *Between Two Shores/Tra Due Sponde* (plate 3-4) graphically depicts the immigrant crossings from the lava of Vesuvius to the city grids and skyscrapers of New York. The pickax heads, irons, and workers' gloves become the boats traversing the ocean between.

There was so much trafficking back and forth between the ports that the immigrants were called *rondini di passaggio* (birds of passage). The Italians crisscrossed the ocean more than any other immigrant group—returning to their home villages in the low seasons of work—hence their moniker. Here, the gloves, always a symbol for the missing person, fly like birds, from Naples, west, to New York, and from New York, east, to Naples. They become an integral part of the twenty-eight-foot-wide *Delirious Naples* diorama (plate 3-5), which celebrates the vitality of the city of Naples. The graffiti-inspired writing forms the twin peaks of Vesuvius, which overlooks the city and the bay. Flame-colored lava stones punctuate the illusionistic ocean.

In terms of my creative working process, the addition of color was an enormous step. After many months of painting each found piece with as many as twelve coats of preservative, it was ready to be integrated into the entire assemblage. It was then that the finishing touches were carefully applied, once again in several layers. The different hues were brushed on lightly against the textured surfaces to bring new life to the battered found pieces that most people call trash and I call treasure. This is a delicate process and, if you look closely, you will see that the original strata are still visible—even the dirt from the street is preserved! One hopes for a transformation of the mundane into the sublime—a transmutation of straw into gold. Each element is archivally preserved, like a fly in amber. These ordinary pieces of reality, barely noticed in their former life, become transcendent symbols of what was and what might become. Each piece, such as *Heart of Naples/Hands of New York* (plate 3-6), so ordinary, so precious—is a reflection of the human condition, how much we take for granted, what we value when it is gone, reminders of our transient passage and the constancy of change.

Like illuminated manuscripts, where ordinary letters are enhanced, the common street elements undergo a transmutation. I thrive on the interaction of an inner dialogue and the formal challenge of transforming such disparate materials into a work of art so that the entire piece becomes a kind of weaving. There is a constant search for a balance between a personal reality and the demands of the increasingly complex world in which we find ourselves.

The finished assemblages are like palimpsests, with layers of images, texts, and street materials revealing both the history and sociology of fertile immigrant life. Like present-day immigrants, the objects exist in the shadow of modernity, inextricably tied to an inevitable transience. What tells more stories about a populace than what it throws away? Like the shadow side of what is customarily preserved, it completes the whole, complementing the bella figura of art, antiques, and prized personal possessions.

In *Roots, for Montefalcione* (plate 3-7), the old sifter still holds some of the seeds and grain that were present when I found it in my paternal grandparents' village of Montefalcione. The signs of its wear and humble origin are obvious, but also its simple, elegant construction enhanced by bits of iridescent layering. What is "refused" or refuse, that is, detritus, bears scars and wounds that are generally hidden. To take these elements, lovingly preserve them, and make them into art is a true transformation, a healing of the incongruent realities that surround us, both personal and societal.

*Window to a Wider World (for Montefalcione)* (plate 3-8) comes from the same town. The central window was abandoned, found leaning against one of the stucco buildings as the *paese* modernized. The central element, a casting of the Easter *tarallo* (pastry) from the town, speaks to a circle of change, as does the view through the small window to the patterned maps of both Naples and New York. The sculptures evolve in the midst of this panoply of sources to create a sense of wholeness out of the myriad parts. Is this not the task we face every day in this increasingly intricate world?

NOTES

1. Enormous gratitude is due to Mary Brown of the Center for Migration Studies; Charles Sant'Elia; Stefania Rinaldi of the San Carlo Opera House, Naples; Ernie Rossi of the historic E. Rossi & Co.; and the John D. Calandra Italian American Institute, Queens College (CUNY), who gave me permission to use images and words from their archives of Neapolitan music; to Susan Benevento, Fred Gardaphé, Norris V. Hardy, Larisa Lawrence, Joseph Sciorra for contributing materials included in the artworks; and to Otis Kellogg, Ethan Mitchell, and Don Ramey for technical assistance.

2. *Chist'è New York: The Mark Pezzano Collection of Neapolitan Sheet Music from New York*, an exhibit at the John D. Calandra Italian American Institute, CUNY, March 19–June 26, 2009; curated by Rosangela Briscese and Joseph Sciorra; see their chapter in *Neapolitan Postcards: The Canzone Napoletana as Transnational Subject*, ed. Goffredo Plastino and Joseph Sciorra (Lanham, MD: Rowman and Littlefield, 2016), 81–96.

3. See the English translation, Simona Frasca, *Italian Birds of Passage: The Diaspora of Neapolitan Musicians in New York* (New York: Palgrave Macmillan, 2014).

FOUR

## Auratic Detritus/Sublime Trash: "Rough Magic"; or, The Art of Transfiguration in B. Amore's *Naples/New York* Installation

*Pellegrino D'Acierno*

> Se gira 'o munno sano,  We can travel the globe
> se va a cercà furtuna,  in search of good luck
> ma quanno sponta a' luna  but when the moon rises
> lontana a' Napule nun se  we can't stay away from our
>   pó sta!          Naples!
>
> —E. A. MARIO, "Santa Lucia Luntana"/"Faraway Santa Lucia"

*The Place of Wonder*

Just as she did in *Life Line—Filo della Vita: An Italian American Odyssey 1901–2001*, her celebrated exhibition for the Ellis Island Museum that memorialized and sacralized the emigrant/immigrant experience,[1] B. Amore created, at the behest of the Hofstra University Museum, a site-specific work—*Naples/New York*—that transformed its exhibition space into a place of wonder, a site of transfiguration in which the viewer marveled at the sea changes that B. Amore's "rough magic" has wrought on degraded, derelict, and forlorn objects retrieved from the streets of Naples and New York as she assembled and elevated them into rich and strange artistic configurations, charging those lumpen objects with wonder and endowing them with the force of epiphanies.

## Eureka!

There can be no vade mecum or preparation for the aesthetic experience of wonder because it operates through the suddenness of surprise. Hence, my primary advice to the viewer of the installation then and to future viewers[2] is to turn on your imagination's eureka radar and be prepared to receive the gifts in the form of countless surprises and eureka (I have found it!) moments that B. has embedded within her intricate assemblages. These constellations of found materials will lead you to notice the unnoticeable as did B. when she first sensed the presencing of those ordinary and downtrodden objects hidden in the streets and then imagined their transformation into luminous aesthetic objects that, despite their eventual transfiguration, would never violate or disguise the elemental force of their prosaic materiality.

It is a truism that anything looked at closely becomes wonderful. This needs to be rewritten in the case of B.'s art; anything doubled or crisscrossed becomes wonderful: the sensed and the imagined, the imagined and the remembered, the here and the there, the now and the then. Each of the ten assemblages and the installation as a whole engages us in acts of doubling, whether they take the imaginal form of doubling back to the original sensing of the found object; the geographic form of doubling Naples and New York, which perpetually crisscross and exchange places in the topography of the installation and its mental mapping of the diaspora; the cultural form of remembering the transatlantic transits of the emigrants/immigrants whose journeys are reenacted or doubled by the orbiting of objects within the installation. And through these acts of aesthetic doubling, we find the "parable of the crossroads" that B. has embedded within the spatial and temporal story set out in the installation: the parable of the diasporic identity and the human sensibility of the immigrant who is as downtrodden as those lost and found objects; a doubled subject/object crisscrossed or perhaps "double-crossed" by the Old World and the New World.

My other advice to the past and future spectator is to accept the invitation to voyage extended by the installation. It will take you into a visual territory marked by the aesthetic experience of pleasure. As a voyage of discovery and self-discovery, it will involve you in imaginary transits, at once spatial and temporal, between Naples and New York, in which the boundaries between those extravagant cities become blurred. As you will also see, this imaginary transiting will oblige you to transform your practices as a viewer, especially the lateral movement ritually imposed by the postmodern display and exhibition. In following the itineraries of those "birds of passage," which are placed in the diorama and the centerpiece and represented by street-found gloves that B. has endowed with the power of flight, you will enter—repeatedly losing and finding yourself—within the installation's endless circulation and recirculation of objects and signs, always experiencing the pleasure of the unexpected (see plate 4-1). And here we approach the parable of spectatorship that B. has embedded in the installation and its spatial story of migration: you must perform it as a transient, as an "art-immigrant," for the stranger is particularly attuned to the solicitations of wonder.

*Wondering about Wonder*

Is it still possible to speak of wonder when confronting contemporary art? Our current Age of Irony—call it post-postmodernism—has almost banished the term "wonder" from its aesthetic lexicon, and my use of it to describe the aesthetic experience generated by a decidedly contemporary art work such as B. Amore's installation is intended to be provocative. The term harkens back to an aesthetic experience grounded in a deep and authentic involvement with art informed by a "dialectic of depth—inside/outside."[3] Now that "the death of the subject" has occurred—at least according to Fredric Jameson—the subjectivity and interiority that attune to the aesthetic experience of wonder seem to have been liquidated, displaced by the aesthetics of shock and by a postauratic art that presents itself all too often as a superficial game.

B. Amore clearly works within the tradition of postmodern art as display and collection, employing the format of the site-specific installation and those well-established techniques and processes—assemblage, collage, combine, synthetic relief construction, "sculpture manqué," and, above all, bricolage, her governing technique—that originate with the avant-garde experiments of Picasso and Marcel Duchamp and have become standard operating procedures for contemporary artists.

I use "wonder" to get at the difference at work in B.'s art, as a way of asterisking it and setting it apart from the all-too-typical art of our current installment of spectacle culture and the hyper-aesthetics, "anaesthetics," and anti-aesthetics that dominate it. B. refuses, above all, the aesthetics of shock—shock as the last aesthetic experience. The shock is a resounding slap in the face; wonder is a soft and silent explosion that goes off in the imagination when it is surprised by the unexpected, by the "instressed" and countering experience or art object. B. would never even dream of attaching one of her humble "street-made" gloves to the hands of Mona Lisa à la Duchamp's moustache for that would be to desecrate the integrity of the glove—not Leonardo's masterpiece!

In this age of weak art, B. is committed to the radical and original experimentation of strong art. Hers is an art of tactics, an art of making do with poor materials and with the poor tactic of bricolage; tactics are always opposed to an art of strategies, the strategies of the masterpiece and the art of the masters—dominant art. Tactics are necessarily political for they counter the strategies of official and commodified art. Whether viewed as tactics of a poor art concerned with everything that has been marginalized and forgotten or as the tactics of a woman artist concerned with declaring her attunement to wonder (for there is something strongly feminine in wonder), her poor art of bricolage stages one of the strongest artistic encounters with our contemporary condition of homelessness and placelessness as prefigured by the immigrant experience and now realized in the globalization of what Rem Koolhass terms "Junkspace."[4] By transfiguring the most ordinary and dirt-breeding of objects and constellating them into striking assemblages, she reminds us of the capacity of contemporary art to engage us in auratic forms of aesthetic experience by which, in this age of distraction in which the subject is put to death by incessant tweeting, we become, whether as creators or as spectators, "subjects."

*Deconstructing the Collection Zone*

This is in no way to suggest that B. has created a wonder-room or cabinet of curiosities dedicated to the Disneyfication of lost-and-found objects. Although she has refined and purified—alchemized—those "street-made" objects, rendering them luminous, and aestheticized them by placing them in complex multilayered assemblages in which their conjunctions/disjunctions impart a new vibration to them, she is not concerned with spectacularizing them or presenting them as extraordinary or magical objects meriting placement in a wonder-box. On the contrary, she is concerned with preserving their ordinariness as far as possible for, in B.'s exercise of "rough magic," it is the most ordinary—even the extreme ordinariness of trashed and abject objects—that becomes itself the most extraordinary. In B.'s art of transfiguration, the advent/event of wonder is precipitated by the ordinary as it comes to be displaced by the extraordinary, something that will require the spectator to at once step back in wonder at the outbreak of the extraordinariness of the ordinary (to use Heideggerian language) and to double back to the streets to refind those objects in their original condition in order to gauge the transformations they have undergone. It is through their ineradicably rough and gnarled ordinariness that B.'s transformed objects resist the utopia of the display and bear witness to the urban fabric and the placelessness it has conferred upon them.

B. sets those proletarian objects to work in the installation where they are prevented from slipping into ornaments or souvenirs and made to undertake (and to elicit from the viewer) passage-work, narrative-work, and memory-work by which—as objects tattooed by the streets of Naples and New York—they keep secret their small and unutterable stories of ownership and abandonment and, as figures of and in transit, narrate the grand stories of the perpetual migration of bodies, identities, culture, and destinies between Naples and New York; of the placelessness and homelessness definitive of the diasporic condition; of the materiality of cultural identities; and of the great "Junkspace" in which we now live.

## The Madonna of Gloves

Walking the streets of New York with B. Amore involves a strange form of flânerie as I immediately learned while accompanying her on a stroll through Chelsea one January in the late afternoon. Indeed, B.'s art of walking eschews the idling and dandyish practices of traditional flânerie: our walk would involve no "botanizing on the asphalt," to refer to Walter Benjamin's description of window-shopping in the Paris arcades; and the flâneur's/voyeur's threshing of the crowd in search of a beautiful but briefly glimpsed face prompting "love at last sight" would be transposed into a rabid scavenging of the asphalt in search of the "beautiful ugliness" of urban detritus, particularly as embodied in discarded and sullied gloves, the obscure objects of B.'s artistic desire.

That dreary and arctic day perfected winter, and there was no need for a snow alert for it had rewritten T. S. Eliot's famous line in the most brutally literal way: "January is the cruelest month." A counterthought perversely came to mind—"sun alert"—as I realized that the mood of the day had distanced our spirits irremediably from the City of the Sun, where it never snows. Nonetheless, delirious Naples, the place of both our origins, remained as always the topic of our infinite conversation. Her animated improvisations *alla napoletana* triumphed over distance, compelling my imagination to keep traveling back and forth between the streets of Naples and New York and obliging my cultural memory—triggered by her anecdotes of the *rondini* (swallows)—to retrace the migrant journeys of the "birds of passage," those nomadic singers and musicians of the Great Immigration who brought the repertory of volcanic and passionate Neapolitan songs to the New World. So as we strolled I secretly kept pace with the rhythms of those remembered songs.

But this proved impossible, for to drift with B. means to trudge along with your head lowered like one of those penitents in Dante's *Purgatorio* and with your gaze directed downwards toward the ground scrutinizing and interrogating the dead silence of debris and litter, waiting for a chance encounter with a unique and uncanny object that cries out for transformation and redemption through art. This search for lost objects was no easy task for B. because it involved something more than a casual exercise in the connoisseurship of street trash bent on locating interesting objects that struck her fancy. It involved an intensive targeting or scoping of the object that penetrated its core and located its invisibility. This was brought home to me as she discarded object after object as being unsuitable. Finally, the eureka moment occurred. Finally, the Madonna of Gloves encountered an object that revealed its secret, an object worthy of inclusion, as Yeats would have it, "in the foul rag and bone shop of the heart."[5]

I shall never know whether she found the object or the object found her.

It was, of courses, a mangled worker's glove lying in the gutter of West 27th Street (see plate 3-1). She scrutinized it intently, in a way that made me see it through her eyes, giving me lessons in both the phenomenology of perception and the impure poetry of things. The glove was squashed—*schiacciato*, as she said, which made me think of Donatello's *rilievo schiacciato*. It was an indexical sign still bearing the shape of a worker's hand, even though the tattoo of the streets and the passing traffic had twisted and disfigured it, with three fingers extended and the other two scrunched against the palm. Despite this rough treatment, it remained recognizable as one of those "eccentric souvenirs of human shapes" that Wallace Stevens writes about.

She put me in the place of the glove. The glove required a double or triple take. It concealed its wonder, but by concealing that wonder it disclosed it, thereby issuing its summons to B.'s imagination. So the glove was, in effect, a subject and not simply an object. Its ephemerality demanded to be transformed into a *monumentum aere perennius* (a monument more lasting than bronze). And at this point I began to understand B.'s obsession with gloves: workers' hands (immigrants are those condemned to do manual labor); the hand and signature of the artist; the artist self-defined as worker (art as hard work); the artist as creator of a "poor art," poor in its materials and poor in its thematization of the immigrant condition, a "minor art" (in the nonpejorative sense of Gilles Deleuze and Felix Guattari) because it refuses the art-language of the masters and thus is immediately political.

But the glove also demanded to be paired or coupled with another glove, her way of restoring it to its owner. This pairing, which can be seen to be the dominant aesthetic tactic in the installation, is exactly what would happen, for in the "Piedigrotta Passione/Chelsea Passeggiata" assemblage it would be paired with an elegant diamond-studded evening glove found on the streets of Naples (see plate 3-2). And this pairing and juxtaposition of a poor glove and a rich glove unleashes the play of resemblances and differences that surprises the spectator into wonderment.

B. deposited the glove within the pages of a copy of the *Village Voice* for safekeeping. After all, many of her found gloves also demanded to fly, to be transformed into those birds of passage that wing their way through the installation. All the objects she scavenged that day in Chelsea have now found their place in the "Piedigrotta Passione/Chelsea Passeggiata" assemblage. All of the assemblages punctuated, as they are, by paired gloves, will oblige the viewer to return to the primal scene that B. enacted that day in Chelsea and repeated elsewhere. On the art walk she left behind the Duchampian search for the ready-made for the glove had already been "assisted" by the streets and endowed with its own uncanniness, an uncanniness that would be intensified and perfected by its placement within the assemblage where it would collide with a host of other objects and where it would be at once in place and placeless. As one wanders/wonders through the installation, remember that the origin of the work of art is in the street.

## *Performing* Naples/New York: *An Invitation to Voyage*

The redemption and transformation of objects that have no place and have lost their use-value—urban detritus and found objects (e.g., a red envelope bearing a love letter, a wishbone, the sole of a shoe, and, above all, gloves); fragmented materials, whether natural or humanmade (from lava stones to fragments of the tar roof blown off the old Ellis Island building); remnants and souvenirs of all sorts—is only a small part, albeit the most riveting and essential, of B.'s art of transfiguration and the aesthetics of wonder informing it. Her "rough magic" is more inclusive, operating as well on archival documents, maps, images, and texts, such as the exquisite Belle Epoque song covers and the sheet music of countless Neapolitan popular songs. As a result, the exhibition becomes at once a lost-and-found depository of the present and a memory box of immigration history documenting the transmission of Neapolitan musical culture to the New World. But B.'s musical archive, brimming with the titles of beguiling Neapolitan songs, elegant images of divas and panoramic views of Naples—the Diva of Metropolises—is also put to work, thereby countering its ornamental or picturesque effects.

The archival material is presented as a collage/montage upon which the relief constructions are superimposed. The collage serves not only as a ground for the reliefs but also as a source of visual contamination that releases all sorts of montage effects or "editing effects"—surprises and collisions—both within the montage itself and between the levels of the assemblage. In the vertical organization of the assemblages, the higher or foregrounded level is given to the material culture of the streets and everyday reality while the lower or background level is given to Neapolitan spectacle culture as represented by the musical documents and their images of the soigné universe of the *café chantant* and the spectacular Naples of *vedutismo* and the panoramic postcard—the "see Naples and die" iconography that emerged with the invention of the stereograph and the camera. In her structuring of the assemblages in this way, B. carnivalizes the two levels or domains of culture, mirroring the carnivalization at work in the reliefs themselves in which her art of transformation elevates trash into the sublime and infuses detritus with an aura.

By placing these lost-and-found (and sometimes given) objects and other materials into ten intricate assemblages and within the orbit of the installation itself as defined by the diorama and centerpiece, she has created a liminal space or in-between in which these objects are made to "travel" perpetually—albeit virtually and as propelled by the imaginary journeys of the spectator—back and forth between Naples and New York.

And here the problem of the spectator's response to the installation emerges, for the viewer as voyeur/voyageur will also undergo a sea change as he or she undertakes the "passage-work" imposed by the exhibition, even though it is confined to a single room. The installation presents its viewer with an invitation to journey between Naples and New York. To perform the installation the viewer/voyager must transit like those "birds of passage" figured in the panels of the diorama and the centerpiece (see plate 4-1). The birds of passage in the form of gloves emblematize the nomadic journeys of the old immigrants and the "songbirds" or Neapolitan musicians, both of which shuttled back and forth between the two cities. The birds of passage also serve as emblems of the viewer's performance of the installation. Because the installation has embedded within it a circular journey or even a strange loop, it will change our practices as viewers, obliging us to become voyeurs/voyageurs and to find counter-paths to the lateral movement imposed by the conventional display or collection. This is to say we view the installation as transients.

## Point(s) of Arrival/Point(s) of Departure

Although there are hundreds of little themes embedded in the individual assemblages—each of the assembled objects is a theme or little story—they are inscribed in an overarching spatial story that is marked ostensibly by the port cities of Naples and New York, with Naples as the point of departure and New York as the point of arrival, as in the original mapping of the Great Immigration and as in B.'s remapping of it in plate 3-5 in which Naples, represented by a diagram of Vesuvius in the shape of an *M*, is positioned as both a point of departure and return. But the installation creates an imaginary space in which Naples and New York are constantly crisscrossing, transiting with those objects or fragments, which are indexical signs physically linked to the two metropolises; palimpsests that the city-streets have written upon, imprinting them with marks and traces that bear witness to the force of place and locality. (For example, cardboard that bears the diamond-shaped imprint of paving stones or *pietrini*.) In the imaginary space created by the installation, Naples travels to New York and New York travels to Naples in a way that blurs the boundaries between them.

And here B.'s great theme emerges: she installs within the exhibition the spatial story of immigration and a figurative mapping of the psychogeography of the diasporic condition. The objects migrate within the installation where they crisscross both spatially and temporally—temporally, for recently found objects are made to collide through montage with memory objects and archival documents, as previously mentioned. This transiting of objects mirrors those "voyages without" undertaken by the immigrants of the Great Immigration, or B.'s *Return to the Stones of Naples* (plate 4-2). Even when executed as homecomings—real or imaginary (imaginary as in the lyrics to "Santa Lucia Luntana" by E. A. Mario cited above in the epigraph, in which the mere sight of the moon elicits a return to Naples)—those journeys remain without return because the immigrant has become a stranger unto himself or herself, a liminal being condemned to exist betwixt and between the Old and New World and in a transitional state in which identity must be reconstructed in terms of the irreversible loss of the homeland and the impossibility of going home again.

Is there a more powerful metaphor for the immigrant than that of detritus or *garbaccia*/trash? The immigrant is the detritus of the nation and the refuse of class, a negated and displaced object condemned to oscillate between the Old and New World, a liminal or marginal subject confined to an eternal state of homelessness and placelessness. Conversely, is there a more powerful metaphor for the hybridized, transcultural, and transgeographical identity that results from the diasporic experience than the transfiguration of detritus—that which has no proper place—into artwork?

*Place Names: The Name and the Place*

Since place/placement/displacement is such a fundamental theme in B. Amore's installation and its attempt to confront and map out the psycho-geography of emigration/immigration, it is well worth considering the place and space of the installation along with the litany of proper place names that define it and that circulate within it, most explicitly as titles for six of the ten assemblages or combines lining the gallery's walls: *Heart of Naples/Hands of New York* (plate 3-6, originally titled *Marechiaro blu*), *Floating between Liberty and Vesuvius* (plate 3-3), *Return to the Stones of Naples* (plate 4-2), and the three pieces named for the ancestral homes of the families of B.'s mother and father: the Lapio piece, *Place of the Heart* (plate 4-3), and the two pieces dedicated to Montefalcione (plates 3-7 and 3-8, both towns located in the province of Avellino, to the northeast of Naples. These three pieces are of great personal significance to B. because they bypass the metropolis and link her directly to her motherland, where she must confront the traumatic dialectic between the village and the diaspora.

Place names are also constantly brought into play by the song titles, which are often celebrations of specific places or landscapes. Place names are monumentalized in the *Delirious Naples* diorama, where Napoli is written out in graffiti-inspired writing suggesting the flames of an erupting Vesuvius and superimposed on the diagram of Mount Vesuvius in the form of an *M*, a pictogram representing its two peaks the huge caldera between them (see plate 3-5). Vesuvius, which always sleeps with one eye open, is, of course, a metonymy for Naples, as are the fragments of lava stone that flow through the installation.

These proper place names are crucial to B.'s mapping out of Naples and to her marking out of the spatial story of migration. As J. Hillis Miller writes: "The place names seem to be intrinsic to the places they name. . . . The place is carried and becomes available to us there. You can get to the place by way of its name."[6] This is particularly true for the Neapolitans of the Great Immigration for whom place names had a talismanic power capable of transporting or returning them to the beautiful landscapes and seascapes of Naples. This nomenclatural and topographic power of names is at work in the titles of numerous popular songs involving place names such as "Turna Surriento" and "Marechiara." Naples, promised land of the popular song and the postcard, has a huge repertory of songs dedicated to it in which the invocation of its name transports the listener to its bay and its alleys. One might even say that Naples as a city has the power of a *zahir*, a place or place name that has "the terrible power to be unforgettable, and whose image eventually drives people mad," to refer to Borges's definition of *zahir*.[7] The *zahir* is the best way to cut the interior distance of exile, as evidenced by the audience of emigrants that ritually attended the performances of Gilda Mignonette, the female Caruso, in New York City. They would constantly entreat her to sing of place: "Gilda, *per carità*, a song about Mergellina!"; "Gilda, I beg you, a *canzone* about Posillipo!"

And this gets us the problem of the functioning of the two major place names: Naples and New York, both of which are nomenclaturally "new cities" (Neápolis or New City), both of which lie on the 48th parallel, both of which are cities of mass migration defined by supersyncretic cultures, both of which are cities of extravagances, both are, of all the cities in the world, perhaps the easiest to visit without traveling to them because they travel to us through clichéd images and a vast array of cultural texts. In other words, they are doubles, and the installation is constantly pairing and comparing them, coupling and disjoining them, and always dialogizing them. For example, in *Heart of Naples/Hands of New York*, the heart of Naples is represented by the sole of a shoe, found in Naples and etched with striations (see plate 3-6). It is superimposed upon a crushed gold box also found in Naples, whereas Vesuvius, again in the shape of an *M*, is constructed from the fragments of the tar roof of the old Ellis Island building, thereby indicating how in the immigrant's imaginary the substance of each city shifts place. The wishbone, placed beneath the "heart" and framed by two gloves (one bronze, one blue), signifying the "hands of New York" and the regime of hard labor the immigrant has entered, also involves a doubling of desire, referring to both the Neapolitan emigrant who desires to voyage to New York to find work and to raise himself or herself up, and the estranged immigrant who wishes to return home to Naples. The contradictory interior life of the emigrant/ immigrant is also indicated by the crumbled piece of notepaper placed to the left of the "heart," a reminder of the pragmatic tasks to be performed as a stranger in the land of opportunity. The relief structure—a mini-lava bed, *schiacciata pizzicata*, collapsed soufflé, or what have you—is a multi-stable figure with the top half shaped like Vesuvius and the bottom half and the entire relief suggesting the shape of Manhattan island. The relief is placed on an ocean of song covers and sheet music predominantly tinted blue, suggesting the "diaspora blues" and the patina that has formed around Naples as a distanced object of desire. That ocean of songs in dialect, particularly "Cartulina 'Napoli" (to be discussed below), embody the soul-work and the soul-storms of the immigrant as liminal and crossed subject.

In these exchanges and doublings of materials, we can see how the assemblages are articulated as crossroads at which Naples and New York meet, combine, and exchange places as homelands. And embedded within this spatial and temporal story of crossing over and crisscrossing, in which cultural and urban identities meet and cross and blend and become one another, is a profound fable of the diasporic identity and the interiority of the exile. And here at the crossroads, the geography of place names is confounded and destabilized, found and lost in the chaos of traces, as they were in the immigrant imaginary.

## *The Transatlantic Tarantella/Crossed-Rhythms/Birds of Passage*

The installation needs to be heard or listened to. It has a jukebox effect or, to be less anachronistic, a gramophone effect. The collage of sheet music and covers and other musical documents requires the "viewer," whether by the force of the synesthesia in sight-reading the scores or by the arousal of the memory of the songs and the voices of their singers, to enter into the rhythms of the songs through which the pathos and worldview of Naples traveled to the New World and the immigrants maintained their Neapolitan and Italian cultural identities.

One of the primary figures in the installation is that of the "birds of passages" (*rondini*, or swallows) as emblematized by the gloves assembled in the side panels of the diorama and the centerpiece. Although they represent the immigrants as nomadic subjects who travel back and forth between Naples and New York, they also refer to the "birds of passage," those equally nomadic singers and musicians of the Great Immigration whose history has been documented by the musicologist Simona Frasca in *Birds of Passage: I musicisti napoletani a New York (1895–1940)*.[8]

These "songbirds"—Enrico Caruso, above all—brought Neapolitan popular music to America, where many of the songs would enter the American repertory. Late-nineteenth and early-twentieth-century Naples was avant la lettre the Tin Pan Alley or Nashville of world music. Those Neapolitan musicians made Little Italy into a Piedigrotta where they would create a new transnational repertory of songs *alla Napoletana* that confronted the immigrant condition and embodied the joys and blues—the *rimpianto*—of the diasporic experience. Some of those songs, especially those by Eduardo Migliaccio, were influenced by American musical culture and became exemplary sites of hybridization and creolization that imparted a new direction to the conventional Neapolitan song. Others preserved the essence of the Neapolitan song, and they—the so-called postcards from Little Italy—traveled back to Naples, along with their singers, where they were welcomed into the repertory.

Perhaps the most exemplary of these songs was "Cartulina 'e Napule" ("Postcard from Naples"), which was written by Giovanni De Luca and Pasquale Buongiovanni and made famous by the *sciantosa* (chanteuse) Gilda Mignonette, the "Queen of the Emigrants." The cover of the song is appropriately placed in the *Heart of Naples/Hands of New York* assemblage (plate 3-6). Although sentimental by current taste, the lyrics embody the soul-storm experienced by the immigrants in their exile from the motherland:

M'è arrivata stammatina
'na cartulina;
è 'na veduta 'e Napule
ca m'ha mannata mammema!
Se vede Capre, Proceta,
se vede Margellina,
'nu poco 'e cielo 'e Napule . . .
che bella cartulina!

Napule! . . .
aggio scritto pe' tte chesta canzone
e pe' ricordo 'e mammema
aggio chiagnuto lacreme 'e passione.

This morning I received a postcard:
It is a view of Naples
that my mother sent me!
You can see Capri, Procida
you can see Mergellina,
and a little bit of the sky of Naples.
What a beautiful postcard!
Naples!
I wrote this song for you
and for the memory of my mother
I have cried tears of passion.

In her heart-wrenching and throat-lacerating rendition of the song, Mignonette becomes the Diva of the Diaspora and the Neapolitan-American version of Bessie Smith, the Empress of Blues. The song, in Mignonette's emotive cantillation of it, has a duende that distances it from such cliché-ridden songs as "O Sole Mio" and "Maria, Mari" ("Oh Marie"). It bears witness to the crucial way in which Neapolitan songs in the dialect served the immigrant not merely as tokens of nostalgia and memory but, more importantly, as transitional objects by which they negotiated their separation from the motherland and the mother's body and their adjustment to the estrangement and assimilation imposed by the Law of the Father as embodied in the imperative to define themselves in terms of hard work. The immigrant as the Other maintained his or her personal and cultural identity through these songs that carried in their rhythms the whole Neapolitan universe of signs—music, language, texts, body language, soul language, and so on. Mignonette's song itself becomes a postcard, one of the *cartolina da Little Italy* that the birds of passage send back to Naples. In the ocean of the collage in which all the Neapolitan and Neapolitan-American songs pulse, there is set out the entire immigrant imaginary, a world of desire expressed through an amorous discourse in which the songs address the distanced and lost beloved—the mother, the ever-receding motherland, the left-behind beloved, the individual places. The only way of reaccessing them is through song and specifically the amorous discourse marked by the passionate inflections of Neapolitan dialect, the language of the skin and libidinal desire.[9]

## Farfariello, the Trickster of the Diaspora

The other figure embodying the dislocation and alienation of the immigrant condition who circulates within the installation is Eduardo Migliaccio, better known by his stage name, Farfariello (Little Butterfly). He was the King of Italian American vaudeville and an avatar of Pulcinella through whom the Neapolitan sense of humor/sense of survival and body image traveled to America in the form of *macchiette coloniali* (colonial sketches) that involved all sorts of culture-clashing and tongue-twisting greenhorn encounters with the Nuovo Mondo. But he was much more: a cultural hero of the immigrant experience, a trickster who always found himself out of place or in the wrong place and yet he confronted his placelessness through humor and carnivalized the angst of the stranger into laughter and the silence and linguistic alienation of the immigrant into a fractured language through which he expressed his agency.

One of the most significant of his songs or *macchiette* is "'Mpareme 'a via d' 'a casa mia," sometimes shortened to "Portame 'a casa" ("Show me the Way Home"), the title of B.'s assemblage in which the cover sheet of the song, with a photo of him upon it, is placed in the upper right-hand corner of *Cracked Immigrant Mirror* (plate 4-4). You may be familiar with the melody of the song, composed by Irving King, from the definitive rollicking Roaring Twenties version of it by the California Ramblers or from its many cinematic recyclings in such movies as *Cat on a Hot Tin Roof* and *Jaws*. It is a ditty about drunkenness but, in Farfariello's version of it, the drunkenness is induced not only by booze but, more significantly, by the intoxicating yet disorienting experience of Manhattan. Indeed, it represents the immigrant condition as a form of drunkenness in which Farfariello has lost all his bearings. Here are its lyrics in Neapolitan dialect and in English translation:

> Non so perché pensaje
> d'andare a Broduè

nun c'ere state maje
vulette andà a vedè.
Migliara 'e lampetelle
girano accà e allà,
te giren' 'e cirvielle,
c' 'a forza 'e alluccà
Portame a casa mia
me voglio andà a cuccà
me ne sò asciuto iere
non saccio cchiù addò sta
M'ha fatto male, i' crere,
quell'urtemo bicchiere
Chi m'empara pè cortesia
'a via d' a casa mia.
Trovai 'na naise ghella
Che disse "mi know you"
Pareva tanto belle
Pittata rossa e blù
Nu vaso le cercaje,
nun me dicette no,
'a sacca me tastaie
poi disse "c'atro vuò?"

I don't know what possessed me
to go to *Broduè* (Broadway).
I had never been there
and wanted to go and see
the thousands of bright lights
that flicker here and there.
They make your head spin
until you scream.
Show me the way to go home
I want to (go home) and go to bed
I went out yesterday
and don't know any longer the way back home
That last drink must have
gone right to my head.
Will someone please show me
the way to go home?

I bumped into a *naise ghella* (nice girl)
who said to me, *"Me know you"* ("I know you").
She was so pretty
all made up in red and blue
I asked her for a kiss
she didn't say no
she felt my pockets
then she said,
"What else do you want?"

Although Farfariello appropriates the original tune and some of the lyrics, he completely Neapolitanizes the song by performing it in a raucous Neapolitan voice and by converting the lyrics into the dialect punctuated by terms in "Italglish." He removes the song from its original setting in a train and locates it in the streets of the metropolis, the supreme site of modern alienation, where he tells the story of the impossibility of homecoming. The line "Show me the way home," in fact, refers to the double impossibility of returning home; he cannot find the way home to both his house in America and his home in Naples. He encounters a prostitute but does not immediately recognize her as such. And these opening strophes are only the start of his misadventures that will culminate in the arms of the police and before a judge where he will be charged with public drunkenness. Farfariello's disorientation is also reflected in his language, which interrupts the Neapolitan dialectic with a number of linguistic disfigurations: "Broduè" (Broadway), "naise ghella" (nice girl), "Me know you" (I know you), which convey his estrangement from English or perhaps his attempt to territorialize it. Whereas the American version is a drinking song about the familiar condition of drunkenness sung by a wanderer who finds the comfort of home in the singing of the song as a supplement to a bender, Farfariello's version, instead, is about the existential condition of the immigrant lost in the New World and a stranger unto himself who cannot go home again. His only defense against alienation is the performance of the song *alla napolitana*, his way of carnivalizing the diaspora blues. The song is one of the first and best examples of hybridization and one of the most poignant of the postcards from Little Italy for it bears witness to the irreversible loss of the homeland and the impossibility of going home again.

## A Litany for the Madonna of Gloves

We owe a great debt to B. Amore for creating a place of wonder that transports us into the ordinary rather than away from it and that thrusts her collection of impenetrable, damaged, crushed, impure street objects into the sanctuary of the gallery space as a way of contesting the great divide between the exteriority of the city and the interiority of the museum. By relocating the "aesthetics of rare experience"[10] in the streets and in the everyday world of ordinary and poor objects, B. has recast the aesthetics of wonder. For her, art requires the creator and the spectator to notice the unnoticeable and to experience the presencing of the ordinary object. This means becoming responsible to the sublime that is concealed or overlooked in the mundane object and, as a corollary, refusing to violate the object whether by romanticizing it or turning it into one of those ersatz art games that commodify and mystify junk and trash. This is no easy task at this moment in which the omnipresent exclamatory adjective "Awesome!" has deleted through parody our capacity for ordinary wonder.

By way of concluding, I want to express formally my deep gratitude for the gift of the installation, especially since it is also event-specific, linked as it was to "The Delirious Naples Conference" sponsored by the Hofstra Cultural Center. In a sense the installation and the conference are mirror-images of each other in that both are concerned with staging an encounter—at once critical and celebratory—with historic and contemporary Naples and with exploring the ways in which Naples, as a visible and invisible city, and its vibrant culture have traveled to New York and throughout the world.

## NOTES

1. The exhibition opened November 4, 2000; see B. Amore, *An Italian American Odyssey: Life line—filo della vita: Through Ellis Island and Beyond* (New York: Center for Migration Studies, 2006).

2. The exhibit traveled to the Museo dell' Emigrazione, Sant'Angelo dei Lombardi in the province of Avellino, near Naples, in 2016–18.

3. Homi Bhabha, "Postmodernism/Postcolonialism," in *Critical Terms for Art History*, ed. Robert S. Nelson and Richard Shiff (Chicago: University of Chicago Press, 1996), 316.

4. Rem Koolhaas, *The Harvard Design School Guide to Shopping: Project on the City* (New York: Monacelli Press, 2000).

5. W. B. Yeats, "The Circus Animals' Desertion," in *The Poems of W. B. Yeats: A New Edition*, edited by Richard J. Finneran (1933; repr. New York: Macmillan, 1961).

6. J. Hillis Miller, *Topographies* (Stanford, Calif.: Stanford University Press, 1995), 4.

7. Jorge Borges, "The Zahir," in *Collected Fictions*, trans. Andrew Hurley (New York: Penguin, 1999), 246.

8. See the English translation by Simona Frasca, *Italian Birds of Passage: The Diaspora of Neapolitan Musicians in New York* (New York: Palgrave Macmillan, 2014).

9. See *Neapolitan Postcards: The Canzone Napoletana as Transnational Subject*, ed. Goffredo Plastino and Joseph Sciorra (Lanham, Md.: Rowman and Littlefield, 2016).

10. Philip Fisher, *Wonder, the Rainbow and the Aesthetics of Rare Experiences* (Cambridge, Mass.: Harvard University Press, 2003).

FIVE

## One Early Twenty-First Century Summer in Naples

*John Domini*

*Caldo Africano*, that was the name for it: the African heat. In Naples, as across all of Europe, the temperature and humidity made headlines throughout the summer of 2003. Many died, in particular the elderly. In fact, other Italian cities, inland cities, better known, suffered worse than Naples. The southern seaport got the benefit of the shifting air currents off the Tyrrhenian Sea—the same cooling relief known by the long-gone Greeks who settled nearby Cumae, by the Romans in Pompeii, the Saracens on Capri and Ischia, the Normans in Amalfi, and many another influx of peoples who came in time to consider themselves Neapolitans.

You could catch a hint of the sea air in the piazzas of downtown, the palm and eucalyptus leaves trembling amid the baroque filigree, even though the city now ranks as the most densely populated in Europe. Officially, it's the third largest in Italy, after Rome and Milan. Metropolitan Naples contains more than three million inhabitants, and that's without reaching as far north as Cumae, or as far south as Pompeii. Nor does that number, large as it is, account for many of the most recent immigrants. Many newcomers remain off the books, their legal and social position effectively captured by the slang term *clandestini*. And this shadow status, to be sure, generally means a shadow skin color. Undocumented aliens tend to be African in the Italian south. Here, the volcano-troubled geology that created the hairpin turns of the Amalfi Drive also left the coastline notched with inlets sheltered enough for wading ashore by moonlight. Such nooks and crannies lie only two or three long nights' sea voyage from the likewise hidden embarkation points between Tunis and Tripoli.

Not surprisingly, estimates on immigration vary widely. One Italian newspaper claimed, over the summer of 2003, that some 200,000 newcomers were now coming into Italy every year; this included both legals and illegals, those who stay and those who move onto other parts of the Continent. On the other hand, the official 2002 immigration figure, which counts those with documents only, was roughly a tenth as much—but even that was up steeply from the 12,000 who made the census books in 2001. In both years, too, the greater percentage of *immigranti* were African. Back in the 1990s, Balkan refugees had attracted international attention, fleeing the devastation around Sarajevo and Tirana, but newcomers like those, nominally white, were arriving in far lower numbers now.

In Africa, over the same decade, troubles had continued to mount. Early in 2003 Liberia saw the U.S. Marines step in, as the Rangers had done a decade earlier in Somalia, but these were only the high-profile crises, the stuff that makes headlines. In other countries, less newsworthy problems such as the lack of jobs carried an impact just as devastating. Of course, Europe has been attracting economic refugees from among those Franz Fanon called "the wretched of the earth" since before he first published his book in 1961. But if the twentieth century has been a nightmare for countries north of the Mediterranean, now it appears that those of the twenty-first will occupy the lands to the south.[1]

More and more these populations have begun to search for a better life in Italy. On the lower boot, African emigrants can count on a climate not terribly unlike the one they left. In the city a vendor can hawk his wares until 2:00 a.m., and year-round he needs little more wardrobe than a presentable *djellaba* and a strong pair of sandals. Out in the country, the olive and lemon orchards, the vineyards, the fields of tomatoes and greens: all these need short-term pickers and haulers. The dairy ranches need extra hands too, as they process *la vera mozzarella* from the milk of the local water buffalo. Water buffalo—something else you'd never find in earlier immigrant boomtowns like London or Berlin.

Then there's a less sunny fact of southern Italian life luring the *clandestini* traffickers. Any crook knows that the farther down the coast of Campania and Calabria he lands, the less he has to worry about the law. These regions now suffer the most laissez-faire attitude toward organized crime in Italy. Neapolitan gangs are known collectively as the Camorra and, all too often, are accepted with a shrug. For a fee, they can arrange a landing free of Coast Guard interference. And once the goods are ashore, the real profit-taking begins. The black market in prostitution, naturally, captures the media spotlight. But the mob has got their hooks into just about anything these transients might buy or sell, from knockoffs of Gucci leathers to counterfeit passports.

Now, a few of these African newcomers might be aware of the ancient cultural connections across this stretch of the Mediterranean: between Imperial Rome and the Pharaohs, or between seventh- and eighth-century Amalfi and "the Moors." A few of the post-2000 arrivals might even understand that they're participating in a rare social watershed, in which the Italian South has shifted from a place *di emigrazione* to one *di immigrazione*. For a full century before this—roughly between the Italian unification of 1860 and the decade following my own father's departure for New York in 1948— men and women raised in the shadow of Vesuvius abandoned their homeland in droves. The region suffered both the manpower drain of recurrent wars (including little-known Italian squabbles) and the worst odds against making a living in Europe. Now, however, the country belongs to the G8, the richest nations on earth. And a homeless Eritrean couldn't care less about fine distinctions between the Italian North (the seat of the economic boom) and the South (the seat, to simplify egregiously, of the Mafia). For most *clandestini*, too, the last thing on their minds is some journalist's irony, or even less a sociologist's, about comings and goings over the last thirty or forty years.

All in all, this darkening blur at the population's margins appeared an inescapable subject as I returned again to my family's native city. The African heat, the African semi-citizens: I found both impossible to avoid. I was a frequent visitor by then, and I knew something about the new immigrants. I knew as well that in August 2002 their situation had gotten more complicated thanks to a fresh set of regulations known as the "Bossi-Fini law."

Bossi-Fini was named for the legislators who'd shepherded the bill through the tricky Roman parliament.[2] In the summer following the law's ratification, I was there trying to gauge its effect, as well as to assess the general changes wrought by yet another new wave of Neapolitans. The news isn't good. Especially unsettling is the state of denial in which I found many natives and immigrants. But as it happened, the story of the new African presence in southern Italy was for me unexpectedly illuminated—profoundly illuminated—by the spectral glow of those who had left. Ghosts out of my own family's past.

My late father grew to manhood in this city. Before he became one of the *emigranti*, his defining experiences were Fascism and "the war"—an expression that could only mean one thing to Enzo Domini, though he lived more than half a century beyond 1945. Indeed those two words always signified the same to the man's children, and to most other Euro-Americans who came of age during the postwar decades, decades otherwise said to be revolutionary.

And that war, for my father, had little in common with the warm glow kindled by American myth-mongering like the "Greatest Generation." To inner-city Neapolitans the conflict was a brute business of deprivation and dying: random, pointless, constant. If Mussolini didn't have you carted away to a German camp (before his regime collapsed in July 1943), and if the Nazis didn't gun you down (after they put the city under martial law), then the nightly Allied bombing would obliterate you while you slept. On top of that, mortality levels from disease and starvation were unmatched anywhere west of the Polish ghettos, and continued for many months following the Allied liberation in October 1943. Under these nightmare circumstances, it hardly mattered to my teenage father and his younger, smaller brother—an uncle I will call Gigi, diminutive of Luigi—that they took part in one of the most heroic guerilla actions of the European conflict.

This battle, well-nigh unheard of in the United States, is known as "The Four Days of Naples." Between the 26th and 30th of September 1943, a spontaneous citywide uprising, in which many of the combatants were teenagers like my father, accomplished what no other community on the Continent could manage: they threw out an occupying German force. Much of the fighting was close-quarter, face-to-face. Neapolitans first took to the streets with little more than kitchen implements, and with only one way to get their hands on real weapons. Yet on the 30th the Nazi field marshal sued for peace, meeting with an ad hoc civilian leadership to arrange a safe withdrawal from town.

Hindsight makes clear that the decision to pull out was also strategic. The Wehrmacht set up its next line of defense along the Volturno River to the north, where it cost thousands of lives to dislodge them. Nevertheless, the Naples resistance dealt a significant blow to the Axis. During the first weeks of September, the Germans had set civilian crews tearing up the downtown, stringing barbed wire and planting mines, preparing for a battle along the lines of Stalingrad.

A number of those mines went off after the Allies moved in. Many died again (one such explosion provides a defining scene in the best book about that time and place, the memoir *Naples '44*, by Norman Lewis), and so for my father, like thousands of his fellow citizens, "the war" remained only that growl in the throat; years later, his bookish son heard the words as eerily similar to "the horror" of Conrad's Kurtz. Young Enzo's days and nights as a guerilla ran together into nothing so compelling as another reason, perhaps the best reason, to get out. Such madness never afflicted happy America, and he could take English at the university.

Yet the decades that followed, in the country he'd willingly adopted as his own, never proved entirely free of my father's early trials, hand-to-mouth and hand-to-hand. In the middle 1960s, Pop was among the first in our greater New York community to oppose the escalating conflict in Vietnam. "You Americans," he told one buzz-cut WASP acquaintance, "you don't have any *idea*." Later that decade he startled me with his willingness to share a joint, and he especially enjoyed hashish. Over a toke or two (such times are among the happiest memories I have of him), it came out that on bad nights in 1942 or 1943, hash was the only thing he and Gigi had to keep hunger at bay—hunger, cold, and the all-pervading fear.

More disturbing reminiscences emerged more slowly. My Italian grandfather, a man I knew as a witty master of gesture and aphorism, for instance, had made a barefoot escape, in the foothills of the Alps, from a train bound for Auschwitz. But it was only after Nonno's death in the early 1970s that Pop opened up about the episode, and about the old man's anti-Fascist troublemaking. Then in the mid-1990s my father suffered a near-fatal heart attack—who can say how much his weakness owed to the damages of teenage years?—and in the days afterward he told me for the first time the full story of the nuns who'd given him and Gigi shelter in their convent crypt, during that same late summer of 1943.

Some of this story was long familiar, like the bowl of soup the nuns gave him and his brother. Only a half-dozen churchwomen remained on the grounds, holdouts from some missionary Austrian order, and they proved sympathetic to a pair of Catholic boys on the run from conscription in the labor crews. The soup had mushrooms, I'd often heard, Enzo's and Gigi's first hot food in days. Also I knew how the boots of the local German commander had sounded that night, echoing above the boys, as my father and uncle turned over, literally, in their graves; the nuns had hidden them in the sarcophagi under the church nave, first clearing out the bones of their former colleagues. But only after Pop's heart attack did I learn what he'd seen the next evening, when he and his brother returned to the convent. The officer in charge had found out what the nuns had done, and he'd needed to make a point. All six were strung up from the chapel rafters.

My father offered just one more confession about wartime trauma, his worst yet, a few months before he died. He lasted into the first year of the current century, and succumbed to his second attack with merciful swiftness. In the heat-saturated Naples of summer 2003, what more private insights I gleaned about immigration and emigration came from his younger brother. Gigi, during the years of my father's increasing debility, had taken precautions about his own aging. Let me call his doctor son Marco Aurelio since my Neapolitan family, like nearly all the Africans I spoke with, asked that their actual names be kept out of this essay. Family and *immigrati* alike found it one thing to share their private shaping and reshaping with a lone sympathetic American, and another entirely to have strangers overseas horn in.

In any case, my cousin Marco Aurelio had arranged, over the last decade, for Uncle Gigi to have a bypass. During one of my previous visits the man had boasted to me that he had "the heart of a twenty-five-year-old." But in

July 2003 my investigations around the city were interrupted by the news that my uncle had gone into the hospital.

In time I learned that Gigi had liver cancer, and that if he made it through the current crisis, he might last as much as another year. But once again the whole truth was withheld for a while. At first my cousins would tell me only, as families do, that no one could say.

Perhaps the sweetest response to the news about Gigi came from an African immigrant. He was golden brown, with a close-cut 'do and the trim build of a former lightweight boxer. In his mid-thirties, he was still making his living on his feet, and I'll call him Leo, a natural name for anyone who's seen his catlike amble. Leo's Italian was flexible too, with some of the melody of the French he'd grown up with back in Morocco. Every time we met, and though I nearly always found him with native Neapolitans who'd known far longer, Leo was the first to bring up my uncle and to offer some good wish for the family. In the least European among the people I knew, I encountered the greatest Old World *politesse*.

To be sure, this paradox seems familiar: it's the one far from home who bends over backward to fit in. Besides that, Leo might've at first suffered the delusion that his friends' American friend was rich or well connected. But the man was no dummy. Once Leo and I got further into our midnight conversations (life in the piazzas goes on late in Naples, especially for a man who runs a street-stall), I began discovering my own misconceptions. I had expected more aggravation among the darker-skinned Neapolitans; I'd expected anger over the Bossi-Fini laws. But none of the Africans I spoke with expressed much displeasure with their adopted country.

"I have no problem here," Leo would tell me, in limpid street Italian.

But he had so few rights, I pointed out. And now if the police wanted to make trouble . . .

"The police know me and I know them. When they want to look at my documents, it's no problem."

Moroccans like Leo, I've learned, are among the best-off Africans in southern Italy. They began to make the crossing before most other national groups, and Leo was no *clandestino*, in danger of deportation every time the police give him a second look. He carried a folding piece of heavy paper, which in the United States would be called a work visa: not a document of citizenship, but a license to turn an honest euro. And it was only this document that brought out the least hint of intensity in Leo, something like fear of consequences.

"I cannot show it to you," he insisted, his language suddenly formal. "I pray you, I cannot."

And in another minute he was asking that I avoid using his name, in whatever I might write about him.

Nonetheless the pervading tone of our exchanges remained more than cordial. Leo wasn't fazed even by my questions about the Camorra. Wouldn't the mob, I wondered aloud, take an interest in his growing success? Leo after all had achieved the status of a vendor entrepreneur, by now selling leather goods with the help of a couple of employees, one his cousin. His booth holds an established space in a rhomboidal piazza along the fringes of what are now known as the *quadri neri*, the "black blocks." But, thanks to Bossi-Fini, Leo had even less protection against the rackets than most Neapolitans.

The Moroccan's smile, in response, was easy to read. *You Americans don't have any idea.* When he spoke, he almost chuckled.

"This is Naples," he said.

Evasion, denial, was the norm even for the compassionate Leo. Yet from his side of the schism created by a change in homelands, as from mine, the Bossi-Fini regulations must have felt unfair. The law stipulates that the prime minister will set an annual limit on the number of immigrants allowed in the country and requires that any lower-skilled labor (most of the bill's provisions exclude the highly skilled and well-educated) arrive with a "residence contract," a *contratto di soggiorno*, signed by both the Italian employer and the incoming worker. This contract must guarantee not only housing of some kind, which the employer must underwrite somehow, but also funding for the return to the home country. For no residence may last longer than two years. Even those with a *contratto* are fingerprinted on arrival in Italy, and should they wish to stay longer their file will be thoroughly reviewed; this would happen no fewer than seven times, even in an ideal case, before the person achieves citizenship.[3]

And full vestiture requires no less than fifteen years of documented residence, no matter the immigrant's skill level. Applicants must show tax records for every single year, something many native Italians couldn't manage. Worse, at no point during that decade and a half does any immigrant have the right to vote. The highest office they can hold is *consigliere*, an advisory position within the local office of immigration.

These restrictions have but one exception, a classic loophole: marriage to an Italian citizen. Bossi-Fini also allows a grace period for immigrants already in country to "regularize" their status. But when it comes to *clandestini*, the new law turns draconian. It decrees swift deportation, without appeal. Suspected illegals can be rounded up any time, anywhere.

In short, my friend Leo lives with anxieties far more disturbing than his late-night affability would suggest. And yet, to be fair, he and others like him aren't simply refusing to face facts. The southern metropolis can indeed feel safe and homey to an African newcomer, and not just because of the flora and fauna. The black blocks, for instance, suffer nothing like the isolation and decay of an American ghetto. The neighborhood occupies an easily reached swatch of the city proper—not the oldest part of the *centro*, with its medieval palazzi atop the original Greek blueprint but, rather, a nineteenth-century development near the train station. There's decent building stock in predictable quadrilaterals, and I walked its streets with less trepidation than I have other sections of the downtown. The vendors certainly get weary, but never less than amiable, and the races mix more than you'd see in the States. Several white farm families choose to sell on these blocks, avoiding the cutthroat competition of the older and more crowded *mercati*. There's a Vietnamese presence too, and Indian (not so much Pakistani), and it must be said that these fulfill some sort of stereotype, running dry cleaners and tailor shops.

The Africans too bear out something of an immigrant cliché: they'll sell anything. They perch on beach stools beside bootleg CDs, t-shirts or jewelry (now and again vaguely African), flimsy sunglasses or flip-flops, plastic lighters or water pistols. On those rare occasions when it starts to rain, in a matter of minutes there's no escaping the rock-bottom deals on fold-up umbrellas.

If they have a specialty, it's Leo's, the leather belts and bags and sandals. These tend to be decorated in the woven detail one associates with northwestern African cultures (the cultures that, in general, made up the U.S. slave population), but the majority of the more recent immigrants come from the other side of the continent, what used to be called "the Horn." Of

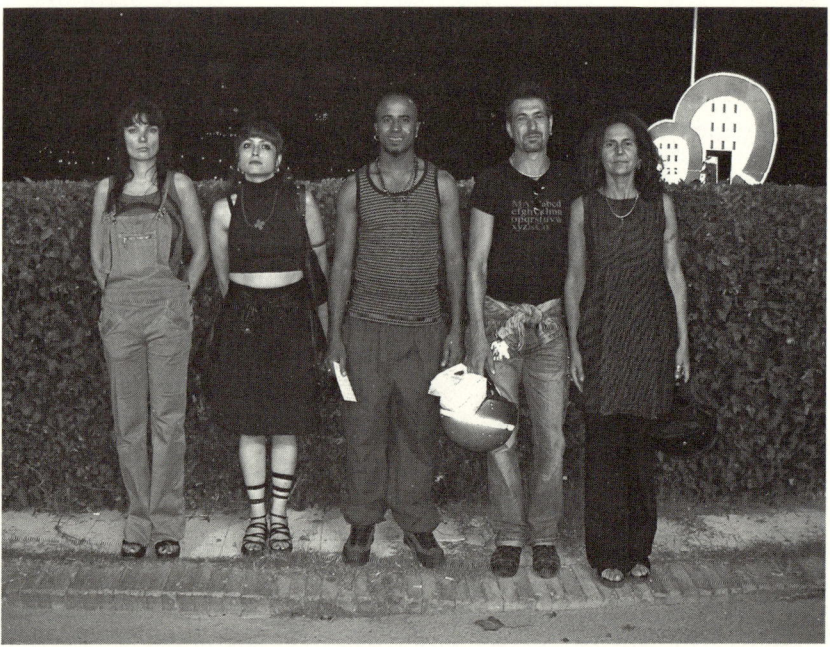

Figure 5-1. Neapolitan friends, 2004. (John Domini)

course, such countries as Ethiopia and Somalia have suffered one convulsion after another. More than that, these were places with an Italian colonial presence. Rome held sway over much of the eastern Sahara and sub-Sahara, as recently as when my father and uncle were children. It's not uncommon for a person from that region to have a smattering of Italian and half an idea what they're getting into; in the Somali novels of Nuruddin Farah, the torture victims dream of linguine and *vongole*.

On top of that, arrivals from the southern continent often have friends or family waiting in Naples. Any informed assessment of the increasing African presence in Italy must conclude that it's no longer composed entirely of the solitary and dispossessed. Leo has his cousin, and the proliferation of leather shops proves that immigrants can count on a network beyond the Camorra. When I first inquired about a pair of parti-colored Senegalese balloon pants, the young women at the front of the clothing stall deferred to a hefty backroom seamstress they called "Zia," (aunt). Such incidents hardly mean that the fundamental motives for coming north have changed. Undoubtedly life in the *quadri neri* remains better than in shell-pocked Mogadishu. Undoubtedly, the black vendors, not to mention the prostitutes and farm laborers, include those who have no better option and no one to help. But these days the experience of transmigration occurs in an ever more complicated rainbow of nuance.

The two sons of my uncle Gigi, in their way, also defy the stereotype. Both are worldly yet law-abiding family men, with multiple degrees and good incomes, precisely the sort of people on whom a livable city depends. Both are also quick to express compassion for the plight of recent immigrants, Africans especially. It's a great crisis, one will say, the greatest difficulty facing our country just now. Marco Aurelio, the doctor, pointed out that when he visited hospitals in Paris or New York, he could see at once how much more progress *i neri* had made toward professional status in those countries.

"In those places, the staff is nearly all African," he pointed out. "The receptionist, the nurses; if they're not African, they're Chinese, Indian."

I finished the thought for him: but not in Italy.

Marco Aurelio and I were nosing along one of the pedestrian-only zones, seeking a pizzeria he had in mind. Earlier that evening I'd learned about Uncle Gigi's cancer, and my cousin had let me know as well, without dissembling, that the old man's prognosis remained touch-and-go. He might have just a few days left, or he might go into remission and last several more months. But as Marco Aurelio found the restaurant he wanted and we took a seat, he went on speaking about the newly arrived Africans.

He explained that Italy lacked the *mezzi*, the established career tracks of schoolwork and apprenticeship by which a foreign-born person could achieve a career more reliable than selling in the street or freelancing in some other field. Immigrants depended on such *mezzi*, in other countries. Perhaps in the Italian North, too, things were beginning to open up. I pointed out, however, that the Bossi-Fini regulations tended to limit the possibilities for businesses to develop such career tracks, or for a foreigner to get on one. Now more than ever the costs of contract labor had fallen on the private sector, which left them few resources for research and development, and at the same time immigrant labor had been legally codified as transient, as an assembly-line piece to be replaced every two years. At that, my cousin fell back on a very Neapolitan response.

This city, he said, had seen three thousand years of newcomers. "They all found their own way, sooner or later," he assured me. "And these Africans will too."

The answer is a kind of default setting for the whites around here. In the late 1990s I interviewed then-mayor Antonio Bassolino, a politician who had effected a number of significant changes, bringing about something as close to an urban renaissance as Naples had seen in the entire century. But the mayor too had availed himself of the comforts of history. Naples has always been a melting pot, Bassolino declared, a meeting ground for diverse cultures.

I've learned, since, to turn the cliché back on the speaker, to give it some bite. The Africans, I told my cousin, certainly found their way with this family. Look at our wide lips, our kinky hair . . .

Now, I must add that Marco Aurelio has adopted a son with skin darker, and hair knottier, than that of any blood relatives. The boy, Americans would say, is black. Not surprisingly, then, my cousin didn't rise to the bait. He merely rolled his eyes and seemed to change the subject, mentioning that in the hospital today, his father had been talking about the war again. After another moment he made the connection: both the Germans and the British (who took over the city's reconstruction following the Four Days) had referred to their Neapolitan laborers as *neri*.

Of course the racist epithets of fair-haired overseers, back in 1943 or 1944, hardly mean my family shares a genuine kinship with contemporary *neri* (the connotation isn't far from "nigger"). The African in the southern Italian's closet is hardly a secret; it's turned up in everything from movies by Spike Lee to short stories by Italo Calvino, but the thousands of latter-day arrivals from the far side of the Mediterranean have, I repeat, little use for such ironies. Boat people and legal immigrants alike realize they're crossing a color line. Even in Naples, even the dark-skinned newcomers who claim to "have no problem," must live with a primitive chill; inevitably they're seen as alien.

So the nastiness my uncle endured sixty years ago in no way made me a soul brother. In no way. Rather, what the old man accomplished, lying in an ugly hospital ward and revisiting the terrible days that had ineradicably stamped a life now ending, lies at the heart of this essay: he opened my nerve ends to their freshest experience yet of the immigrant's hard choices.

My church visits that summer seem relevant. If I found a cathedral open, I often took a seat and offered silent bilingual prayers. From time to time I stopped in for Mass, taking the wafer as the city began to cool with evening. Attendance tended to be sparse, and there were services when the Africans outnumbered the Europeans; the Roman Church is currently suffering a steep decline in adherents in its home continent, while finding more and more converts among Fanon's wretched of the earth. The faith after all derives from a brown-skinned visionary out of the Middle East, one who preached that the individual wandering soul is worth more than an empire. As a missionary friend of mine put it recently, "Christianity no longer wears a white face." But my Neapolitan family, whatever you'd call its color over the centuries, has always had a strong connection to the Church. Our very name provides evidence of priests and friars among my forebears, going back to medieval times. I needed to take that summer's concerns to some consecrated space, repeatedly.

Yet as I sat praying, I realized too that in all my life I'd never seen my father set foot in a Catholic place of worship. And more: the most intense things he'd ever had to say about church and churchgoing had come when he'd at last told me the whole truth about hiding in the convent—that and the aftermath.

"Nuns," he kept saying, at that time, in a broken whisper. "*Nuns.*"

In the years that followed the Four Days, in another country, the man's children had been raised blandly Congregational. Pop came along, to choose an American expression he always liked, once in a blue moon.

Once, speaking of the tomato pickers in the fields south of the city, one of my most enlightened and good-hearted Neapolitan friends told me, "White Italians won't do that any more." This man knows better than I do—he's an educator working with children at risk, and a sensitive writer—but then again, in the 1930s and 1940s, my family had felt the pinch of a similar poverty, and none of them worked the fields. Likewise, most of the Africans out in the sunbaked farm-rows have some degree of choice in the matter. Most have someone else's coat they might pull.

In Leo's case, his friendliness never extended so far as an invitation to visit him and his cousin at home, a telling omission perhaps. But one day I did climb up into an apartment building above the black blocks, and the feeling around the stairwells and in the kitchen seemed entirely friends-and-family. This was about those pants, marvelous baggy West African slip-ons in a vivid print; I was visiting the square-built woman who ran the clothing stalls. Beforehand I'd made clear to her and others that I was coming in for a look, only, and I carried no daypack, nothing that looked like real money. I was still a scared white boy, oh sure, even when indulging the hipster pleasures of multiculturality. But once inside the woman's palazzo, my concerns seemed silly. I caught a whiff of hashish from the smokers on the balcony, but none of the woman's visitors was looking for more than a good dinner. She served up paired frying pans full of something like lamb jambalaya, and nearly every African who got a plate called her "Zia."

One of these relatives or seeming-relatives was an espresso-dark bull of a man in a spectacular dun-and-ocher wrap. He announced, or boomed, that he was down just for the weekend, flying back to Venice on Sunday: anything for his Zia. I had to wonder about the paperwork of travel by air, the government ID required. But no one in that kitchen had a bad word to say about "white Italy." No one had been denied a plane ticket, or a credit card, and when I ventured a tougher question, mentioning the Mafia traffic in false documents, Zia proved as expert a dodge as Leo. Would I like to try, she asked, some palm wine from Ghana? Likewise the hostess wasn't offended in the least that I found her suit prices a bit high. She never lost her smile while she detailed her overhead costs, and what she could and couldn't hide from the tax collectors.

The latest wave of immigrants knows these things. In Leo's case, his boxing skills helped to pay for a year or two of college, and he claims he could've settled in Paris. Options like his, which entail education well above some backwater mission school, are available even among the *clandestini*.

Only three or four of the newcomers I spoke with would admit to truly illegal status, and all but one had a relative or old family friend somewhere in the greater metro area. The one exception, wouldn't you know it, was the most willing to talk, the most articulate. He and I got to know each other by swapping songs on his guitar at a rooftop garden party. The get-together was otherwise entirely white, and I thought he was some neighborhood rock star, in dreadlocks down to his shoulder blades and a suede jacket that seemed, in this heat, a sacrifice for fashion. Yet the young man freely admitted, after soaking up a round of applause for "Redemption Song," that he was an illegal alien. What's more, he was a wanted man in his home country (let's say Sierra Leone).

This was a *clandestino* who'd nearly finished an advanced degree in film-making. And he too had caught a plane to come to Naples, a flight paid for by a study grant. That grant, however, had provided him an escape in the nick of time; the master's thesis documentary for which he'd won the money had offended his country's thug regime. The authorities had rounded up two or three others on his film crew, college trained, still in their twenties. My guitar-strumming friend hadn't heard from them since, and he'd seen no better option than to pocket the money set aside for a return.

By now, he went on with a toke of his spliff, he saw no reason to risk returning. He had work in the film community (at the end of the last century, Naples was a center for independent film, with celebrated work from, among others, Mario Martone and Paolo Sorrentino).

But his work, I had to ask, under Bossi-Fini . . .

The young man pulled a face. In the movie business, in music, they always found a way to pay.

But he was in danger, I pointed out. He was just the sort of person the new code called for deporting.

We were interrupted by the arrival of fresh sea-salad, purple coils of chilled octopus. The chic fugitive took a small plate and, smiling, handed me the guitar. He asked if I could show him "Like a Rolling Stone."

Did my father live in similar denial? Avoiding the Church, keeping his combat experience a secret from his children. Should I pathologize this behavior with words like "post-traumatic?" Certainly it was Gigi, his brother in the trauma, who more than anyone else brought my father back to a re-engagement with the agony. Certainly Naples never lost its core importance for Enzo Domini. Italians tend not to let go of the Old Country, of course; I wonder if any transplanted American group endures such a poignant closeness to the native culture. My father, as he grew into a bona fide "uncle from America," took to returning more and more often. On one such visit, as he and Uncle Gigi sat with their families by the central thoroughfare Spaccanapoli, the younger man startled everyone with a less-than-happy reminiscence.

"But, don't you remember, Enzo?" he asked. "This is where we sat and shot Germans."

Their long-ago sharpshooting, as Gigi may have surmised, proved something that Pop could open up about. Back in September 1943, once the two boys had found rifles and the cover of an overturned trolley, the threat hadn't seemed quite so terrible. And almost sixty years later, as the two old men exchanged an innocuous sentence or two about the experience, anyone listening could see that, just as there's no telling the toll of such hard times, there's no telling the healing possibilities a personality might hold. Instead of therapy, my father had, like many of his long-married generation, my mother. This woman's easily worthy of an essay herself; she was Pop's greatest resource, no question. Also he had his own mother, a woman who, among other accomplishments, brought in a useful second income by interpreting dreams. Again, I'm not talking about psychoanalysis. I mean rather that my *nonna* held a salaried position with the national lottery, helping ticket buyers by consulting that unique Neapolitan text the *Smorfia*, a compendium difficult to find in other Italian cities. The book translates the details of a dream into numbers and sequences.

Pop had his resources. My father too, as Gertrude reminds Hamlet, lost a father. But as his final heart attack drew near, some urgency began to prompt him. I may as well add that this period was my own closest brush with mystic experience; the few months before and after his passing, I had prophetic dreams, I heard voices. As for my father, for the first time he shared with his children some part of the worst he'd endured back when he'd been, as we would never be, entirely Old World. The most memorable storytelling came at a moment quintessentially American, a Thanksgiving in Boston.

I don't remember just how Pop got onto the subject; perhaps by way of the soup, rich with mushrooms. But he began relating how he'd helped Gigi get some shoes, many an autumn day ago, in a city full of different ways to die.

The brothers had stopped looking for places to hide and instead joined a band of young partisans. These heroes of the Four Days tended to be a rough crowd, naturally: teenagers known then as *scugnizzi* and now, perhaps, as gang-bangers. Enzo and Gigi, conversely, were church kids, school kids. My father had to beat up one of the other boys to prove he wouldn't be a liability. Only after that would the "unit" help the younger of their two new recruits find some shoes, a life-or-death matter in that place and time. Also the way these *scugnizzi* went about it seems like another harsh rite of initiation. They didn't waste time trying to scavenge. Rather, they went to the same source from which they got the rifles Gigi and my father used later in the battle; the Germans had the real weapons. The partisans knew of a bar frequented by soldiers off-duty, and they had Gigi darken up a bit, so he looked all the more like a harmless "little monkey." A beggar without a home. Then they sent him inside to find a man who wore the right size shoe.

Over the bones of his turkey, that last Thanksgiving of his life, Pop's look wasn't clouded or inward. He kept meeting our gaze, striving to get across. He said that when he saw his little brother come back out onto the street, it made no difference that the unarmed soldier with him was hardly more than a teenager himself.

"First thing," he said, "is you cut his throat so he can't call for help."

He and his new comrades were quick. As soon as the German's shoes were off, no doubt while his carotid was still spurting, they started on cleanup. To leave the body of a *Tedesco* lying around, even evidence of a body, would invite all kinds of trouble. At the least, the local commandant would retaliate ten for one, picking out neighborhood men, women, and children.

"You cut him up," my father explained, "so you can get rid of him."

At times during this past summer I asked myself how many of the recent African arrivals were driven by horrors like my father's. From Rwanda, the Sudan, and elsewhere across the southern continent have come recent stories of depressing similarity: execution by machete, or lopping off an arm to teach a lesson. Not that any of the immigrants I spoke with shared such stories. The fashionable *clandestino* who swapped songs with me, for instance, wouldn't even go so far as to speculate on what had happened to his grad-student friends. But if people like this would-be filmmaker in fact live in denial, they have a good reason. They're all about the new, here in Naples, about reconstruction of the self and its community. Them I could understand—but not the Italian government, which seemed to have plunged into a considerably deeper denial of immigrant reality.

Regarding Bossi-Fini, the most knowledgeable Neapolitans I spoke with criticized the new legislation as, above all, unrealistic. "These regulations," declared one man, a lawyer, "speak to phenomena that don't exist." A woman, a social worker, put the point more bluntly: "The law is surreal." Hyperbole springs eternal when southern Italians talk politics. Even those who attack the Bossi-Fini law acknowledge that it builds on processes for regularization laid down by a 1998 decree (under a more welcoming, left-leaning administration). Everyone agrees that employers who rely on foreign-born labor should shoulder some of the responsibility for keeping a roof over their heads, and everyone admits, too, that the Italian legal system was late and slow, overall, in responding to the immigrant challenge. Nonetheless the very names on the 2002 legislation smack of rank politicking, the protection of vested interests, more than anything more civic.

Umberto Bossi founded the Northern League, a party that called for the prosperous territories up by the Alps to secede from the rest. Leaders of the League considered anything south of their own hardworking "Padania" a welfare state infested by the darker races; Bossi himself, until a couple of years ago, gave speeches that appealed to the lowest anti-immigrant denominator. As for Gianfranco Fini, he was the leader of the National Alliance. This bland designation masks an outfit so far to the right that as recently as the mid-1990s it proudly claimed direct descent from Mussolini's Fascists.

But over the first half-decade of the new century, both Bossi and Fini were careful to soften their rhetoric (Fini, for instance, disavowed any allegiance to Il Duce), in the process aligning themselves with the then prime minister, Silvio Berlusconi. Most Americans know the smiley face Berlusconi for his steadfast support of the Iraq war; they don't know his vast and not-quite-legal wealth, and his hardly coincidental promotion of protection for the long-standing economic powers over whatever might be good for a changing majority of citizens. Hence the cold shoulder given to the immigrants and those who hire them, engineered by two of his arch-conservative accomplices. Hence what I saw that summer: a situation as difficult for immigrants as any in Europe.

And given the tangled plumbing of the politics, small wonder that many blithely dismissed the crisis, no matter their sides of the lines of color and citizenship. They sank into the heat, saying, *Africans will find a way somehow*; saying, *we have no problem in Italy*. While the fingerprinting issue prompted one or two demonstrations in 2002 and 2003, its challenges were swiftly funneled off into constitutional court, where decision making could drag on for years. Yet much as everyone in the Neapolitan *mercati* and *piazze* might present an air of business as usual, this could never entirely hide the

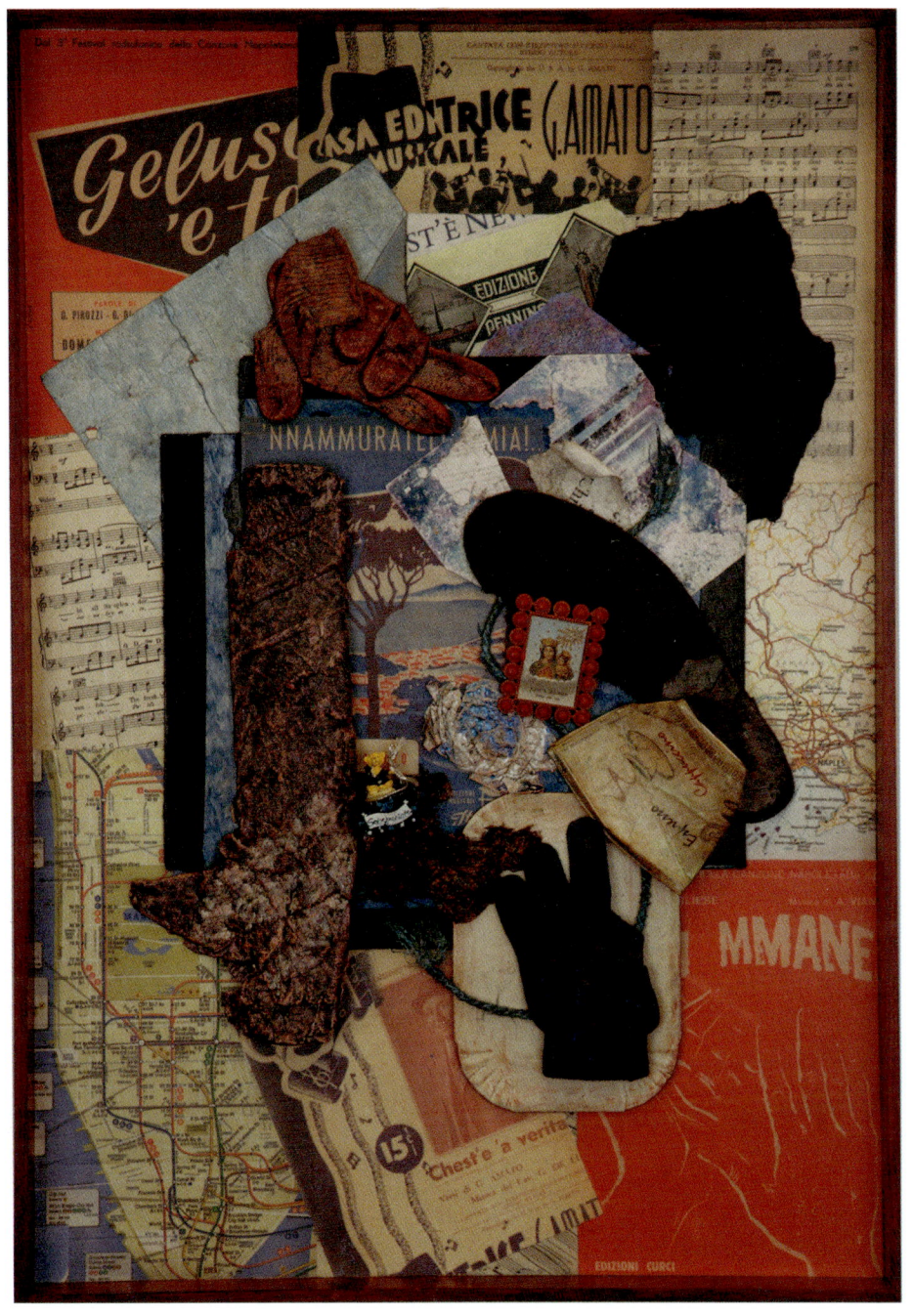

Plate 3-1. *Holding the Street in My Hands / Sti Mmane*
Rick Odell

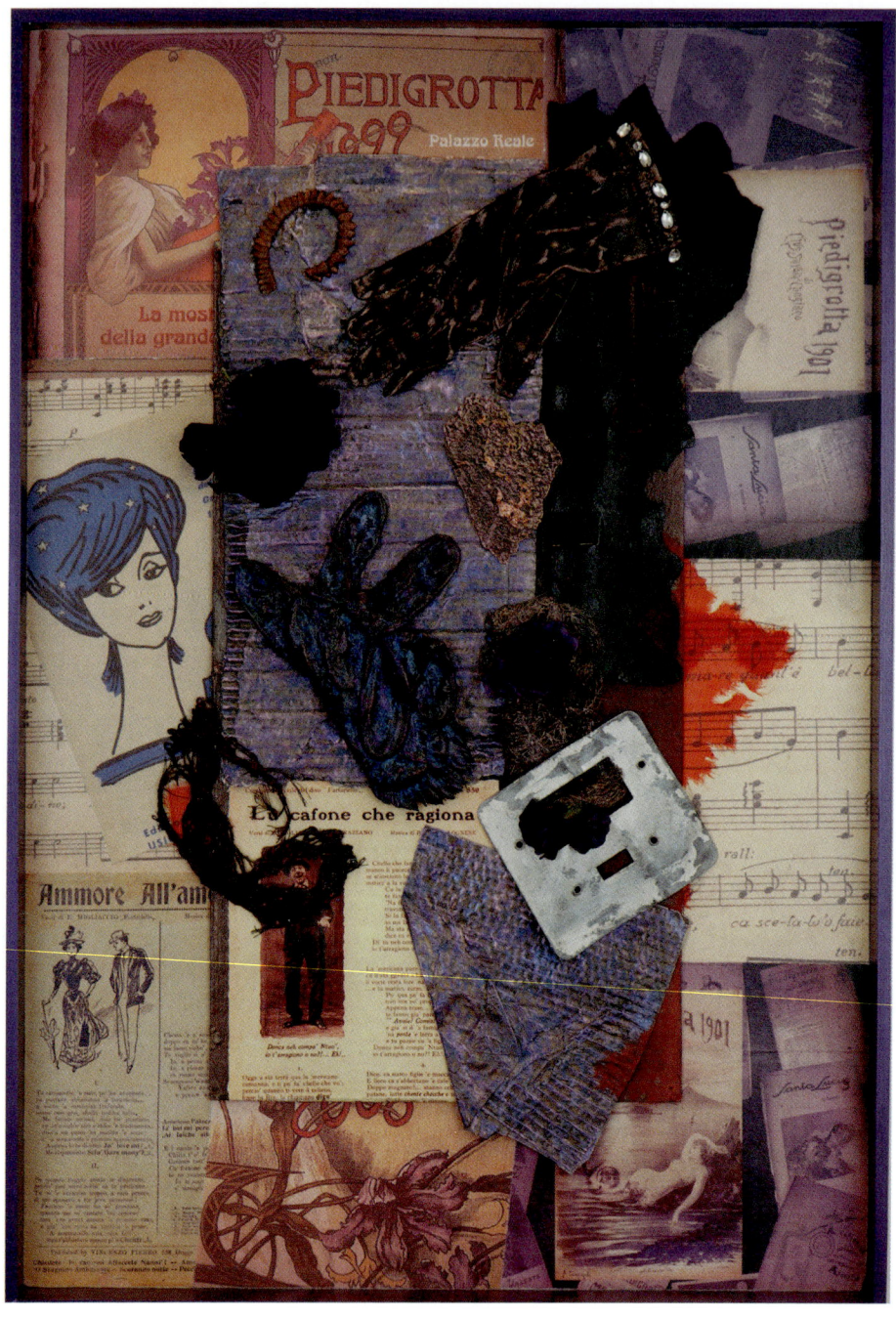

Plate 3-2. *Piedigrotta Passione / Chelsea Passeggiata*
Rick Odell

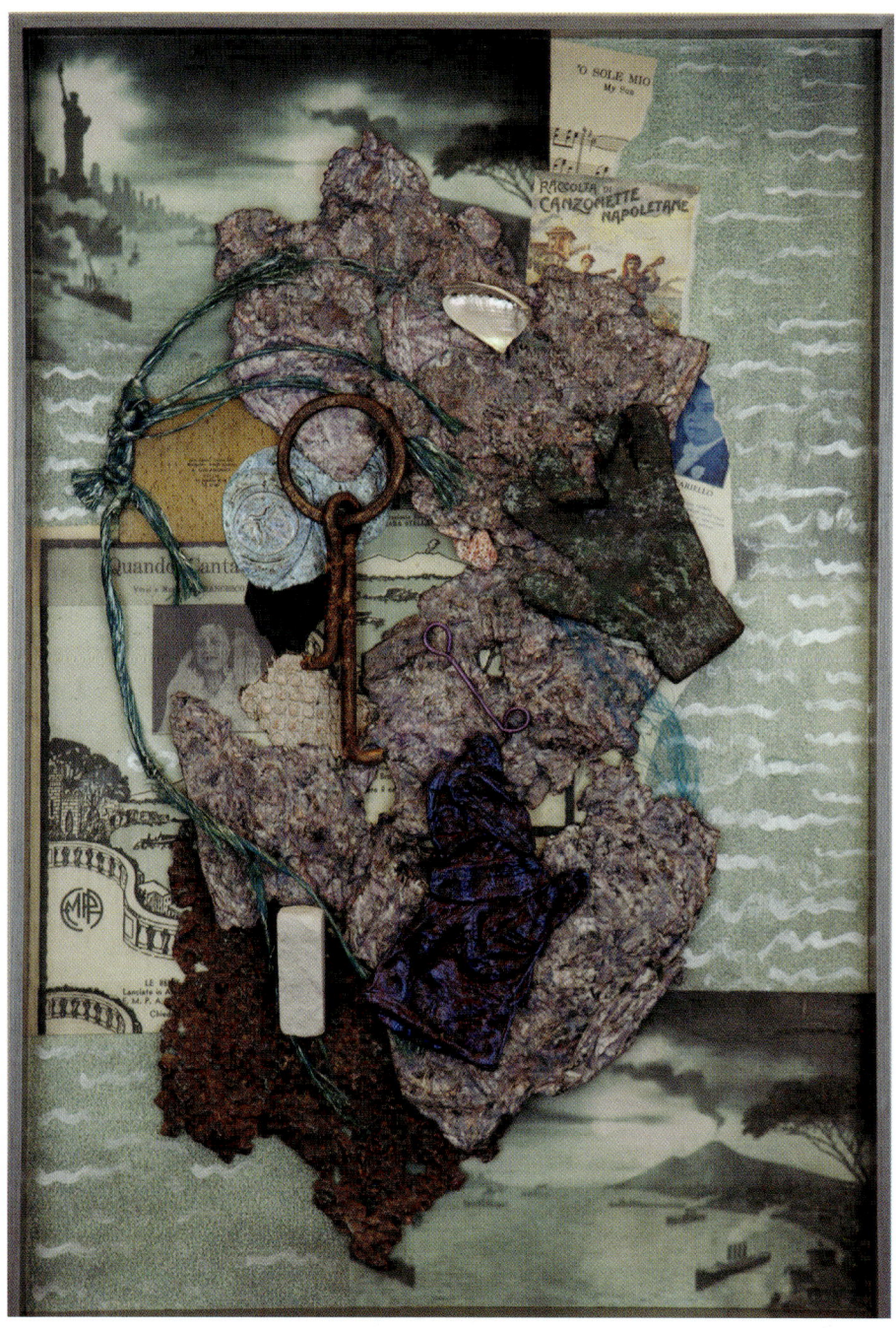

Plate 3-3. *Floating between Liberty and Vesuvius*
Rick Odell

Plate 3-4. *Between Two Shores / Tra Due Sponde*
Rick Odell

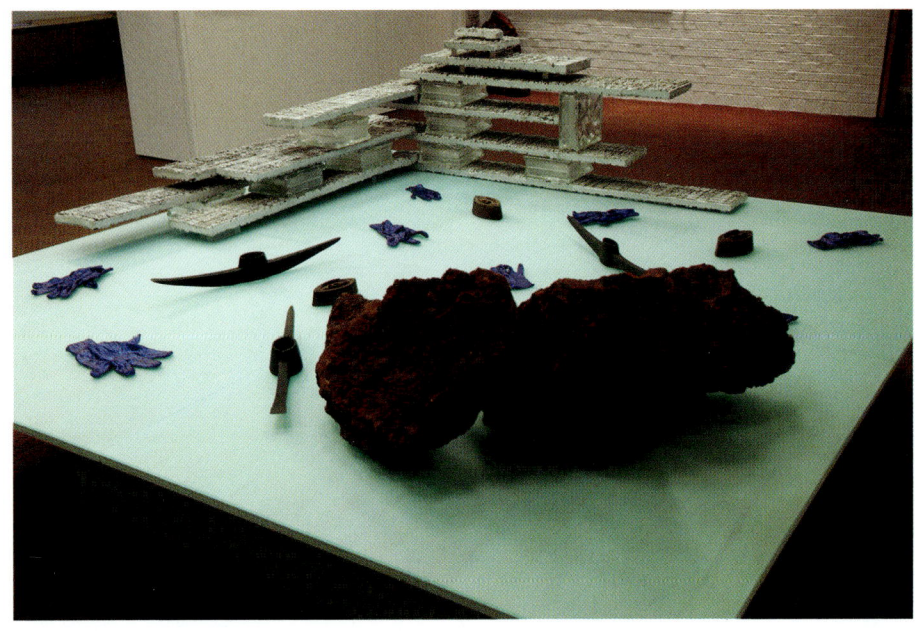

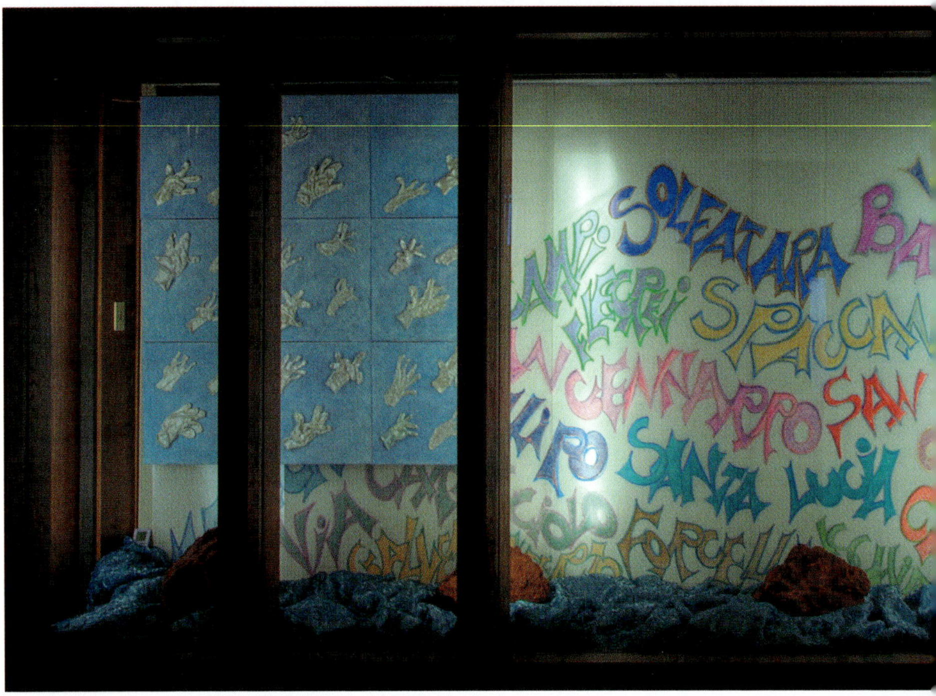

Plate 3-5. *Delirious Naples with Birds of Passage / Napoli Delirante con Rondini di Passaggio*
Rick Odell

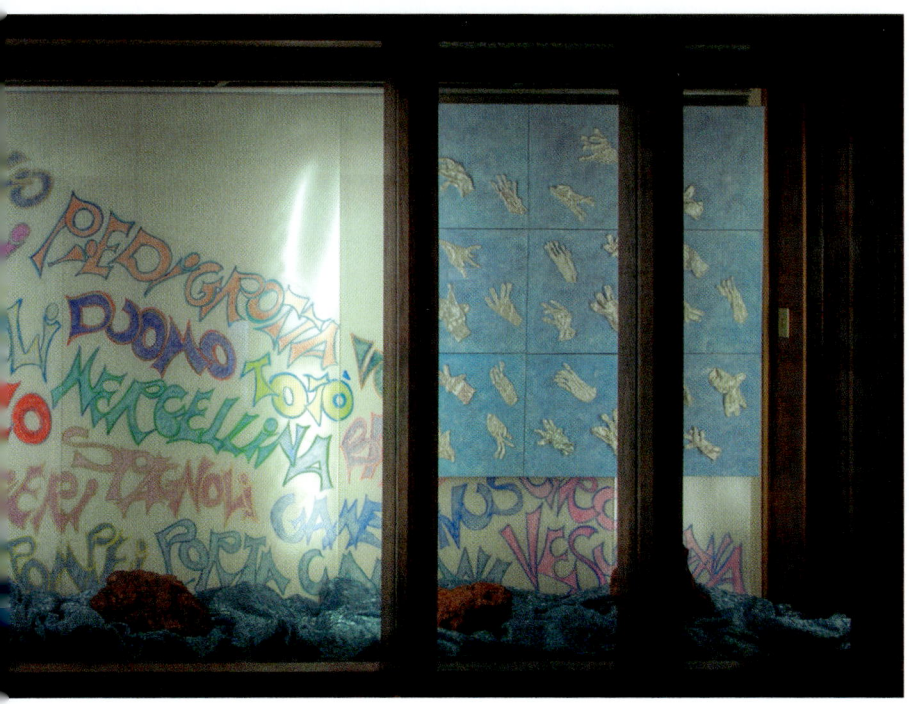

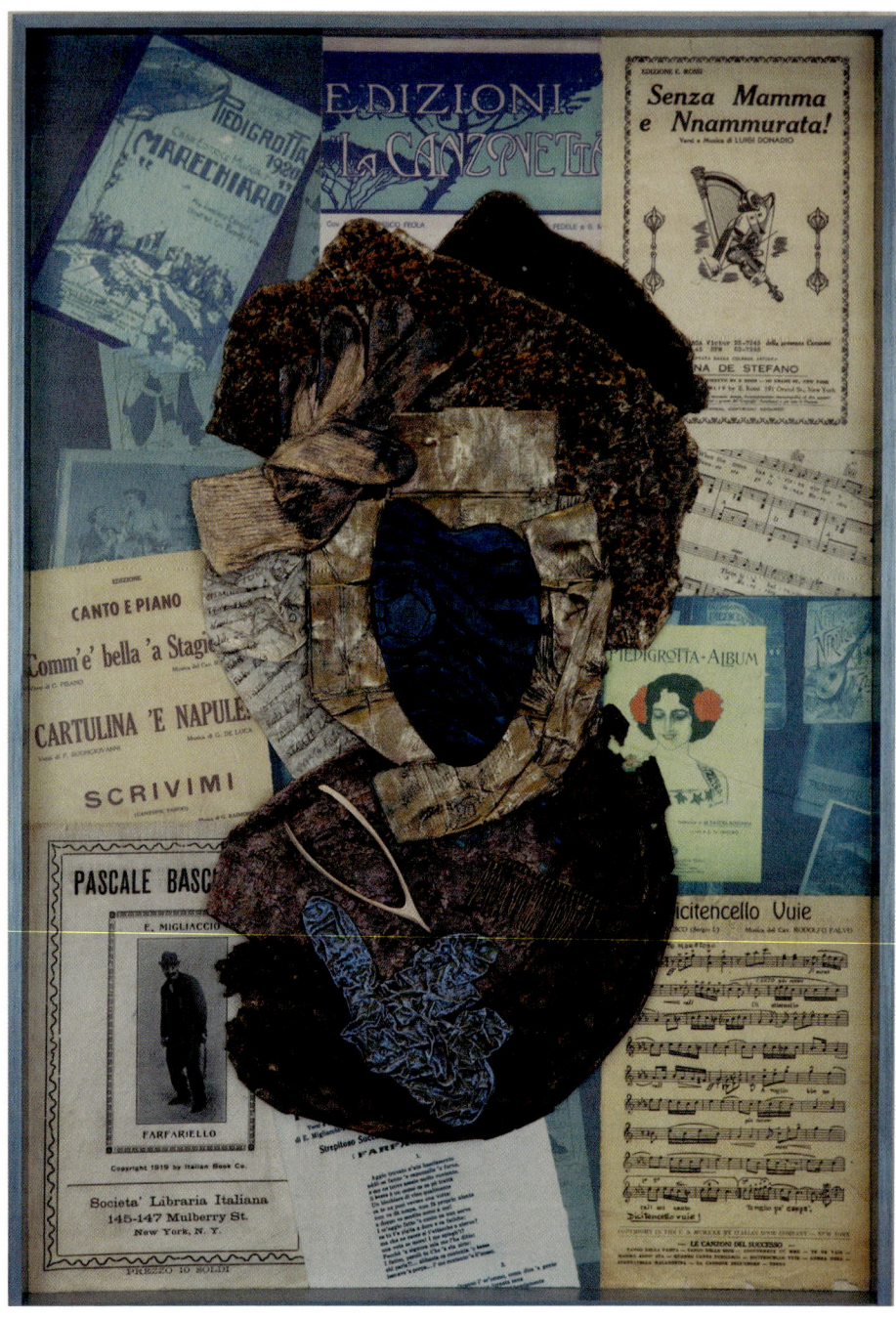

Plate 3-6. *Heart of Naples / Hands of New York*
Tad Merrick

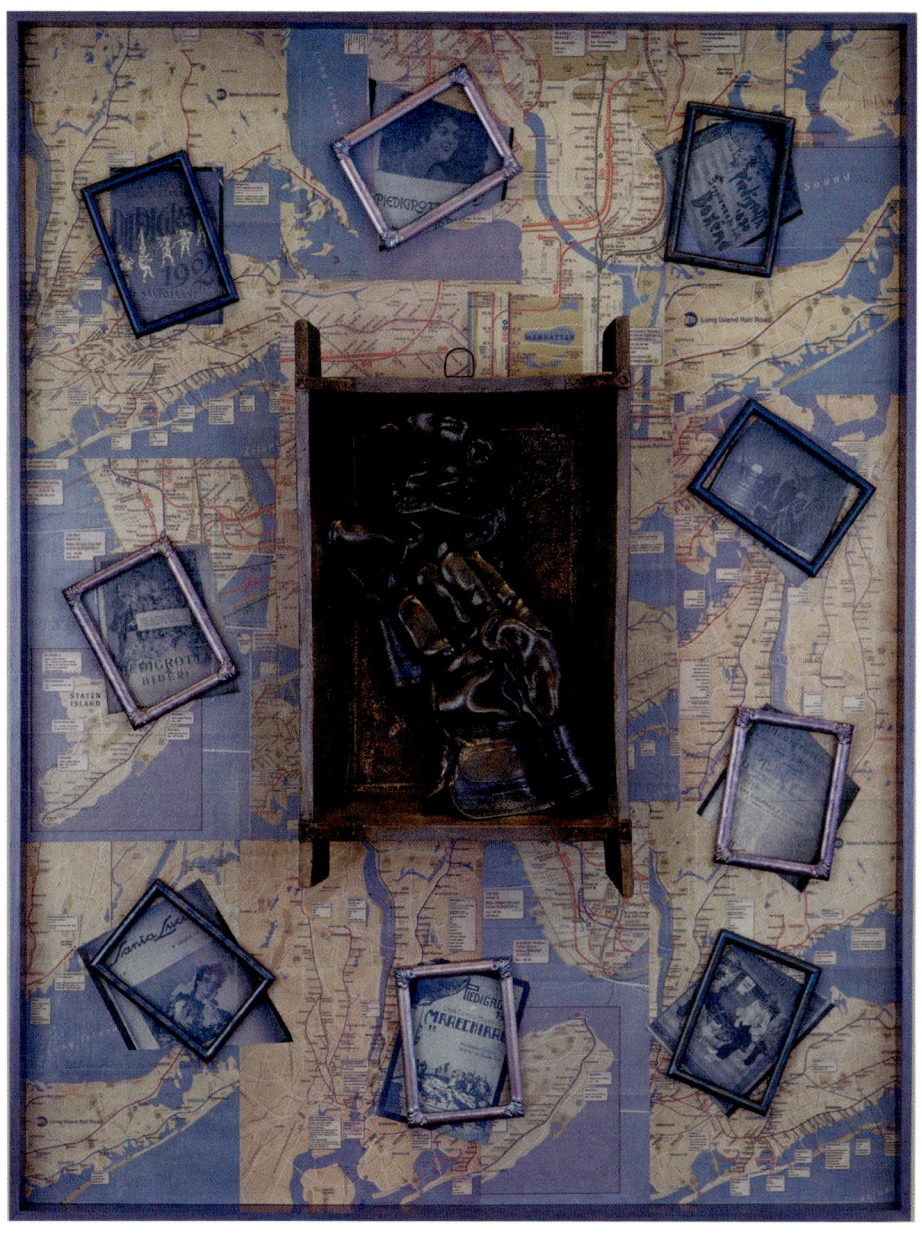

Plate 3-7. *Roots, for Montefalcione*
Rick Odell

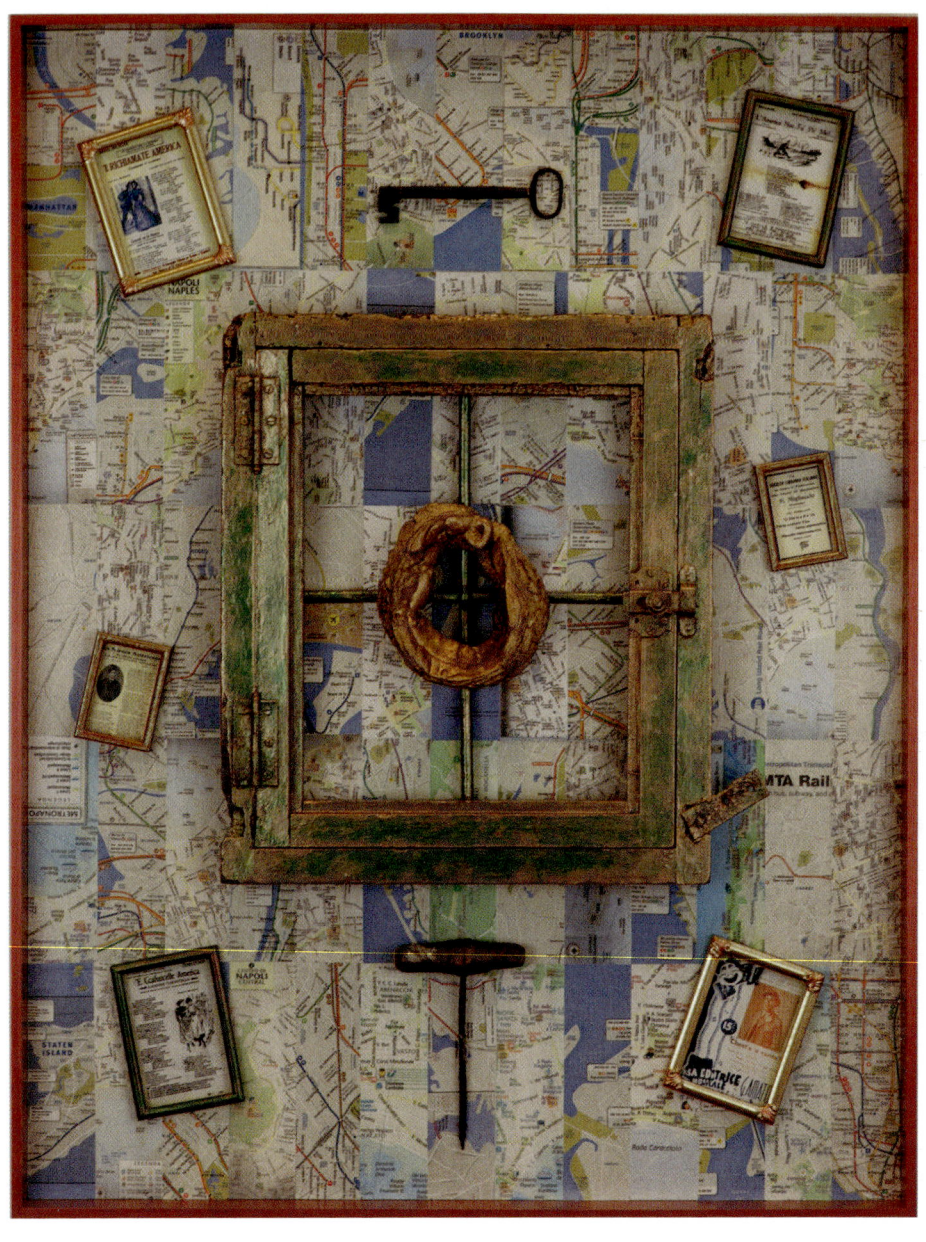

Plate 3-8. *Window to a Wider World (for Montefalcione)*
Rick Odell

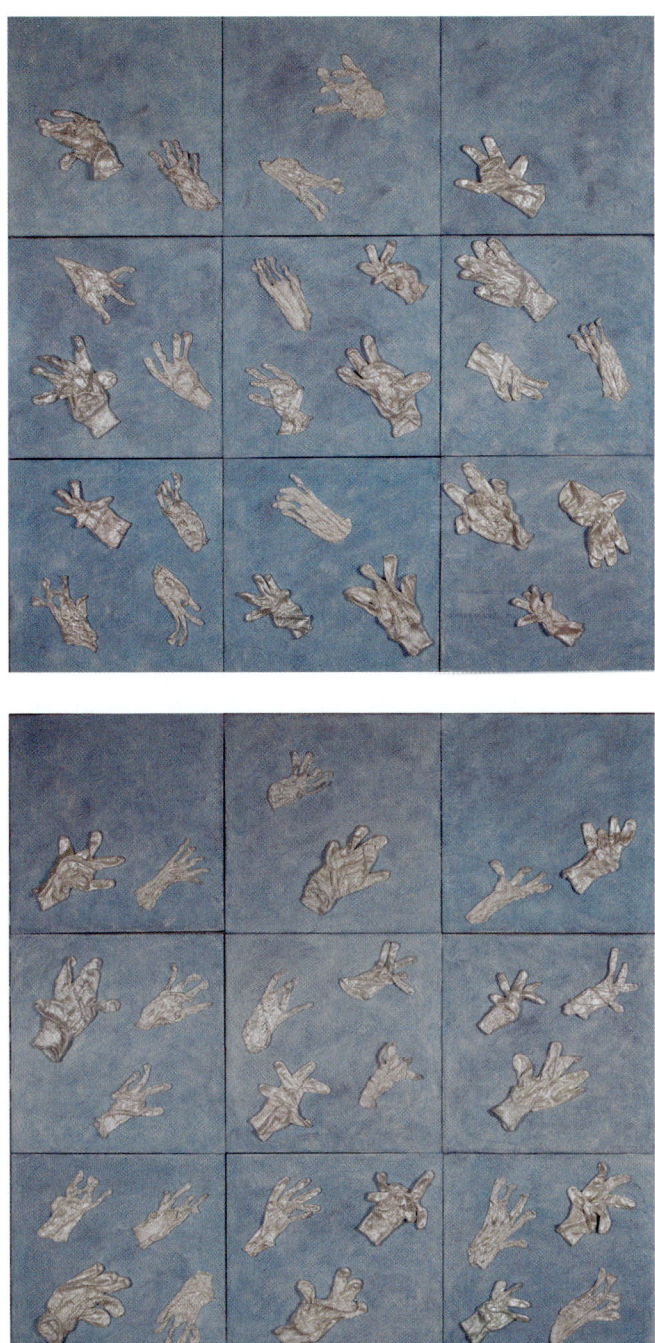

Plate 4-1. *Birds of Passage Naples/New York* (B. Amore)
Rick Odell

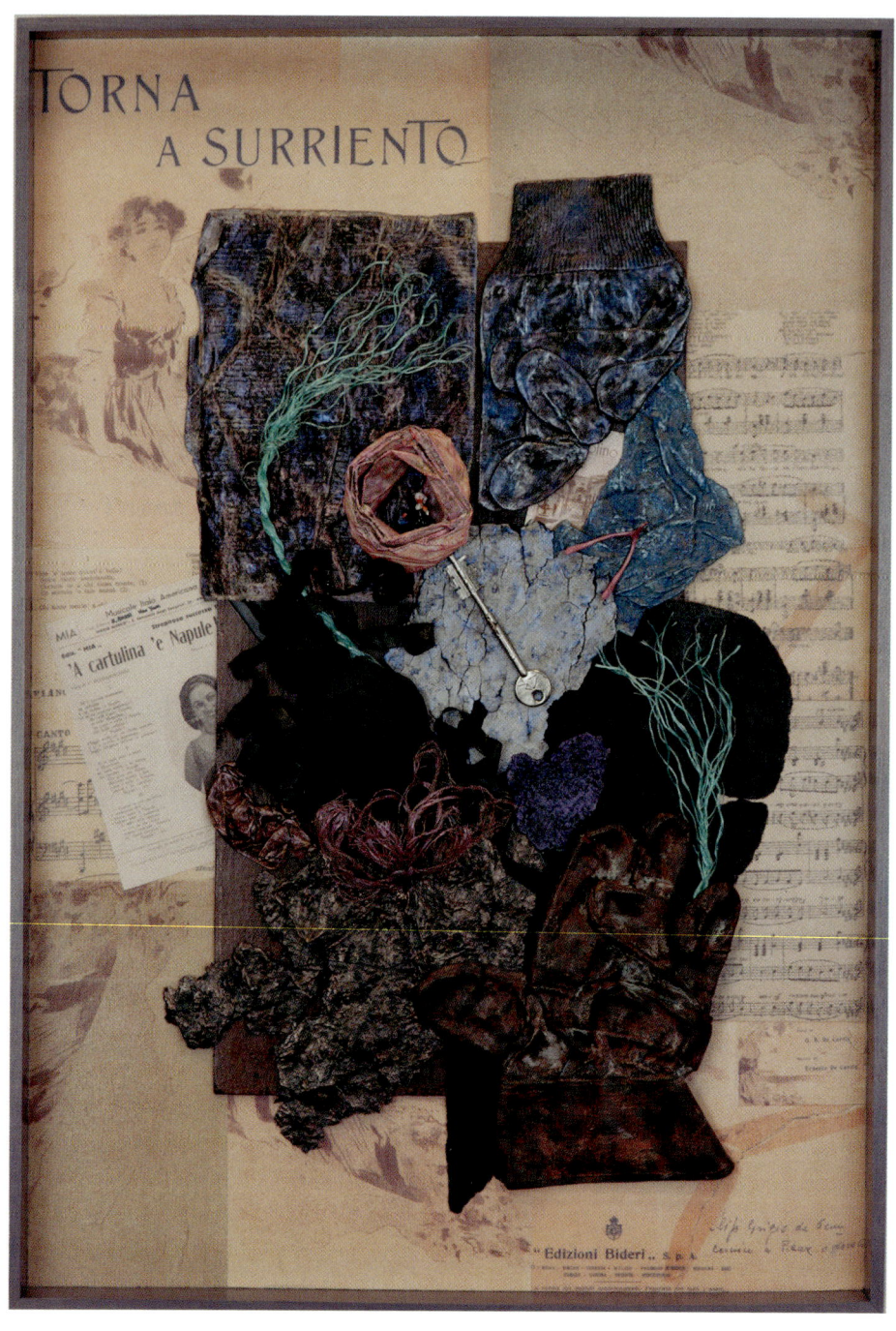

Plate 4-2. *Return to the Stones of Naples* (B. Amore)
Rick Odell

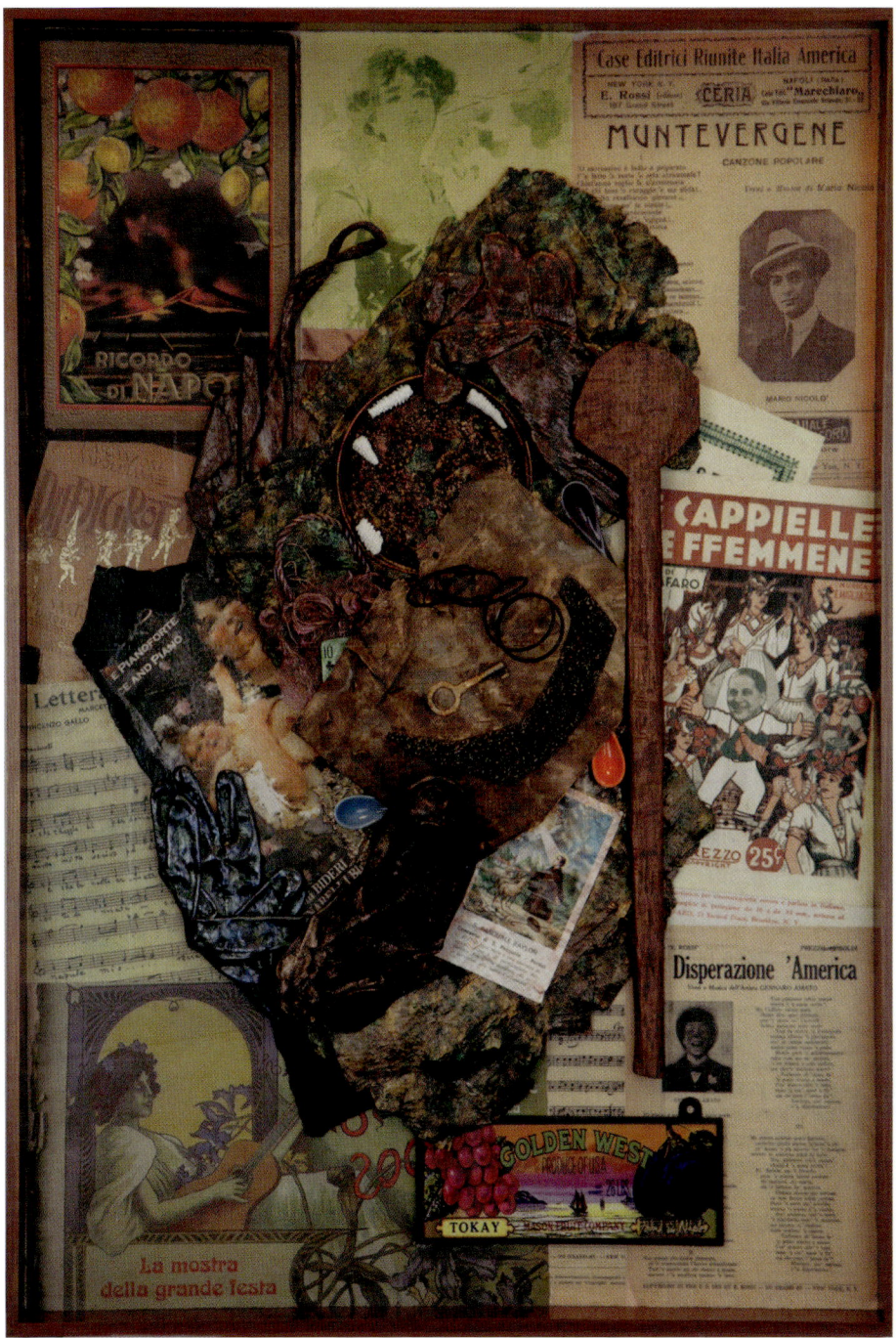

Plate 4-3. *Place of the Heart (for Lapio)* (B. Amore)
Rick Odell

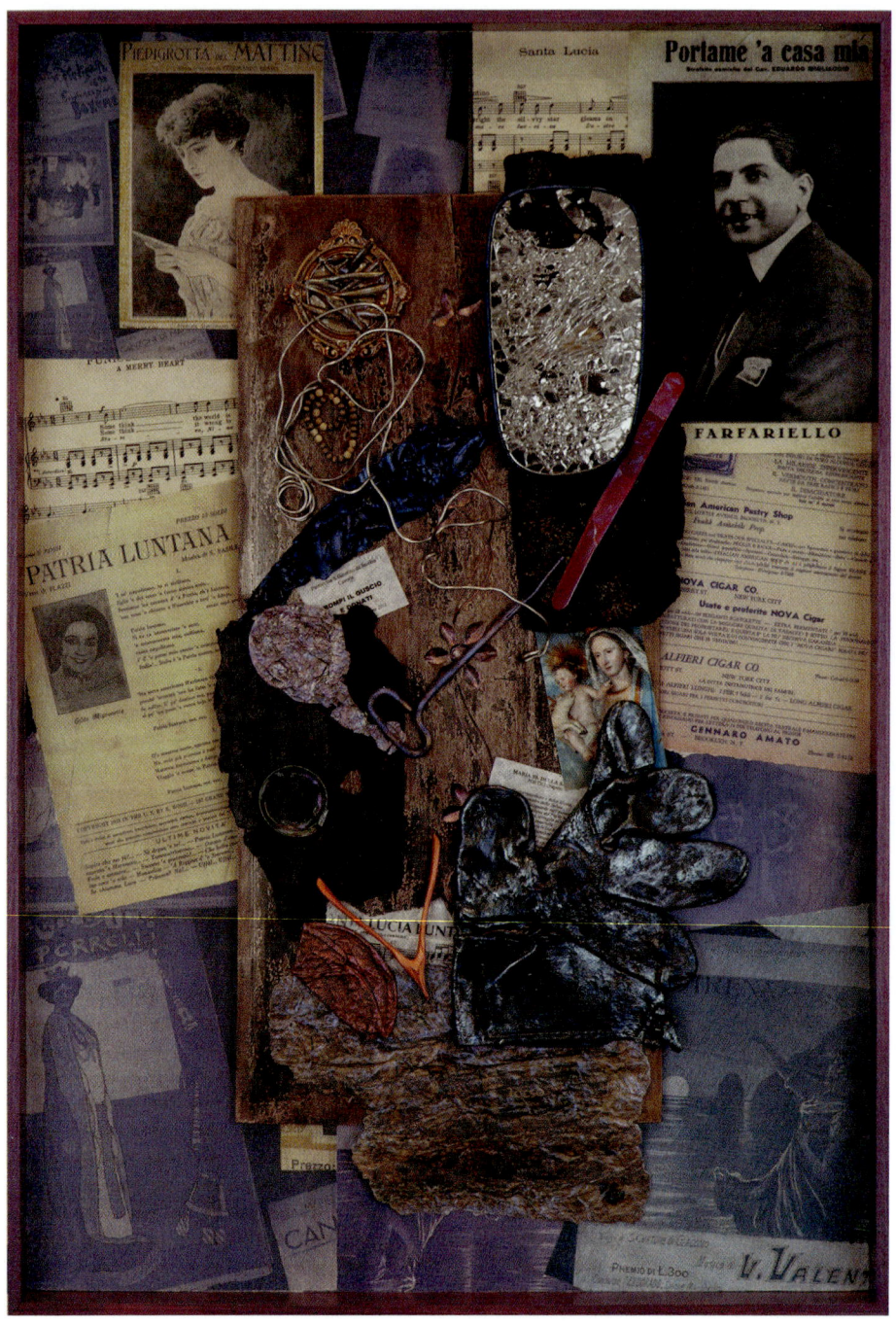

Plate 4-4. *Cracked Immigrant Mirror* (B. Amore)
Rick Odell

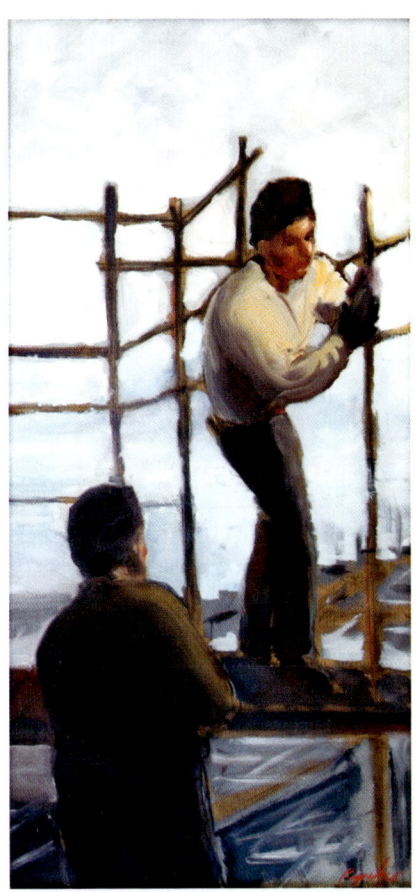

Plate 7-1. *Ship Builders above Vesuvius, Castellammare di Stabia*
William Papaleo

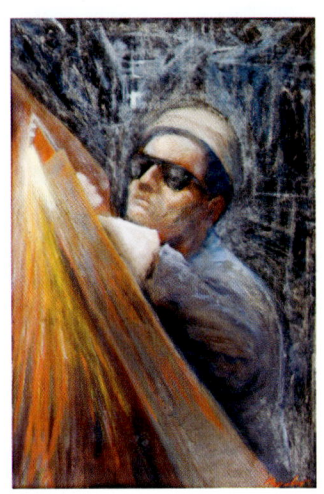

Plate 7-2. *Shipbuilder, Welder, Castellammare di Stabia*
William Papaleo

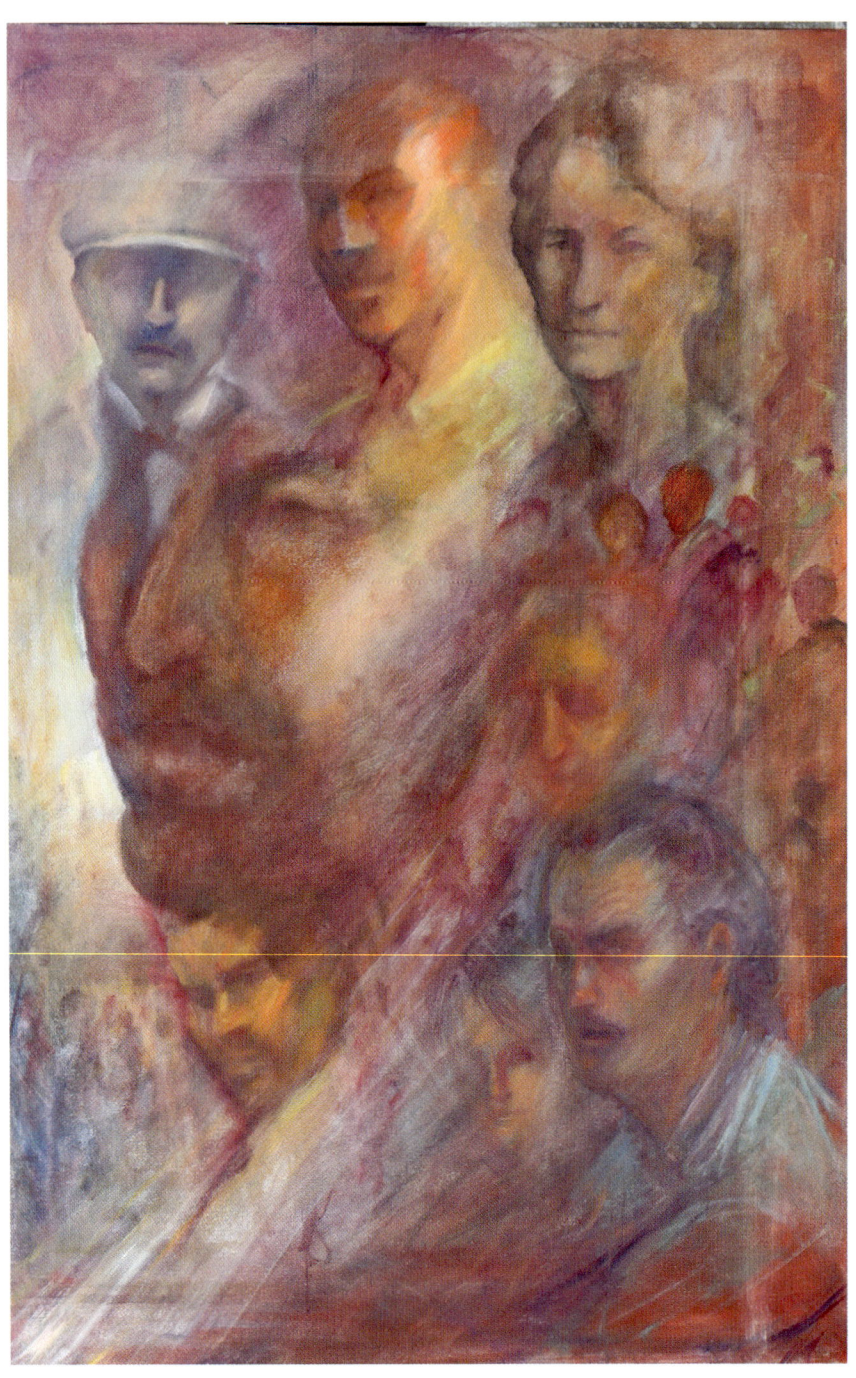

Plate 7-3. *Immigrants/Emigrants*
William Papaleo

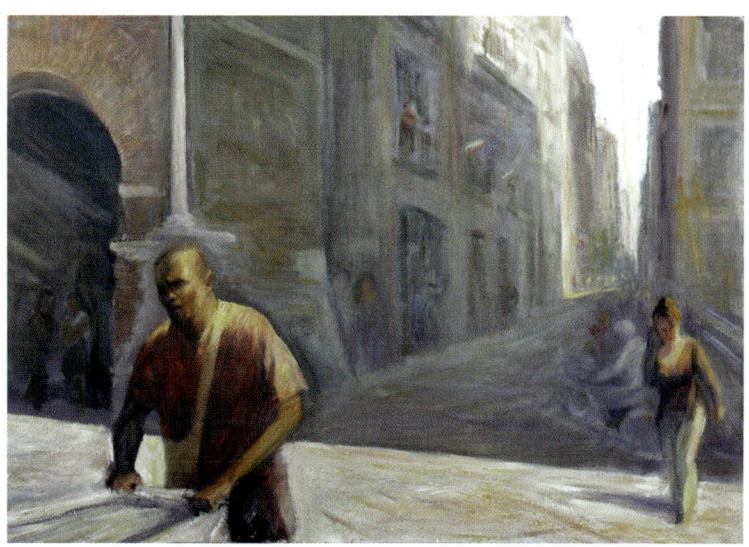

Plate 7-4. *Nigerian in Naples*
William Papaleo

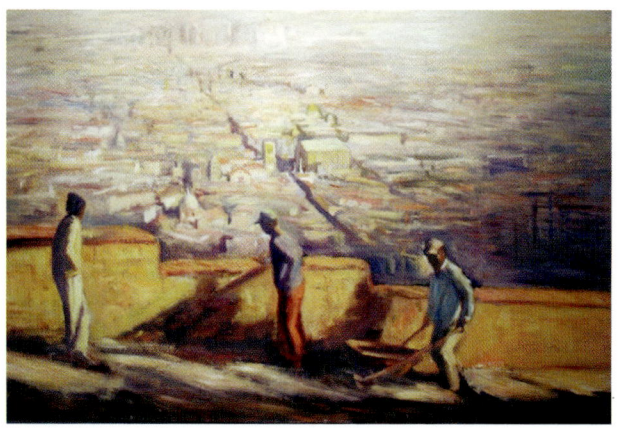

Plate 7-5. *Nigerian Workers above Naples*
William Papaleo

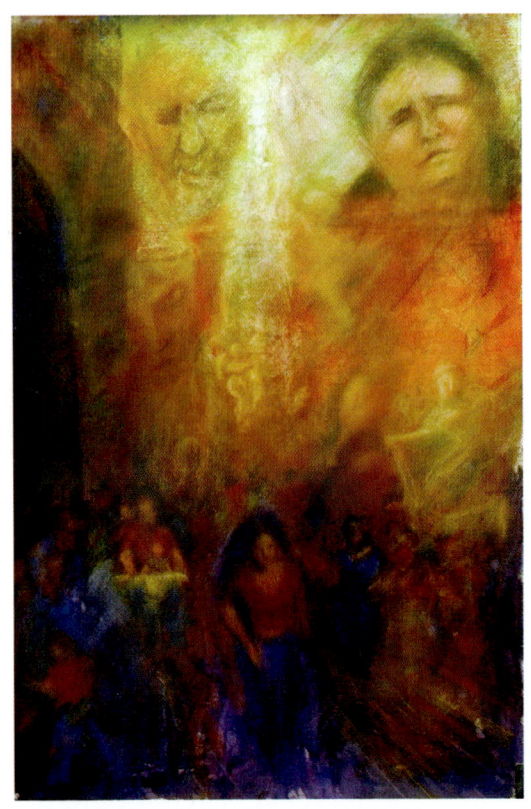

Plate 7-6. *Miele e Fiele* (Honey and Bile)
William Papaleo

mutual suspicion and fear. Every time I talked with an African, we soon skidded on the black ice of silence and evasion.

But the most disturbing examples of growing distrust that I saw came from the white, Italian side of the ongoing encounter. At the bus stop or the Metro station, it wasn't uncommon to see a pair of police close in on any passenger with dark skin and a duffel bag. Papers were demanded, and once I witnessed a rough frisk (I was with my cousin and never got a chance to find out the circumstances). Especially shocking were two July 2003 letters to *La Repubblica*—a left-wing paper, not a Berlusconi mouthpiece. One correspondent flatly declared, "among the immigrants are . . . terrorists, thieves, prostitutes." The other, angrier, complained, "we let them in our country and in return they rob us," and ended with a *moviola* fantasy of kidnapping and murder at the hands of *clandestini*. But to me the most damaging piece of writing in the paper that day was the response from the editor (a regular feature). This read like sweet nothings, swiftly dissolving to spit: "We live in an era of Biblical changes . . . ; we can ask only that [they] be responsible and controlled." The editor even tacked on a jingoistic puff about America growing "great" by taking on refugees from Europe, "the Italians at the top."

The news, in short, wasn't good. Who could blame the new arrivals and those who worked with them if they turned to the classic alternative of *arrangiarsi*, making arrangements? In Naples, most of the time, this means another envelope of cash for the Camorra.

Then there's the rising potential for something worse: for smashing windows and breaking heads. Doesn't violence seem the inevitable result when you have an ever-growing population with ever less to lose? Hasn't it come to that elsewhere, most memorably in London? And southern Italy, no matter how thick it paints on the sybaritic gloss, cannot hide its history of street war. In my mind inner-city riots loom as a very real possibility, since it was this same tension—between longtime have-nots and those with no greater value than maintaining control—that tore apart these streets when my father and uncle were as badly off as many of the Africans.

But this conclusion seems too harsh, finally, and not just because I don't want to sound like one of those letters to *La Repubblica*. More than that, my worrying fails to credit the many ad hoc and extra-governmental efforts that creative people across this unique city have been making, from both sides of the immigrant struggle. In one of the very places where the apathetic may drink and doze, Café Arabo in Piazza Bellini, I found citizens taking action. The Arabo owners are a pair of Palestinian brothers who founded an Arab Council of Naples, a group whose pro bono activities seem all the more heartening given the terrorist fears raised, after 9/11, about any such organization. The Council has had to work under close observation by the *carabinieri*, yet in January and February 2003 its efforts enjoyed a public validation in a highly sensitive case. At the beginning of the year, twenty-eight Pakistanis were arrested in Naples, accused of plotting some sort of terrorist attack; then in less than six weeks (this latter news received next to no attention in the States), all charges were dropped and the Pakistani government was threatening to sue the Italian, arguing the men had been framed.

That case drew the attention of many others besides the Arab Council of Naples, to be sure, but there can be no denying the group's ameliorative impact for those arrested, and beyond that for all immigrants, including Africans. Petitions circulate out of this café, and small loans are made. Perhaps most usefully, these relatively sophisticated downtowners help disseminate key information about licenses and contracts, reaching even the half-literate menial workers in the fields. If Bossi-Fini is to be made workable, it will only happen via careful attention to the paperwork.

Whites in Naples (and I hope that by now such a phrase seems simplistic) have also taken steps, improvising around the regulations in a way at once inveterately Neapolitan and entirely twenty-first century. The lawyer and social worker I spoke with were but two of a growing network of younger professionals setting up *gruppi* and *associazione*. A store near Piazza del Gesù Nuovo, Il Mercato Equosolidale, features the kind of socially responsible crafts and foods one would find in the United States at Ten Thousand Villages, and twice a week they have legal counsel on hand for immigrant drop-ins. The store has become, like Café Arabo, an aid center; visitors can find names, phone numbers, and explanations free of legal jargon. Here too you learn about the many immigrant-friendly concerts and arts events, Africa-Drum for instance. To judge from the flyers in the store and the posters all over downtown, such shows were almost a weekly feature in July and August, and entailed cooperation at the municipal level. So, too, it's become easier to make contact with support organizations, both those that have more of a within-the-system approach like Dedalus Cooperative, and those more radical and freewheeling, like O'Pappacé.

That last name, not coincidentally, derives from an aphorism about subversion. *Pappacé* (PAH-pah-CHAY) is dialect for a worm, the sort of worm that burrows in fruit, and according to this expression, no matter how shiny the apple, in the end it belongs to the humble creature under the skin—kindred, clearly, to Marx's old mole. And I must add, finally, that I saw Neapolitans undermining the fleshy barrier between native-born and immigrant in another way, more informal but perhaps more transformative. I mean that I saw more interracial couples than ever.

Leo had hooked up with an old friend of mine, a woman I'll call Nunzia, a freethinking artist who works in terra-cotta. She had no thought of helping Leo achieve citizenship via the marriage clause in Bossi-Fini. She still had a husband, in the eyes of the Catholic Church at least, and as for the former Moroccan boxer, the one time I raised the issue of what marriage might mean, he merely laughed and frowned at once: you Americans. But this American had some idea, at least, about the couple's new excitement, their pleasure staying up until dawn, for instance, dancing at one of the African-music events. Though I could see that such concerts brought together a community, and allowed it a moment of carefree belonging, I was enough of a Woodstock victim to doubt the summer performances would have lasting impact. Nunzia, however, believed the shows meant something more, something her lover too accomplished; she said they showed her "a new beauty," and had restored her "ideals."

Idealism also seemed the essence of the relationship between the Dylan-curious *clandestino* and his Naples girlfriend, a technician and designer with one of the film studios. While her boyfriend and I were swapping tunes, she told me she refused to believe that her country would ever do something "so shameful" as to deport "a man of this talent and intelligence."

I nodded, then as innocently as possible mentioned Bossi-Fini's marriage clause.

She made a face she appeared to have learned from her boyfriend. She refused to believe, she said, that any woman in Naples could do something so disgraceful.

Is that young woman only showing us one more form of denial? Or can we trust in her idealism, and in a more intimate communion developing between north and south of the Mediterranean? My "evidence" hardly deserves the name, scattered and haphazard as it is. Statistics do confirm that interracial marriage is on the rise in Italy, but that's true all over the former First World. Nonetheless the phenomenon was impossible to miss for someone who knows Naples. Seeing so many blacks and whites together, or rather browns and olives, I couldn't help but take it as a tonic to the more pernicious effects of the region's "Biblical changes." But my happy interpretation of these transgressive loves, I have to admit, reveals still more traces of bias. My glasses were tinted rose long ago, as the product of a mixed-blood Neapolitan father and WASP New York mother.

They met on the Italian side of the Atlantic after she arrived in 1946 to work at a camp for the war children. My father was the Italian in charge, the one who spoke English. To hear my mother tell the story, and judging from old photos—and according to Gigi after he went into remission and was let out of the hospital, allowing him months more of reminiscing—Enzo had so palpable a sexual vitality it made the American women blush and laugh. Then who can say what most drove Pop to change homelands? Was it the old nightmare or the new love? The need to emigrate or the desire to immigrate? In any case, those twinned impulses come in a rainbow of nuance, and what I experienced over these weeks of African heat was more of its colors than ever, made more brilliant by contemporary pressures, and revealed finally as unknowable, enough to talk about for a lifetime.

Yet (speaking of endless mutability), I now must turn against that last insight; it strikes me as rather too zen. When it comes to Africans in southern Italy, contemplation must take a back seat to action. The inequities of Berlusconi,[4] and of self-satisfied Euro-America generally, demand to be addressed. If we may say that the great challenge for the middle of the previous century was the war, defeating the evil embodied by a racially driven Holocaust, then can't we make the case that the overriding challenge for the present is that of true integration, and the extension of genuine opportunity to all? Such seems the historical argument made by my discoveries in Naples. As for the philosophical argument, the zen, the issue is whether any of us with a hyphen in our makeup—in a world ever more a compound of tent cities—ever gets to the bottom of the enigma of transplantation. We beat on against the current, borne back ceaselessly into the past.

NOTES

1. The situation described here, indeed throughout the essay, has worsened since, in particular after the "Arab Spring" of 2011, and the subsequent Libyan war.

2. Their "Bossi-Fini law" was enacted by the government in July 2002, and my essay considers the chilling impact of the law generally. More specifically, Bossi-Fini imposed sanctions on persons either illegally entering the country or returning after expulsion.

3. This situation, too, has grown worse since. In 2009, Italy ratified a "security package" that ranks with the most draconian anti-immigrant measures in Europe. The subject of repeated court challenges, it's proven difficult, if not impossible, to enforce.

4. At the end of 2011, Mario Monti replaced Berlusconi. Monti's new "technocratic" government, however, changed next to nothing concerning Italy's immigrants, and the following administrations, even under the more progressive Matteo Renzi, continued to struggle with the political and economic implications of immigration. In Naples itself, the current mayor, Luigi De Magistris, has proposed granting honorary citizenship to the children of immigrants.

SIX

# Investigating Gilda Mignonette as a "Newpolitan" Approach to Popular Culture

*Simona Frasca*

In the second half of the last century there were many radio programs devoted to Italian music and culture. From one of them, one could hear the voice of Gilda Mignonette singing "Facimm' Pace," a tune recorded for the label La Voce del Padrone in 1940. The radio program was made right after Mignonette's death in 1953, and the female announcer who introduced her was the actress Mimì Cecchini. When giving homage to the singer, Cecchini recalled that she was a child actor when she first met Mignonette and was playing the role of the young daughter in "Balocchi e Profumi," a *sceneggiata* piece based on the song by E. A. Mario and written in 1929. Just before his death, Tony Giangrande, one of Mignonette's most intensely devoted supporters, played the recording of that program for me years ago during our meeting in his museumlike house in Brooklyn. He was an elderly man of Italian descent with a real passion for Neapolitan singing and especially for Mignonette's. During his life, Giangrande spent most of his free time organizing shows and musical events dedicated to the Italian singer, and over the years he collected more than a thousand of her recordings, creating in the United States one of the largest known private musical archives devoted to Neapolitan music outside Naples, now archived at UC Santa Barbara.

Giangrande's intense interest evidences the capacity of Mignonette's life and voice to symbolize the Italian immigrant experience in the United States. In Italy the cult of Mignonette would certainly have been less developed if she had declined the opportunity to go to America, and she possibly would have remained just one singer among many. Mignonette is known as the most recognizable name of what we can call a new wave of Neapolitan voices. That she was dubbed the *Carusiana*, honoring her attempt to establish continuity with the tradition represented by Enrico Caruso, and the Queen of Immigrants testifies to her enormous popularity in the United States. Among Neapolitan artists on either side of the Atlantic Ocean, she had one of the most active recording careers during the earliest years of the sound recording era, beginning with Italian-American labels, and in particular Geniale Record, and then moving on to larger companies such as Columbia and Victor. The singer was very receptive to American musical influences, performing onstage in Latin American costumes and singing tunes arranged as foxtrots, tangos, shimmies, and other rhythms inspired by Latin American or African American musical trends. Her continuous traveling between the United States and Italy (as well as South America) allowed for a fruitful exchange between the countries and specifically helped to modernize the Neapolitan repertoire.

During the very first decades of the twentieth century, a vocal style emerged within the Neapolitan song tradition that existed in tandem with an older, academic operatic style. Setting the stage for this new way of singing and acting were the *posteggiatori* (street singers), whose musical practices constituted the conditions that made possible the birth of the modern urban vocal style. During the last decades of the nineteenth century and the very first of the twentieth, the *posteggiatori* were crucial intermediaries between the literate song tradition and the frequently anonymous, popular repertoire. When poets such as Salvatore Di Giacomo, Libero Bovio, and Ernesto Murolo appeared on the Neapolitan stage, the enormously rich popular musical traditions[1] (constituted by such forms as *tarantella, canzoni satiriche, serenate, canti politici* and *canti d'occasione*) were displaced by new practices of popular song consumption in an urban context. The vast array of vocal styles and musical forms (i.e., parodies of famous songs) that the *posteggiatori* proved to handle very well faded away in the face of the arrival of music addressed to an urban bourgeois market (*musica di consumo*) in the early twentieth century. Although according to testimonies of poets such as Filippo Sgruttendio, the urban vocal style belonged to a very long history in Naples, dating back to the seventeenth-century, if not earlier, singers of the repertoires of the earlier urban style, and the *posteggiatori* shared the same approach to their songs: the singer was simply the channel of the tradition which manifests itself through him or her, without dramatic musical interpretation or any particular expression on the face, in a sort of statuesque pose.[2]

In the modern musical world shaped in the early twentieth century, these practices and techniques—together with their accompanying motivations and social values—that I have briefly described were flattened to favor a style that gave prominence to the individualism of the performer, emphasizing his or her more dramatic qualities. Mignonette was one such figure of this rising tide who conceived of a new approach to singing Naples and its song history. We find evidence of this even in characteristics such as a peculiar vibrato, nasalization, or the Neapolitan pronunciation of some groups of consonants, such as /ND/ for /NT/ in Mignonette's singing, which are in fact leftovers from a Neapolitan vocal tradition.

As was the case for many artists and singers of that time, Gilda Mignonette was a stage name, her real identity being Gilda Andreatini. She was born in Naples, in either 1886 or in 1890. (The year of her birth has long been debated because the old sources state it was in 1890[3] and the modern assure it was 1886.[4]) Her debut as a singer came at the age of twenty in Catania, Sicily, an important center for the spread of Neapolitan music and theater then as today. Around 1910, after having achieved reasonable success in Italy, Mignonette started to tour abroad: South America, Hungary, Spain, Russia. After collecting some positive experiences in Italy with important companies such as Raffaele Viviani's, she decided to move to the United States, probably following the advice of Roberto Ciaramella.[5] In New York City she married Franco Acierno, the son of Feliciano, the entrepreneur of the Acierno Theater on the Bowery in Manhattan, one of the most interesting Italian stages in New York at that time. There exist several unconfirmed anecdotes that associate her name with Mafia life in the American city.[6]

Let's look at "'A cartulina 'e Napule"[7] as it is representative of her singing style that is marked by the intense use of melismas and vibrato as nuanced devices that bring audiences into the world of feelings and passions she embodies and represents onstage. These elements were part of the knowledge she gained during her training in Naples that contributed to her excellent control of theatrical techniques. Her vocal style was very dynamic and naturally inclined to dramatizing. She seems concentrated on the emergence of each melodic shape in order to maximize emotional tension, and when it is achieved we are captivated by the drama of her voice. She employs an intense, marked vocal emission to generate a climax of the melodic phrase. Mignonette sings *as if* she pushes the emotional tension to the foreground. A peculiar aspect of the technique she uses is the frequent breaking of the sung word *as if* her voice is interrupted by an extra-musical action, coming by surprise, like an unexpected crying or lament, a hardly discernible forewarning.

All this dramatization seems to remain intact when Mignonette worked with other musical genres such as Latin American or those associated with the syncopated dance music orchestra repertoires (tango, maxixe, foxtrot). She preserves the impetuosity of popular song as a peculiarity of her singing. What happens to her voice when the traditional Neapolitan repertoire comes across the new influences of American dance music? The more explicit rhythmic paradigm offered by the American repertoires seems to soften the dramatic intensity of her singing. Such changes occur when she sings in Italian, using sexual themes, ironic language, and smoother sonorities as in "La rumba delle fragole." The song was written in Naples in 1933 by Enzo Bonagura and Giuseppe Cioffi. It was probably composed in the wake of the success of "The Peanut Vendor" (1931) by Marion Sunshine and L. Wolfe Gilbert. This was one of the first examples of American rumba written after the Cuban original "El manicero" by Moisés Simóns. "La rumba delle fragole" sounds less soft than the original Cuban song. The rough and angular characteristics of Mignonette's version are probably due not only to the change from Spanish to Italian but also to the change of mediation of Neapolitan in Italian. Even if she sings in Italian she does totally abandon those stylistic elements derived from popular Neapolitan music.

Mignonette was interested in what happened around her in the big American cities. She dressed in South American gowns with fruits and flowers on her head years before Carmen Miranda became famous for doing so. While performing for an Italian audience on North American soil in a Neapolitan-inflected Italian language she was enacting one of the first experiments of cultural and racial integration in the twentieth century, effectively articulating a transnational space. This is possible because sound has the capacity to create community. Iain Chambers writes that sound constitutes a "home": "For sound narrates and affects an attachment (to a memory, a place, a trace) that elaborates a temporary territory and transitory home in the world. This is to think of the cultural and historical affiliation of music not in the largely static appeal to 'origins,' but rather in the altogether more suggestive, fluid and freer understanding of 'beginnings' that are always haunted by the ghosts of other songs. It is precisely in this key that sounds deterritorialize and reterritorialize cultural landscapes and their inherited histories."[8] Mignonette creates a home for the Italian migrants in the United States using Italian and Neapolitan dialect and not using English; but the titles of her tunes, for example "Fra un tango, un foxtrot e uno shimmy" or "Il tango delle geishe,"[9] reflect her strong attraction to American dance music; she understood the market potential of that repertoire even if her noted patriotism never waned. Her success is a testament to the fact that she represents an entire community that follows her closely along a new musical itinerary.

"Fra un tango, un foxtrot e uno shimmy" is a three-verse song in which a music club, where the song is set, is characterized as an immoral or shady place in the lyrics of the singer. A jazz band's music is associated with filth and degradation, with the dance hall slowly changing into a brothel. It was not uncommon to hear a song based on tango or ragtime rhythm combined with moral corruption. "Il tango delle geishe" by S. N. Tortora (pseudonym of Salvatore Neri) and Gaetano Lama was composed in the same year as "'A cartulina 'e Napule."[10] Both were recorded for Brunswick in New York in 1928 and arranged by Romano Romani. The song sounds like an experiment of grafting a folk vocal style onto popular marketed music. Mignonette's voice is softer than usual, probably reflecting the influence of opera music, especially Puccini's *Madame Butterfly*, whose subject is borrowed. She pronounces the lyrics in a more rhythmical way and sings doubled initial or midword consonants, as in *b*bambole (dolls), fraggili (breakable), *b*bianca (white), and sometimes she changes the letter *p* into *b* as in "pian pian" (slowly), which is pronounced "*bian bian*." Again the secret of her success seems to consist in a peremptory, and at the same time flexible, voice that dramatizes every little nuance of the lyrics, whether they are in Italian or in Neapolitan. Her success probably can be explained much like the success of Enrico Caruso has been described: Mignonette had a voice that sounded "discographically" perfect, and the gramophone—to quote Marsha Siefert— has the peculiar charm possessed by anything mechanical that *faithfully* reproduces any of life's actions. If a machine talks, we are apt to regard it as almost human; if it sings, we look upon it as being artistic.[11]

Continuous traveling from Italy to the United States put Mignonette in a very convenient position to stay abreast of new ideas in both countries. Her schedule anticipated her staying in Naples during Piedigrotta feast days in the autumn season,[12] and going back to America to tour the country for the rest of the year. These back-and-forth movements aided an intense musical exchange that went on until June 1953 when she died of a cerebral hemorrhage. News about her death has been cloaked in a haze for a long time due to a lack of sources and studies.

Among Neapolitan women singers, Mignonette was probably the most active in the studio. The twenty-four recordings she made in Italy were printed in the United States under the label Geniale Record. She continued to record other songs for similar labels before moving on to the most well-known companies. The first masters of those records for Geniale Record date back to the twenties, and in the subsequent decades her recordings for Columbia, Victor, Okeh, and Brunswick were numerous. For these labels, Italian and Neapolitan titles of songs were translated into English: "'A canzone d' 'a felicità" (The Song of Happiness); "Tutta pe' mme!" (All to Myself) (Co 14653F); "Ninna nanna" (Rock-a-Bye Baby); "'O calore d' a staggione" (The Season's Heat) (Br 58008); "'Nterra Surriente" (On the Land of Surriento); "Sulo Dicenne 'Napule'" (Only Saying "Naples") (Br 58089); "Si dormono 'e sserene" (If the Sirens Should Sleep); "Questa è l'Italia" (This Is Italy) (Br 58197); "Serenata Malandrina" (Apache's Serenade); and "Il valzer di mimosa" (Mimosa Waltz) (Br 58198). We don't know for sure whether in addition to Italian immigrant buyers who were able to understand the original idiom there might have also been non–Italian-speaking American consumers attracted by an euphonious language. However, we can be sure that besides aiding the cataloging of masters, the English translations of titles would have allowed a deeper penetration into the growing phono-discographic market.

The vocal and musical style that emerged in the early twentieth century within the Neapolitan song tradition accentuated a deeply felt and *larmoyant* interpretation centered on a sentiment of "suffering" that was part and parcel of the divo/a persona who expresses his or her inner life to a heterogeneous audience. The divo/a, with signature name recognition, offered an inimitable personality as "interpreter" to fans as a form of vicarious escapism. The new voices of singers like Gennaro Pasquariello or Elvira Donnarumma popularized this new style not only in Italy but beyond the national borders through recordings and performances as migratory artists.

Gilda Mignonette is the symbol of a new music; she presents herself as a new-waver with transnational peculiarities; she is perfectly a part of the American musical context of the early twentieth century. Her name is among other women singers and performers in the United States who originated abroad. Many women were rethinking themselves through the channel of the entertainment industry probably earlier than in any other social environment of the last century, and Mignonette was among them. Thus, she participates in the formation of new cultural processes.

Popular culture has often been seen as the antithesis of folk culture, not as emanating from within a community but created for a community or, rather, for the masses who no longer have an organic community capable of producing culture. My position is to consider popular music as a popular culture text, and with this perspective it is a matter of negotiation between the author, the present, and the audience in a way Lawrence Levine has pointed out:

> The audience's role in popular culture, as it is in folk culture, is not the passive reception of a given text but rather a question of translation; fitting the text into a meaningful context. Whether it is the creator's intention or not, it seems inevitable that the audience's imagination will be kept busy by any work of expressive art simply because so many expressive works are by their very nature incomplete, filled with interstices that need connecting, ambiguities that need resolution, imprecisions that need clarity, complexities that need simplifying. In this manner, folklore encourages listeners to become not merely participants but even creators of meaning when the message is not explicit; to project themselves into the text in order to invest

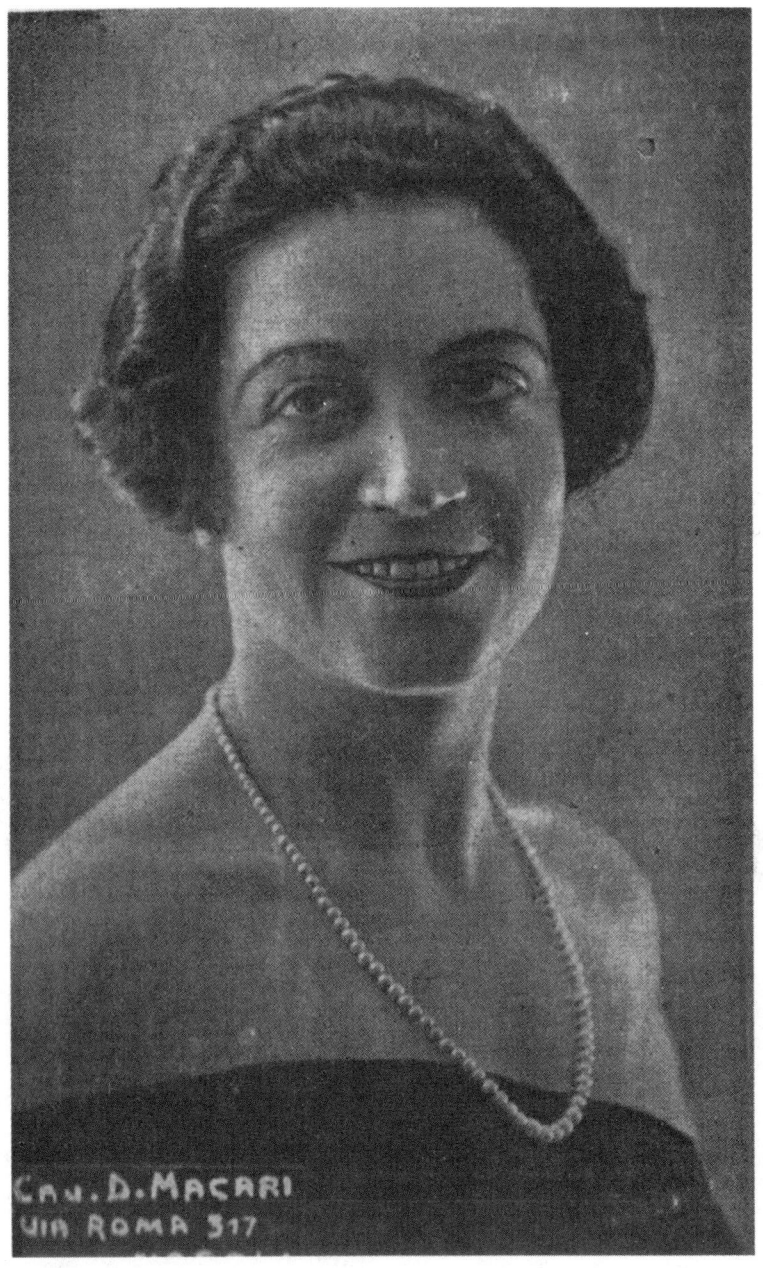
Figure 6-1. Gilda Mignonette. (Courtesy of Antonio Sciotti)

the empty spaces with meaning. Precisely the same process occurs in popular culture.[13]

Levine argues that the process productive of a musical text creates a relation between listener and creator in such a way that the listener is actively engaged, following the model of an "open text," as elaborated by Umberto Eco. An open text, Levine writes, "mandates the cooperation of the audience by compelling them to make a series of interpretive choices that invest the text with meaning and significance. While such choices are obviously not infinite, they are, as Eco puts it, 'more than one,' and they transform the reader or viewer into 'an active principal of interpretation,' who becomes 'a part of the picture of the generative process of the text.'"[14]

Let's see how this theoretical approach finds its space in the Neapolitan context. Mignonette's artistic training took place in a Neapolitan folk cultural context, in which the relationship between audiences and creators is tight. She is able to integrate her musical sensibility on American soil thanks to the presence of the Italian diaspora. The dynamic that she creates with the Italian community through her performances, sounds, and lyrics safeguards precisely one of the key defining aspects of folk cultural contexts, that is, the dialogical relationship between audience and author/artist.

Alongside Mignonette, there exists a variety of female singer-performers hailing from South Italy (Campania, Sicily, Calabria) but none of them gathered such unanimous approval as Mignonette. Singers such as Teresa de Matienzo, Rosina De Stefano, whose artistic activity recount a late–nineteenth-century Italian feminine dimension anchored in an existence limited to roles of mother and wife. According to this model, the woman was mother and life companion, but rarely did she become a dynamic part of an extra-family social process. Italian women singers' lyrics and their interpretations on stage and on recordings produce an unconventional image of Italian women who modernize themselves through the experience of emigration and the social climate with which they come in contact.

In the "jazz era" and later on during the thirties, musicals welcomed women artists onto syncopated and light music stages and all-girl bands were very popular. Groups such as the Blue Bells, the Ingenues, and Helen Lewis and Her All-Girl Jazz Syncopators played all around the major American cities with very exciting onstage shows; dozens of saxophones, clarinets, trumpets, accordions, banjos, and drums were all together on stage spreading the new wave of syncopated music—and all of them played by women. In 1925 Lee DeForest, known as one of the pioneers of the electronic age, filmed Helen Lewis and her band using his short-lived Phonofilm process.[15] All-girl bands were active in vaudeville, variety, and early sound films during the twenties. This new tendency in American music probably had a positive impact on immigrant communities in terms of an increase in the recording, touring, and marketing of their music, and music was revealing its great potential thanks to the new technology of mechanically reproducing tunes for listening comfortably and in the relaxing comfort of home. There was a notable drive to record ethnic music, and many performers went into the studio to record in their own languages. Tunes originally written in English and versions of preexisting stock arrangements were frequently translated into immigrants' languages. One of the most popular of these was "Show Me the Way to Go Home" by Irving King (a pseudonym used by the two songwriters Jimmy Campbell and Reginald Connelly), which became famous in 1925 and was played by countless bands in many different languages and circulated in a variety of ethnic contexts.

Many of the performers were female singers like Rita Abadzi from Greece who performed Rembetika, Lydia Mendoza from north-central Mexico, Toña La Negre from Chile, and Mignonette from Italy. Many of the recordings of that time were realized with a mobile recording unit, as has been documented in photos and in recent movies.[16] The trend to record immigrant female singers underscores the depth of interest in marketing popular, ethnic, and folk music repertoires. Mignonette and these singers shared the same labels, studios, social dimensions of the audience, and circuits of music distribution and touring.

Mignonette depicted herself as a diva in the way Angela Dalle Vacche has defined the term. The figure of the diva is closely related to Italian silent film and is a combination of the femme fatale and the modern woman, but unlike any other European or American star of her period, she also exhibits a strong mater dolorosa aspect that taps into Catholic-mystical artistic and religious traditions.[17] Furthermore, the word "cinemelograph" proposed for some cinematic experiments by Anton Giulio Bragaglia during the age of futurism, refers to a kind of kinetic writing in which words melt into music. This points to a sort of marriage between cinema and music in the silent movie era, which can explain the similarities on a theoretical and aesthetical level between the worlds of image and sound.[18] The complex mixture of different female types contained in the diva character is something that is discernible in Mignonette as well—in her sexual appeal when dressing in Latin American gowns and when dramatizing her voice and body onstage like a saint or Madonna. If we go back to her above-mentioned song "Fra un tango, un foxtrot e uno shimmy," if we think about the lyrics and the moral environment described through the words, we can easily grasp that in the background there is a strict and severe Catholic education that controls women, sex, and entertainment in a way that can be rigorously felt in South Europe. In fact, Dalle Vacche asserts something that again is perfect in describing Mignonette and other women singers of that time: the diva's acting was often apparently without restraint, spectacular, and operatic instead of psychologically motivated and introspective. This is because her character's sense of self does not stem from personal entitlement but, rather, from the approval of family and society at large.[19] Also, the escapist, aristocratic, transgressive component of orientalism that Dalle Vacche considers peculiar to Italian silent cinema is present in Mignonette's repertoire. It is sufficient to consider her song "Il tango delle geishe."

Gilda Mignonette perfectly embodies the contrast between old and new models of social and cultural life. Performing in a vocal style with many characteristics of Neapolitan folk singing, she represents the old and traditional; while touring around Italy and the Americas, incorporating new musical models and genres, she contributed to the spread and syncretism of different repertoires. She also stands for the entire Italian nation torn between old and new. It is her specific kind of modernity that could shed light on the rise of Italian light music and how much it owes to the nascent Italian community in the United States and to foreign repertoires for its development. The musical life of Mignonette offers us the opportunity to highlight musical interaction between different minority ethnic groups in the United States during periods of mass migration in the nineteenth and twentieth centuries. It furthermore helps us uncover a rich cultural space ripe for the consideration of the ethical thrust of Alan Lomax's notion of cultural equity as a productive way to investigate the languages of music in a modern world made complex by deterritorialization and reterritorialization, and by a hybridity of styles shaped by migrations and new modalities of commercial production.

NOTES

1. With this term I mean the music made, produced, and spread by lower-class rural people, and with the term *popolaresco* ("popularesque"), I refer to the music inspired by that same popular cultural context but written by trained composers and poets.

2. As evidenced by Giovanni Vacca, "L'arte della posteggia," *Alias*, weekly supplement of *Il Manifesto*, December 13, 2003, 14–15.

3. Ettore De Mura, *Enciclopedia della Canzone Napoletana* (Naples: Il Torchio, 1969), 2:255.

4. Emelise Aleandri, *The Italian-American Immigrant Theatre of NYC* (Charleston: Arcadia, 1999), 86; Antonio Sciotti, *Gilda Mignonette, Napoli-New York solo andata* (Naples: Magmata, 2007), 9.

5. Ciaramella, born in Naples in 1887, was an actor, singer, author of comedies and songs. Together with Silvia Coruzzolo, Mimì Maggio, and his sister-in-law, Mignonette, he founded one of the first companies of *sceneggiata*. Ciaramella had close relations with the Italian American impresarios Alberto Campobasso and Feliciano Acierno. It was with them that he started touring the United States, as the numerous recordings bear witness. One of the most interesting *sceneggiata* movies, *'O Festino o La Legge*, produced in the immigrant community and directed by Bud Pollard in 1932, had a discographical edition made by Compagnia Ciaramella.

6. Sciotti, *Gilda Mignonette*, 80.

7. "'A cartulina 'e Napule" is considered the musical manifesto of Italian immigrants. The song was composed in New York in 1927 by Pasquale Buongiovanni and Giuseppe De Luca. It was performed for the first time by the young male singer Mario Gioia but it became canonic when it was interpreted by Mignonette.

8. Iain Chambers, *Mediterraneo Blues: Musica, malinconia postcoloniale, pensieri marittimi* (Turin: Bollati Boringhieri, 2012), 21.

9. "Il tango delle geishe" was published in 1927 by La Canzonetta; then the song traveled to New York and was published in United States by the Italian Book Company. In 1928 Mignonette recorded the song in America. "Fra un tango, un foxtrot e uno shimmy," composed by Enrico Battiparano and Eugene Mignone in the same year, seems to have been created for the Italian American audiences because it is hardly known in Italy.

10. In New York Mignonette became famous for her interpretation of the song "'A cartulina 'e Napule," her first successful recording. The song added to her celebrity for different reasons but probably mostly because it has all the elements of the *larmoyant* canon typical of the Italian migrant repertoire, which Mignonette is able to offer back intact and pure to the audience.

11. Marsha Siefert, "Aesthetics, Technology, and the Capitalization of Culture: How the Talking Machine Became a Musical Instrument," in *Technology: Aesthetics, Politics, Culture*, ed. A. J. Rieber and M. Siefert, *Science in Context* 8, no. 2 (1995): 430.

12. Piedigrotta was an annual musical festival in Naples where publishers presented new songs. Festivities reached their peak on the night between the seventh and eighth of September as a commemoration of the Virgin Mary's birth

13. Lawrence W. Levine, "The Folklore of Industrial Society: Popular Culture and Its Audiences," *American Historical Review* 97, no. 5 (1992): 1384 passim.

14. Ibid., 1382.

15. The film is now in the Maurice Zouary Collection at the Library of Congress.

16. One of the most interesting is *The Soul of Man* by Wim Wenders (USA, 2003).

17. Angela Dalle Vacche, *Diva: Defiance and Passion in Early Italian Cinema* (Austin: University of Texas Press, 2008). On the topic see *Non solo dive. Pioniere del cinema italiano*, edited by Monica Dall'Asta, Bologna: Cineteca di Bologna, 2008, proceedings of the international conference "Non solo dive. Pioniere del cinema italiano," Cineteca di Bologna, December 14–17, 2007.

18. Regarding this issue, the cinema of the Neapolitan director Elvira Notari helps to redefine the role of women in film and cultural production in the Neapolitan and Mediterranean area during the early twentieth century and the interconnection between cinema and other cultural fields such as popular music and theater.

19. Ibid., 6. This statement finds support in what Ellen Koskoff writes about musical success in a male-dominant culture, considering that in societies where males were or are the main patrons of musical performances or where male-dominated political, religious, and economic spheres call for young female performers, musical behaviors that heighten female sexuality are the norm. Ellen Koskoff, *Women and Music in Cross-Cultural Perspective* (Urbana: University of Illinois Press, 1989), 6.

SEVEN

## Go Make Naples: New Perspectives from Italian American Artists

*Fred Gardaphé*

> There's an arcade in Naples that they call the Galleria Umberto. It's in the center of the city. In August, 1944, everyone in Naples sooner or later found his way into this place and became like a picture of the wall of a museum.
>
> —JOHN HORNE BURNS, *The Gallery* (1947)

I first learned of Naples when my grandfather told a friend of his, "Vattene; va fa napoli."

I could tell from the tone that this was something bad, if not the language (for whenever this grandfather wanted me not to know what was going on, he'd switch into Italian). From that day on I paid particular attention whenever someone used that phrase, and it was often. I heard it again and again when people wanted to tell someone to get out of here, or in crude terms, "Go fuck Naples." Now I understood why the 'mericans would use the words "Go fuck yourself," but I couldn't for the life of me figure out why most of the men in my neighborhood (except for the Napoletani) would say, "Go fuck Naples."

I asked a Neapolitan friend, "In Naples you don't use 'Va fa Napoli,' do you?" "No," he said, "We say 'Go fuck everyone else.'"

I asked the same question of an old man who used to hang out in my grandfather's tavern, and he explained to me that people say that because

Naples was once the richest city in Italy; then after the "Great" Risorgimento, people started to rob Naples, and it began to lose everything; Naples turned into a terrible place, a place like hell, and so, instead of telling people to go to hell, all you had to say was "Go to Naples."

I had to study Italian on my own in order to make sense of the little Italian and lot of Barese dialect I used to speak thinking it was Italian. During that time I came to realize the flexibility of the verb "fare" and thought if you translated "Va fa Napoli" literally it could mean, "Go make Naples," and I thought, who would you say something like that to, and who would take it literally? The answer I came up with was immigrants. For it is fitting that a city made by immigrants would continue to be remade by successive immigrations.

This essay is the result of my search for the appearance of Naples in American literature and art. I had a tough time finding serious, extended depictions of one of Italy's largest and most important cities. Database and Google searches turned up little when I typed in "Naples in American literature."

I had been familiar with depictions of Naples by John Domini, an Italian American writer who had set a couple of his novels in Naples, but beyond him it was hard to find any American writer who had seriously dealt with the city in his or her fiction. Thanks to leads from Domini, I found John Horne Burns's spectacular novel of World War II entitled *The Gallery* (1947), and the Australian Shirley Hazzard's 1970 novel, *The Bay of Noon*. He also reminded me that Naples turns up in Saul Bellow's *The Adventures of Auggie March*, and the writings of Jay Parini and Joseph Papaleo, but there is very little in these works that does Naples justice. Two other novels that are set in Naples, and that present somewhat realistic depictions of the city are Susan Sontag's *The Volcano Lover* (1992; set in the eighteenth century) and Joseph Caldwell's *The Uncle from Rome* (1993; set in the twentieth century).

This caused me to wonder why, when Italy had played so strong a role in the works of many English and American writers, had Naples received very little attention. And why most of the attention came from voyeuristic perspectives, as though Naples had to be kept at a distance from the observer to keep from contaminating the writer. It's as though the old adage "Vedi Napoli e mori," (see Naples and die) actually killed the possibilities of more penetrating prose about the city that was once considered to be a jewel of

Europe. The goal of this essay is to examine the role that Naples plays in the fiction and art of Italian Americans. For the purposes of focus, I present Naples as found in the writings of John Domini and the paintings of William Papaleo.

Most Italian American writers use Italy to set up a sense of the past and reconnect to it through travel. Their art, more often than not, focuses on the family and their own reactions to returning to the home of their ancestors.

What I have found in these two artists is something new, something all other Italian American writers have not dealt with and that is the role of the immigrant in today's Italy. For both the writer Domini and the painter Papaleo create a Naples void of the old country sense created by ancestors as it becomes the new country through their art and through the way both artists use the subject of new immigration.

In "One Early Twenty-First Century Summer in Naples," Domini provides some insight as to why he has chosen to write fiction that focuses on Naples's new immigrants: "The story of the new African presence in Southern Italy was for me unexpectedly illuminated, profoundly illuminated, by the spectral glow of those who had left. Ghosts out of my own family past."[1] Both of his later novels spend much time on the plight of these African immigrants, and both contain dramatic portrayals of the real characters he discusses in this essay: "They're all about the new, here in Naples, about reconstruction of the self and its community. Them I could understand—but not the Italian government, which seemed to have plunged into a considerably deeper denial of immigrant reality."[2]

Nominated for a Pulitzer Prize, *Earthquake I.D.* (2007) is the first in the author's Naples trilogy. In it he spins a tale around Barbara Cantasola Lulucita, a wife and mother who discovers that her family's trip to Italy is not what she thought it would be. The surprises and mysteries cause her to doubt everything she holds dear, and pushes her into places she's never been physically and spiritually. The connection between Italian American and Italian has never been more obvious and tenuous in the same character. Barbara is on the verge of losing everything she ever wanted and in many ways has never been happier. Her husband, Jay Lulucita, is a CEO who leaves his U.S. job to head up NATO-sponsored earthquake relief efforts in Naples. When he gets his head bashed in during what seems to be a routine tourist mugging, the family's documents are lost and they become paperless like many of the *terremotati* (earthquake victims). When these ugly Americans find themselves hostage beneath the ruins, they come to learn more about each other than they have in the nearly twenty years of their marriage through their encounters with the new immigrants to the city.

The geographical and economic contrasts of Naples reflect the contrasts that Barbara learns to see inside her self and the "normal" life that she had been living so simply and uncontemplated until this trip. Naples, above and underground, is rendered in exciting detail, and casts some interesting light onto Italy's immigration issues, especially the *clandestini*.

Barbara's first thoughts of Naples come to us through her observance of a map of Naples that she examines before the family leaves the United States.

> The water was a brilliant ceramic blue, a color that attracted the twin eight-year-olds. The two girls had to touch, cooing, but meantime the mother's bewilderment gave way to worse. Against the ubiquitous sea the city center was always depicted in yellow, whether shown from a distance or in close up, and either way, to Barb it started to look like a gaping way the color of pus. The few highways that threaded the area were blood red, and the metropolis itself presented lips spread wide for a love-bite. There was a bit of tongue, the peninsula on which stood the Castel Dell'Ovo. Barbara stood faced with a soul kiss of disease.[3]

The resulting uneasiness expresses itself in her early fears of the city, and through more personal encounters these early fears give way to more sober realizations, such as "A lepers' city, a city full of crooks, a city for the end of everything . . . no. The Naples Barbara encountered over the next couple of days proved impossible to label and file away. At times it did seem a city of prayers. But more often she could be certain of the appearance of prayers ex voti."[4] The juxtaposition of the problems faced by these privileged Americans to the solutions provided by the novel's immigrant characters helps us to better see through the stereotypical surfaces of Naples and deep into the heart of a Naples that these immigrants remake.

In his second novel, *A Tomb on the Periphery* (2008), Domini presents Fabrizio, a young Napolitano *settebello*, who dabbles in the black market, and who meets a beautiful and mysterious American woman. In an effort to woo her—and to show off his Neapolitan street smarts—he helps her sneak into an archeological dig and rob a tomb of its jewelry. What should have been a simple braggadocio's theft soon brings in the police, Camorristi, illegal aliens, NATO officials, and ghosts. In this novel, the storyteller spends more time in the neighborhoods controlled by the Camorra, populated by the "clandestine," and damaged by the earthquake than any other area. It is in these dark quarters that the light of hope shines for Fabrizio, whose skills as a jeweler learned through his father are honed by the black market's need for forgeries of ancient treasures that sometimes find their way out of Paestum's archaeological digs.

Domini's creation of the world of African immigrants is vivid and sincere. Whether it's the repartee of a pair of street thugs, the wise advice of a professor, or the cat and mouse verbal and physical play of two young lovers, Domini renders real highly imaginative scenarios that keep characters real and the plot moving without a slip.

> The real power around Naples and its periphery; the way so much unstable living could be jammed into the cavities of a single long moment, past and present and future all bursting through the seams of the same moment, so that a single mistaken step would leave you out of time, down some clotted and inescapable hole. One bad move could make you history. Here any person who sought to remain on top of some game or other needed to recognize that essential of citified play, the unstable tectonic pressure on the rules, the shakeups. . . . The metropolis could delude you with it sempieternal figures made of skin or stone or society, pretty figures, intriguing which seemed to cycle round endlessly, inevitable as sinning itself.[5]

Once again, the novel's protagonist is aided and saved through his interaction with immigrants.

In his latest fiction, the immigrant takes center stage in the short story "Catwalk Plastique" (2007). Two new immigrants who want to be terrorists are rigging a bomb on the rooftop catwalk of the city's Galleria Umberto I—considered by many to be the commercial heart of Naples. The two are met by Risto, a Moroccan who had immigrated to Naples before them, who questions their intentions. One of them responds: "Naples, it's time these people learned—Naples is Mogadishu." Risto replies: "'Naples is a city, that's all. Could be the land of opportunity.' When Risto freed a hand to gesture over the Opera House below, the People's Piazza beyond, he discovered how hotly he'd been gripping the rail. Still: Naples in this century, he went on, could be for the Africans what New York had once been for the Italians."⁶ And one responds: "You don't understand. The gold of the city, the figures in gold, all that taunting obscenity? Isn't that precisely why we have to take down the Galleria?"

> This too came to seem like something Risto could work with, the thinking that had brought these men here. They hadn't just imagined the catastrophe of the flying glass and steel, across these thronging downtown crannies, but they'd grasped how the target itself made a statement. Unique among the ancient city's landmarks, the Galleria had nothing to do with the church or the law (immigration law, in particular). It served, rather, as the shoppers' Duomo. A resonating candy egg, it rose over a skewed X of storefronts. The decorations that covered the floors and walls might well have included some number off an old-fangled cash register, written in gold. What's more, other than a couple hunks of Fascist urban renewal, the bigger places around the centro were all either Gothic or Baroque. This however was a piece of fin de siècle Paris. You could imagine one of the Impressionists setting up a canvas in its cavernous interior. Peopling the scene, to be sure, would be the well-born and the servants who carried their purchases. The Galleria was the closest that crumbling Naples came to the Euro-dream of swank and entitlement.⁷

The Gallery, which was featured in the Burns novel as the heart of black market commerce that had been bombed by the United States and Germany during World War II, is used by Domini to represent the oppression of the new immigrants, and their attempt to destroy it becomes yet another page in the history of remaking Naples. There is much more to be said about the use of Naples in Domini's writings, but I want to shift attention to an American artist who has, like Domini, used immigrants in creating his portraits of Naples.

William Papaleo is the son of Italian American writer and professor Joseph Papaleo (1925–2004). Over twenty years ago, William moved to Naples to practice the art he had learned in the United States. Recently he contributed a presentation to a conference at the University of Salerno, and I take from his soon-to-be-published writings some of his thoughts on the use of African immigrants in many of his Naples paintings. "Of all the TV and film images that have been presented . . . by masters such as Scorsese, none of their characters are identifiable to my experience or sensitivities in even the slightest sense. The vast panorama of images and ways of seeing for an Italian American have not really been explored. Italian workers that I have met and painted have often been well-read and aware politically."[8] Papaleo spent time portraying these workers in several paintings such as *Ship Builders above Vesuvius, Castellammare* (plate 7-1), and *Shipbuilder, Welder, Castellammare* (plate 7-2).

In both of these paintings, Papaleo focuses on the bodies of these workers, featuring especially their faces and the concentration that they apply to their jobs. He writes about this in his essay: "This would certainly not fit into any Hollywood stereotype of Italians. However, we know that Italians were in the forefront of many of the labor movements in the early part of the 20th century."[9] Papaleo is careful to point out the dignity in the faces of these men who, for the most part, remain invisible to the world outside of work.

In another painting, *Immigrants/Emigrants* (plate 7-3), Papaleo mixes the images of Italians who immigrated to the United States with those Africans who immigrated to Naples, blending them into a historically impossible group portrait that comments on the role that immigration plays in renewing cultures. Papaleo tells us: "Landscape and the environment has an importance for me as an American but why not also as an Italian? Why would I want the claustrophobic sense of space often associated with the Italian American provincial families and art? Why can't an Italian American embrace the grand view of landscape and give nobility to nature as we have with figure and portrait."[10]

Unlike the many images we have of America's Italian immigrants in horizonless scenes, be it photos, paintings, or films, Papaleo paints the African immigrant into his cityscapes of Naples, and by doing so, as in *Nigerian in Naples* (plate 7-4) and *Nigerian Workers above Naples* (plate 7-5), forces the people who are often on the margins of society into the center of our perceptions of Naples.

In these paintings, the African Italian workers seem to be alone against the backdrop of city scenes and urban landscapes, bringing attention not only to their work but also to their place in contemporary Neapolitan society. Papaleo points out the motivation for his work and some of the reasons he chooses to remake Naples through images of the new immigrants:

> In a sense, I am life imitating art. My father's inner conflict between success and inferiority, the desire to assimilate, and the resistance to lose his American and Italian cultural identity gave energy to my own desires to choose the Italian

road less travelled. When I came to Italy to paint, it was often like the call of an unconscious memory. I was not here to simply study the grandeurs of the past, the "old world" seemed strangely contemporary to me. The juxtaposition of pagan and Christian imagery along with the confusion of the teeming, traffic-filled streets seemed a lyrical way to jump into the 21st century cultural and artistic, identity search.[11]

In a final image, *Miele e fiele* (Honey and Bile), (plate 7-6), Papaleo presents a haunting image of contemporary Neapolitan immigrants against a cityscape that is composed of the faces of earlier Neapolitan workers who were no doubt a mixture of migrants and natives of the city.

Some of the most revealing scenes of Naples today come to us through the children and grandchildren of Neapolitans who had immigrated to the United States. These Italian American artists show us through immigrant sensibilities and images that one man's version of hell might function as another's vision of heaven. Through their art, they have given us new insights into Naples by seeing it through the filters of the new citizens who have left their homelands, lead by the call to "Go (re)make Naples."

## NOTES

1. John Domini, "One Early Twenty-First Century Summer in Naples," in *Delirious Naples*, Pellegrino D'Acierno and Stanislao G. Pugliese, eds. (Fordham University Press, 2018), 98.
2. Ibid., 111.
3. John Domini, *Earthquake I.D.* (Pasadena, CA: Red Hen Press, 2007), 1–2.
4. Ibid., 29.
5. John Domini, *A Tomb on the Periphery* (Arlington, VA: Gival Press, 2008), 190–91.
6. John Domini, "Catwalk Plastique," *Del Sol Review*, no. 17 (Spring 2011), http://delsolreview.webdelsol.com/dsr17/Domini.htm (accessed November 13, 2011).
7. Ibid.
8. William Papaleo, "'Color and Horizons of Memory': Words and Images on Italian American Identity," University of Salerno, 2012.
9. Ibid.
10. Ibid.
11. Ibid.

EIGHT

## You Want to Be Americano?

*Robert Zweig*

No matter how easily I slipped into "Naples mode" when I arrived each summer in the streets of *bassi* (street-level apartments) to take up residence, I was always the "Americano." Although I wore the shirts and sandals of the boys on the street, spoke with a tinge of a Neapolitan dialect, ate the same foods, played with the same toys, and wanted the same things all the other boys did on the Via Pizzofalcone, no one was deceived.

In fact, everyone knew that I wasn't from the neighborhood or anywhere near it. The haircut, the accent, the knowledge that I wasn't around the rest of the year gave me away. Everyone in Naples was a *ficcanaso* (one who sticks his nose in things–a busybody) and they knew I was the grandchild from Il Bronx, Nuova York.

Another summer of my youth in the 1960s.

"Roberto has arrived," someone in my grandmother's building would call out, and word got out fast. Immediately I was pelted with questions. "How

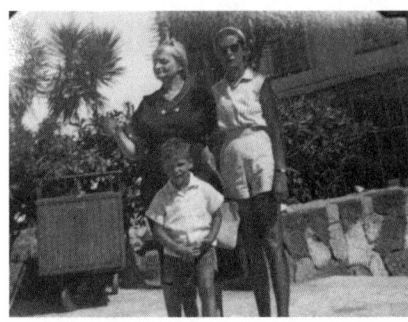

Figure 8-1. Young Robert Zweig with mother and grandmother in Naples, circa 1960. (Bruno Herrmann)

was the trip? How long will you stay? You grew a lot this year, more than you did last year."

Our neighbor Mrs. Malvese, peering from her tiny apartment, called out, "Another summer, Robertino, welcome. There will be some life out here now in the courtyard. How are your momma and your dad?"

In the first few excited hours after each arrival, people slowly came out to see me, called from the window, or transmitted greetings through others. The "Americani are here for the summer," I heard someone call from the building.

Maria Teresa, who was my age, lived just below my grandmother. She appeared before me one year just after my arrival with *tamburrelle*–a set of two tambourine-like drums that hit a small rubber ball back and forth—along with bocce balls. "They're brand new," she assured me. "Are you too tired to play later today?" Maria Teresa wasn't really interested if I was American or not. She was interested in playing in the courtyard, especially during the afternoon "siesta" when the adults were sleeping.

It may seem unusual that an American boy in the 1960s in an Italian city of over a million people should be such an interesting phenomenon. However, Naples had a different relationship with its tourists and foreigners than did other Italian cities. In Rome, Florence, and Venice, tourists—in those days, mostly Americans—came in large numbers and wandered all the neighborhoods and *vicoletti* (little streets). They could be seen taking cabs and sitting in the cafés and restaurants, their Japanese thirty-five-millimeter cameras and Kodak Instamatics dangling from their necks.

American tourists to Italy often avoided Naples altogether, or came from Rome for the day, then went straight to Pompeii or Sorrento. Groups of Americans could be seen huddled in front of the *aliscafi* (hydrofoils) or *vaporetti* (ferry boats) waiting to go to Capri or Ischia. I knew they were American by their brightly colored shirts and blouses.

Other tourists sidestepped Naples because of the *scippatori* (muggers). Most guidebooks advised avoiding Naples altogether or stopping only for the day in order to get to the sites outside the city. Those who insisted on staying were advised to hold tightly to cameras, luggage, and pocketbooks to avoid youths on Vespas who would grab whatever they could.

The sixth fleet was stationed in Naples and the destroyers and aircraft carriers were anchored in the bay. But even the sailors stayed near the port or limited their excursions to a few downtown shopping streets. They usually walked in small groups or in pairs, their white hats easily standing out in crowds.

Besides this local insularity that made me an intriguing and foreign presence, the cult of American power and culture was very marked. The Cold War had ideologically divided the world between America and Russia, with Italy in the middle. There were many communists in the country, but most Italians clearly were on the side of the Americans.

One verse of a popular mid-sixties song in Neapolitan dialect was:

Tu vuo' fa' ll'americano
mericano, mericano . . .
ma si' nato in Italy
sient a mme: nun ce sta niente 'a fa'
ok, napulitan!
tu vuo' fa ll'american
tu vuo' fa ll'american.

(You want to be American
'merican, 'merican
but you were born in Italy!
listen to me, there's nothing to do
OK, Neapolitan!
you want to be American
you want to be American.)

The song spoke of rock 'n' roll, whiskey and soda, and baseball. Because of its catchy tune, I sang it around the house every day for an entire summer. Little did I know that the lyrics actually held a spark of truth from those times. The Platters, Elvis Presley, and Gene Pitney could be heard in every Neapolitan jukebox.

*Via col vento* (*Gone with the Wind*) was shown repeatedly on television, and there were long lines outside theaters when *West Side Story* opened in a few select Neapolitan theaters.

Jack "Limone" came to Capri to film a movie and the papers were full of his pictures.

Tonino from the courtyard chewed Brooklyn Bridge Gum with the image of the bridge on each wrapped piece. "How beautiful it looks," he would say. "I'm going to see it one day."

And when a Chevy Impala was parked in front of the American Embassy, people stopped to stare at it in amazement.

Ah, America!

Most people in my grandmother's neighborhood spoke to me about America with admiration, but they also teased me about the eccentricities and pomposity of America's proud claims. At the tender age of twelve, I had the difficult and unwanted job of being the "American ambassador" to the Via Egiziaca and vicinity.

"Roberto, come here," urged Renaldo, our local baker. "I want to talk to you about New York. Is it true that the buildings are so tall that the tops are always in the clouds?"

I remember saying yes to impress Renaldo.

"And the cars are the size of three 600's?"

"Yes, very true."

"And the streets are so very wide that ours are a joke in comparison?"

"Yes, that's true, too," I admitted, hoping not to offend.

"And I hear you also have Coca Cola there?"

"Yes. That's American," I said confidently.

"It was invented in Naples," he corrected me, "And it was stolen and taken to America. And of course," Renaldo said, "You have the *krapfen* that we make here in Naples. That is very common in America, isn't it?"

"Well, no, we don't have that," I admitted.

"Such a big country and no *krapfen*? How can that be, Roberto? It's not possible."

I felt somewhat defeated, so I decided to tell him about baseball, pasteurized milk, and peanut butter.

"Butter from peanuts? That doesn't sound very good, Roberto."

And to finally put Renaldo in his place, because he was a baker, I told him that we had Mr. Chips chocolate chip cookies, which were way better than the Pavesini so popular in Italy. In return, he laughed and gave me a hot roll just out of the oven, the big, crusty thirty lire kind, and I took it, feeling a little foolish that I had been so earnest in my defense of America.

"Ciao to your Nonno," he said as I walked away, chewing away at the crusty little lumps at the top and the middle of the roll.

Some people had distant relatives who had moved to America many years before, and harbored confused notions about life in America. The barber near the Pallonetto told me that a great aunt had moved to America and complained that people only ate cereal for breakfast and that the coffee was like poison.

"Why is the coffee so bad?" he asked me seriously.

I couldn't answer, since I didn't know anything about coffee.

"And why do people eat steaks every night?" I didn't know the answer to that one either.

"And is it true that there are no fresh vegetables, only frozen ones?"

"And what is better, Il Bronx or Brookolino?"

I told him that I thought the Bronx was a little better.

His aunt had lived in Brooklyn, he told me.

"Well, parts of Brooklyn are better than any parts of the Bronx," I replied diplomatically. This was becoming rather tricky.

"Maybe you know some of the family? Esposito, from Brookolino."

I didn't know anyone from Brooklyn, I told him.

"Why do Americans have such thin hair?" he asked.

"I have no idea," I answered honestly, but decided this might be worth looking into.

A taxi driver told me all about his family in "Newaaark, New Jerzzz." His uncle was a baker who introduced the superior Neapolitan method of baking to "New Jerzzz." Through his cousins he had also become a Yankee fan, the only one I ever met in Naples.

"Mel Stottlemyer, a grand pitcher, but not good enough," he said in halting English.

I was only eight years old in 1963 when President Kennedy came to Naples in early July. My grandmother couldn't walk well and would therefore not see him in his open limousine, but she urged my mother and me to go to the Piazza Plebiscito early that morning to find a good spot to see him when he passed by.

"Go down by Gambrinus. From there you might have a good view. How much I like him. I wish I could go too."

The newspapers and magazines had pictures of him, the RAI television news had a segment about his life, and plates with an image of his face hung in store windows all along the Via Roma. Pictures of the president and first lady were being sold in the street along with small American and Italian flags.

My mother held my hand tightly as we made our way down the street and down the steps to the piazza. We were an hour early for his appointed pass-by, but already the piazza was filled. The pigeons had no place to land and twirled in circles above.

After staring at the back of gray jackets and elbows and legs for what seemed an eternity, a roar rose from the crowd and I climbed the base of a lamppost to get a clear view.

It was him! He was tall and impressive, standing up in his car. Next to him was a much shorter man; this was Segni, my mother said, the president of Italy. The men waved and smiled, waved and smiled, while behind the car children were running and waving to the crowd as well. In a few minutes the crowd dispersed, but the excitement remained.

We walked back home and people congregated in small groups, talking about Kennedy. One woman was remarking what a *bel' giovanotto* (Good-looking young man) he was.

I remember being happy that he was so much taller than Segni. I felt that I was a little taller that day too. When I got back to my grandmother's house, I told her all about it and how tall he was and she was excited that we had had a clear view of him.

For the rest of the day, many of the people from the building were talking about Kennedy and asking me questions about how he looked and what he did. As a proud American, I was awash all day in the residual glow reflecting from him.

That night we were all eager for the *Carosello*—a show made up of intricate commercials—to end, and for the RAI news to begin.

"Let's see, let's see how they show Kennedy and whether he had anything to say about Naples at the airport when he left," said Aunt Adele.

When the news came on, Kennedy was seen filmed from a camera behind the car. The little *scugnizzi* (ragamuffins) were between the back of the car and the camera, and most were looking back at the camera, laughing, jumping up and down, and making faces. Some were jumping on and off the car's fender.

One yelled out to the camera, "Hey, momma." I thought it looked like fun, but I saw that Aunt Adele was not pleased.

"How disgraceful! The president of the United States is in town and look at these kids. What are they doing? What will people think of us?"

My grandmother nodded in agreement and my grandfather just shook his head in wordless disapproval of the scene.

That night I was happy to be American, just like Kennedy. I wondered if, when he was in Italy, he ate Italian food like I did, or if someone brought him peanut butter and white bread so he wouldn't be homesick.

By the 1970s, Naples was much less isolated than it had been. Everyone owned a car, travel to all parts of the world was common, and the icons of American life were everywhere. I could not have imagined the song "You Want to Be Americano?" having the cultural force it had ten years earlier.

I was still the "Americano" but was no longer exotic. Now, I was asked questions about all the problematical aspects of American life.

"Is it true that there are so many poor people practically starving in American cities? Is it true that blacks and whites hit each other in the middle of the street?"

Now I was old enough to offer a thoughtful answer to these pressing concerns.

I was in Naples in 1974 when President Nixon resigned. People were perplexed that a scandal like Watergate could lead to the resignation of a president. After all, here in Italy political intrigue was a normal and accepted way of life. I was told that Americans were moralistic and naïve about so many things.

Over the years, American popular culture became more dominant while America itself became a less exotic place. On my last visit, *Seinfeld* and *Tutti Amano Raimondo* blared from the windows while Dodger caps, Houston Rockets sweatpants, Timberland shoes, and t-shirts with both absurd and profane language on them hung in the windows of the fancy stores. I wanted to buy a t-shirt that read, "Seattle Supersonics Electrical Supply Company" before I found out it cost forty dollars.

I thought of the song "You Want to Be Americano?" The world had become smaller and so many Neapolitans seemed not too different than many "Americani."

**History, Memory, and Mercy**

NINE

## Words in Journey: Echoes from Pompeii

*Angelo Cannavacciuolo*

I believe that within all of us two types of memory reside: a "small" memory that concerns us quite intimately and draws from our tangible past—from the place where we were born, from our family, and from our personal recollections—and a "historical" memory that, unconnected to our specific worldly experience, witnesses our existence in wide and enduring ways. A historical memory, dormant within us, that we often forget we possess and that, unbeknownst to us, guides our choices and alternates and contrasts with the small one. And there are, as such, certain places that represent those memories and that are elevated to being a topos of one or the other; it even happens at those times we choose to belong to one place rather than another because we sense that our soul dwells there. You see, I believe that within me historical memory dominates, and Pompeii, for some reason or other, must be my place of preference.

I also believe it is possible for me to affirm that my love for Pompeii is almost visceral, just as I am sure it happens with many other people (writers, artists, intellectuals, from the past and from the present), whether born or not in the shadow of Vesuvius. And it was precisely this sentiment that predisposed me to a desire that has followed me in the course of time and that has often fed my creativity—one of those desires rooted in a simple resolution that, even now in my part of the world, almost always ends up assuming the flavor of something heroic, of a titanic endeavor, that is to say, literary composition. It is a desire for impossible dreams long relegated to the page, especially for a writer who lives the reality of this area protected by the inviolability of its own isolation, aware of the myriad complexities, presumed or real, that torment the day-to-day life of these localities.

In the excavations of Pompeii, however, in the clarity of a late October morning some years ago, one that was still full of the relish of summer, in the vineyard uncovered after two thousand years, something unexpected occurred: that which I had long considered to be an unhealthy temptation was, as if by a spell, turning into a tangible opportunity. And it was thanks to a man speaking to a large crowd of journalists, gathered there, just like me, for a press conference at which they were introducing a mysterious wine produced through the reactivation of ancient vines: Villa dei Misteri. Behind him, Vesuvius stood out clearly against the indigo colored sky; and that person whom I had never met—whom later I discovered to be the deputy commissioner for the archeological areas of Naples and Pompeii—immersed in rows of vines, spoke in terms of passion, of dedication, of strategies with which one might preserve for the entire world our cultural roots and the splendors of Pompeii, so that from a dead city it might be transformed into a living one. Around these parts, I have heard all too many proposals for this or that project. Yet, the more he spoke, the more I felt that desire break through my diffidence and seize me; break the levees of any reluctance toward institutions and bureaucracies, toward the futility in which we find ourselves floundering in this part of Italy. And when he finished speaking, for some unknown reason, historical memory came to my mind, and I fancied imagining that the speaker, like me, must have chosen—and not just because of the office he held—Pompeii as his place of preference.

When the crowd had dispersed, among the stalls meticulously staged with delicate libations that were to promote the region's local products, I did the simplest thing that could have been done: I spoke to him about my dream. And I did this in the simplest way I could have, there, among the guests who milled about tasting a glass of wine or a wedge of cheese. But the most surprising thing was that, with just as much simplicity, this man demonstrated an unanticipated interest. During a subsequent encounter, which he took care to organize in the superintendent's office, I spoke to him of my dream of putting words themselves on a journey, to have them travel from one far-off place and have them arrive in Pompeii, and if it was possible, have them return to the place in which they had been conceived. I spoke to him of the Grand Tour, of the ambitious idea of assembling writers from every corner of the world and inviting them to write something so that a trace of their own transience might persist, just as that mythical season between the eighteenth and nineteenth centuries had taken place, that had seen our land traversed by the most illustrious minds of the period. And he even urged me further. I told him that, given the narrative aspect implicit in the title itself, the matter dearest to me was to broaden the same concept of narration, bridging the word and the image, with respect to the vast production of pictorial art created during the Grand Tour. A tale would gush forth from the splendor of words, on the one hand, and on the other hand, from the awesomeness of the images. Thus, visual arts would be integrated within the reinvented Grand Tour. And after a number of centuries, what better than photography to embellish a book that might contain both forms of narration? I confided this to this man, finding in him an enthusiasm that was almost touching, that my idea had met the ears of another man who is considered to be one of the most important masters of contemporary Italian photography: Mimmo Jodice. I had already known Mimmo Jodice for a number of years, and many times, without success, we had tried to build a bridge across the many territories of narration, but the opportunity in question seemed to be the exact one with which to finally realize our goal. I could hardly believe it, but there it was: *Parole in viaggio* (Traveling Words). International literary meetings, and the photography book, were born on that same late October morning, when together that man of such kind expression and I dreamed of putting words on a journey.[1]

When our land opens itself with great purpose to the eyes of the world, it almost always succeeds in showing the best aspects it has to offer: culture, art, history, and tradition—past and present; the part of Italy that is indissoluble from any human apparatus that lives the territory with proud awareness of its manifold abilities. Indeed! And I am pleased to reaffirm that our land is

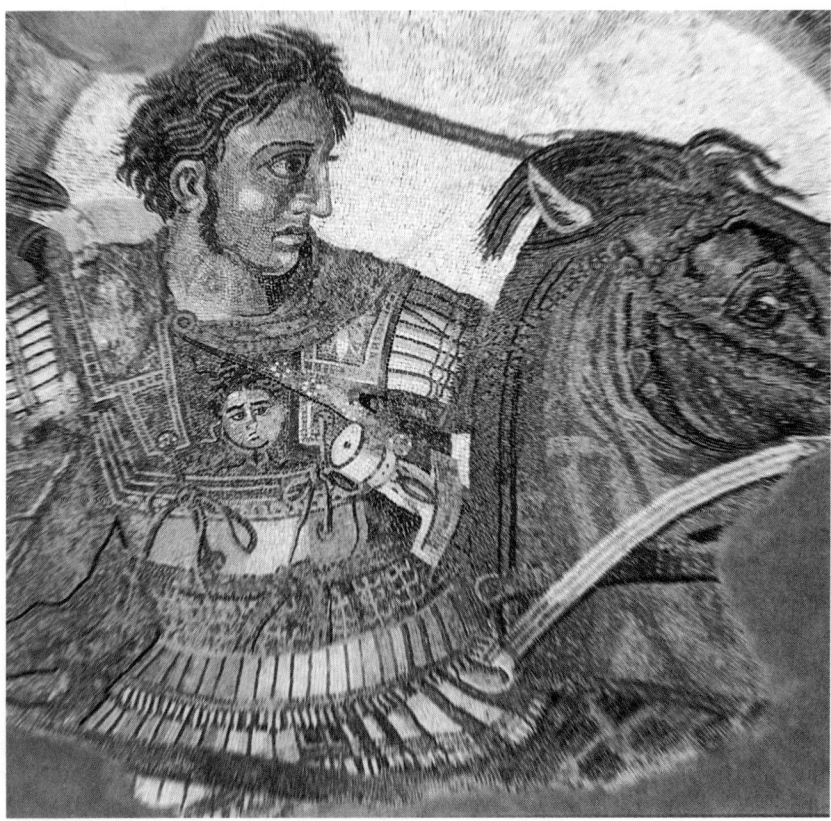

Figure 9-1. Detail of Alexander the Great from *The Battle of Isso* mosaic in the House of the Faun, Pompeii, ca. 100 B.C. (© Mimmo Jodice, 1993)

made of art, of centuries-old culture, of ancient vestiges that are the envy of the entire world. A heritage that at times seems difficult to recognize as our own. And it is in this heritage that I intended to place my confidence, in the attempt to offer a contribution that I can only hope may have contributed to strengthening even historical memory's criteria of objective reassessment; a heritage that also owes its dissemination to a cultural phenomenon of great fascination, of which we have lost all traces. The Grand Tour d'Italie.

Around the seventeenth century in Europe, the fashion of the voyage of personal discovery was beginning to spread. Before long the custom of this voyage became a specific, closed "route"—particularly long and wide and without a break, along with a departure and arrival in the same locale—that might have traversed a number of continental countries but that had as its principal and irremissible end Italy. Thus, the peninsula became the favorite destination of the scions of Europe's most aristocratic houses, those whose sole purpose was the production of young gentlemen, made so through a healthy exercise of comparisons. But it was above all the South that became the favorite place of great artists, writers, and thinkers of the time, who left innumerable written testimonies of their experience. Campania Felix ("prosperous [region of] Campania"), already in those times an "open-air museum," with its mild climate, its beautiful landscapes, the vestiges of an ancient civilization, monumental and artistic riches, became the destination, the absolute protagonist, of the Grand Tour. The close study of our territory by such characters as Goethe, Lamartine, Stendhal, Dumas, Chateaubriand, and the pictorial gaze of such artists as Hackert, Horner, Constable, and Turner, among many others, transform into a narrative tale that enriches and renders eternal our history, our past, resubmitting them to the context of what was effectively the known world in those times: Europe.

In the centuries that would follow, with the advent of an ever-greater development of tourism, of travel routes and of transportation, this type of voyage fell into disuse. The Grand Tour is but a forgotten relic as the world becomes a global village, distances shorten, and tourism conforms to standardization. The narrative tale—written testimonies of great thinkers tied to those places that evoke the past—ends up in a tomb of oblivion. With the exception of a rare few events, now, for the most part, tourist brochures and advertising sound bites take the place of literature in the promotion of our cultural heritage. But if a location such as Pompeii is still one of the most visited in Italy, perhaps one owes this to a rash love for travel, a love for knowledge and for the culture of those great figures of yore who lived and created the *Gran Tour*. And if these artists produced such masterpieces, perhaps one owes that to the magnetic attraction of places like Pompeii.

And, so, what better frame for the *Gran Tour* than Pompeii? What more picturesque place is there within the excavation site than the Teatro Grande? Perhaps the excavations of Pompeii have no need for fringe activities to be brought to the eyes of the world, for they represent in and of themselves a reference point for our cultural heritage—a flower in the lapel not only of our region but of the entire nation. But to place this site alongside literature and photographic art may, to our mind, best consolidate their importance, improving the profile of the surrounding territory.

Hence, here we are, following the tracks of the Grand Tour, with the declared intent of a celebration, a retrospective of that grand epoch. We re-evoke it, therefore, through the alliance between great contemporary writers—so different one from the next, like Gore Vidal, Ethan Canin, Jim Nisbet, and Jay Parini—and a photographic artist of such distinct international renown as Mimmo Jodice. Together, they were invited to play the part of travelers bearing witness to our memory. On the one hand, a revisitation of classicism through literature; on the other hand an interpretation of a place like Pompeii through the photographic lens, with a contemporary context holding the two together. It seems clear, then, that despite appearing unusual, the attempt at commingling two diverse art forms—even from an editorial point of view—is precisely the best way to fathom the depths of our historical memory. I like to imagine, in our case, that literature and photography are two parallels most probably destined to converge, where the convergence, translated into historical memory, nowadays might even become a bridge spanned across uneven territories. Above all, however, I like to imagine that this experience—subsequently brought to the attention of a wide-ranging and thoughtful audience during the four days of the conference, "Delirious Naples"—in its elemental nature, might be remembered as an insignia for a new sort of alliance, a new sort of coalescence, a new accord of love for the arts, for culture and for aesthetic values.

NOTE

1. Mimmo Jodice, *Pompei: Parole in Viaggio*, ed. Angelo Cannavacciuolo (Rome: Contrasto Edizione, 2010).

TEN

## One of These Days

*Ilaria Marchesi and Simone Marchesi*

In the following pages, we present an excerpt from *Live in Pompei*, a portrait of the dead city published in Italian in 2016. The book is a short memoir about a trip we, two college professors from Italy living and working in the United States, took to Pompeii with fourteen grammar-school children in 2014. Written in two distinct but interlocking voices, it contains an account of the three days of seminars at the Villa Vergiliana in Cuma, where the group stayed, and the visits to the archeological sites of Pompeii and Herculaneum. The book, like our trip, combines information about the ancient past of the city, its history, as well as the history of its rediscovery and afterlife in Western culture, with meditations on what elements of that past still matter in our identity today. The Naples area is a constant point of reference for the book. Shuttling between Cuma and Pompeii, our group always gravitated around the central city, with the sense that the ancient ruins we were visiting had a necessary connection with it. A connection that was both archaeological and visceral. Naples, with the Bourbons and their royal palace, now the city's archaeological museum, is part of Pompeii's afterlife to the same extent that Pompeii, the ancient city razed by the same Vesuvius that defines Naples's magmatic history and life beyond the postcards, is part of the city's identity today.

*The gong has sounded. That means breakfast is ready. We leave the room and meet the still-sleepy parents on the stairs, as well as the children who've gotten dressed in a hurry and are racing down the steps before us. We exchange smiles as we head to the dining room. The villa's lower ground floor has a long, narrow room almost entirely taken up by a table big enough for all of us to sit there. It's a windowless room, half sunken underground. The villa's kitchen and utility rooms are also there next to it. The rooms where the gardener and the breakfast waiter sleep must be on this floor too. Maybe the other house staff sleeps here too, but I haven't yet figured out how the other rooms are arranged.*

*I think I glimpsed one of those rooms at the end of a hall, as I was coming downstairs, but I'm not sure. Someone must have forgotten to shut the matte glass door on the landing above, and for a moment I managed to see a corridor behind it with two doors on each side, one of which was open. In the semidarkness of that space, I was able to make out the white of a pillowcase and a sheet on a carefully remade bed, and a chair next to it with clothes hung on the back. On the other side, higher up, a slit of light reflected off the screen of an old TV. I saw something that looked like the bedroom of someone who lives on this floor, although I don't know exactly what I saw. I'm usually fairly good at guessing from outside how houses are inside, especially for those from the end of the last century, but I'm having some problems with this one. There are parts that resist any attempt to match the facade and the interior, the windows and rooms, the balconies and hallways. Especially on the floor that's half-buried beneath the ground. It's not a confused house, but the structure does confuse me a little. So I leave aside my hypotheses as I go downstairs. Especially because I'm hungry this morning.*

*I'm always hungry in the morning, I think, but I quickly correct myself mentally. I know the appetite that made me get out of bed today and tell Virginia to get dressed quickly to go downstairs and have breakfast isn't hunger. And every day I have to remind myself that if I call what I'm feeling in the morning hunger, then I've been rather lucky. If the longest fast I know is the one that's interrupted by my daily breakfast, it means I've never felt real hunger in my life. And that also means that my habit of calling what is nothing more than a little appetite "hunger" is an* ugly habit. And potentially a dangerous one, because I can get used to thinking I know about the rooms that open in the dark hallways of this house, and thinking I'm capable of articulating the truth of who's living in them. And so, out of respect for the truth of whoever is living in those rooms and hallways that I have never been forced to call mine, and therefore out of respect for a truth that I have no right to think of as also being mine, each morning I remember not to call my appetite hunger. For it is simply not true that all lives are the same. I remind myself this today too, as I go gratefully downstairs to the lowest floor of the house for breakfast.

The room where we all meet is part of the atrium onto which open the daytime rooms: the administrative offices, a few studies that turn into bedrooms when the villa is fully booked, the library, the bathrooms. The other half of the hallway is, basically, the conference room. But that's on the main floor; we're below, with the low vaulted ceiling supporting the floor of the room where no one is right now, because we're all here around the table that's been set for us. I immediately realize that, like the attendance register, breakfast at the villa also speaks more than one language— or at least whoever prepared it for us is prepared to adjust for the varied tastes of the center's guests. There are slices of fresh bread next to bowls with cereal, little jars of jam and honey next to salt, pepper, and ketchup bottles, fruit juices alternating with cartons of milk. The children are happy to be able to choose. And they know only too well how to choose. Each of them has a palate that knows at least two languages.

I do a few calculations as I watch them help themselves. There are fourteen children already sitting around the table; some of them still young enough to need our help spreading jam on toast or pouring milk into cups. Two of them have lived in England for a third of their lives; one has dual Italian-American citizenship; one was born in Holland to Italian parents and lives in Switzerland; two live in Northern Italy but spend a month every winter in a different South American country; two more have done all their schooling in German until now. Almost every one of them speaks a language other than Italian fluently and knows how to be a child in another culture. And this, at that age, means simply that each of them knows how to function perfectly in two worlds.

And that's not only clear from how they speak. How they eat also shows that their horizon is different from the one we—their parents—grew up with. It seems they might have less need than we do to experience the ancient world as a chance to learn how to feel at home in another time or place, an exercise in domestication that has, in contrast, been a daily effort throughout my twenty years of living abroad.

*Now, watching them have breakfast and move easily from the eggs and bacon to the toast with jam, from the yogurt with honey to the bread with cheese, from the biscuits to the fruit juices, from the remains of a culture based on oil, grains, and wine to the triumph of another based on milk, meat, and beer, it seems to me that for them the need to have this experience really doesn't exist.*

However, bread is a great invention and sooner or later I'll need to talk to the children about how important it is—even if they already know or saw it right away. To leave early, we need to get up early: I told them that last night, and they understood. So, while the parents have made a huge effort to come to breakfast every day, we've found the children are always very punctual, already sitting at the table and ready for their daily bread. Of course they're not only attracted by the bread: part of the credit goes to the accompaniments. Particularly, I suspect, to the giant pots of Nutella that we find arranged on the lovingly laid table and the continuous production of fried and poached eggs coming from the kitchen. But that's fine: we'll need a lot of energy today too.

In the bus after breakfast, we cross the entire gulf again, traveling along the coast of Naples from the top of the motorway link between Soccavo and Vomero. It takes a while to reach Pompeii from Cuma, but I use the time to do some planning. Besides, the road is empty this morning, and the corridor between Vesuvius and the sea is clear. As we approach the dead city from the Portici and Torre Annunziata side, I think about where we can go today. The plan is to comb through the regions we didn't get to yesterday. There's still a lot to do, and I mentally organize our movements. It's not always easy: some streets are closed off, blocked by metal barriers, so we're forced to take certain routes rather than others.

That's why, when we are back at the excavation sites, we end up retracing some of our steps, and the children notice. On Via dell'Abbondanza, we stop in front of the Fullonica of Stephanus. It's also closed. Too bad. Under restoration, it says. We'll come another time, I say. Let's hope so. What a shame, though. I really wanted them to see it, because the children had immediately loved the idea that there were huge vases outside the door for passers-by to pee in, filling them with urine that the launderers would use to remove stains from clothes. It was their bleach, their OxiClean, their Clorox, their Tide. Going on a trip with children is great. Their parents look for the brothel street or, with the excuse that it's an "archaeological shot," go home with a picture of some young Nebraskan woman in a skimpy t-shirt and even skimpier shorts. But the children keep asking me about pee and poo. They jump from one rock to another at the street crossings, pretending to avoid ancient horse droppings, opening their eyes wide when they hear that some people study the feces found in the Herculaneum sewers to find out about the typical diet in the area; they are thrilled when we get to the latrines at the thermal baths and they see how the Romans—as they call the ancient Pompeiians—sat there, side by side, chatting happily away as they emptied their bowels.

*Children are definitely strange sometimes, I think. On the first day, when we were visiting the acropolis at Cuma, I saw two of them crouched down, scraping the earth where the platform of Jupiter's temple ended. It was Virginia and Guia. When I got closer, I saw they'd dug up crumbs of earth with a big nail and were piling them onto a piece of pine bark. They were talking to each other, but there was too much wind and I couldn't hear what they were saying.*

*So I go up to them and ask what they're doing. They simply answer that they're playing Worm Orphanage. I'm not sure I've understood what this game is, but I don't push it. Sometimes, with children, it's really better not to ask. But I also don't ask any questions because I've gotten a better look at the piece of metal they're digging with. It's not just any nail: it's about ten centimeters long, with an irregular squared profile, and its head is a half-pyramid. It's definitely old. It might not be Roman: the city was a lively one, as it passed between the Greeks, Etruscans, Campanians, Romans, Byzantines, and Saracens until the Middle Ages. But it's definitely old. What should we do? I call my wife and Guia's father over; I explain the problem. What lesson do we want to teach our children?*

*Is it more important that this artifact, one among thousands that the excavation could still turn up, make the experience they're having deeper and truer? Is it more important, in other words, that Guia and Virginia are rewarded in some way for the bit of work they've done, playing archaeologists for the day? Is it useful to show them that there can be a concrete result, an object that represents their efforts and creates a genuine link between the past and the present where they live? Or is it better to teach them that these objects from the past don't belong to any of us in particular, not even to those who find them while playing "dig the worm orphanage" in the earth next to the Temple of Jupiter? That they are, instead, everyone's property, and that there are more qualified people than us who use them to understand the past, institutions responsible for their conservation, and programs through* which anyone who's interested can have access to them? That is to say, that if archaeologists, supervisory administrators, and museums exist, they exist precisely to protect common goods from private appropriation, so that what belongs to everyone really is shared. Should we say that?

The decision isn't difficult. Or it wouldn't be difficult, had one of the adults found the nail. What's giving us pause is the idea that, if we ask them to do the right thing, the enthusiasm sparked in Guia and Virginia when they found a tiny piece of history in their children's hands could also be snuffed out. But if they're big enough to feel the excitement of the discovery, we conclude, they're also big enough to understand the reasons behind a justified "no" that conflicts with their desire to keep the nail in question.

So we explain why it wouldn't be right to bring the artifact home. Instead, we ask them to mark the place where they dug it up with a stick, go back to the little wooden shack where we saw a custodian sheltering from the sun as we came up, and give him what they've found. And that's what they do, obedient and absorbed in the task. We adults stay back voluntarily: this is their thing. From a distance we watch them go down to the shack, get the custodian's attention, talk to him for a moment while holding out a hand, then turn around and race back to where we are, smiles of pure joy on their faces. We don't even have time to ask how it went. "He told us we can keep it!" they call out. "It's ours: we can keep it!" Oh well: we tried. And all in all, not bad for the first day.

But that was the first day, when the sun was boiling hot. An unexpected summer sun that roasted the bald heads of the fathers, and colored the faces of our children while we were at the excavations. Today scattered clouds shade us and make the path easier. Suddenly, though, there's an incredible burst of rain that surprises us just as we're entering the House of the Prince of Naples. The tourists around scatter; swarming, running I don't know where. Maybe to that horrifying Autogrill rest stop that someone had the brilliant idea of constructing along the road that leads to the forum—or rather, of wedging in among two-thousand-year-old stones, by the Arch of Nero, at the border between Regions 6 and 7, its kitchens practically wall-to-wall with the forum's thermal baths.

It's an Autogrill with all the trimmings, just like the ones you find on the highway. The spitting image. Even the sandwiches and tubs of ice cream are the same. An architectural monstrosity that the Ministry of Cultural Heritage has tried to defend as an "indispensable service" for visitors, and which the general manager of Autogrill S.p.A. thinks of proudly when he asserts (and I quote) that "the importance of a site like Pompeii and its ability to attract an international audience merited the attention of a company like Autogrill." I start thinking about the etymology of the word "merit," *meritare* in Italian. It comes from the Latin verb *mereo*; from the same crude Latinism, one we have by now completely digested, we get *merenda*, or "snack." I'm pretty sure—no, absolutely sure—that the Pompeiians would never have used that word in a sentence like the one above. Instead, they would have wondered what they had ever done to "merit" all of this.

We, however, didn't run from the rain. We've stayed put in the House of the Prince of Naples for the thirty minutes exactly of torrential rain. After hours and hours of walking through the crowds, it seems strange being just us again. Alone, with the sound of the rain. I take advantage of this unexpected break and of all the water coming down to show the children how the *impluvium*, the little pool in the center of every Roman atrium that gathers rainwater, works. We've already seen many of them: simple, with mosaics, or adorned with statues—like the one with the faun, so small and yet so powerful that it's almost awe-inspiring. As I was saying, by now they know the *impluvium* well: during the examination, at the end of our trip, they'll even know how to spell out the name. But now we see it in action, and Miriam finally calms down. There really is a lot of water today; it's coming down in buckets, but it's clear it can't overflow: there's a cistern below to gather the excess.

This thing of water entering the house through a hole in the roof is beautiful: beautiful to hear, to see, to touch. Textbooks on the history of architecture say it was used to cool the room down on summer days. But above all, I think, it was beautiful. Romans made their houses beautiful. I'd like to build a similar one, somewhere in Tuscany. Ginevra agrees: she even says she'd like to have lived back then and there. Except for the eruption, she adds quickly. And we look at the door of the house to see how the water flows quickly down the sloped street, and we imagine it cleaning the streets of the dirt from horses and human beings, those open-air sewers that so fascinate Tommaso and Camilla. And we all hope they had quite a few torrential rainfalls to clean the streets and dull the smells.

The adults spread out around the rooms. From the window of a *cubiculum*, someone observes the little temple of the *lares* in the garden; others look at the marble table with winged lion paws; still others study the remains of the stairs that led to the upper floor. But soon after, drawn by a silence that's lasted a little too long (the measuring of silences is one of the senses that all parents develop), I turn and look for my children. Everything's fine: there's no problem. They're just all there in the next room, on the floor of the frescoed living room, sitting in a circle. They're playing a game of cards, waiting for it to stop raining. The oldest children have the youngest sit on their laps and tap the cards lightly with their fingers, showing the little ones which to play. Under centuries of history, not minding the Medusa heads behind them, or the marble inlays where they're crossing their legs, at home within these walls, between Paris and Perseus. As if finding themselves there and making these gestures is the most natural thing in the world. And it is, the entire time it rains.

When it stops, though, we start walking again and find the House of the Painters at Work. This house is so named because in the biggest room they found the remains of scaffolding, jars of gesso, containers for mixing colors, and dozens of little pots, some almost empty, others still with dry paint inside. Basically, all signs that the room was abandoned in a hurry, during the eruption, by whoever was decorating the walls. The ceilings were finished, as well as the upper part of the fresco, but the lower part is clearly incomplete. I've reminded everyone that the eruption did not take the city completely by surprise, that many people had already gone away, but not all of them: some still believed that nothing would happen to Pompeii, that it was a good idea to repair the cracks, spread a new coat of plaster, and paint the walls of the houses. It's here, in this house, that I try to explain another peculiarity of the dead city, which died of a sudden and clean death, that makes it so special to me. Pompeii seems to be resistant to the signs of failure of human industry. In other words, there are no traces of the weariness of one generation, or the emptiness of the next, that are sometimes found in our cities.

To explain what I mean, I give an example that at least the parents will be familiar with. Right after Montelupo Fiorentino station, I say, on the Pisa-Florence line, there's a field between the railway and river, where years ago someone planted fir trees in straight, ordered lines. This wasn't something that could have happened unnoticed: it's not an area of plant nurseries, much less firs. It was clearly an economic development initiative, a decision to intensively farm a plot of land that people had always been happy to think of as a calm arable land with trees. Whoever saw it from the train basically felt as if they were looking at a little modern investment that met the demand for indoor Christmas trees with its selection of dwarf firs. Now, thirty years later, those lines of little trees have been replaced by a hodgepodge of conifers, some of them gigantic, others half-crushed by the masses of vines that have infested them. Nothing catastrophic happened there; and this is the result.

Using that overgrown plant nursery as an example, I try to explain the weariness that follows the energy of one generation, or the void left by a generation that has not continued the work of the one before: because it was distracted by something, because it left, went far away, maybe never existed. In Pompeii, I add, there is no trace of that weariness, that failure of energy that started but did not finish, cared for and then abandoned. There wasn't time, maybe. Or maybe the volcano erased any traces of it. What the ashes and lapilli that fell on the city have preserved is, instead, a feeling of the opposite. It's a cliché in archaeological guides that the dead city allows us to have a glimpse of ancient life, frozen in time like an insect trapped in amber. In a certain sense (at least in the sense that I've tried to explain, succumbing for a moment to the overused Jurassic simile in the guides), it seems to me that this is true when I find myself with the children in the House of the Painters at Work. But it's hard to say. On the other hand, all of this house still hasn't been excavated. It's part of the zone of Pompeii, north of Via dell'Abbondanza, that is still to be discovered.

*As I stand here and look at the compact block of possibilities contained in the unexcavated hill and listen to my wife, who's talking about the inertia that can be seen in a plant nursery left to its own devices, I'm reminded of a framed photo that was on my high school German teacher's desk. It's an old one printed in black and white that shows her, almost posing, in a light overcoat, square-heeled shoes, and a little purse with a curved handle held tight in her hands. It's in Cologne, she's twenty-two, she's smiling. It must be 1946. Behind her, at the back left, you can see the city cathedral. There's at least a kilometer between the figure in the foreground and the church in the background. And the church towers are clearly visible, the second row of glass windows on the façade, the pointed arch of the entrance.*

*My eyes went to that photo every time my teacher, my mother's friend and colleague and our next-door neighbor, invited me over after school for tea in the little living room. This minimalist tea ceremony was really a chance for her to give me stamps, which she steamed off the letters she'd received from Germany, or to pass along a clipping from the* Zeit *or* Der Spiegel *that she thought would be of interest to me, her student. Now that I'm here today, between walls of houses reduced to rubbles which the children lean over to see rooms with mosaic floors, I understand that, more than the newspaper cutouts, it might have been that photograph that drew me in; from the first time I saw it.*

*Something about that image struck me right away. It's something that isn't in the picture and, by not being there, gives it a strange perspective where things both near and far share the surface of the photo. It's the fact that the cathedral, from that distance, shouldn't be visible. There should have been houses between the twenty-year-old smiling woman and the church. And instead, there's nothing. The city had been there, of course, until the English bombers from Operation Millennium completely wiped it out the night of May 30, 1942. I understand, now that I'm here listening to how a plot of land on the bank of the Arno slowly went wild, that there was no trace of weariness in the city reduced to fragments of wall where my twenty-year-old German teacher was smiling; nor did that photo hint at the generational vacuum that would follow hers.*

The hill has not been excavated—and it makes up almost a third of the city—but the border between the revealed part and the as-yet uncovered one is not marked by any kind of exhaustion: it's not a product of surrender. It is, instead, a frugal choice. The archaeologists have decided that in the end it's better to devote themselves to preserving what has so far been discovered, rather than digging further. A very wise decision, in my opinion. Since what stays under the ash at least stays safe, doesn't crumble, fade, or wear out, and doesn't end up on the interminable list of houses "AWAITING RESTORATION," which I'm sorry I can't show the children. What we don't dig today is still available to whoever comes after us. The future archaeologists. This is another expression (on par with the drop of amber) that I try out a little hesitantly. It's difficult to talk about the future. If the future can be judged from the past, we can count on the fact that future archaeologists will be different from us: that they'll have new technologies, and renewed enthusiasm, for revealing to the world what the rest of the dead city is hiding. Most of all, they'll have other ideas about what we're looking for and why we're doing it. And so, to avoid jeopardizing the future, it may really be good to wait and not excavate any more. Or, at least, not too much.

Because maybe there's still something that could still be worth trying to find. For example, for my part, I pray every night that there's a scholar's library in the unexcavated city. And I pray that a few years before the eruption, Petronius's *Satyricon* arrived in Pompeii, "hot off the press." You just need to think about what we have of that strange, ancient manuscript to understand immediately that having more of the *Satyricon* could only benefit Latin literature. I'm not interested in recovering anything else in the canon. On the contrary, I'd like to avoid finding more of Cicero's writings. But I want Petronius; if not for me, then at least for our daughter. And maybe he'll end up giving us another exhilarating chapter like the one with the grotesque, hellish dinner in the house of Trimalchio, the wealthy ex-slave who holds court amidst a crowd of parasites in a city that I like to imagine is Pompeii itself. Sooner or later, a less-mutilated copy than the ones we have so far must show up. Maybe they won't find it here, but outside Pompeii, a little to the north, in the Villa of the Papyri. Maybe the text really is there, one of the volumes in the unexcavated Latin room. And this thought consoles me during the wait. It's good to feel rich for a little while, or at least potentially rich. It's like walking with a lottery ticket in your pocket, a ticket that until the day of the drawing is, like any other ticket sold, the winning one.

Speaking of the Villa of the Papyri. I've told the children the story of this villa outside Herculaneum, on the sea. Built around the middle of the first century B.C., at the time of Caesar and Cicero, maybe belonging to the Piso family. It's famous for having allowed us to find the only practically intact library of the ancient world: a room with more than a thousand papyrus scrolls. They're almost all in Greek, with writings on the philosophy of Epicurus and his followers. It seems they were organized by Philodemus the philosopher, a client of one of the Pisos, poet in his own right and friend of the Golden Age Latin poets (Lucretius, Virgil, maybe Horace). In doing this, it's said that Philodemus made Herculaneum the hub of epicureanism in the Latin world.

The library's papyri are, obviously, carbonized, and since the time when they were found, people have been looking for the best ways to open them and be able to read them without them crumbling. It's not an easy task. We don't even want to begin to think how many fell to pieces during the first attempts at unraveling them by mechanical and chemical means. But the library was not only damaged by technical problems and clumsy attempts at

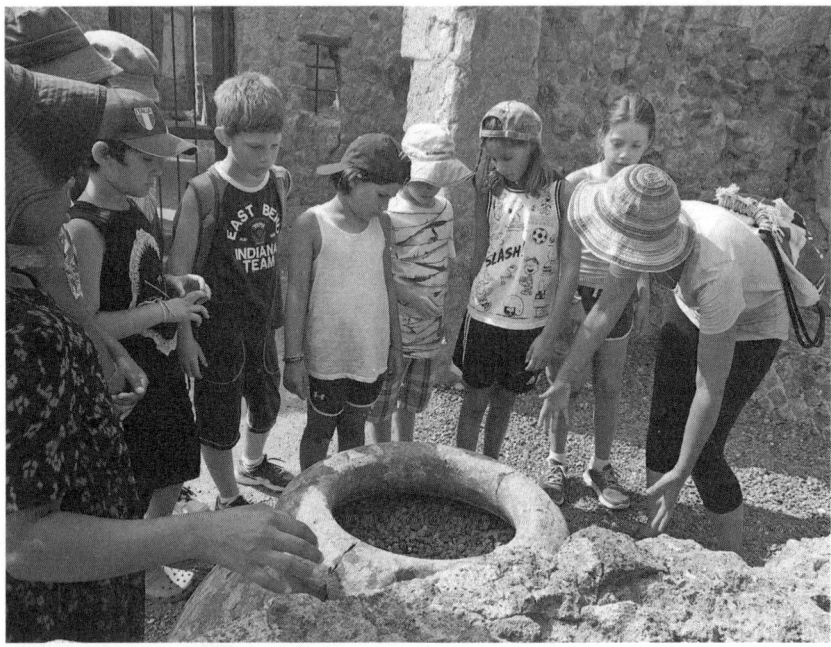

Figure 10-1. Teaching at Herculaneum. (Simone Marchesi)

restoration. Other papyri went in other directions. For example, it's funny to think of those eighteen papyri Ferdinand IV of Bourbon gave to the English royals in exchange for as many kangaroos. KANGAROOS??? Even the children think they've misunderstood. Exactly, children. You've understood perfectly: kangaroos. And not one, but eighteen: one per papyrus, that's right. Well, we don't want to undersell our papyri, do we? The same obviously goes for kangaroos. Eighteen marsupials, to be sent jumping happily through the park of Villa Floridiana: a small gift from Ferdinand to his wife, who apparently loved exotic animals, and who wouldn't have known what to make of those little cylinders of burned wood. We smile at this idea. But that's the way it is: we laugh so we don't cry.

So far about eight hundred papyri have been opened, and, while the reading continues (with continuously evolving methods) in the laboratories, the excavation continues at the villa. Because maybe the famous room with the Latin texts really will be revealed. Roman libraries were organized by language and, if an entirely Greek one was found in one room, it's possible that another will be found, all in Latin, in another room not too far away. And in that one we might also find what's still missing from the *Satyricon*. (I've already said that, I know. I'm sorry: it's an obsession of mine.) But they are digging also because only a few parts of this villa have been explored so far. It's an enormous building, one of the largest private residences ever found in the Roman world. Its front is two hundred and fifty meters long, it was built with three floors, overlooking the sea, and it's buried under thirty meters of volcanic detritus: anything but accessible. The children are calm, though, because children—as everyone knows—have great faith in the human species. From now until when they're grown, who knows how much more of the villa they'll be able to see—maybe in a few years everything will have been excavated. Yes, children, of course: *uno di questi giorni*. One of these days.

And if that doesn't happen, don't worry: because the Americans, as you know, are our allies. And the Americans, even the adults, are children. And some of them are rich. And when children are rich they don't need to throw tantrums. They say "I want this" and they buy it. And if they can't buy it, they make it. Even things that came out wrong. In the Midwest they wanted to remake the Tower of Pisa. With the same incline, although it's half the height: it's called the Leaning Tower of Niles, and despite the name, it isn't in Egypt but in a charming place in Illinois. Niles, that's right. And if you're from Siena, you'll always feel at home on the East Coast: between Massachusetts and Connecticut there are three Towers of Mangia. It seems that one was really popular. And they didn't stop at Italian monuments: they also made the Parthenon's twin. You'll find it in Nashville, Tennessee, and it's an exact replica of the one in Athens. As a sign of respect, the building was reduced by a foot in all three directions but is, in exchange, enriched by the chryselephantine statue of Minerva, which hasn't been in the Parthenon at Athens for a while. By the way, this statue is registered as the "Tallest Indoor Statue in the World" in the *Guinness Book of World Records*. An odd record.

Now, I teach at Hofstra University, a university on Long Island, the giant island that projects New York State onto the Atlantic, toward Europe. Near Hofstra there's a place called Hicksville, a small town at the center of the junction between the island's two main railway lines. At the center of Hicksville is a church, the Trinity Lutheran Church, and on the façade of the

Trinity Lutheran Church of Hicksville, on Long Island, in New York State, are the Ghiberti Gates of Paradise. I found out because some of my colleagues made sure to tell me right away, from the day of my arrival. Because I teach at Hofstra, but I'm from Florence. So, if one day you feel homesick, if you want to feel as if you're going for a walk in the center, in the cathedral square, to the baptistery, this is what they told me: "You wouldn't have to travel all the way to Florence to see the Gates of Paradise. We got them here on Long Island." Yes, right, of course. Maybe not today. Really, one of these days I might go. Not today, though.

So, children, that's why I was saying not to worry if the Villa of Papyri has not yet been completely excavated: sooner or later it will be, and even if it isn't, you can still visit it. In fact, all of us can visit it, tomorrow morning, even. Just don't assume it's near Herculaneum, as all the guidebooks seem determined to remind us. Fly to California, to Los Angeles. You'll find it there. It's not in Hollywood, no. It's not on the set of *Pompeii*, the most recent disaster movie about the eruption of '79, which came out in 2014 and is (I hope) already on the list of cinematic flops and, therefore, consigned to a merciful oblivion here. It's not there: it's a little further in. It's where Paul Getty—one of those rich Americans (no, super-rich: in this case, the richest in the world at the time)—had it rebuilt as an annex of his house, to hold the collection of artworks he'd accumulated over a lifetime of making ends meet.

The children have never heard of Paul Getty, but the parents remember him from 1973, the year when he ended up in all the newspapers and on television. We were young, but it left an impression when his sixteen-year-old grandson, John Paul Getty III, was kidnapped in Rome by the Calabrian 'Ndrangheta. His grandfather—a multimillionaire oil tycoon—refused to pay the initial ransom requested, and the kidnappers had no scruples: they sent a package to the Rome headquarters of the *Messaggero* newspaper with the right ear of the kidnapped grandson, and then also had photos sent of the young man without his ear. Getty gave in and paid: not everything, just what he could deduct from taxes, apparently. A true genius.

On the other hand, this greed, which was questioned at the time of the events, was understandable: he was using the money for more important things. Like—that's right—rebuilding the Villa of the Papyri in Malibu. He'd had this crazy idea a few years before, in 1968. One day he called the architect Stephen Garrett and said, in that deep voice of his, "I want to re-create the Villa of Papyri." When he has told this story, Garrett has always admitted that at the time he had no idea what his client was talking about and that he had to look it up. And so he discovered that it consisted of this enormous estate on the sea on the Gulf of Pozzuoli, possibly belonging to Julius Caesar's father-in-law, which had been buried under volcanic rock and rediscovered by the kings of Naples. A mine of papyri, statues, and other treasures that had so impressed Getty that he was inspired to reproduce it in his backyard to house his Greek and Roman treasures.

And that's what he did: Garrett took the map of the Villa drawn by Weber, the first engineer in charge of the excavations at the time of discovery, in the eighteenth century, and went on countless trips between Malibu and London, where Getty was living, to discuss the details of construction with him. The Villa opened in 1974 as the tycoon's museum of Antiquity, complete with copies of all the statues, frescoes, gardens, and fountains discovered in its double at Herculaneum. Getty died two years later, in 1976, without even having had time to fly to California to see it. But there you have it, thanks to this American of the type that buys something if he doesn't already have it, and that makes it if he can't buy it, thanks to this American that said "I want the Villa of Papyri, and I'll make it for myself," you can go to the Villa of Papyri. But please remember it's not in Herculaneum. Here's the address, for the taxi: 17985 Pacific Coast Highway, Pacific Palisades. And if you want to write to someone there, the zip code is 90272.

*Translated by Erin Brady*

ELEVEN

## Mediterranean Crossroads: Naples as a Model of Southcentric Cosmopolitanism

*Patrizia La Trecchia*

> If it is the North that leads the world, it is the South that sustains it.
> —MARCELLO VENEZIANI, *Sud: Un viaggio civile e sentimentale*

> Naples is extraneous to homologation. It follows the times of a clock that is oblivious to the correct time. Naples is the tropic close to the Autogrill. Garbage and beauty, because this city also has an infamous beauty and, whatever we might think, this is indeed a real resource.
> —FRANCESCO DURANTE, *Scuorno (Vergogna)*

> Whenever, after a long absence, I return to Naples, that beautiful and wounded city, I find myself looking forward to bedtime, to the first few moments of falling asleep. I always stay in one of the more populous quarters, in a room overlooking a steep, narrow street, and as I throw open my window a vast wave of sound floods over me. Settled in bed, I'm disconcerted at first by the sheer volume, by my feeling of floating helplessly in a tide of half-drowned voices, people calling or quarreling, snatches of jokes, television commercials, soccer games, ghosts of songs twisted by the wind; footfalls mingle with rasping scooters, a baby's crying with the honking of horns. Yet, soon the noises soothe me, and suspended between wakefulness and sleep I enjoy a sensation of homecoming, of rejoining a crowd of kindred spirits, faces I have always known.
> —DAN HOFSTADTER, *Falling Palace: A Romance of Naples*

This essay grounds the interpretation of the city of Naples in its centrality in the discourse around the Italian South and the Mediterranean, embracing a discussion of both perspectives on the city and adding this voice to those who have attempted to produce a discourse on the South that renegotiates its common understanding and tries to purge it from the negative stereotypes that have accompanied it over the centuries. Naples will be mapped in the context of a new geography of strategic places that cut across the North-South divide at the global level and are bound to each other by the dynamics of globalization. This introduction to an analysis of this peripheral southern Italian city in connection with a consideration of the multiple social and cultural transformations engendered by the globalization processes has the purpose of concretely viewing the complexities of globalization through a specific place in the Mediterranean that can be empowered with new meaning and new political potential for the formation of transnational identities and communities. While cities are strategic sites for the production of today's cultural discourses, they are also spaces for a whole series of conflicts and contradictions.

In recent years, the city of Naples has been described as the "heart of darkness of Italy." It has appeared in international news as a haunted and devilish place because of events like the Camorra murders as well as the garbage emergency that has plagued the city since 2007, creating the aura of an inhospitable environment and threatening its citizens with the possibility of a cholera epidemic. The stereotypes against Southerners, and Neapolitans in particular, have increased proportionately with the city's deteriorating image in the public eye. This current political and social situation in southern Italy demands a general reflection free from rhetorical denigratory tones or celebratory accounts.

Cities become strategic terrains for thinking about the political implications of globalization. They emerge as sites for new claims and new immigrant workforces. In our global scenario, marginal cities specifically achieve a new geography of centrality where the traditionally disadvantaged actors have the possibility of becoming visible in this new transnational rhetoric. The contemporary global context allows for a recovery of the periphery and the possibility of inclusion for those subjects who lack power but have now acquired presence. The marginal position of the South has gained presence and found a voice in this new transnational geography that fosters a new politics of culture and identity.

The Italian South is a field historically marked by tensions between the local and the global (e.g., the massive diaspora of southern Italians to the United States). At a time when the media, writers, and journalists are turning their attention to the issues of the South, this essay suggests that a paradigm shift is perhaps possible while looking at this part of Italy. Such a perspective goes beyond the favored representations in the media, the old images of patriarchal dominance and backward society, or the rural idyll associated with the Italian South; it is more concerned with its transformation as a geographical and imaginative area that is rich with border crossings of every sort: racial, gendered, regional, and transnational, as is evidenced in the new immigration. There are many visual representations of the South in the nation's consciousness and collective imagination. Most of these circulate in the media and in the consciousness of artists who have portrayed and are portraying the South. It would seem fruitful to consider the South as a theoretical arena that is globally situated with the world's other "Souths." The regional specificities are local but the transnational traits are global. Inserted as it is in this new politics of identity, the South that was almost considered extraneous and a burden to the myth of Italian nation building can now be used as a platform for imagining a different future image of Italian identity that can be constructed on the permeability of its Mediterranean and southern culture. The social transformations in contemporary Naples render the city a Mediterranean model of what we would define as a "Southcentric" cosmopolitanism created through immigration and emigration.

Immigration and emigration are often under-represented and devalued by the dominant culture. As Saskia Sassen notes, they are instead processes that have to do with "the globalization of economic activity, of cultural activity, of identity formation."[1] The patterns of immigration and emigration in the city of Naples envision a global connection between *i Sud del mondo*, the "Souths" of the world, the South of the Mediterranean, and the city of Naples, symbolic of southern Italy and of Europe's "Other."

This essay will elaborate and discuss these issues while making a connection with Francesco Rosi's documentary *Diario napoletano* (Neapolitan Diary) (1992), which is regarded as a social document of Neapolitan political and cultural history, pointing out its political dysfunctions that seem to have grown progressively worse today, and that coexist with the new ethnic and social transformations the city is experiencing. Conveying in images an intriguing osmosis between the official narrations of the city and the more personal experiences and memories of city places, *Neapolitan Diary* captures fragments and traces of a visual mental imagery of the past, present, and future Naples that envisions it as a crucial global crossroad in the Mediterranean.

Rosi left Naples in late 1946 to spend a short period of time in Milan and then soon after moved to Rome. His seminal film, *Le mani sulla città* (Hands over the City) (1963) still remains the most powerful visual manifesto of denunciation against the housing speculation in Naples in the 1950s. Thirty years later, Rosi returned to Naples for a screening of his film at the Department of Architecture of the University Federico II. With his usual artistic mastery and ethnographic vision of life and events, he used the opportunity to write the screenplay for *Neapolitan Diary* with Raffaele La Capria. He also directed and performed in this intensely poetic and politically engaged documentary that is a continuation of his inquiry into the Neapolitan cityscape that began with *Hands over the City*.

*Hands over the City* offers an intense and prophetic portrayal of Neapolitan political and social history as exemplified in its distorted urban development. The tragic consequences of the careless housing speculation promoted by the postwar Achille Lauro administration, and continued by the Christian Democrats with the Gava dynasty and their political allies, offered the opportunity for a lucid reflection and debate on the intricate relationships between economic interests and politics. What is remarkable about *Hands over the City* is that the film goes beyond the scandal of the housing speculation to accuse the political system that rendered it possible. By letting it speak and giving voice to the speculators' "reasons" and those who protected them, it confronts them with the reality of those who suffered the dramatic consequences of the speculation.

*Neapolitan Diary* is a documentary fiction that assembles interviews of famous protagonists of the Neapolitan cultural, academic, and political scene, including architects Bruno Zevi, Aldo Loris Rossi, and Cesare De Seta; historians Giuseppe Galasso and Aldo Schiavone; and director Mario Martone. Rosi revisits the disastrous local choices continued over the last thirty years with his usual polemic verve. The opening traveling shot offers an aerial view of the northern part of the city devastated by the housing speculation. In the fifties it was still a rural area, yet in the seventies housing speculation completely changed its urban definition, reshaping or, rather, distorting its urban space. The huge block of apartments called "Le Vele" (the sails), which are the typical buildings in this area, were originally part of an avant-garde architectural project of renovation based on Law 167, which provided for public housing. The idea had been modeled upon the Scandinavian suburbs with their modern blocks of apartments surrounded by green areas. Because of the strong political corruption of those years (preceding the attempted political and economical renovations of Tangentopoli and Manipulite), there remained only blocks of apartments, and by the eighties the area had become one of the most degraded in the city and the province's main center for drug pushing.

When the director travels by car through the streets of Portici, along the so-called Miglio d'Oro (Golden Mile), he films the entrances of the wonderful villas that used to characterize this once renowned but now rundown neighborhood.[2] He remarks that in Naples, because of these changes, one has to have a "trained eye" to see the old beauty beyond the decay. During the film, the intervention of historian Aldo Schiavone gives a poignant description of the present-day urban social situation using an impressive visual metaphor. The city is described as a "living body" that is compromised by the "bad blood" of drug pushing and the illegal traffic of public money that provokes an "ethical decomposition" of the city:

> La città è vitale di una vita febbrile come attraversata da una modernizzazione perversa. Un corpo vitale attraversato da sangue malato e questo sangue malato sono questi fiumi di denaro pubblico deviato, denaro sporco di droga e altro. Questo provoca decomposizione etica della città ma insieme tenuta sociale, la città tiene meglio di venti anni fa. Il controllo della camorra sta riscrivendo la geografia sociale della città, la storia delle classi della città, via i vecchi ceti borghesi. (*Diario napoletano*)

> The city is alive with a restless life as if crossed by a perverse modernization. A sick body nourished by bad blood. This bad blood is made out from the flow of illegally diverted public money, which has become soiled by drugs and such. This provokes both an ethical decomposition of the city and social cohesion. The city is more cohesive than it was twenty years ago. The control of the

Camorra is rewriting the social geography of the city, the history of the urban social classes, and is destroying the old bourgeoisie.

Architect Bruno Zevi argues that the city would need a courageous act of creativity to get out of its deteriorated state, "something that is risky to even imagine." Instead, it seems that time has passed but things have not changed since the shooting of *Hands over the City*, as Carlo Fermariello, who is present among the audience, says during the commemoration: "Il problema dopo trent'anni è sempre lo stesso, chi fa la legge e in quali tasche vanno a finire i soldi dello stato" (After thirty years, the problem is still the same: who makes the laws and where public money goes).

While denouncing the illnesses of the contemporary city, the director also retraces its rich cultural heritage by strolling around the familiar places of his own past. He invokes collective memories by visiting the *loci officiali*—monuments and historical places around the city—and also giving us glimpses of those unconscious elements in the social memory of the city that cannot be systematically addressed and need instead to be experienced and recounted firsthand through an excursus into its rituals, gestures, dialects, and even culinary traditions. In this context, memory understood as a cultural practice and memory as an individual faculty overlap and intertwine. The nostalgic flashback to the memories of the director's Neapolitan childhood and the fishing of the octopus and the bombings during the war provides relief and comfort to both the narrator and the audience and concludes the film.

In this narrative of past Neapolitan history through the lens of memory, the past is rendered contiguous and its intrusion in the present challenges our unquestioning retention of past events. Those images trace the memories of a past that bears witness to historical moments that have shaped the present events. However, the present is not haunted by the past but understood and resited through the past. Time of memory and time of identity are linked together. In the end, the insertion of memory provides a counternarration of lives and stories that the "well-tempered, disciplined, scales of modernity are structurally unable to register."[3] This counternarration, reenacted through memory, contests our contemporary amnesia of what occurred and perhaps provides a new frame of potential understanding amid the contemporary crisis.

*Neapolitan Diary* shows a complex and layered image of the Neapolitan present that critically presents and breaks through the stereotypes of the South while becoming globally applicable. Over the past few years, Naples has been the object of much political and intellectual debate because of the rise in criminality and the increase of organized crime murders in the degraded suburbs of Scampia and Secondigliano; this is where the Camorra, the Neapolitan-based criminal organization, battles for control of the drug trade. On several occasions, the escalation of violence has required state intervention.

At the beginning of the film, using the camera with an investigative tension, Rosi inserts a cinema verité scene showing a police officer interrogating a group of young boys from the Secondigliano area. He does not ignore the deformities and brutalities of this labyrinthine city and he is able to incorporate them into a lucid and poetic documentary.[4] He approaches the "monster" as a sympathetic insider who has chosen to live somewhere else but still believes that "Naples is a dynamic city that mustn't die and that if Italy gives up here, it will give up everywhere." With the attitude of both a reporter and a modernist flâneur, he strolls through the divided and diverse spaces of the city trying to experience it as a whole and trying to provide the audience with a sensory experience of it.[5] His gaze becomes a privileged one that is able to both take possession of and see from a distance the cultural, geographical, and social landscape of the city.

Naples is a southern city and a crucial crossroad in the Mediterranean that occupies a significant border position between the so-called First and Third Worlds; a space of irreconcilable differences where fear and attraction are both played out; a city that presents a wide array of cultural resources in the visual, literary, and musical fields. It is also symbol of urban decay; a city known for its beautiful scenery and friendly people but also for its brutalities and chronic social problems. Analyzing the deep connection between culture and society, this inquiry tries to capture these two opposing perspectives, the positive and negative imaginaries and realities of Naples, the fascination and repulsion they exert, and the great diversity of thinking and ambiguity they represent. Ultimately, this complex and layered image of present-day Naples critically breaks through the stereotypes of the South while becoming globally applicable.

This conflictual cityscape reinforces an imaginative distance between the observer and the observed, between the privileged observing subject and the marginal object of study. From whose point of view should a chronicle on the city be narrated? Who has the authority to tell or to retell its story? How should it be covered or recovered? Which stories and works should be included and which ones should be left out? How should the notion of being constantly misunderstood and "excluded"—something that Naples has too often experienced, and still experiences in different situations—be approached, treated, and eventually modified? How should the uncomfortable, distorted, and removed Neapolitan Other be brought back in the analytical frame, avoiding the risk of falling into either paternalism, celebratory and folkloristic accounts, or "moral panics"?[6]

These questions are pressing to this inquiry. As Peter Stallybrass and Allon White argue, "what is *socially* peripheral is so frequently *symbolically* central."[7] In other words, the rejection and marginalization of the low-Other at the level of social and political organization is paradoxically accompanied by a symbolic importance of the Other that becomes constitutive of the imaginary repertoire of the dominant culture.

In a broader global perspective, Naples can be viewed as an example of periphery that unsettles and disrupts the hegemony of Western thought and action. The cultural languages it produces and the social and ethnic transformations introduced by the flow of new immigrants can be analyzed as ways that allow to recover the concrete, the localized processes through which globalization exists. This city reopens the view on the South as a controversial space, and at the same time it reveals, culturally and socially, an open complexity that the narrow requirements of modern nationalism and identity are unable to contain.

In a world that is and has been moving toward a world culture of universality where particular cultures resemble one another more and more in their cultural forms and in their struggle to obtain what constitutes the culture of more privileged countries—and this happens paradoxically even when nationalist fervor intensifies—in a world where cultural diffusion, communication, technology have connected us in ways that were obscure to past generations, what does the South—and in this case, the Italian South—represent? What does a liminal city like Naples represent? Is it an example of a disadvantaged periphery that needs to be rethought and absorbed by the center?

Neapolitan culture has been transported and reterritorialized in other parts of the world, for instance in the United States. Naples is the symbol of southern Italian immigration to the United States and the port from which Italian immigrants traveled to New York. The city has attracted people of different backgrounds for centuries and has also contributed to shaping the image of Italian immigrants abroad. Over the last two decades, the phenomenon of South-South migration has become more noticeable in the city, where large groups of immigrant communities coming from North Africa (Morocco, Algeria, Tunisia, Libya, Egypt) and sub-Saharan Africa (Ethiopia, Somalia, Nigeria, Senegal, Cape Verde), from Eastern Europe (Poland, Ukraine), from the Balkans (Croatia, Serbia, Albania, Montenegro), from Latin America (Brazil, Argentina, Venezuela, Ecuador, Peru, Colombia, Cuba, Dominican Republic), and from Asia (Sri Lanka, China, Philippines) have settled and sought integration within the Neapolitan culture.

The expression "South-South migration" is here broadly referring to migration from southern countries to other southern countries. Economists usually refer to the phenomenon of South-South migration to describe the inflows of people from other developing countries that developing countries experience and how this is reshaping the global economy.

As a consequence, the image of Naples that emerges these days is a multiethnic and diverse one. In spite of its internationalization and recognition and because of the everlasting North-South divide, the city is still present as a contested terrain at the national level and is still central in the discourse around the Italian South. Is the South still the "heart of darkness" of our civilization?

It seems that on the one hand we are becoming one world culture and on the other we are resistant to this idea by asserting our cultural difference and specificity with the emergence of local and marginal cultures that struggle against uniformity. What can be a helpful model? Can there still be a southern culture without the social dysfunctions and the backwardness? Is the culture of the South posing a struggle against the tendency toward a northern normative type of uniformity and cultural homogenization?

Our world is far from being an egalitarian global village. What we have are asymmetries of center and periphery. In terms of broader cultural impact, the periphery seems to be more the receiver of cultural meaning than the producer. And the periphery seems to be also where the loss of local identities becomes more visible and tangible. Is the cultural scenario of the future going to be that of a global world culture of homogenization? If so, why do we keep talking about the periphery? In this dynamic of center-to-periphery, the periphery seems to be where the dysfunctions or demons of the center show their traits. The dysfunctions of the periphery provide a relief and almost a celebration of the role the leading center should have in our society. In the end, it is an unbalanced comparison between culture and nonculture, between civilization and savagery that serves to reinforce the ethnocentrism of the center and deflects any critique from itself. In fact, closely observed, this global scenario and dynamics generate debates from the periphery to the center. These debates reinforce a marginal and weak rhetorical vision of the periphery that constructs in the mind of the general public hostility toward the region and its inhabitants, deflects attention away from other equally pressing national issues and events, and ultimately fuels a rhetoric of self-celebration of the center. Admittedly, the reality is more complicated than this schematic structure I have attempted to provide.

In the case of Naples, the periphery shows a crisis of the best values and the highest ideals that the center offers as models of civilization. In Naples the legality is swallowed by the omnipresence of a criminal organization like the Camorra. In Naples, the positive models that come from the center seem unable to become models and seem destined to be destroyed. Recently, newspapers, books, and television programs have alarmed and alerted the public about the recrudescence of criminality and corruption in the city. Looking through my archives of Neapolitan articles and drawing mainly from the Neapolitan newspapers, *Il Mattino*, the *Corriere del Mezzogiorno*, and *La Repubblica*, I can trace a series of worrisome titles dealing with the rise of criminality, with Camorra killings, state intervention, drug trafficking, garbage emergency, Neapolitan companies threatened by the Camorra, and, ultimately, the state intervention in the area of Castelvolturno after the killings of innocent immigrants in September 2008. On December 2006, Giuliano Amato, the minister of the interior, back in Naples for the second time within a few weeks, stated that for the Camorra, "la nottata non deve passare," literally, "the night must not pass," which means that there will not be another day for the Camorra.[8] However, over the past decade, not much seems to have changed.

Naples constantly captures the public imagination as a negative example of a periphery we all should ignore and keep at a distance. The media keeps invoking Naples to rouse indignation, horror, and incomprehension with its sensationalism and deliberately aggrandizes its negative aspects while ignoring the positive ones.[9] This process through which the media has constructed the perception of the South and of the city of Naples is defined as "moral panic" by sociologists. It is a concept that refers to the exaggeration of deviance on the part of official institutions in order to achieve firmer social control. It is often used to turn public attention away from other issues of equal gravity and national concern and to enhance citizens' support of conservative legislations or restrictions.

Turning to the city of Naples and to its location in the Mediterranean opens an interrogation on an ongoing simultaneous division—between northern and southern Italy, between the modern North of the world, on the one hand, and the South of the planet, on the other hand—and connection, such as how the formation of Italy and Europe depends profoundly upon this negated space. Many voices have attempted to produce a discourse on the South that tries to purge it of the negative stereotypes that have accompanied it over the centuries and that renegotiates the prejudiced understanding of the South. The city's cultural history as presented in Rosi's documentary is still relevant to the contemporary social and cultural crisis and its current "shame," as Francesco Durante defines it in his book *Scuorno*.[10] The social crisis in Naples cannot be easily evaluated, or solved without practical interventions. However, it is possible to examine the social history of the city in order to attempt a new framework for the analysis of this southern city that is often considered a synecdoche for the Italian South.

In order to produce balanced scholarly research, the terrain on the South should be freed from the commonplaces, expectations, and negative visions that still inform and keep influencing the discussion. Symbolically "traversing" the open territories of the South, analyzing its social crisis, and acknowledging the social transformations brought by the flows of people who are currently occupying its territory might introduce an element of contestation that would allow a move away from the surface of inherited categories and accepted ideas about the Italian South. Significant social, ethnic, and cultural transformations are taking place in the Neapolitan territory. The rising number of immigrants coupled with the economic and social instability in the region sets the scene for a cosmopolitan metropolis of the South with rapid population growth, growing unemployment, and falling incomes. This mass influx of immigrants comes from the South, particularly from less developed countries of the Mediterranean rim and sub-Saharan Africa. In many cultures the South represents poverty as well as ethnic and racial discrimination. These reflections implicitly address the idea of marginalization and exclusion of the Italian South, which led to the Italian diaspora to the United States.

The dominant discourse about the South revolves around a "spatial-geographical" perspective that has constantly structured representations of the South's marginal position in Italian society since the century before the unification. However, this perspective has become increasingly challenged and reconfigured by the present-day social and cultural transformations that are working with and against the social crisis and these accepted cultural constructions creating an alternative perspective in the dominant discourse. The cultural Southcentric cosmopolitanism brought by the immigration flows and by contemporary cultural practices becomes a counterspace, a site of oppositional readings that is able to deconstruct mythologies about itself.

Traditional political discourses refer to specific spatial terrains, but this specificity and its complicity in reproducing modernity's dominant, territorial imaginary has often been unrecognized and underestimated. An example is how the North and South's binary opposition is articulated in terms of a spatial paradigm. In order to challenge uncritical historical narratives through which the dominant imaginary is reproduced and legitimated, it is necessary to obtain critical distance from a simplistic ethical thinking that projects one specific way of shaping the world on the spatial basis of political and cultural discourses.

Fredric Jameson refers to "ethical thought" that "projects as permanent features of human 'experience,' and thus as a kind of 'wisdom' about personal life and interpersonal relations, what are in reality the historical and institutional specifics of a determinant type of group solidarity or class cohesion."[11] This refers, for instance, to the claim of a particular social, cultural, or geographical group to ethical and moral superiority over another group.

One can argue that the same process that Jameson describes is also applicable to the cultural discourse that emerges from certain cultural texts that strive to maintain an unambiguous space that, in the end, serves to support an unchanged and homogeneous image of society. As a result, the same practices of exclusion and inclusion are found in the discourses of much of the culture produced within a certain community or nation that tends to eliminate alternative voices coming from its subcultures. But what is suppressed within the dominant cultural "cartography" emerges in alternative texts that oppose the dominant moral geography by showing the conflicts and the many contending voices that are repressed in the dominant culture. At the level of discourse, this becomes translatable as the need for the recovery of alternative voices that destabilize discursive hegemonies attached to spatial configurations, while overcoming the invisibility of their marginal positions through re-inscription on the cultural map.

For Naples, both mediatic and public discourse manipulate and interpret social values in a preconceived mode. As mentioned earlier, the discursive consciousness within the dominant culture verbalizes the underlying values of the society as a kind of unspoken ideology. Certain key words that appear as leitmotifs in the definition of the city of Naples or the South exemplify the values of the time around these issues. These discourses have an impact on the way in which society organizes the perception of the city or even its legitimization in the dominant discourse. For instance, there is a rhetorical creation of meanings that magnify the reality. However, the contemporary cultural and social transformations in the city have produced a shift in its representation both in the artistic domain and in the dominant discourse.

After a long period of oblivion, when global attention had been directed toward the North and western Europe in general, southern and Mediterranean issues are receiving renewed interest. They are now present on the national cultural and political agenda, and, in the case of Naples, are not exclusively limited to concerns related to Mafia, Camorra, or criminality. The return of the South in the global arena acquires meaning not only when it allows us to wonder about growth and development but also when it raises an interrogation of the national future and the memory of its past, especially in the contemporary historical moment dominated by technology and communications—what we could define as the "new media orders" of high modernization. The South has contributed to modernization with the workforce of southern emigration.[12] The radical questioning that comes from the South concerns some of the crucial issues that are implicit in our modern society and in its model of growth: the relationship between public and private wealth, between public poverty and private prosperity; issues of social cohesion, social order, and societal foundations; dependence and development of local capabilities; and the dichotomy between growth and development.

All the dysfunctional aspects of modernity are present in different forms in the dynamics of southern society as well—unequal development and disproportions in wealth and poverty. Such universal themes have a local specificity reconstituting the same "perverse" mechanisms of modernity such as the law of the jungle, disinterest for the collective, and lack of trust. More than simply economic growth, which requires a large investment of capital and public resources, it is necessary to correct the present process of growth toward a new path of development that could lead to those social and institutional qualities that allow democratic and free living for all citizens. Is it possible to find alternative routes for the development of the South in light of the contradictions of modernity?

In our present-day condition dominated by the myth of the benefits of technology and a blind trust in the invincibility of progress, sociologist Franco Cassano wishes for reconciliation with the Mediterranean tradition. In *Il pensiero meridiano* (Southern Thought) (1996), he articulates what I define as a strategy of "looking and thinking South." It is a strategy that understands that the South has to be "looked at and thought about" from its own perspective, from the inside, and not from an external point of view that views it as the troubling Other. This approach finds a consonance in what is emphasized by the permeability of the Neapolitan tradition and contemporary cultural and social transformations. It seems that "looking South" thus becomes a necessity—linguistically and theoretically. The Italian South becomes a metaphorical South: the South of the entire world and not necessarily only the Neapolitan South. "Looking South" becomes the place from which to start thinking in a new way, beyond the rigid parameters imposed by a certain normative thought.

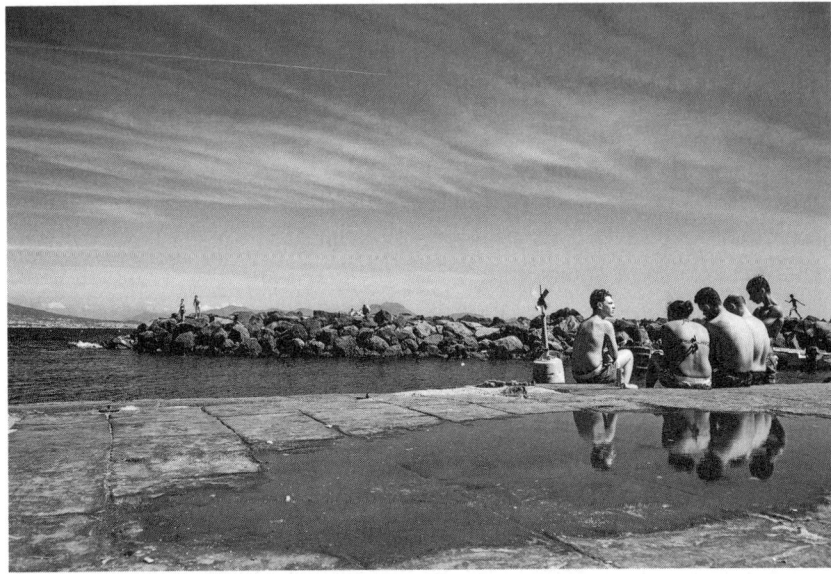

Figure 11-1. At the Bay of Naples. (Luca Di Martino)

Thanks to this new attitude toward the South, it has become possible to show the limits of traditional studies that have perpetuated a derogatory critical vision of the South as an undeveloped and backward land of sorrow, magic, prejudices, and negative stereotypes. This vision underestimated the relevance and the vitality of these apparently negative aspects to southern culture and, indeed, to Italian culture more generally. By invoking the Neapolitan rich literary, cultural, and linguistic traditions and building on the capital brought by immigrants, as the human embodiment of globalization, one begins a process of "legitimization" of the South that insists on an ethic of respect and that aims at giving a new confirmation to the dignity of southern history and to its long-suppressed "otherness."

A city has a million stories. It is not possible to tell all of them. With these reflections I wish to give testimony about the city that goes beyond the apocalyptic views in which it is described as the image of all that is wrong with Italy, and beyond the sentimentalized and romanticized views in which its real problems are overlooked. This is the account of an intellectual with a sense of exile and a sense of roots, who lives far from the eye of the storm and who wants to understand the stories and the flows of people that have shaped and are shaping the city.

As a concluding personal remark, I will say that Naples is not my city, it is not the city where I was born, but it is the city that has become a symbol of my "southern" roots. When I chose to navigate the space of Naples, I realized that its familiar space encountered the terrain of affects. My narrative of this city is inspired by my own origins and by the memories of the years I spent in Naples. From the distance of my current life in the United States, I have realized that over the years I have been listening for voices and stories that have eventually made their way into my writing. I have tried to engage myself with these stories of places and people I know deeply without losing myself in the process. The story I am narrating is a story of marginality, a story of a people who, although part of an industrialized nation, had and have to endure an existence of marginalization and exclusion.

NOTES

Epigraphs are from Marcello Veneziani, *Sud: Un viaggio civile e sentimentale* (Milan: Mondadori, 2009), 3; Francesco Durante, *Scuorno (Vergogna)* (Milan: Mondadori, 2008), 57; and Dan Hofstadter, *Falling Palace: A Romance of Naples* (New York: Random House, 2005), 3. All translations from Italian into English are mine.

1. Saskia Sassen, *Globalization and Its Discontents: Essays on the New Mobility of People and Money* (New York: New Press, 1998), 168.

2. The coastal region between the towns of Ercolano and Torre del Greco is commonly called Miglio d'Oro. It used to be an affluent area punctuated by villas, palaces, and gardens descending toward the sea like a "golden" area. In Portici, King Carlo III, the Bourbon monarch, built his summer residence, around which many other famous figures built their summer villas. Villa Nava is one of the oldest of the Vesuvian villas. The owner, Bernardino Martirano, was the secretary of the kingdom under King Carlo V. La Favorita can be found on the way to Ercolano. In 1799 it was the Accademia Militare di Marina (Navy Military Academy), and after the Neapolitan republic and the return of the monarchy, it became the *regal dimora*, the residence of the king. In that same area, after the Ponte della Maddalena (Maddalena Bridge), at the mouth of the Sebeto river, there is the building called Edificio dei Granili (Grain Building), built in 1799 by architect Ferdinando Fuga to be used as a barn. In a later era, during the

Neapolitan revolution, it was transformed into a prison. It is used as the setting for Anna Maria Ortese's short tale "La città involontaria," in *Il mare non bagna Napoli* (Turin: Einaudi, 1953).

3. Iain Chambers, *Mediterranean Crossings: The Politics of an Uninterrupted Modernity* (Durham, N.C.: Duke University Press, 2008), 58.

4. His gaze is that of a male subject.

5. I am referring to the idea of the flâneur, the city stroller, initially developed by Charles Baudelaire and drawn upon by numerous other thinkers such as Walter Benjamin, Georg Simmel, David Harvey, and Susan Sontag as a referent and detached observer for understanding urban phenomena and modernity.

6. See Stanley Cohen, *Folk Devils and Moral Panics* (St. Albans: Paladin, 1973). I will return to the definition of "moral panics" later on in the essay.

7. Peter Stallybrass and Allon White, *The Politics and Poetics of Transgression* (Ithaca, N.Y.: Cornell University Press, 1986), 5–6.

8. Amato is quoting Neapolitan-born playwright Eduardo De Filippo's famous line that concluded his 1945 drama, *Napoli milionaria*. Eduardo's line was in the Neapolitan dialect, "adda' passa 'a nuttata" (the night will have to pass, or there will be a new day), as a message of hope and renewal in the aftermath of the Second World War.

9. Among other things, Naples is an important manufacturing center. It has been defined as the Mediterranean version of New York in men's fashion. Everyone knows that the shows and shops in Milan are where people go to see top fashion, but many are surprised to discover that some of the most prized designers and producers either live and work in Naples or came from Naples. Men's fashion has reached its highest level (and certainly its highest prices) in Naples, from Marinella ties to the super-chic ateliers of Borrelli, Isaia, Attolini, Kiton, Barba, Rubinacci, and others. It may seem counterintuitive that a city famed for mass misery should simultaneously be a world center of luxury men's fashion, but the "Naples look" now dominates the top-of-the-line market throughout the Western world, from New York and San Francisco to Hong Kong, St. Petersburg, Tokyo, and Dubai. Roberto Saviano's reportage, *Gomorrah* (2006), has disclosed accurate information about the connections between Naples and the high-fashion industry in the chapter entitled "Angelina Jolie."

10. Francesco Durante, *Scuorno* (Milan: Mondadori, 2008). The word *scuorno* is Neapolitan dialect for the Italian *vergogna*, shame. The Neapolitan word also expresses the sense of frustration, depression, and impotence experienced by Neapolitans for being unable to do anything to rescue their own city. As Durante explains, the waste emergency has depressed Neapolitans because it has a great symbolic meaning (see Chapter 2).

11. Fredric Jameson, *The Political Unconscious: Narrative as a Socially Symbolic Act* (Ithaca, N.Y.: Cornell University Press, 1981), 59.

12. Italy, especially southern Italy, has traditionally been a country that supplied immigrants to other countries. Many Italians left in large numbers in the late nineteenth and early twentieth centuries in search of work, migrating mainly to the United States. In the 1960s, over four million Italians—one million of them from the region of Sicily—migrated to northern Europe. And two million more emigrated to the so-called Italian industrial triangle comprising the cities of Milan, Turin, and Genoa. These migration flows shifted toward the South during the mid-1970s when Italy became a destination country for emigrants leaving Africa, Asia, and Eastern Europe. As a consequence, Italy shifted from being a country of net emigration to one of net immigration.

TWELVE

## The Delirium of the Neapolitan Baroque

*J. Nicholas Napoli*

No one captured the delirium of Neapolitan baroque sculpture like the British art historian Anthony Blunt (1907–83). His book *Neapolitan Baroque and Rococo Architecture* (1975) was the first modern study to present the Neapolitan baroque to an English-speaking audience. While he wrote for a specialist audience, his characterization of the architecture of this era in Naples, exemplified in the Cacace Chapel in the Basilica of San Lorenzo Maggiore (see plate 12-1), deserves quotation at length.

> The architecture of Naples is like its inhabitants: lively, colorful, and with a tendency not to keep the rules, or rather, to have its own rules, which are not those of other cities or of other countries. If you go to Naples expecting its architecture to behave like that of Rome, you will be as surprised as if you expected its traffic to behave like Roman traffic, though you will be in less physical danger. On the other hand, if you go prepared to play according to Neapolitan rules, you will enjoy both—the architecture and the traffic—because Neapolitan drivers, like Neapolitan architects, are virtuosi in their

own art, but as the architect likes to torture the marble to the limit of endurance, so the driver likes to exploit the nerves of his pedestrian to just short of the breaking point; but both are experts in knowing how to stop in time to preserve life and marble.[1]

Neapolitan architects, like the cab drivers in the modern city, seem to relish pushing their materials and the nerves of their audiences to a point of no return, a breaking point, or, to consider the definition of "delirious," to go outside the furrow. Even more importantly, Blunt's analogies between Neapolitan baroque architecture, the people of Naples, and the drivers of the city suggest that the careful observation of art and architecture reveals broader cultural insights.[2]

This essay considers how Anthony Blunt's observations had a counterpart in seventeenth-century Naples. Its approach is inspired by the British art historian's lighthearted but astute analogy of the Neapolitan baroque and the potential of visual description as a vehicle for unlocking meaning in culture. The act of visual description—what art and architectural historians call the analysis of form—is central to how we make sense of the world and come to terms with its contours.

In the seventeenth century the act of describing architecture was a critical operation in the assessment of work completed and the payment of architects and building specialists. These descriptions were documented in written form as professional appraisals, and they served as a legal document that helped verify the sums of money owed to architects and builders upon the completion of a construction initiative.[3] The vocabulary used to describe architectural projects in the city of Naples, especially the work of the sculptor-architect Cosimo Fanzago (1591–1678), like Anthony Blunt's analogy of the Neapolitan taxi driver, takes unusual turns and departures from the more common phrases to be found in the reports.

## The Language of the Appraisal

From Sir Christopher Wren to Gianlorenzo Bernini, the professional appraisal was acknowledged to be a tedious and difficult but essential part of architectural practice in early modern Europe.[4] As a task of precise measurement, appraising architects needed a vocabulary to describe and name the numerous units of architectonic sculpture in order to write the appraisal. Not surprisingly, they employed the Vitruvian vocabulary. Generated in the *Ten Books of Architecture* by the ancient Roman architect and theorist Marcus Vitruvius Pollio (c. 80–70 B.C. to c. 15 B.C.) and propagated and codified by the architectural treatise writers of the Renaissance, this vocabulary allowed architects to combine the operations of measurement, evaluation, and judgment.

Where the Renaissance treatise writers sought to conceptualize and even codify a logic of assemblage that obeyed humanist principles of proportion and rhetoric,[5] the seventeenth-century appraiser internalized this logic, using a working knowledge of these components to parse often complex ensembles into simpler and more easily measurable units. Where the Renaissance treatise writer saw each architectonic unit as a component to be subtly integrated into a larger whole, the appraiser saw these units as a connoisseur rather than a composer: each piece was a work of sculpture that presented varying degrees of difficulty in manufacture and quality in execution.

Written statements about how an appraisal was performed, signed by the leading architects and builders of seventeenth-century Rome and Naples, are conserved in the archives of the Vatican and Naples. They are part of the documentary record surrounding Naples's preeminent sculptor-architect, Cosimo Fanzago, and his most famous project, the remodeling of the Carthusian monastery in Naples, the Certosa di San Martino.[6] In these statements, the marble workers in Naples and the architects in Rome presented remarkably similar strategies for measuring architectonic decoration in a completed project. They describe three operations performed by the appraising architect. First, the appraiser assessed the columnar unit by using the Vitruvian terminology to identify architectonic units and to parse the column into its component parts of capital, shaft, and base.[7] Second, they measured these units using a measuring line, recording both circumferential and vertical dimensions of the component. Third, the appraiser took into account the pricing for different architectonic pieces: flat work is less difficult to carve than pieces in the round such as columns, capitals, and other types of molding. The Neapolitan appraisers took care to point out that the molding at the base of a column, with its tightly tiered layers of convex lips, or *toruses*, and concave dividers, or *scotie*, is particularly difficult to carve.[8]

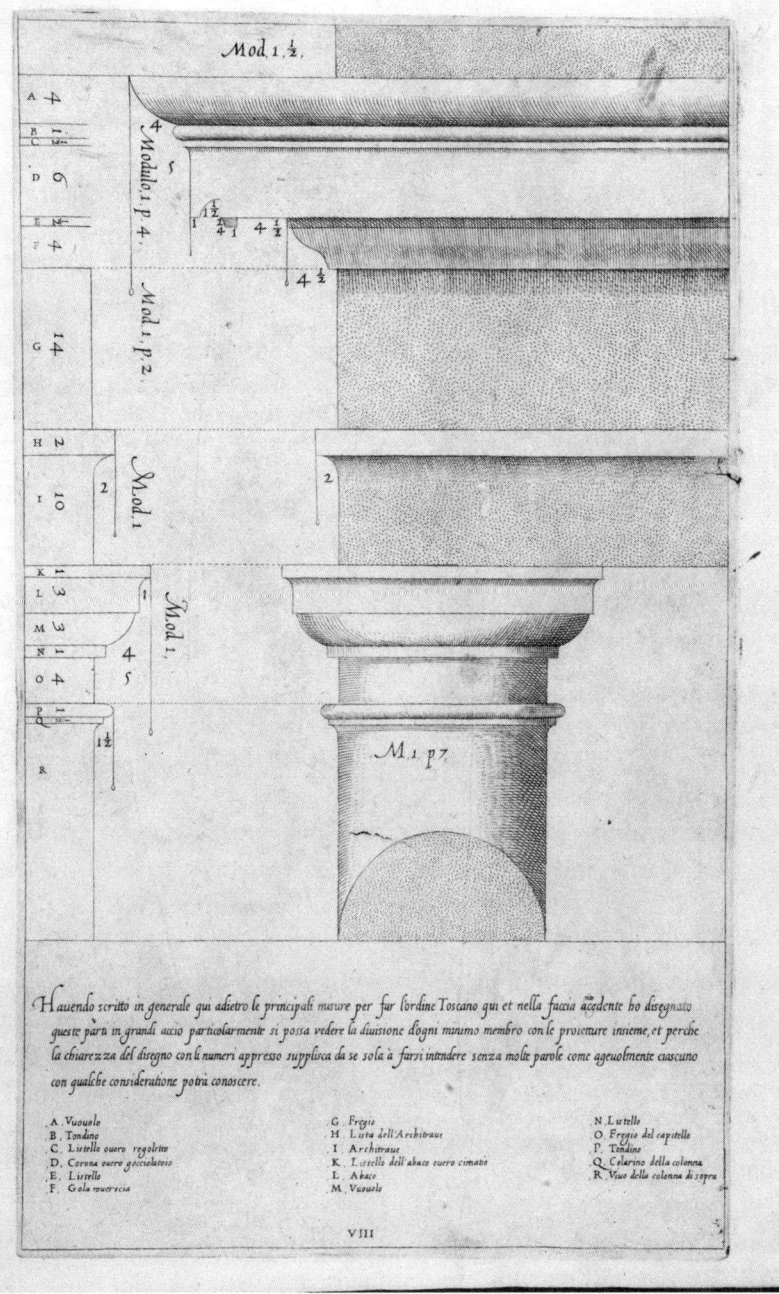

Figure 12-1. Giacomo Barozzi da Vignola, capital and cornice of the Tuscan order, pl. VIII. (Marquand Library of Art and Archaeology, Princeton University. Presented by Allan Marquand, Class of 1874. Photo by John Blazejewski)

Even though the statements appeared in the documentation without any illustration, they seem to have been made with illustrations of the orders, like those found in the treatises of Serlio and Vignola, in mind (see figure 12-1).

In their use of the terms "echinus," "abacus," "collar," "imoscapo," "scotie," and "toruses," the Neapolitan and Roman appraisers drew directly from Vitruvius and the Vitruvian tradition of the Renaissance treatises on the orders. In his description of Ionic column bases, capitals, and entablatures, Vitruvius used the terms "upper torus," "lower torus," "scotia," and "fillets" (the combination of the scotia and the fillets was called the "trichinous") to describe the complex of convex, concave, and flat moldings that cap the plinth and support the column. He called the flared lip that capped the capital of a column the abacus.[9] The placement and sizing of each of these components on the columnar unit was based on a complex system of ratios based on the diameter of the column shaft on its base.[10]

## *The Language of Appraisal in Seventeenth-Century Naples: The Challenge of Cosimo Fanzago*

The task of appraising Cosimo Fanzago's interventions at the Certosa di San Martino in Naples presented a momentous challenge to appraising architects. Fanzago, known as the "Cavaliere," a title bestowed upon him in the 1620s, had been working at San Martino for over thirty years, refurbishing everything from the monks' cloister and cistern system to revetting the interior of their church in polychromed marble and procuring paintings for the church (see plate 12-2). He ultimately claimed that he was grossly underpaid by the monks, igniting a lawsuit that lasted for over forty years. Given the volume of work he completed and the still large number of sculpted components that he left behind without assembling them, there were ultimately five appraisals of the Cavaliere's work at the monastery. All of the intricacies of an estimate—classification, pricing, and quality—awaited the appraising architects.

The first appraisal, conducted by Fanzago's former assistants, Pietro Antonio Valentino and Pietro Sanbarberio, concluded that the Carthusians owed Fanzago 13,908 ducats for his interventions at the monastery.[11] They itemized 106 features that included inlay work and sculpted pieces, from marble festoons to column capitals, that were installed alongside the inlay. Measurement of features like the marble architraves of the nave were relatively simple, but other features of the decorative ensemble became much more difficult to assess, let along measure. In a 1631 liquidation of accounts between Fanzago and the Carthusians, the architect Cristofaro Monterosso and the marble worker Jacomo Lazzari described the different carved pieces in the cloister of the monastery and the nave of the church. For most of these descriptions, they did not even include measurements or make attempts at valuation, and the vocabulary used by the appraisers attests to how Fanzago's decorative ensemble stretched the Vitruvian vocabulary of architectonic units to its breaking point.

The doorways and sculpted frames in the large cloister, framing the bust-length portraits of leaders in the Carthusian order (see figure 12-2), were described as follows:

> The seven large portals in the four corners of the cloister, all of them with their ornament above with the hollowed-out ovals made of *bardiglio* where the half-statues are placed with surrounding un-wrappings/cartouches (*fatti cho scartocci atorno* . . . ) and with panels of wrappings and incised festoons, with the ovals filled with *bardiglio* surrounding the afore-said portals. The cutting, squaring, cleaning, and incising to have them adjusted and retouched when installed and the assistance in constructing them is appraised (all seven together) at three thousand ducats with the declaration that all of them should be of the perfection and form of the two that are at the entrance of the afore-said cloister by the entrance of the cell of the Most Reverend Father Prior: 3000 ducats.[12]

The description of the sculptural-architectonic ensemble of the doorway is intriguing. They speak of the half-statues surrounded by *scartocci*. The word *scartoccio* appears to be a variant of the word *cartoccio*, which derives from the Latin term *charta* (map or charter) from which derives the French term *cartouche*: a scroll-like tablet that provides an ornamental frame for inscriptions.[13] While not a Vitruvian term, it became part of the decorative vocabulary of the visual arts in the sixteenth century. Andrea Palladio actually derided its use in architecture in the first book of the *Quattro libri dell'architettura*.[14]

Like cartouches, the elements of Fanzago's doorframes include scroll-like curves of marble, but they do not frame an inscription—the designation of

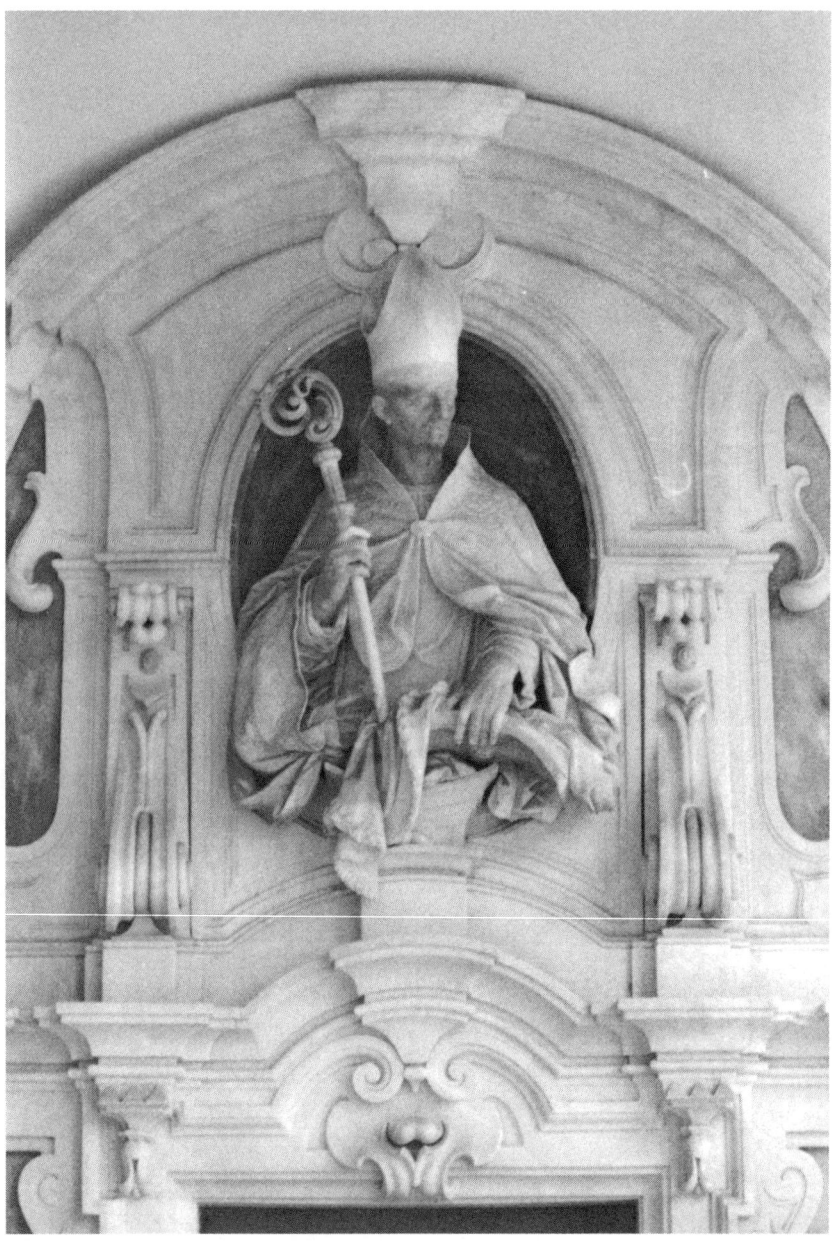

Figure 12-2. Certosa di San Martino, bust and frame of Saint Anselm, sculpture by Cosimo Fanzago and workshop, 1631–56. (Ministero dei beni e delle attività culturali e del turismo, Polo Museale della Campania, used with permission. Photo by J. Nicholas Napoli)

"cartouche" only approximates the forms. There is another Italian word, however, that is even closer to the term used in the appraisals: the verb *scartocciare* means to unwrap or to unhusk (as with an ear of corn). With this definition in mind, scartocci would signify "unwrappings." The meanings of these terms evoke both the forms and the function of Fanzago's framing elements. They describe the scrolling forms of the brackets and teardrop volutes and allude to how they frame the half statues.[15] Neither term, however, provides a perfect description of the brackets and moldings of Fanzago's doorways—the slippage between vocabulary and form suggests a passage where the Cavaliere's work begins to transcend the classical language of architecture.

The term appears again in a later appraisal (1676) of Fanzago's work in the church of San Martino (see plate 12-3). Describing the framework that surrounds Jusepe de Ribera's portraits of the prophets Moses and Elijah, Pietro Valentino and Pietro Sanbarberio wrote the following:

> First there are two ornaments where the pictures of Jusepe Ribera are placed, that are Moses and Elijah. Because these two ornaments are contained by their frames both above and below, it is understood however that the thin arms of verde antico marble, that go up to the collarino of the capital, are excluded. All of these are measured, but the ornament one understands as the framing inside and outside, that on one side [outside] has a shell [*gusso, guscio*], and the other side an ovolo with its flat surfaces and its *cimacie* [projecting rings] with studs and triangles, with mischio of breccia di francia, with the background of breccia minuta, that joins to the framework with drops (*gocciole*), little brackets (*menzoletti*), cartouches/unwrappings (*scartocci*), half jars, and a *cimacio* in the framework. And within the jars here and there [on both frames] there are inlays of verde antico marble, with thin strips of white and black, and a background of breccia di francia. If the ensemble of these ornaments can be appraised all together so as not to confuse the components/materials, this should be sufficient.[16]

Valentino and Sanbarberio's concluding statement confirms the complexity of the assessment: after his description of the ornamental ensemble that frames the Ribera panels, all of the pieces should be appraised as a single unit to avoid confusion. In the description the appraisers frequently shifted between the Vitruvian vocabulary of architectonic components to a descriptive terminology (frequently based on forms found in nature such as shells and drops, but also using the term for "unwrappings" or *scartocci*), attesting to the fluid relationship between architectonic components and sculptural components in Fanzago's ensemble. The sculptor employed the Vitruvian vocabulary in a loose manner: he identified the *collarino* of the pilasters as being a part of the capital rather than part of the shaft, and a *cimacio*— normally the crowning ring (also called the echinus or abacus) of a capital— designated any ringlike prominence that framed the ovolo below or the cornice of the frame above.

The description calls attention to two extraordinary features of Fanzago's work. First, he combined several different types of marble in an intricate fashion to compose an architectural framing piece. Second, he crafted these materials into forms that pushed the Vitruvian language of classical architecture to its limits. In its place, the appraisers resorted to a descriptive vocabulary making analogies to shapes and forms found in nature, to more aptly describe Fanzago's sculpture. In this passage the delirious language of Neapolitan baroque architecture emerges prominently.

## *The Broader Implications of Fanzago's Delirium*

Even art and architectural historians, when they seek to cast an analytic eye upon the figurative and architectonic sculpture of the city and to chart the changes in its forms from generation to generation, are challenged by the undulating curves of Neapolitan sculpture. When describing the inlaid-marble work of Neapolitan churches, art historians have often resorted to the word "phytomorphic" to describe shapes, seemingly derived from a plant or animal form, that have then been transformed into otherwise unidentifiable shapes.[17] The words and analogies employed by modern art historians in their descriptions evoke intuitive observations about Neapolitan baroque sculpture and architecture. As a creative endeavor, the Neapolitan baroque starts from a nature-based model and transforms it to the limits of recognition. Keeping in mind the observations of Anthony Blunt, this manner of sculpting suggests a deliberate bending of rules and conventions that is discernible in other sectors of Neapolitan society, even in the service industry of taxi driving in the present day.

*The Delirium of the Neapolitan Baroque* 199

The documents surrounding Fanzago's work at San Martino also cast the production of sculpture and architecture as a professional practice with large-scale financial implications. They reveal the professional, social, and economic contexts of producing art and architecture in baroque Naples. Fanzago was not the only artist who disputed the compensation of the monks, but their cases were not as lengthy or as complex. Considered together, however, they attest to the common difficulty of determining the just compensation for a decorating artist and to the delicacy of establishing a professional relationship that would be satisfactory to both artist and patron.[18]

The financial stakes of Fanzago's lawsuit were exceptional. While Fanzago originally sought an additional 20,000 ducats from the Carthusians, the first appraisal concluded that the Carthusians owed him only 13,908 ducats. The monks paid his daughter Vittoria 7,364 ducats in 1687, an adjusted sum based upon the new appraisal made in the same year.[19] Combined with the payment of 1,700 ducats in the year 1700, the Carthusians paid Fanzago and his heirs 9,064 ducats, nearly 4,000 ducats short of the amount sought after the first appraisal.[20] To give these totals a frame of reference in terms of cost of living, it has been calculated that renting a small apartment on the fashionable Via Toledo in 1640 cost 45 ducats a year. Should rent be considered 20 percent of one's living expenses, then a comfortable living in Naples in 1640 would require an income of 225 ducats a year.[21]

These sums were not necessarily the profits of Fanzago's enterprise; instead, they represented the labor of an extensive team of building specialists. The surviving documents from San Martino reveal that Fanzago supervised and collaborated with no fewer than twenty-two different specialists in marble cutting, *piperno* (a local Neapolitan stone) cutting, and *rotatori* (specialists in cylindrical sculptural components like balustrade shafts).

The monetary figures linked to Fanzago's activity at the Certosa di San Martino remain impressive even when compared against kingdomwide figures generated from contemporary industries. The Dogana delle Pecore of Foggia, the principal wool exchange of the kingdom of Naples, averaged 140,000 ducats of wool sold per year in the seventeenth century (1625–84).[22] Given that Fanzago was paid a total of 57,000 ducats over the course of thirty-three years of work at San Martino, he produced an average of 1,900 ducats worth of architectural sculpture at one site per year. With these figures in mind, Fanzago's production at one institution in one year is statistically significant, 1.4 percent, compared to the aggregate wool production in the entire kingdom of Naples. The value of Fanzago's work at the Certosa is impressive by both micro- and macro-economic standards.

The professional relationship between Fanzago and the Carthusians ultimately embodied the challenges faced by the civil authorities of Naples in regulating the economic activity of the kingdom. The problems and the potential solutions for the kingdom become explicit in the economic writing of Paolo Mattia Doria (1667–1746), Antonio Genovesi (1713–69), and Ferdinando Galiani (1728–87)—the leading figures of the Neapolitan Enlightenment.

NOTES

1. Anthony Blunt, *Neapolitan Baroque and Rococo Architecture* (London: Zwemmer, 1975), 5.
2. Blunt's passage and its insights into Neapolitan culture were discussed in J. Nicholas Napoli, *The Ethics of Ornament in Early Modern Naples: Fashioning the Certosa di San Martino* (Burlington, Vt.: Ashgate, 2015), 277–78.
3. The architectural appraisal is discussed at length in John Nicholas Napoli, "The Art of the Appraisal: Measuring, Evaluating, and Valuing Architecture in Early Modern Europe," *Memoirs of the American Academy in Rome* 54 (2009): 201–44.
4. For more on architectural appraisals, see ibid., 201–41.
5. This concept is articulated in Alina Payne, *The Architectural Treatise in the Italian Renaissance: Architectural Invention, Ornament, and Literary Culture* (Cambridge: Cambridge University Press, 1999), 52.
6. The following documents include printed and handwritten transcriptions of the appraisals and court rulings related to the case. At the Archivio Segreto Vaticano they include the following: S. R. Rota, *Positiones*, 622; R. P. D. Benincasa, *Neapolitana Mercedis pro Haeredibus Eq. Cosmi Fanzaga. Sumarium* (Rome, 1686); S. R. Rota, *Positiones*, 622; R. P. D. Benincasa, *Neapolitana Mercedis pro Vener. Carthusia S. Martini. Summarium* (Rome, 1686). The following documents are at the Archivio di Stato in Naples: Archivio Notarile, Notai del Seicento, Felice di Attano, 599/22, pp. 128v–152r, 162r–163v. *Conventio inter Regalis Monastero Sancti Martini Victoriam Fonzaga Joseph, et Alexandrum Corrado*; Monasteri Soppressi, Fascicolo 2051; R. P. D. Guaxardo,

*Neapolitana prætensæ Mercedis pro Ven. Carthusia Sancti Martini Neapolis. Summarium* (Rome, 1683).

7. Napoli, "Art of the Appraisal," 212–13. The architects parse these elements of the classical column into even smaller units. The Roman appraisers note how the height of the capital is measured from the lip of the top of the column, the collarino, to the crowning band of the column capital, or abacus. When measuring pilasters, the Neapolitans focus on the delicate molded components that form the crown and the base of a column or pilaster: the collarino above and the imoscapo below. While they measure the shaft of the pilaster itself, this dimension is set aside because it manufactured by workmen and not trained marble workers. They do note, however, that the shaft of a column actually has a double curvature: it is round in plan and has curvature in its elevation.

8. Napoli, "Art of the Appraisal," 212–16.

9. Vitruvius, *Ten Books on Architecture*, trans. I. D. Rowland (Cambridge: Cambridge University Press, 1999), book 3, chap. 5.2:51–52.

10. While the proportions follow a principle of commensuration, (*symmetria*), the actual numerical ratios that express *symmetria* become complex. Ingrid Rowland's translation of Vitruvius uses the word "symmetries" to express the proportional relationships of the components to one another and to the column as a whole. To give an example of the complexity of these ratios or symmetries, the abacus (the capping ring) of the capital of the Ionic order was to be the equivalent of the diameter of the shaft at its base, plus one-eighteenth part of that diameter. The height of the capital would be half of that measure. This would calculate to 19/36 the diameter of the column shaft at its base. See ibid., book 3, chap. 5.5:52. The symmetries are not consistent throughout Vitruvius's treatise. In book 4, chap. 1.1:54, Vitruvius comments that the height of the Ionic capital is one-third the diameter of the column. Also see Payne, *Architectural Treatise*, 41–45.

11. The testimonies of a sculptor, Giovanni Battista Cappelli, and a stone cutter, Antonio Caputo (Mastro d'Ascia), assert that both Pietro Sanbarberio and Pietro Antonio Valentino worked with Fanzago at the Monastery of S. Martino and the Church of the Gesù Nuovo and were considered to be the *discepoli* of the Cavaliere. Guaxardo, *Summarium*, art. 4.

12. The description of the large portals is as follows: "Le sette porte grandi nelle quatro cantonate dello inchlaustro tutte cho li loro ornamenti sopra cho li ovati sfondali fatti di bardiglio dove vengono le meze statue fatti cho scartocci atorno e cartelle cho scartoci e festoni intagliati cho li ripieni di bardiglio atorno ditte porte e segatura e squadratura e pulitura e intagli cho averle agiustate e ritocate in opera et assistitoci a fabbricarle si aprezano unite tutte sette insieme ducati tremila cho dichiaratione che tutte abino da

esse di quella perfezione cho forme alle due che stanno alla entrata del ditto inchlaustro dalla parte della cella del Reverendissimo padre priore dicho—3,000." In Archivio di Stato, Naples, Monasteri soppressi, fasc. 2160, f. 26. N. 24. It was previously published by Mario De Cunzo, "I documenti sull'opera di Cosimo Fanzago nella Certosa di San Martino," *Napoli Nobilissima* 6, fasc. 1–2 (1967): appendix 1, 104–6.

13. Margherita Azzi-Visentini, "Strapwork and Cartouches," in *The History of Decorative Arts: The Renaissance and Mannerism in Europe*, ed. Alain Gruber, 347–432 (New York: Abbeville Press, 1993), 350.

14. Palladio considered the use of the cartouche as contrary to what nature teaches about the simplicity of creation, and so it should be avoided. See ibid., 349.

15. The English definition of "cartouche" was taken from *The American Heritage Dictionary*, Second College Edition (Boston: Houghton Mifflin, 1985). The Italian definitions of *cartoccio* and *scartocciare* were taken from *Il nuovo Zingarelli Minore: Vocabolario della lingua Italia*, 11th ed. (Bologna: Nicola Zanichelli, 1987).

16. "In primis ci sono due ornamenti, dove stanno le pitture di Gioseppe Ribera, cioè Moisè, et Elia, e perche questi doi ornamenti sono centinati delle loro cornici tanto sopra quanto sotta, intendendosi però eccetuate li membretti di verde antica, che vanno sino all'colanino [collarino] del capitello. Questi sono tutti misurati, ma l'ornamento intendendosi le requadrature dentra, e fuora, che ad'una via ha un gusso [guscio], et l'altra un ovolo con suoi piani e sue cimase, con borgie e triangoli, con misco di breccia di francia, con il fondo di breccia minuta, che fà fuso alle requadratura con gocciole, menzoletti, scartocci, mezze giarre, cimasa in centino, e trà le giarre di qua, e di là vi sono commessi di verde antico, con listello bianco, e nero, e fondo di breccia di francia. Si che quest'opera di questi ornamenti si può apprezzare tutta insieme per non confondere la materia, e questo basti." Archivio di Stato, Naples, Monasteri Soppressi, fasc. 2143, fol. 315.

17. The word continues to be used in the emerging work of Paola D'Agostino, *Cosimo Fanzago scultore* (Naples: Paparo Edizioni, 2011), 209; and Sabina De Cavi, "Applied Arts in Naples: Materials and Artistic Techniques from Micro to Macro Cosmos," *West 86th: A Journal of Decorative Arts, Design History and Material Culture* 19, no. 2 (2012): 196–230.

18. The sculptor Giovanni Michelangelo Caccini; the painters Giovanni Battista Caracciolo, Giovanni Lanfranco, Jusepe de Ribera, and Viviano Codazzi; and the silversmiths Giandomenico Vinaccia and Gennaro Monte also believed that they were underpaid by the Carthusians. For a summary of these cases, see J. Nicholas Napoli, "Artists, Patrons, and Trust in Early

Modern Naples: The Case of the Certosa di San Martino," *California Italian Studies* 3, no. 1 (Fall 2012).

19. A. S. N., Archivio Notarile, Felice d'Attano, 599/22, f. 139v.

20. "Nel Tribunale della Nuntiatura compare il Procuratore del Monastero di S. Martino, e dice, come per parte del Cavaliere Cosmo Fonzaga gli è stata notificata un'Istanza, nella quale domanda ordinarsi alli Padri, che faccino rivedere à loro spese un'asserto apprezzo in virtù dell'accesso fatto ultimamente super faciem loci, & anco, che pro nunc paghino ducati 6695. di pretese partite indifficultabili." R. P. D. Guaxardo, no. 8, September 16, 1675.

21. Nino Leone, *La vita quotidiana a Napoli ai tempi di Masaniello* (Milan 1994), as cited in Michela Mantovani, "Moneta ed economia pubblica del Regno di Napoli e Politiche dei Beni Culturali nell'Area Napoletana," *Studi per una Rivalutazione Economica e Culturale del Mezzogiorno*, no. 69 (2000): 20.

22. This figure is taken from John Marino, *Pastoral Economics in the Kingdom of Naples* (Baltimore: Johns Hopkins University Press, 1988) 204–5.

THIRTEEN

# The Sansevero Chapel: A Case Study of the Neapolitan Enlightenment

*Salvatore Napolitano*

This essay examines the Chapel of Santa Maria della Pietà in Naples, better known as the Sansevero Chapel, and generally associated with Raimondo di Sangro, VII Prince of Sansevero, patron and brilliant inventor of the complex iconography of the chapel. A significant moment of convergence between art, patronage, philosophical and cultural trends, and even scientific experimentation, the chapel significantly embodies the delicate transition from the late baroque era to the early Neapolitan Enlightenment (see plate 13-1).

The Neapolitan Enlightenment accommodated two trends that coexisted in an uneasy detente: reverence to tradition and the impulse to modernize. Because of this problematic coexistence, the Enlightenment in Naples never reached the antireligious zeal and subversion of cultural and social hierarchies of the radical Enlightenment magisterially described by Jonathan Israel.[1]

Ultimately, the Sansevero Chapel represents a prime case study for the analysis of the two key terms of the Enlightenment's cultural ideology, reason and religion, which coexisted in a peculiar way in Naples, like in the Neoplatonic *Coincidentia oppositorum* first theorized by Nicola Cusano in the fifteenth century, and then recovered by Giordano Bruno for his *Mens insita omnibus*.

## *The* Pietatella

The origins of the Sansevero Chapel are more a matter of legend than of archaeological testimony. A legend testifies that the chapel was built on the ruins of the Temple of Isis, and Cesare d'Engenio Caracciolo, author of one of the most successful city guides of the seventeenth century, the *Napoli sacra*, states that in the late sixteenth century a man was unjustly sentenced to prison and while passing in front of Palazzo di Sangro saw the collapse of a part of the wall of the garden, and the image of the Virgin miraculously appeared to him. Declared innocent and released, the man commissioned a votive image depicting the *Pietà* as an act of devotion to the Virgin.

This image immediately became a sacred place of pilgrimage and an object of devotion. Shortly after, in fact, a seriously ill Giovan Francesco di Sangro, Duke of Torremaggiore, devoted himself to the *Pietà*. Healed, he built a chapel in her honor, named the Santa Maria della Pietà or Pietatella.[2]

In the early seventeenth century it was his son, Alessandro di Sangro, archbishop of Benevento, who commissioned major reconstruction in order to turn it into the family chapel. Of this first phase, there only remained the perimeter, some marble in the apse, and the image of the Virgin (see figure 13-1). The chapel's current configuration is the result of the commitment and the dedication of Raimondo di Sangro, who from 1745 began to invest massive efforts and money into the project.

The chapel has one nave with eight side chapels and a barrel vault with six windows. Originally, a suspension bridge connected the church directly with the Palazzo Sansevero. The current entrance that opens directly onto the nave was originally walled up. The original entrance was the Porta Nord. On top of this side door we can still read the inscription that effectively summarizes the significance of Raimondo's endeavor:

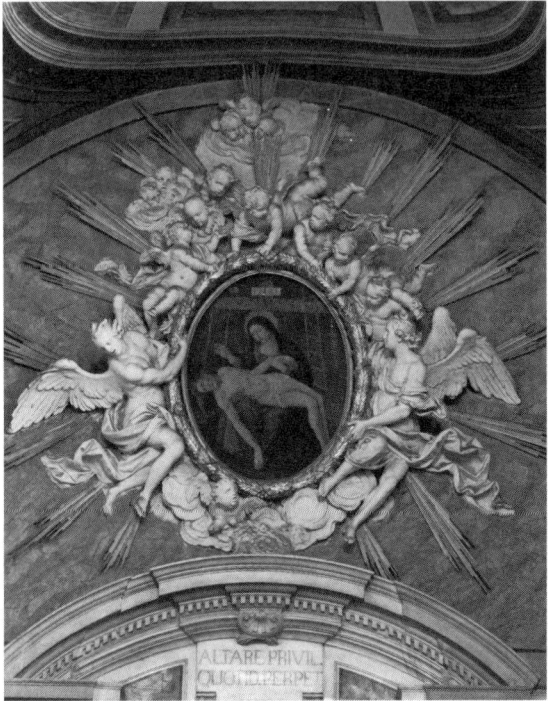

Figure 13-1. Unknown, *Pietà*, second half of the sixteenth century. The oval was framed in a starburst of stucco angels by Paolo Persico in 1769.

Whoever you are, traveler, townsman, countryman or foreigner, enter and piously pay homage to this prodigious ancient work: this noble family chapel, long since consecrated to the Virgin and greatly enlarged by the illustrious Prince of Sansevero, Don Raimondo di Sangro, to the glory of his forefathers and to immortally preserve his ashes and those of his family, in the year 1767. Observe with attentive eyes and veneration the urns of the heroes endowed with glory and contemplate with wonder this precious homage to the Divine work and the tombs of the departed, and when you have honored them, profoundly reflect and then proceed on your way.

Clearly, there is the glorification of the Prince and his family, but the inscription prompts also basic but important questions. What would the viewer have found in the chapel? What would cause the viewer to "profoundly reflect"? What was Raimondo di Sangro's deeper message? In order to answer these questions, we would have to reconstruct the activities and the interests of Raimondo di Sangro.

### Raimondo di Sangro, VII Prince of Sansevero

Raimondo di Sangro was born January 30, 1710, in Torremaggiore (Foggia, Puglia), where the Sansevero family had most of their possessions. His mother, Cecilia Gaetani dell'Aquila d'Aragona, died in December of that year. His father, Antonio di Sangro, following the death of his wife, indulged in the high culture of the aristocratic courts of Europe, so Raimondo was taken in by his grandfather Paolo di Sangro, VI Prince of Sansevero, and moved to Naples, where his ancestors had established their home in an impressive building in Piazza San Domenico Maggiore.[3]

Raimondo was educated in Rome at the Jesuit College, as was customary for young people of the most influential families of the time. The Roman years profoundly affected his interests. He was able to visit the extraordinary museum of Athanasius Kircher, an authentic *Wunderkammer* (cabinet of wonders) and a wonderful encyclopedia of the world.[4] Together with the study of philosophy and languages, Raimondo devoted himself with particular passion to the natural sciences and military architecture, on which he composed a treatise that remains unpublished.

Upon his grandfather's death in 1726, Raimondo found himself at only sixteen years of age the head of one of the most powerful families in southern Italy. He settled permanently in Naples, which had become the capital of an autonomous kingdom with the coronation of Charles of Bourbon in 1734. Raimondo initially had an excellent relationship with the new king, culminating in 1740 with his appointment as Cavaliere dell'Ordine di San Gennaro.

The king was particularly benevolent to him because of Di Sangro's loyal commitment in military actions against the Austrians, utilizing his extraordinary inventions and machinery. For example, in 1739 he invented an innovative hydraulic machine and a rifle capable of firing with compressed air, and in 1741 a cannon, more powerful and lighter than those normally used at the time. His expertise in the military arts, which also earned him the admiration of the principal European courts, was finally formalized in his publication of *Pratica di esercizj militari per l'infanteria* in 1747.

In addition to his work as a military engineer, Raimondo already had nurtured a proper interest in the literary arts. In 1743, he had been admitted to the Accademia della Crusca with the nickname of "Esercitato," while the following year he obtained permission from Pope Benedict XIV to read the *Libri proibiti*. He also studied the French *philosophes*, as well as scientific treatises and texts of alchemy and the Masonic tradition.

Di Sangro cultivated an extraordinary passion for many different experiments, ideally reconnecting with the southern experimentalist and empiricist tradition. In Naples, these traditions saw the peculiar coexistence of scientific phenomena, geological activities, and the mythological fascination variously related to the presence of Vesuvius and its activities.[5]

Among his most amazing inventions were a fully waterproof fabric; a *lume perpetuo*; fireworks of colors never seen before; drugs that earned him a reputation as a magician, healer, and portentous soothsayer; artificial stones; colored marbles; and a revolutionary polychrome printing process made possible by a machine that he built in the basement of his own palace.

These scientific and literary achievements earned him great fame but fomented derogatory rumors and legends about his interest and abilities in sorcery and magic. His affiliation with Freemasonry, culminating with his investiture as Grande Maestro della Loggia Napoletana in August 1750, further provoked rumors.

And so in 1751, when he published his *Lettera apologetica*, focusing on the analysis of an ancient system of signs (the Quipu) used by the Incas of Peru, but rich with references to heretical authors and to the world of Freemasonry, the condemnation by the religious authority was inevitable.

Although presented as an apology for the effectiveness of the communication system of the ancient Incas, and composed following the recent publication of the *Lettres d'une péruvienne*, published by Françoise de Graffigny in 1747, the *Lettera apologetica* included broad praise for free-thinking and praise for unorthodox theories about the origin of the world, of humankind, and writing. Judged as heretical, and harshly attacked by several pamphlets, the work was banned by the *Congregazione dell'indice dei Libri proibiti* in February 1752, and even the publication of a *Supplica* sent to the pope by Raimondo one year later did not serve to exclude the *Lettera* from the list of *Libri proibiti*.

Isolated by the court entourage, and by the same king who back in July 1751 had formally condemned the Masonic lodges, Raimondo devoted himself almost completely to scientific experiments, literature,[6] and particularly to the renovation of the family's chapel, personally developing a complex iconographic project.

He made his final public appearance in spectacular fashion in July 1770 navigating the coastline of the Gulf of Naples on board the *Carrozza Marittima*, a boat of his own invention, which proceeded faster on waves through an ingenious system of blades that looked like wheels. He died March 22, 1771, at Palazzo Sansevero.

## The Chapel

Having reconstructed Raimondo's intellectual and biographical profile, we can probably better understand his most important commitment, and finally his own intellectual testament: the Sansevero Chapel.

As mentioned, since the 1740s and until his death, Raimondo devoted his energies almost exclusively to the chapel. In 1752, driven by strong and new ambitions, he called Antonio Corradini, a sculptor of European fame and a Freemason, to Naples. However, the sudden death of Corradini that year marked the arrival of other artists to the chapel, including Francesco Celebrano, Giacomo Lazzari, Paolo Persico, Francesco Queirolo, Fortunato Onelli, and Giuseppe Sanmartino, the sculptor of the *Veiled Christ*.[7]

I will not dwell on the many issues of attribution related to the individual works of art, but we would rather try a comprehensive interpretation of the cultural and ideological value of the chapel. In order to do that, I identify three different levels of communication, coinciding with as many as three different chronological and conceptual phases: the vault (*The Glory of Heaven*), the statues of the Virtues, and the labyrinthine floor.

## *The Vault*: The Glory of Heaven

Signed and dated 1749 by Francesco Maria Russo, the fresco that covers the vault represent *The Glory of Heaven* (see plate 13-2) and is one of the first works commissioned by the prince for the chapel.

The artist still is little known, but some archival documentation ensures that Russo had already been in contact with Raimondo in 1743, when—under his direction—he painted the anteroom to the sacristy of the Chapel of the Treasury of San Gennaro.

Still strongly influenced by Francesco Solimena's style, Russo painted a powerful fresco with illusionistic architectural structures, sudden glimpses, angels and figures ideally converging toward the center. The dove of the Holy Spirit stands out in a burst of light, crowned by a triangular nimbus.

All around the chapel, six windows illuminate *The Glory of Heaven*, and between the windows are the portraits of the saints of the di Sangro family. On the ceiling, an illusion of a dome completes the scenic decoration. The bright and radiant colors used by the artist are the result of a formula invented by Raimondo.

Despite the expressive power of the fresco, the prince was dissatisfied with the result. Raimondo, in fact, recommended to his son Vincenzo to commission—without changing the subject represented—the painting to the "best artist that *he* could find," in order to realize a "nicer fresco" conforming with the quality of the other works in the chapel. However, Vincenzo di Sangro left this wish unfulfilled.

Particularly significant in the fresco is the triangle that dominates the center of the scene together with the dove. In fact, this geometric figure has multiple meanings: for the Christians it represents the Trinity; in the Pythagorean system, the capital letter delta—triangular-shaped—is the symbol of the Cosmic Birth; and in the Masonic culture it is a distinctive sign of the *Gran Maestro*.

## *The Tombs and the Statues of* The Virtues

The chapel has one nave, and the end of it opens to the apse with the altar. At the sides are the tombs of the male members of the di Sangro family, and leaning against the piers that separate the arches are the sculptures dedicated to the women of the family (except the *Disinganno*, erected in memory of the Raimondo's father, Antonio di Sangro).

According to the intentions of Raimondo, the famous *Veiled Christ*, currently at the center of the nave, would have been placed in an underground cave (kind of *succorpo*) designed to accommodate the future graves of the family members, ideally illuminated by two eternal candles—the *lumi perpetui*, invention of the same Raimondo, which are placed at the head and the feet of Christ.

The statues of *The Virtues* are therefore the true heart of the iconographic project designed by Raimondo. I will analyze only three statues, truly exceptional for their artistic quality and for the same complexity of their iconographic messages.

### CHASTITY

Corradini's extraordinary abilities are highlighted here by the veil, gently resting on the body of the woman with an extreme elegance and naturalness, as if the vapor exhaled by her breath contributed to making it moist and extremely adherent to her skin. The expression of the woman, the tree of life, the broken headstone, are all symbols of a life ended too soon (see figure 13-2).

The bas-relief on the base also refers to the relation between life and death, with the *Noli me tangere* in which Christ appears to Mary Magdalene as a gardener.

Some scholars have also proposed interpreting the woman as an allegory of Wisdom. Rosanna Cioffi notes that the *Veiled Truth* engraved in the frontispiece of the *Encyclopédie* highly resembles the Chastity of Corradini (an active Freemason). In support of this hypothesis, the scholar stresses that the same oak tree growing out of bare rock could legitimately be considered as an allusion to the *arbor philosophica*.[8] According to this perspective the reference to the Veiled Isis, goddess beloved by Freemasonry, seems quite natural. The popular tradition that believes that the Chastity was located in the same place where the statue of Isis once stood in Νεάπολις (ancient Greek Naples), is highly suggestive, but it has no basis in historical documentation.

### DISILLUSION

Executed by Francesco Queirolo between 1753 and 1754, *Disillusion* is dedicated to Raimondo's father, Antonio di Sangro, who finally expiated his lush and rakish lifestyle after his return to Naples by converting to the monastic life.

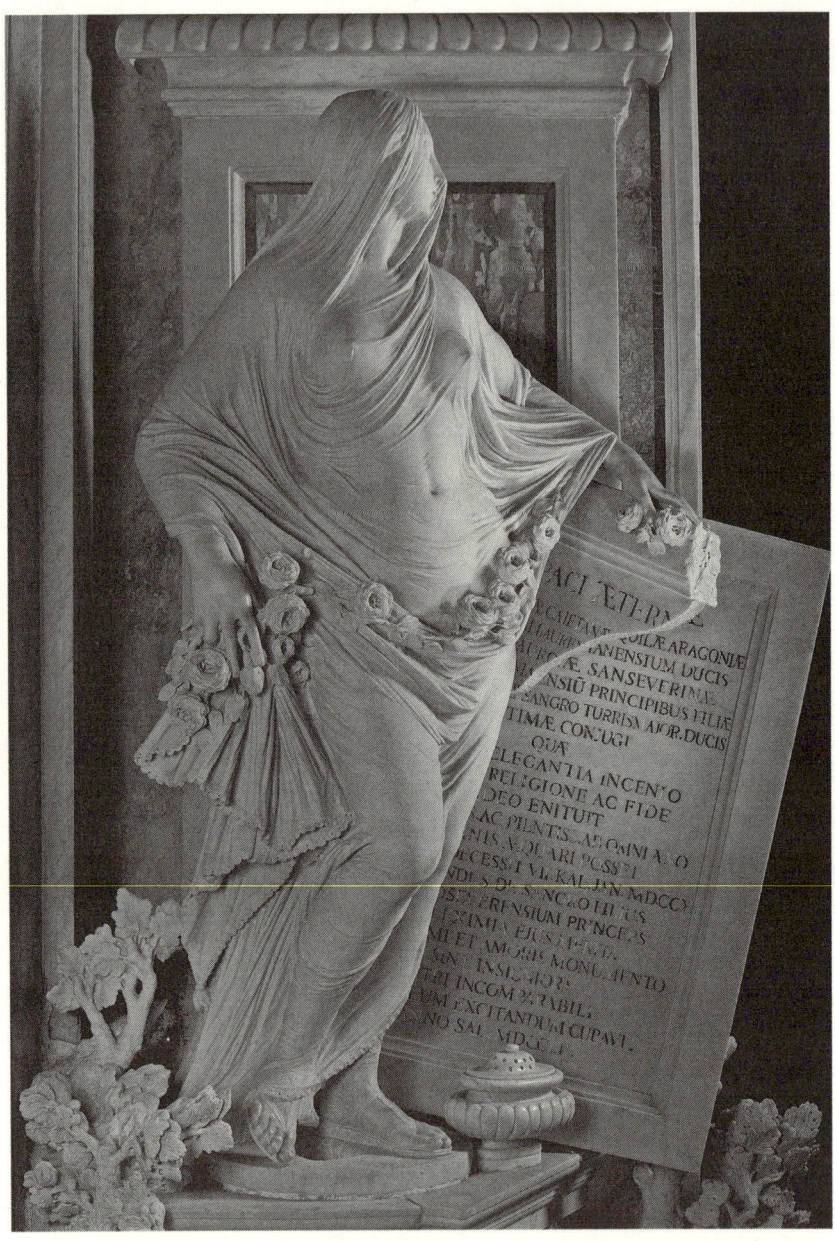

Figure 13-2. Antonio Corradini, *Chastity*, 1752. The statue is dedicated to the memory of Raimondo's mother, Cecilia Gaetani dell' Aquila d'Aragona, who died when he was not yet one year old (December 26, 1710).

The sculptural group depicts a man trying to liberate himself from his sins, represented in the extraordinary and astonishing net realized by the artist. A winged spirit, bearing a small flame on its forehead, symbolizes human intellect and assists the man in liberating himself from the tangled mesh, while indicating the globe at his feet, symbol of worldly passions. The globe supports an open book, the sacred text of the Bible, but also one of the three "great lights" of Freemasonry (see figure 13-3).

The bas-relief on the base, with the episode of "Jesus gives sight to the blind," accompanies and reinforces the meaning of the allegory: there are some things that human reason can neither understand nor explain.

The *Disillusion*'s iconography, as Giangiuseppe Origlia contends, is absolutely innovative and was a creative invention of the prince.[9] The reference to the contrast between light and darkness, evoked by the allegory on the bas-relief with the phrase "Qui non vident videant" (Those who do not see shall see), and by the biblical passages inscribed in the open book, seems to be a clear reference to Masonic initiations, in which the beginner ritually went blindfolded, and then opened his eyes to the new light of truth kept by the Lodge.

Raimondo wrote a wonderfully heartfelt dedication, in which his father's life is placed as an immortal example of "human fragility, which is not allowed to have great virtue without vice."

### VEILED CHRIST

The third work is undoubtedly the most impressive: the *Veiled Christ*. Initially conceived by Antonio Corradini, who only realized a terra-cotta sketch, the work was finally carved by a young and talented Neapolitan artist, Giuseppe Sanmartino (1720–93). Sanmartino demonstrates his artistic autonomy, creating an original and technically outstanding sculpture (see figures 13-4, 5 and plate 13-3).

The most powerful point of interest is the veil that covers the body of Christ, lacerated and crucified, yet still seemingly pulsing with life. The swollen vein on the forehead, the wounds of the nails on the feet and hands, his side pierced by the Roman soldier's lance, his last liberating death, are in fact all signs of intense and extreme scientific research.

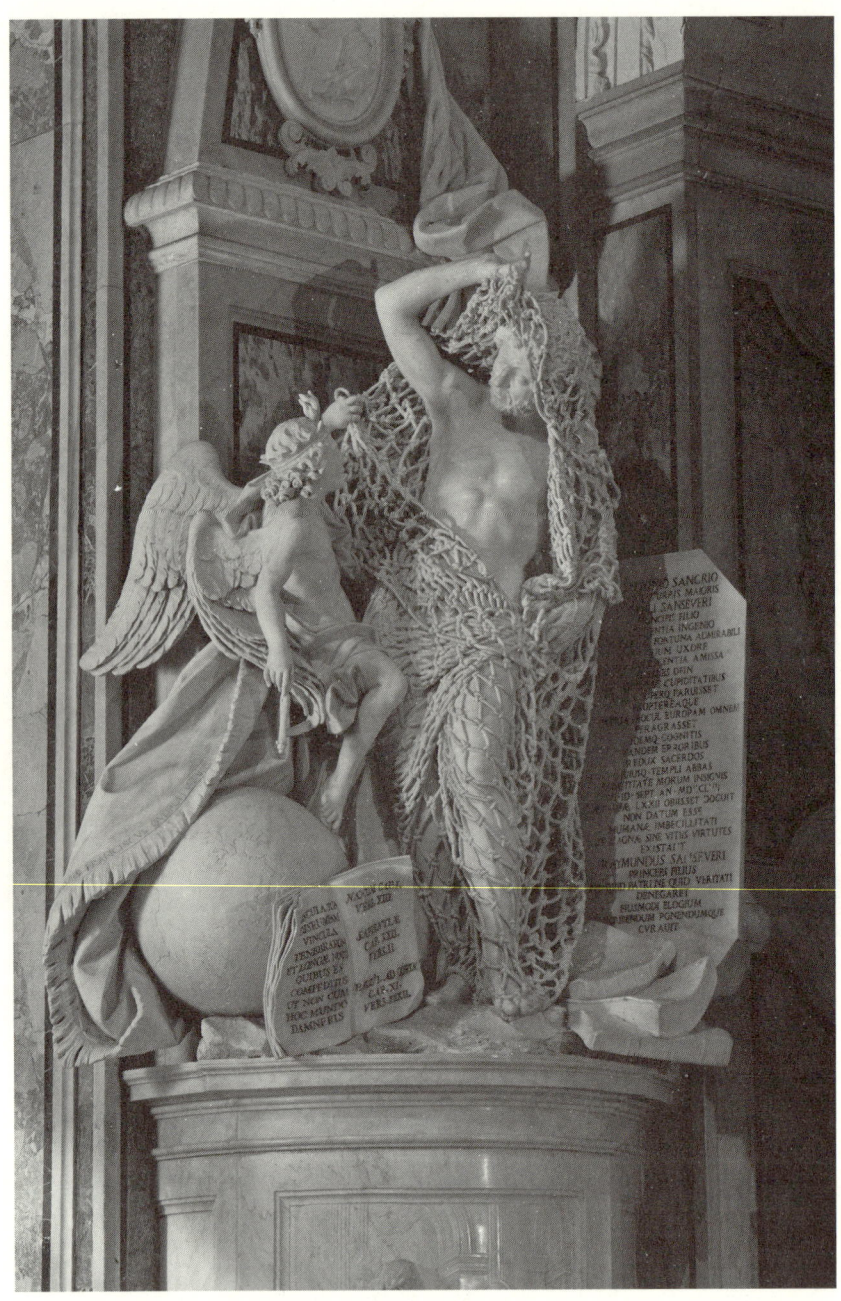

Figure 13-3. Francesco Queirolo, *Disillusion*, 1753.

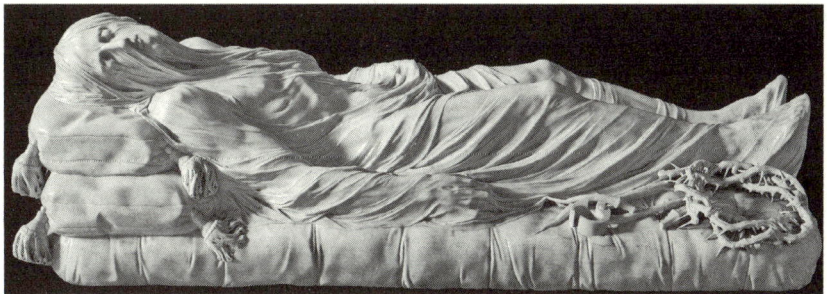

Figure 13-4. Giuseppe Sanmartino, *Veiled Christ*, 1753.

Sanmartino's art is solved here in a dramatic evocation, which finds in Christ's suffering the symbol of the redemption of all humanity. I find it very significant, finally, that in this work Raimondo and his artist give more emphasis to direct communication with the viewer—to the physical evidence of life and death—rather than obscure codes or inexplicable intellectual iconography.

Here is all the evidence of a moral message that Raimondo wanted to offer to the future members of his family, who—as I mentioned—would have been buried in the underground cave where the *Veiled Christ* was originally intended to be. Having shown a series of *exempla virtutis* variously connected to the theme of wisdom and reason as guides for humankind, Raimondo offers here a powerful and inescapable *memento mori*, through this dramatic and impressive humanization of the divine.

Not surprisingly, the stylistic perfection of the veil generated many legends, some describing it as the result of presumptive experiments made by Raimondo, instead of considering it as an authentic masterpiece of Western sculpture.

*The Labyrinthine Floor*

Finally, the third level of our analysis: the labyrinthine floor. By the mid-1760s, Raimondo envisioned an intricate and multicolored marble labyrinth floor for his chapel, finally commissioned to Francesco Celebrano. The design involves alternating swastikas with concentric squares placed in perspective and an infinite white line. The polychrome inlays have different

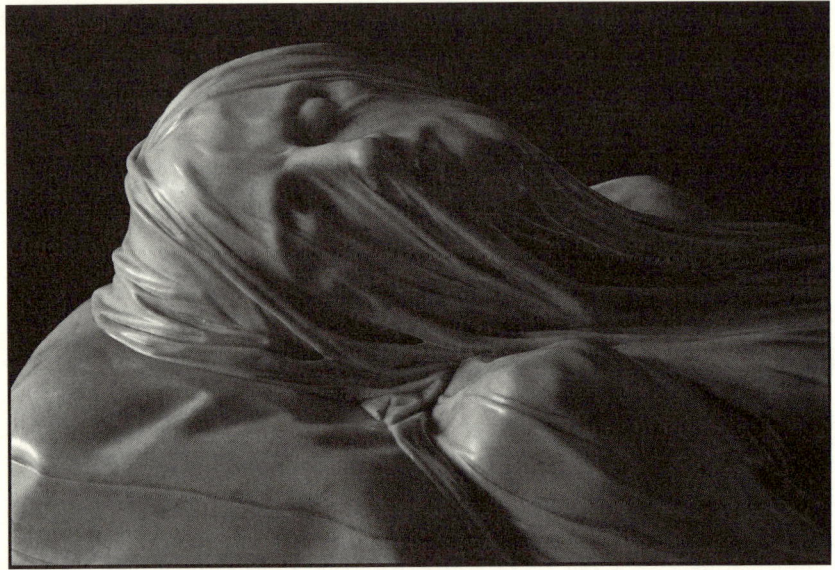

Figure 13-5. Giuseppe Sanmartino, *Veiled Christ*, 1753, detail.

shades, from blue to white, giving depth to the composition. The choice of the labyrinthine floor fits perfectly with the allegorical itinerary designed by the prince for his chapel (see figure 13-6).

The maze pattern, already used in the classical tradition, and rich with references to the hermetic tradition, represents the difficulty in attaining knowledge. Dating back to the great astral myths of the ancient world, the swastika symbolized the cosmic movement; the concentric squares, alternating with swastikas, allude to the four squares of the elements.

Generally, the labyrinth, found in many Gothic cathedrals and in all the "dwellings of the philosophers," are the alchemical image of the *Grande Opera*. As Raimondo says in his will, the execution was extremely complex, but it was eventually finished, as testified by a nineteenth-century engraving. The floor of the chapel had been changed in the late nineteenth century, when a collapse of the south wall severely damaged the original floor.

However, some of the original floor slabs have survived and are still visible in front of the tomb of Raimondo. Others are exposed in the underground cave and in the sacristy. Finally, also in relation to the messages expressed through the statues of *The Virtues*, I think that Raimondo intended

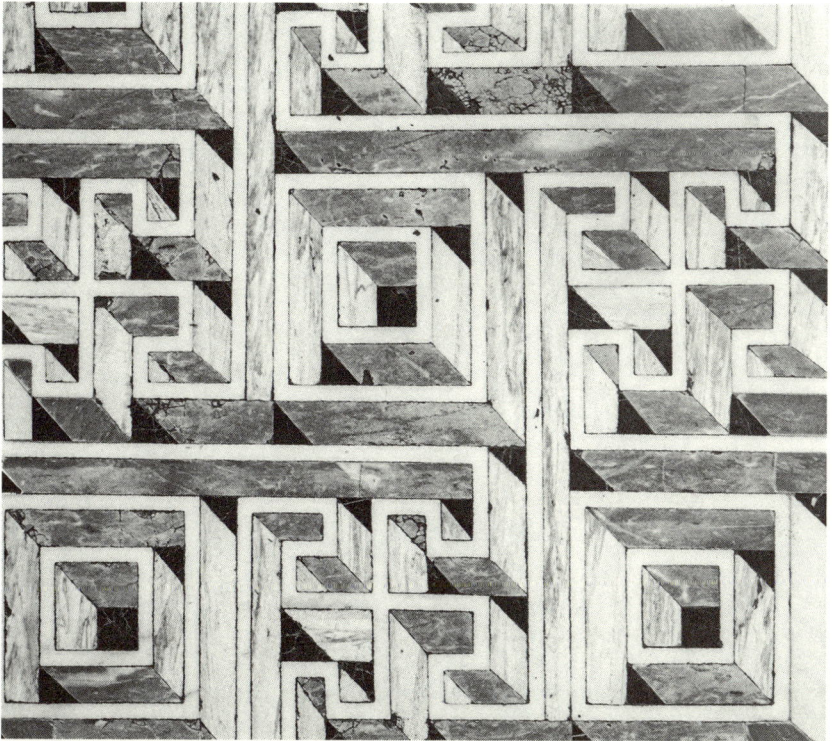

Figure 13-6. The labyrinthine floor.

to express, on the one hand, the difficulties of gaining ultimate knowledge, and on the other the unpredictability of life and fate.

*Raimondo di Sangro's Theological Vision: "Reasonable Faith"*

We could read the chapel from this perspective: to access the Eternal Glory (the Vault), humans must walk through the labyrinth of life, inspired by the *exempla* provided by the di Sangro family members (the Statues of the Virtues), never forgetting the tragic sacrifice of the son of God, who became man to atone for the sins of the world.

Therefore, the previous view of Raimondo di Sangro as exclusively devoted to Masonic science should be slightly reconsidered. His theological

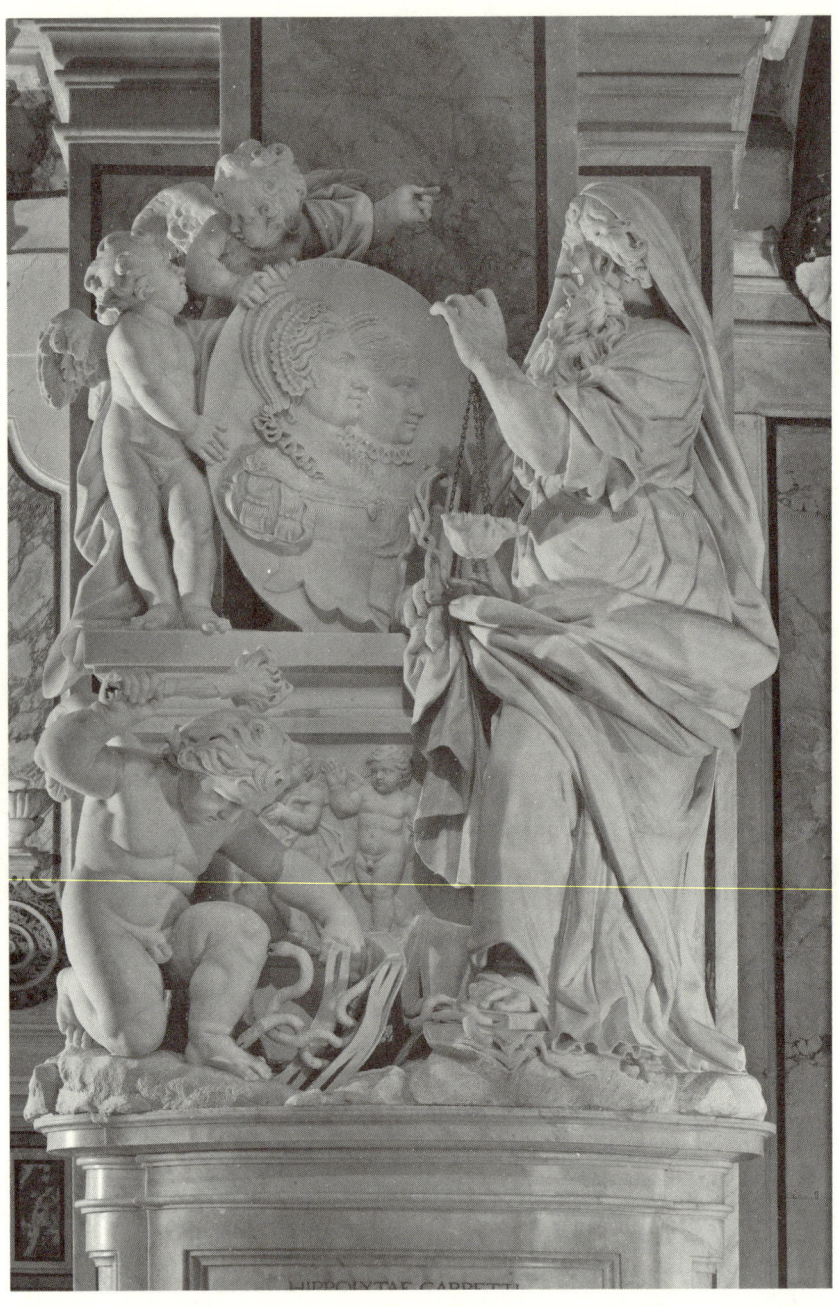

Figure 13-7. Fortunato Onelli, Francesco Celebrano, *Zeal of Religion*, 1767.

vision seems authentic and profound, as—among other things—could be proved by the *Zeal of Religion* (see fig. 13-7). One of the last works made for the Chapel in 1767 by Fortunato Onelli, it is usually described as the more "orthodox" of the sculptures.

Perfectly aligned to his times, Raimondo seeks to overcome the contradictions between reason and religion, finally conceiving religion as a sincere and extreme act of surrender; and trust in a divine that completely incorporates the vast universe of the irrational. Thus, there is no contradiction between reason and religion; on the contrary, they live here without apparent contradictions, mutually reinforcing each other.

But what inspired Raimondo in this pursuit of reconciliation? In the midfifteenth century, the Neoplatonic philosopher Nicola Cusano, intending to demonstrate the impossibility of knowing God rationally, conceived him as a *coincidentia oppositorum*, or a union of opposites. Using a parallel with the figure of the circle, Cusano concluded that God is the point in which all the opposites coincide. In God coincide the light and darkness, the true and the false, the black and the white, men and women, because they are finally identical with each other.

Continuing along this line, Cusano proposes a distinction between reason and intellect, in which the latter, assuming a value very close to the imagination, fall under the divine, enabling human beings, through intuition and mysticism, to perceive things inevitably contradictory at a logical and rational level.

Reason, therefore, remains on a human level, while the more broadly conceived intellect now becomes an instrument to be enlightened by God and to enlighten the truth. After more than a century, a similar vision will inspire Giordano Bruno (1548–1600) and his extraordinary *mens insita omnibus* (mind present in all things) as the first principle of Nature. Both of these metaphysical visions refer directly to the relationship between God and humanity, which tends to legitimize a vision of the world in relation to God and a vision of God in relation to the world.

The nexus between Bruno's and Cusano's theories on the relationship between God and world was quite clear during the eighteenth century. In particular, the most prevalent of Bruno's interpretations during the seventeenth and eighteenth centuries derived from Pierre Bayle's reading in his *Dictionnaire* that presents the philosopher as a pantheist.[10] This interpretation also circulated in the Neapolitan context surrounding Sansevero, as clearly demonstrated by Antonio Genovesi's *Metaphysicarum elementa* (1764).[11] Along with these elements, I want to stress again the crucial importance of the years spent by Raimondo in Rome at the Jesuit College, and the decisive influence of Kircher's cultural model.

I consider these cultural references to be decisive in Raimondo's reception of Bruno's and Cusano's philosophies, finally orienting him into seeking a new dialogue between reason and religion, particularly important after the extraordinary changes initiated by the scientific revolution of the late seventeenth century.

In fact, following this revolutionary historical and cultural junction, with decisive implications for religion, Kircher declared Holy Scripture and modern thought entirely reconcilable based on the extraordinary potential of the human intellect in its understanding of the world.

Faced with the problem of the infinitude of the universe demonstrated by modern cosmology, with the subsequent destruction of the creationist theories on which the Christian church founded its political legitimacy, Kircher recovers Bruno's thesis on the infinity of the universe as the explanation of the infinite power of God.[12]

According to this prospective, Bruno's role is therefore crucial because it allowed interpreters of the time to rethink the relationship between the Platonic tradition of medieval theology and Renaissance philosophy in the light of the new cosmological discoveries of the late seventeenth century. Also, Cusano's and Bruno's philosophies offered a concept of *mens* [mind] as a measure of all things precisely because it is a direct emanation of the divine mind: as it produces all things, so the human mind was potentially able to know them all. In this way, human reason was presented as a supreme ordering reason.

We can thus better understand the exceptional project of Kircher's *Wunderkammer*, a wonderful encyclopedia of the world and an extreme effort to rationalize reality at precisely the moment when contemporary scientific innovation was profoundly changing the perception of reality and the classification of knowledge.

It is therefore perfectly legitimate to assume that Sansevero reconnected these cultural and philosophical concerns, which also took into consideration libertine literature, during his stay in Rome.[13]

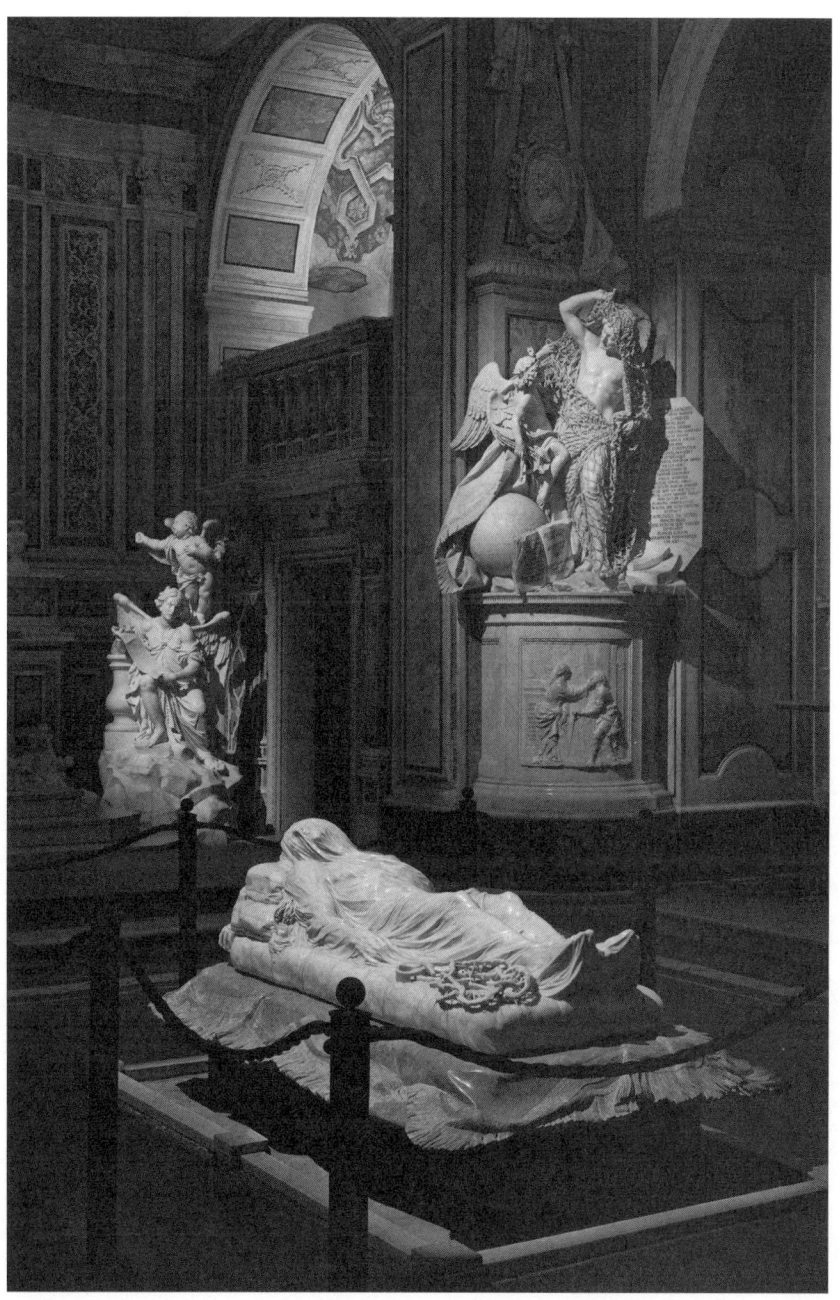

Figure 13-8. San Severo Chapel with *Veiled Christ* and *Disillusion*.

In the early Neapolitan Enlightenment, therefore, through this particular cultural tradition, which I have briefly tried to reconstruct, both Cusano's and Bruno's metaphysics had appeared to Raimondo di Sangro as the ideal solution to overcome any possible theoretical—and moral—contradiction between reason and religion.

This philosophical framework allowed him to effectively transform a legitimate and declared personal glorification into a genuinely authentic and profound religious action, in which the human experience of family members become the paradigm of a global history, which deals with the meaning of the life and the beyond, and ultimately with God and humanity.

For a "famous investigator of the most recondite mysteries of the Nature" (even human nature), Raimondo di Sangro truly struggled with this unstable balance between two eras. This was vividly brought to life in the extreme humanization of Christ embodied in Sanmartino's extraordinary *Veiled Christ*. It was to be perceived as the more "reasonable act of faith," and the final solution to the problem of human limitation in a rational understanding of the mystery of religion.

## NOTES

I am grateful to Fabrizio Masucci, president of the Fondazione Museo Cappella Sansevero, who allowed me to publish all the images used in this essay. I'm deeply indebted to Stanislao Pugliese: his guidance and mentorship have been priceless in these years, helping me grow both culturally and personally. The translation from Italian and the emphases are my own.

1. Jonathan Israel, *A Revolution of the Mind: Radical Enlightenment and the Intellectual Origins of Modern Democracy* (Princeton, N.J.: Princeton University Press, 2011), and *Democratic Enlightenment: Philosophy, Revolution, and Human Rights, 1750–1790* (New York: Oxford University Press, 2013).

2. Cesare D'Engenio Caracciolo, *Napoli sacra* (Naples: Ottavio Beltrano: ad istantia de Francesco Buonocore, 1623), 262–64.

3. The main source for the biographical reconstruction of Raimondo di Sangro is the second volume of Giangiuseppe Origlia's *Istoria dello studio di Napoli*. Additional information is available in the anonymous *Breve nota di quel che si vede in casa del Principe di Sansevero* (first edition, 1776; enlarged, 1767), and clearly in Raimondo's literary works. Together with these sources, we can add information contained in the reports of travelers and guides, in letters, literary texts, and archival documents variously related to the activities of the prince.

4. Paula Findlen, *Athanasius Kircher: The Last Man Who Knew Everything* (New York: Routledge, 2004).

5. Pietro Vivenzio, *Sepolcri Nolani*, ed. Salvatore Napolitano (Bologna: Il Mulino, 2011), vii–lxxxviii.

6. At the same time, he maintained correspondence with the greatest exponents of the contemporary République des Lettres, adhering to the Società Colombaria of Florence, publishing the *Dissertation sur une lampe antique* in 1756, and between 1764 and 1767 funding the publication of a new edition in five volumes of the Cesare Ripa's *Iconologia*, a very important iconographic treatise, published for the first time in 1593.

7. Rosanna Cioffi, *La Cappella Sansevero: Arte barocca e ideologia massonica* (Salerno: Edizioni, 1994).

8. Ibid.

9. Paolino Giovanni Giuseppe Origlia, *Istoria dello studio di Napoli* (Naples: Giovanni di Simone, 1753–54), 366.

10. Pasquale Terracciano, "'Nemici et impazienti di poliarchia': Riflessioni sul rapporto tra Giordano Bruno e Shelomon Ibn Gabirol," in *Sogni, favole e storie: Seminario su Giordano Bruno*, ed. O. Catanorchi and D. Pirillo, 551–75 (Pisa: Edizioni della Normale 2007).

11. Saverio Ricci, *La fortuna del pensiero di Giordano Bruno 1600–1750* (Florence: Le Lettere, 1990), 345.

12. Danielis Georgi Morhofii, *Dissertatio de sole igneo* (Kilonii, 1672).

13. An important element that confirms this reconstruction can be traced in Raimondo's publishing activities. In 1751, in fact, he printed *Il Conte di Gabalì ovvero Ragionamenti sulle scienze segrete tradotti dal francese da una Dama italiana, a' quali si è aggiunto in fine il Riccio rapito poema del Signor Alessandro Pope tradotto d'inglese dal Signor Antonio Conti* (London [but Naples] 1751), proposing the translation of a well-known forbidden text of the esoteric literature of the seventeenth century: *Le Comte de Gabalis*, published in Paris in 1670 by Nicolas de Montfaucon de Villars. Sansevero's translation was probably solicited by the publication of a new English edition in 1742, in which *Le Comte de Gabalis* was accompanied by another Villars work, the *Nouveaux entretiens*, in which the main character is very significantly the master "Jean le Brun," proposed as the hypothetical descendant of the reformer of Christian morality, Giordano Bruno. Saverio Ricci, *La fortuna del pensiero di Giordano Bruno 1600–1750* (Florence: Le Lettere, 1990), 175.

FOURTEEN

## Caravaggio's Mercy in Naples

*Terence Ward*

Outside my window, the swollen Arno surges under Ponte alle Grazie or Bridge of the Graces. A thick autumn mist slowly wraps its gray shroud over Filippo Brunelleschi's cupola. The orange jigsaw of terracotta roofs, domes, towers, spires, pigeon roosts, and satellite dishes soon vanishes from sight. Below, shrewd merchants bargain with foreign shoppers while the few surviving artisans scurry to appointed rounds, heels clicking crisply on stone-laid medieval alleys.

Each day, this once-refined Renaissance city buckles under the weight of mass tourism. Last traces of jewelers, sculptors, artists, and the dying silk trade of Florence lie submerged under a flood of Chinese plastic knock-offs, t-shirts, kebab takeouts, and postcards. Ambulant vendors sprawl out their wares for countless busloads of travelers. Troupes of Senegalese unfurl sheets laden with fake Prada and Gucci bags. Young Moroccans lay down posters of saccharine landscapes and iconic David with his anatomical wonder. Chinese hawkers dangle counterfeit scarves from their arms. Only in the evening, when the hordes of modern-day Visigoths march back to waiting buses with their cheap trinkets of plunder, only then does the city exhale in relief.

I find myself here, far from the concrete canyons of Manhattan, or the lofty Tehran where I grew up in the days of the Shah, or in the anarchy of Athens where I was based as a cross-cultural consultant for a decade working across the Persian Gulf. All of that changed when I met Idanna, whose magnetic voice seized me one evening in the East Village.

We had both been invited to a storytelling dinner at an Iranian friend's flat. Ironically, each of us had separately decided not to go to the gathering, but because of my friend's melodramatic insistence over the phone—he threatened to throw himself from his third-story window—he was able to lure us there.

So I arrived at the candlelit table and when my turn came I offered the story of Nikos Kazantzakis—author of *Zorba the Greek*—who defied his excommunication by Orthodox priests by carving on his gravestone perched in the hills above Heraklion, "I hope for nothing, I fear nothing, I am free." When we circled the table, Idanna spoke softly, poetically, and told us about a world where Asia spilled into the green Pacific waters. This island was her home. Struck by her words, I knew that I had to know more. Two years later, we were married on Madison Avenue and 25th Street in Manhattan in the Italianate Appellate Courthouse during a blinding December blizzard that blanketed in a white cloak the city for days.

Here in Italy, I've seen that Idanna carries a wide, cosmopolitan vision that sets her leagues apart from the smug Florentine society that has been feeding off the city's legacy for centuries instead of preserving the best of the past for the sake of the future. Idanna's style differs dramatically. She chooses to play it low-key, unpretentious, and understated.

Peering through the Florentine fog from my desk, I gaze beyond the old cypress in a nearby garden. My eyes fall on two aged figures standing by the bridge staring down at the Arno's rising waters. They do not move and stand transfixed. Decades still have not washed away their memories of November 4, 1966. On that morning, the Great Flood breached the embankments, submerging the city in surging waves and an avalanche of mud.

A burst of rain lashes at the windowpanes. Suddenly, I turn to find Idanna standing silently behind me. On winter days like these, a deep melancholy overwhelms her. Her mood changes when the humid chill seeps through our walls and settles in. And she is not alone. Most of her ever-feuding Guelphs and Ghibellines succumb too. Pushing back her chestnut-hued hair, she sighs.

"My Neapolitan grandmother rarely smiled, but when she was bedridden, I remember that all I had to do was to utter the word *Napoli* and a sudden spark would light up her dark blue eyes."

Though I never met Idanna's grandmother, I know she had two remarkably different sons. Each reflected life's great extremes. Her first, Emilio Pucci, shocked the dreary postwar fashion world and exploded into the sixties with succulent colors—hot pink, turquoise, and lime—in psychedelic prints drawn under a Tuscan sky. Her second son, Puccio, chose the opposite trajectory. After separating from his young wife who left for Africa, he closed his palace doors and chose to retreat in solitary seclusion.

So Idanna grew up in a shadowy world with random bursts of sunlight when her uncle's models preened on the palazzo roof for photo shoots with the Duomo in the background. At eighteen, uncle Emilio helped her escape to New York where she worked at Saks for two seasons. But once she understood that fashion was not her path, she set out for Southeast Asia and settled on an Indonesian island. There, she studied Balinese mythology and then wrote a book, *The Epic of Life*, about the ceiling paintings of the ancient Royal Court of Justice of Bali inspired by an episode from the *Mahabarata* that hauntingly reminded her of Dante's journey into the afterlife.

They say her grandmother, *nonna* Augusta, was a religious woman, quietly severe, who carried the scars of polio from childhood. Yet, sometimes, *nonna* would amuse her granddaughter by recounting memories of a Pompeii-red villa flooded by magical sunrises, when eastern light poured across the great jade bay circling from Sorrento to Posillipo.

Staring out my window into the mist, Idanna's words about her *nonna* linger in the air. "You know, in my family," she says, "the word *Napoli* always conjures up light."

For myself, Naples holds another pocket of illumination, the Istituto Universitario Orientale, set in the historic center, which happens to be one of Europe's finest centers of Near Eastern studies. A leading expert on Persepolis, Adriano Rossi, teaches there. I have urgent need to speak with him about my book on Iran.

"Adriano just wrote," I reply. "He's back at the Orientale."

"Yes, *andiamo*, let's go!," she says without missing a beat.

Next morning early, we drop by to bid our farewells to Idanna's father seated behind his desk in the darkened office. A single desk lamp casts its rays downward on his documents. Hearing about our journey south, he raises his eyes and smiles. Puccio was born in Naples.

Speaking in his clipped British accent, he asks me, "You know what they say, old boy?"

"No, tell me, Puccio," I coax him.

"Below Rome, they say, Italy ends and Africa begins."

Then he pauses, negating the words he just uttered. "Terribly mean, all that. Well, don't you listen to them, old boy! I adore Naples. Haven't been back there since the war. It has been such a long time . . ."

Drifting off in thought, he then catches himself and waves his finger sternly: "Now, for heaven's sake, don't leave anything in your car!"

I nod respectfully and we turn to leave.

By the time we pass into Umbria, the rain slackens. The fog begins to lift. Rolling hills topped with fortress citadels float lightly above the highway. Soon, green plains of Sabina surround us. We circle Rome's immense periphery with massive Autogrills offering inedible fast food and quick coffee injections, and enter into the land called *il Mezzogiorno*: "High Noon." I follow all arrows pointing south to Napoli.

Idanna sleeps as I pass the invisible line that splits one mentality from the other—the work ethic of Milano from the *arrangiarsi* of Naples or "the art of making do." A look of contentment has settled over her face. Recounting her country's layered culture, she has guided me over the years through the labyrinth of Italian customs, where blunders can often end with final judgment.

By late afternoon, the sky dims with twilight streaks of violet and coral. Our long journey comes to an end on a corniche that hugs the sea cliffs of Naples in a quarter called Posillipo, from *Pausilypon* in ancient Greek: "respite from worry."

We park in front of grandmother Augusta's aging villa overlooking the magnificent bay. Scanning the horizon from this promontory, the gulf spreads out before us. To the west drift the isles of Capri and Ischia. Across the bay, migrations of fishermen sail home like birds in flight with the day's catch. I watch Idanna sigh and fold her hands quietly. Her thick braid falls behind her soft shoulders. I sense that memories of *nonna* are flooding back.

Originally built by the Duke of Frisio in the eighteenth century, the villa was purchased by Idanna's great-grandfather, who gave it his family name: Villa Pavoncelli. Regrettably sold in the seventies by the last heir, it is now an exclusive apartment building. At the entrance stands a doorman in polished uniform. The gate is firmly closed. A sense of pride for its preserved beauty crosses Idanna's face. From the sloping garden soar giant pines and palms like silent sentinels. She stares at the grand verandahs that descend toward the private beach.

"There!" her hand points down to a white sand cove. "That's where my father and my uncle played each summer as children." She holds the moment briefly. Then it all fades away with the last light.

Further up the cliffs, we arrive at Paola Carola's home. An old friend of Idanna, she welcomes us into her world filled with bohemian sensibility. Now in her seventh decade, she still exudes a magnetism that is the touchstone of all muses. Her admirers include a collection of writers and artists: Arthur Koestler, Gregor von Rezzori, Raffaele La Capria, and Alberto Giacometti. On her bureau stands her bust by the sculptor, along with an autographed portrait of beloved Neapolitan playwright Eduardo de Filippo, who stares out seductively with his smoky eyes.

Paola first discovered her bohemian side in Paris after she divorced her wealthy elderly Armenian husband, a great art collector. She had met Monsieur Giacometti and then enrolled at the Sorbonne to enter the field of the unconscious with the Freudian disciple Jacques Lacan. Much later, she would return to her native city where she still practices as a psychoanalyst.

"Neapolitans are deeply superstitious," she confesses. "They don't greet psychology with the open mind of Parisians."

Bound by taboo, mental problems in her city often carry public stigma. Personal torments remain tightly bound in private inner family walls. Her patient visits must be shrouded in secrecy, unlike in Manhattan where having an analyst is a badge of honor.

Next morning, Assunta in her sky-blue apron brings to the breakfast table a pitcher of warm milk to add to our brewed espresso steaming in porcelain cups. Light illuminates the dining room that faces the rippling great bay where a shrill sun reflects its silver sheen on the jade-blue expanse. Vesuvius's twin craters lift high above delicate nesting clouds. The grand marine arc stretches from our host's terraces to the far cliffs of Sorrento. Marmalade from Ravello lemons covers our toasted bread. Idanna leafs through the heavy volume *La cucina Napoletana*.

"It's by Jean Carola, Paola's mother. Listen to her words," she says. "This book is dedicated to the grandchildren of all the Neapolitans scattered around the world. How can I, neither a scholar nor a writer of literature, express my love for this most unfortunate city, so rich in its past and poor in its present?"

Standing at the door in her burgundy silk dressing gown, Paola savors every word. Then, she takes her place at table and recalls how the Carola family meals often ended with her father's biting remark that his own mother's cooking was the best in the world.

"Hearing those unpleasant words, my mother always fell silent. But slowly, with persistence, she managed to surpass her mother-in-law's reputation. She abandoned the typical Neapolitan recipes and ventured into a level beyond her rival's reach—the territory of the legendary *monsù*."

These alchemist-chefs exist now only in legend, but once they reigned in the aristocratic kitchens of Naples. After the French Revolution, they fled Paris and came south to offer their services to the nobility. Over time *monsieur* morphed into *monsù*.

Paola describes with great relish the world of her mother's kitchen where preparations took entire days. *Pasta frolla* filled with fresh shrimp and mussels; miniature boats of buttered *pain carré* with parsley; fried sliced *zucchini a' scapece* dressed with fresh mint; chestnut and cacao balls coated with caramel, candied orange peels, chocolate truffles . . . Each meal became a cornucopia of delicacies, breaking new ground. "And, finally, in triumph, my mother published her book," she says, "Now it's known as the 'Bible of Neapolitan cooking.'"

As Paola pulls away from the table she announces that it is her wish to escort us into the quarter of ancient Neapolis.

"To . . . day, I will show you *una mer-a-viglia*," she purrs, tasting each syllable. "A true wonder. There is the Cara-vag-gio, you must see . . ."

"How lovely." Idanna says.

"But remember," she says sternly, "leave your valuables behind. Carry nothing." Paola echoes Puccio's warning.

We dutifully prepare. I assist Paola in the ritual of closing up the house. I bolt each shutter while she carefully shuts every window. Slowly darkness swallows room after room. When the last window is closed, the illuminated outside world retreats completely. Then she sets the alarm.

We follow her through the shaded garden of palms, cactus, pomegranate bushes, and then climb the stairs that lead to the gate and the road of Posillipo. Harsh sunlight blinds us with its white uniform haze. We leave behind one face of Naples and descend into another.

A half hour later, our taxi driver pulls up in front of the imposing Duomo of San Gennaro and we step out. Idanna whispers in my ear, "Inside there, the relics of the city's patron saint are stored. When his blood miraculously becomes liquid twice a year, Naples goes into a complete frenzy."

Over two millennia ago, Greek colonizers laid down the grid pattern of the city's "historic center." Spaccanapoli. *Spacca* meaning "cut." And slicing through the heart of ancient Napoli is Via dei Tribunali—the Street of the Tribunals. First laid down by Hellenic founders, this ancient artery cleaves the old city in two. It still follows its original trajectory in spite of layers of urban chaos where buildings have risen and crumbled and risen again for centuries. Here dwells a sea of humanity pressed together like sardines. Underground extends a vast network of caves and tunnels carved out since the Roman epoch from the soft volcanic *tufo* that was quarried to build the city's structures above. Beneath the old city rests a negative space mirroring what stands above.

This living archeological site, the writer Curzio Malaparte describes in his book *The Skin*: "Naples is the most mysterious city in the world. It is the only city of the ancient world that has not perished like Ilium, Nineveh, and Babylon. Naples is a Pompeii that was never buried. It is not a city: it is a world—the ancient pre-Christian world—that has survived intact on the surface of the modern world."[1]

Navigating through the dense crowd, we enter a jumbled forest of once-proud palaces and timeworn tenements. I marvel at the anarchy. Along a stretch of broken pavement and down a side street we step into a tiny piazza, and pull up before a forlorn church façade. At the entrance, a gap-toothed woman sits quite comfortably behind her makeshift table hawking cigarettes. A speeding Vespa with a sixth sense maneuvers in around me in a split-second, scraping at my ankles. I hurriedly follow the ladies inside. And, as the wooden door closes behind us, the bedlam subsides. A quiet hush.

Before us, a tiny wooden sign reads "Le sette opere della misericordia—The Seven Acts of Mercy." My eyes slowly rise to the grand painting above the dimly lit altar. I step closer, drawn in by the eerie chiaroscuro, with figures so lifelike. I've never seen any painting like this. Startling. Magnetic. Strange. In the painting, an old man suckles a woman's breast as she turns her face nervously toward a grim alley. What's happening here? Costumed men grapple in the darkness. Who are they? Someone holds a torch, two dirty feet stick out from under a sheet, a sword blade shines, a half-naked body kicks up some dust. From above, a mother and child peer at the chaos below. Two angels fall to earth, grasping each other. Their wings bat against the walls. Yet, they look more like Neapolitan street kids. I don't understand (see plate 14-1).

I turn to Paola, but she offers no explanation. Instead, she sits content on a scarlet cushioned chair, delighted that she's offered us this unfathomable painting. After lingering for a while, Idanna turns to leave. I do the same. Paola rises too.

Suddenly, a voice behind us echoes off the walls.

"*Ma che fate*, what are you doing?!"

A thin man with silver hair and blazing eyes moves toward us through shadow and light. "*Non andate via*, Don't leave," he cries out.

"Listen . . . !"

"Listen! If you've got time, I will explain the painting," insists the thin man with fiery eyes.

His loud words stop us in our tracks.

He draws nearer, looking at me quizzically.

"You're not Italian?" he asks, "American?"

"Yes," I reply.

"And you, signora?"

"From Firenze . . ." answers Idanna.

"Ahhh, I worked in Grosseto many years ago," he says, smiling.

"I am Neapolitan," interrupts Paola abruptly. "These are my friends."

He turns quickly in her direction, welcoming her.

"Grazie, signora, for coming here with your guests."

His face holds a battery of emotions with a pair of bright blue eyes gleaming behind his glasses perched on an aquiline nose. His wiry torso is charged with the tension of a compressed spring and energy to burn. Standing before the painting, he asks.

"Do you know what it means?"

As he begins to describe what we have not seen, I somehow understand him through his thick Neapolitan accent.

"It's from the Gospel of Matthew," he says, "These scenes could be happening, just around the corner, in one of these alleys."

The man's cadence is gripping. Our eyes are fixed on the painting. As he speaks, the figures seem to stir alive. All the noises, smells, and loud intensity of the streets outside now pulsate from the canvas. Strong, raking light picks out each character.

"Look on the right side. We should begin there." He points over to a young woman and an old man's head reaching out from prison bars.

"Isn't she beautiful? And what is she up to? You won't believe it. She's breastfeeding her father. Look, she's raised her skirt and put it under his chin for comfort but also to prevent the milk from spilling. In those days, families had to provide food for relatives in prison. So you see, this scene combines two acts of mercy—feeding the hungry and visiting the prisoners." He pauses in admiration. "Of course, it's also about honoring your parents and the elderly no matter how and what."

Then, he carefully guides us through all the acts, one by one, pointing out that Caravaggio ingeniously managed to place all seven in one narrative. "With so little space, how did he do all this?" he wonders out loud.

Idanna and I both exchange glances. The passionate erudition that flows out of the humble man is unnerving. As I listen to his delivery, I realize that this is no textbook rendition. It's coming from a deeper place within him. Like most Neapolitans, he seems to have a natural gift for theatrics and pacing.

When he stands back and takes a breath, I offer him my bottle of water. "Prego..."

"Grazie," He takes a sip. "You see Caravaggio suffered so much in his life. The Vatican wanted his head. A man had been stabbed to death," he stresses in a hushed tone, handing me back the water. "Come nearer, and look down in the lower left corner."

I crane my neck but don't see anything. Idanna stares in concentration on that spot of the canvas.

"The painting shouldn't be seen in artificial light," he says firmly, "but sometimes it helps." He reaches behind the curtain and flicks a switch. The scenes glow brightly in the electric light.

"Under that sword, you see?"

I recognize a small figure crouched in shadow behind the blade, hands folded.

"That's his anguished soul, I'm sure. This entire painting is his cry for forgiveness and compassion in this mad world. But, isn't that what we all want?"

Idanna reaches out and touches his arm.

"Excuse me, but what is your name?" she asks suddenly, changing the subject and looking straight into the man's crystalline blue eyes.

"Angelo Esposito," he replies. "I am the guardian here."

Paola, who has been silent, plucks out some money from her purse and gestures for him to take it.

"Signora, please!" he steps back offended.

"For your next coffee . . ."

"No, absolutely not! This is my duty and my love."

She lowers her hand.

He then flips over the lapel of his jacket to show us a silver badge with the words: *Comune di Napoli*.

"I work for the city," he announces proudly.

"And how long have you been here?" probes Idanna.

"Almost five years."

"And before?"

"I worked fifteen years in the Sanitation Department," he answers candidly.

"Really?!" Idanna exclaims. "Not . . ."

"Yes, in the city sewage system. But then they moved me over here to culture."

He smiles at our startled expressions. From the cupola, a stream of sunlight flashes on his sharp nose and firm chin.

We thank him warmly and shake hands. His eyes sparkle as he walks over to switch off the electric light.

Before pushing the door, I turn back to take one last look. The thin guardian stands dwarfed underneath the painting.

Outside, an old woman offers us cigarettes and a big toothless smile. Motorcycles roar past.

Idanna asks Paola, "But how can he know so much about Caravaggio?"

"I have no idea . . . this is Naples," she answers dismissively.

We cross over Piazza San Domenico and Idanna disappears inside a bookshop. I wait outside with Paola who seems eager to return to her home on the cliff. Soon, Idanna surfaces with a book in hand.

That evening, she sits absorbed and lost in the pages of her new acquisition. Paola has long since gone to bed. After some time, she looks up as if surprised to find herself here still in the living room. I close my dog-eared copy of Robert Byron's *Road to Oxiana*.

"Since my childhood days in Florence," she tells me, "I've seen many spells cast on travelers, but today . . ."

"Yes," I agree, "He is possessed."

"Tomorrow, I want to go back there . . . ," she pauses, "to the church."

Harsh dawn light batters the wall with white streaks. Careening seagulls cry as Idanna peers out into the glare. Curtains of Indian muslin wrap around her like wind-blown sails. She gazes out at her grandmother's bay. But from her eyes, I know she is still thinking about our encounter with the guardian and the painting of "mercies."

From the cliffs of Posillipo, we head past *nonna's* Villa Pavoncelli down to Mergellina and then along the promenade all the way to the medieval Castel dell'Ovo or Egg Castle that floats offshore—still oozing its curious history of subterranean intrigue and murder.

In Santa Lucia, facing the sea, we stop for a coffee. At the next table, a couple of men in suits pompously chat away. They look like political operators and fixers trading their harvest of jokes, puns, and double entendres. Their obedient drivers stand by government-issued "blue cars" parked at the curb. In any just society, such shady rogues would be locked up. Yet, here in Italy, they enter politics. The party hacks climb up the ladder of their parties and over time, thanks to an endless stream of brown envelopes passed under tables for government contracts, they become rich. In the end, the system is rigged. Everyone is bound to them for favors at a price—a job, a building permit, a license, a contract, and more.

Idanna looks at them sternly. "Just imagine, Italy has only been united for about 150 years, when the North conquered southern Italy. Since then, two secret organizations have kept the country in suspended animation—the Mafia and the Freemasons. After the war, some would add a third—the Vatican's Opus Dei.

"And these politicians?"

"They just do their bidding. Idiotic governance hand in hand with the Mafia, holds everything hostage. Corruption, nepotism, and inside deals ruin this beautiful country. Have a look at those faces and you know why Italy will always be in a mess."

I scan their expansive waistlines, Prada glasses, slick hair, Rolex watches, and glistening Gucci shoes. One lifts a morning prosecco. Another puffs his cigar.

Even under the bright morning sun, this improvised entourage clouds over any *dolce vita* fantasies with *chiaroscuro*. These toxic characters—straight out of central casting—seem all too happy to illustrate modern Italy's curse for us.

From Santa Lucia, we trudge up to Piazza del Plebiscito and the Royal Palace before descending into Piazza del Gesù Nuovo, which faces the heart of the old city. Slowly we re-enter Spaccanapoli's jumbled forest of architecture from all ages and seasons. On dark and pungent San Biagio dei Librai Street, I hear swarms of voices speaking rapid-fire, laden with nasal drawls so similar to Alexandrian or Beiruti cadences in worlds east of Naples where I had spent a decade in those Middle Eastern lands of broken hopes and dreams.

A familiar warmth sweeps over me as we walk wedged between battered relics of palaces and historic buildings, long since decayed, and shedding their cracked and wrinkled skin. Ambling along Via dei Tribunali, Vespas weave maniacally in and out between cars. Anxious drivers honk their horns, asserting their manhood. A young kid puffs on contraband Marlboros and casually tosses firecrackers into the traffic. Idanna grabs my arm.

Finally we find our way back, retracing our steps into the little piazza. Standing before the weatherworn façade of the church, I spot the woman hawking her cigarettes who recognizes us and grins her gap-toothed smile back in our direction. A speeding motorbike deftly skirts around Idanna. She holds her purse firmly. We pass through an iron gate and push open the wooden door. At times, churches in Naples are not so much places of spiritual comfort as places of refuge from the blaring noise of the narrow streets.

A cool draft of wind blows over us.

The church is empty. And the door closes behind. All the chaos of the street outside subsides. A quiet hush. Peace. The grand painting looms above the dimly lit altar. Drawn by its mysterious beauty, we step closer. In silence, I count the characters: sixteen. Who are they?

Then, I hear his voice.

"I'm happy to see you again," Angelo says with an air of surprise. His eyes glow as he moves toward us across the black and white marble floor.

"I found this book by Mina Gregori," Idanna pulls it out from her bag. "She's a friend of my family in Florence . . ."

"*Che bello!*" He holds it, and his smile lights up when he sees the title, *The Age of Caravaggio*. "You know, you can get hooked on him, if you're not careful," he jokes.

"I can imagine," she agrees.

He thumbs the pages of the book. "No painter can be compared to him. Not even Leonardo. At least this is what I think. But if you want to go deeper, you have to look for the symbols," he stresses. "You have to use biblical and classical eyes."

Idanna is impressed by his erudition. "Excuse me, Angelo, that woman up there. Who is she?" She points to the only female in the painting.

"Ever heard the story of Pero and old Cimon?"

"No." She shakes her head.

"In ancient Rome, there was a young woman called Pero. One day, her father was arrested for some reason I don't remember. Well, she goes to his rescue and keeps him alive."

"Breastfeeding her own father!" Idanna gasps.

"Look closely . . . she's afraid that somebody may see her. But her papa is so famished that he has even spilled two drops of milk."

Sure enough, I see the drops on his beard.

"What she fears most are the prison guards." Angelo raises his hand. "But when the guards come out, they will be so moved by her daring that they'll open the prison doors. Her father will walk out a free man!"

The guardian waves his hands in triumph. Idanna stares at Pero's face glistening with light.

"Caravaggio always shocks us," he emphasizes, "pushing us beyond taboos."

Angelo is so right. Caravaggio takes stories that are so remote and gives them a familiar immediacy. What is so far in time seems to happen next door.

"And who's the pudgy man?" I ask, pointing up. "The one in the corner."

"An inn-keeper."

"He looks German, a heavy beer drinker."

"Good guess. In those days, the whole world came to Naples. And everyone passed through the Cerriglio, Caravaggio's favorite hangout.

"Does it still exist?"

"Of course, but now mostly students from the Orientale go there. But look, he's inviting two pilgrims into his tavern, giving them shelter. One has a red beard and a walking stick. The other, we can only see his ear and a leg."

I then ask him about the red-bearded pilgrim.

"See the small conch on his hat?" he replies. "That's the clue. It's the symbol of the famous pilgrimage site, Santiago de Compostela, and also of Saint Rocco, the most popular saint of Southern Italy."

"And who's that man with a torch?"

"That's a priest looking down at a corpse. When Caravaggio arrived in Naples, death was everywhere. Those two feet belong to a victim from the famine who is being carried away."

"Burying the dead?" Idanna prompts.

"Yes," he nods. "You see, each figure in the painting is separate and yet moves in unison with the others. Caravaggio catches them in action and freezes the moment."

"And the young knight with the shining sword?" I ask.

"He's cutting his cape to give it to the cripple on the ground. He's Saint Martin."

I look intently at the naked man who is pushing his body closer to the passing knight, with the little strength he has.

"Clothing the naked and healing the sick. Martin's gesture is powerful."

"That's when the weather changes suddenly and it becomes warm," recalls Idanna.

"Yes, on his name day, always in November, the summer of Saint Martin. It usually lasts a week."

"Indian summer," I say.

"Look, he's given up his cloak, so God blesses him with warm weather," smiles Angelo.

Two angels fly above the street scenes in wonder. Their wings churn in a whirlpool of feathers, holding up the mother and child.

"And," Angelo puts a question, "where to do you think Caravaggio got the idea of the white flowing fabric wrapped around the angels?" Not waiting for our reply, he grabs my arm.

"Come!" He rushes us outside and around the corner and points at the clotheslines high above our heads.

"See those sheets up there?" The wind lifts the dangling white fabrics just like in the painting. "So you see, Caravaggio didn't have to go too far. He just had to observe life right here in Spaccanapoli."

The sheets sway between the decaying buildings and the brilliant sky. The guardian clearly enjoys seeing us hang on his every word. He moves with agility as he spins around the cigarette seller.

"Giovanna!" He blows her a kiss.

"Grazie! Angelo!" she cries as we are swept back into the chapel.

Inside, I ask about one last character. "And who's that fellow drinking?"

The tavern's light spills on his rugged face. The guardian beckons us to move closer.

"Samson. He's quenching his thirst. 'Water to the thirsty.'"

"Exactly, drinking from the jaw of an ass . . . But, he's also cleansing his soul from the blood of all the enemies he has killed."

Angelo lowers his voice, "I think it's Caravaggio's self-portrait. I told you how he stabbed a thug who had provoked him in Rome."

"But didn't he also have big problems with the Church?" I prod.

"Of course," Angelo replies. "He couldn't stand their hypocrisy. The papal police were after him too. In the end, his art isn't about bishops in silk robes giving handouts to the needy. It's about simple people helping one another. He's the artist of the poor. Our artist! There's no one else like him. It's all there! *Cosa volete di più?* What more do you want?"

His voice echoes in the chapel. His eyes, enlarged by his spectacles, are lit with flame.

NOTES

Editor's note: This essay is excerpted from Terence Ward's *The Guardian of Mercy: How an Extraordinary Painting by Caravaggio Changed an Ordinary Life Today* (New York: Arcade, 2016). Reprinted by permission of Arcade Publishing, an imprint of Skyhorse Publishing, Inc.

1. Curzio Malaparte, *The Skin*, trans. David Moore (New York: New York Review of Books, 2013), 39.

# Malanapoli: From the Lazaronitum to Gomorrah/Camorra

FIFTEEN

# The Contact Zone: Where Organized Crime and Everyday Life Meet

*Jason Pine*

A man with a deep-lined charcoal tan is leaning against the wall of a corpulent, prerationalist-style palazzo at Piazza Nolana. Once white, now covered in soot, the building's two marble caryatids (figured as Mercury the trickster, messenger of the gods, patron of commerce, and guide to the underworld) can barely hold up the second-floor balcony. Next to the man lies his filthy blanket of ceramic trinkets, rusted alarm clocks, and twisted shoes that look like the evidence of unseen violence. He is gesturing with outstretched, needle-marked arms at a man propped against a dented blue car. The other man is talking to him loudly, elongating his vowels and finishing his sentences with intonation that sounds like bellicose whining. A third man is squatting beside his own discolored blanket, which is littered with box sets of pliers, nails, shiny watches of dubious working quality, and limbless nude Barbies. He is playing with a pair of long, black-handled scissors, opening and closing them, entranced by the *slice-slice* of the blades.

Passersby pick their way through the crowded, narrow sidewalk, some choosing to step off the curb into the busy street, bypassing the motley assortment of undesirable objects for sale and the piles of ashen newspapers leftover from the street fires that warm heroin junkies at night. Their main destination is the market known as 'Ncopp' 'e Mmura (Above the Walls), the magnificent fish market that begins at the crumbling fifteenth-century Aragonese city gate, Porta Nolana, one of whose towers (the Tower of Faith) bears the weight of a modern three-story apartment building that someone likely built without a permit. Through the arch and past the gate, women with large green plastic bags make their way to the wide shallow crates of mussels, clams, oysters, squid, sardines, anchovies, swordfish, grouper, cod, bass, and eel. Their sacks are stuffed with kilo-loaves of hard, crusty bread, long-stemmed artichokes, leafy lemons, and knotted bags of mozzarella balls in cloudy white water. A woman stops before a vendor who, with already bloodied hands, majestically takes hold of a live octopus, lifts it into the air and, with a long shout and a swing of his machete, massacres it. He promptly cleans it while calling out in song for the next customer.

The windows of the shops flanking the market are lined with bottles of olive oil and the sulfurous wines of the region, split bread loaves, and inverted dangling bouquets of salami with skin blotched powdery-white with age. Inside the shops are stacks and stacks of pasta—long, short, twisted, ridged, smooth, toothed, rounded, fat, and bulbous. It's lunchtime, and every other pedestrian has some kind of delicacy in hand, wrapped in yellow paper napkins, half peeking out: oily bread filled with prosciutto, provola, and tomato or mozzarella and red peppers, a square slice of pizza, or a buttery phyllo-dough treat filled with escarole and olives. Some are standing and eating while talking on cell phones, gesticulating with food in hand. Others are walking slowly, weaving leisurely through the kinetic fervor as they go.

A stray dog with patches of missing fur is arching its back, keeping its hind legs close together as if preparing for a graceful Olympic dive. Instead, it shits on the cobblestones, already strewn with pedestrians' grease-stained napkins. Around a corner in a narrow *vicolo*,[1] a young man, shirtless and in shorts, is sitting on the threshold of his *basso* (ground-floor dwelling).[2] He points a bottle at his baby's mouth, and the infant gulps hungrily. The bottle slips, and with a slurp the nipple and infant separate. In an instant, the baby lets out a wide scream. It sounds in tune with the numerous other extended

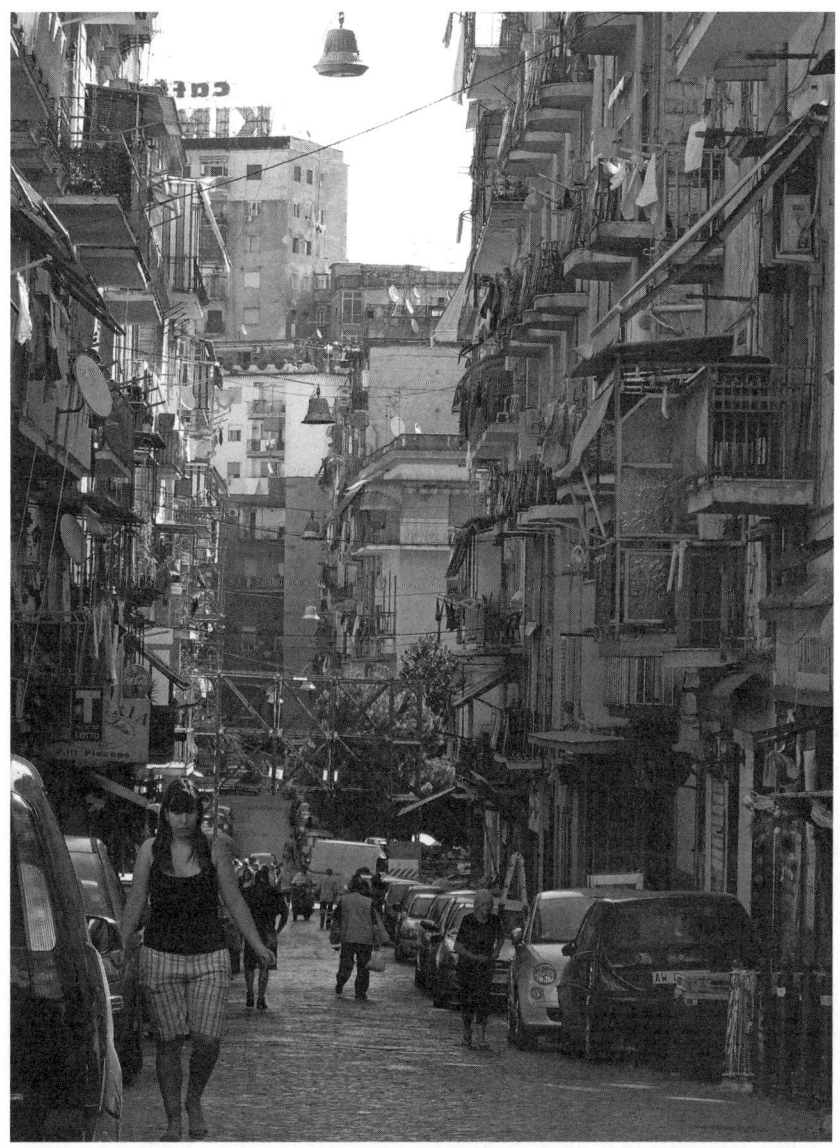

Figure 15-1. The Forcella district in Naples (Jason Pine)

vowels sung at full throttle by market vendors announcing in aggressively plaintive, undulating tones, "Fresh fish! Lemons of Sorrento!" The vocal performances are so extravagant and competitive that they seem just as orchestrated as that of the sexy, olive-skinned thug in tight pants who sings "The strength to decide" to a full-figured teen strutting by in an even tighter ensemble of low-cut jeans and a half-shirt. Effortlessly, she ignores him. Or it may be that his melodramatic serenade is for the young man walking behind her. "What I don't have/is the strength to decide/I'd erase you if I could/from my heart."[3]

These life-scenes might convey to visitors that Naples is flush with the sensory intensities that smolder mainly in the "lower bodily stratum."[4] Indeed, many Neapolitans say that 'Ncopp' 'e Mmura is part of the "belly of Naples," as the popular writer Matilde Serao famously described the city's poorest quarters in 1884.[5] To me, a white, middle-class American man, 'Ncopp' 'e Mmura, host to both heroin packets and baby bottles, sumptuous foods and animal filth, the avid shouts of vendors and the naked songs of lovers, felt precisely like the "promiscuous public space" identified by the nineteenth-century European bourgeoisie who sought to circumscribe it.[6]

The fish market, however, is not merely a place where undisciplined passions and interests run amok.[7] Here a brutal and occulted territorial system undergirds these forces. 'Ncopp' 'e Mmura, and the *quartiere* (quarter) Mercato in which it is situated, is dominated by a crime clan that, together with several rival and allied clans that claim other parts of the city and the wider Campania region as their territories, are commonly called the camorra. For now, the dominant clan in Mercato goes by the surname of its leaders: Mazzarella.

The heroin comes to Piazza Nolana by way of the Mazzarella clan, which shares with other clans the services of independent broker-traffickers to import the drug from the Balkans. When the broker arrives with the delivery, each clan takes its share, then cuts, packages, and sells the heroin to the *spacciatori* (drug dealers) who work the piazzas in its territories.[8] *Spacciatori* usually operate as independent entrepreneurs who pay *tangenti* (tributes) to the crime clan affiliates in whose territory they conduct business. Additionally, uncountable tons of the market's fish are defrosted or contaminated contraband coming from Tunisia, Turkey, Thailand, China, and Australia. They are sold by vendors in 'Ncopp' 'e Mmura who label the fish as "fresh" and "from the Gulf of Naples."⁹ Moreover, some of the vendors are affiliates of the Mazzarella clan, which owns a fishmonger's shop in the neighborhood. The clan's affiliates also run an extortion racket by paying nonaffiliated residents to demand access fees from the drivers of fish delivery trucks and parking fees from anyone else wanting to use the area's public lots.

Heroin and counterfeit fish are just two of the many illegal goods that change hands in 'Ncopp' 'e Mmura. The DVDs and CDs of Neapolitan, "Italian," English, and American videos and music that men and women lay out for sale on card tables among the fish vendors are counterfeit and pirated. In fact, the *quartiere* Mercato is a major hub for the mass reproduction, warehousing, citywide distribution, and sale of these recordings.¹⁰ Since at least the time of the audiocassette, the barons of this illicit commerce even certify, whether ironically, earnestly, or arrogantly, the authenticity of their pirated products. Until the late 1990s one locally renowned mixtape "brand" label contained the "mixed message": "Warning: Tapes with photocopied inserts are not mixed by Erry, the ideal dimension for clean listening."

The dominant genre of these recordings is *la musica neomelodica*. Its voicy Neapolitan-language lyrics, disco-pop tones, and melodramatic (and ironic) melodies resound through 'Ncopp' 'e Mmura and many of the city's poorer quarters in its center, in the urban *periferia*, throughout Campania and other southern Italian regions, such as Sicily, Puglia, and parts of Calabria. Neomelodica music and musicians also circulate in southern Italian diasporas in northern Italy, Belgium, Germany, and other countries.¹¹

Neomelodica music can be heard anywhere in Naples and its surrounding provinces, and well beyond. Adults sing along with the radio at home or in the car, and kids play songs to one another on their cell phones while at school. Singers perform neomelodica music at modest baptism celebrations and at ostentatious wedding parties, and they lip-synch their songs on local private television broadcasts and sometimes on nationally popular television talk shows. In addition, neomelodica music is the inspiration for transnationally circulating, low-budget, Neapolitan-language musical films. It even dominates the soundtrack of Matteo Garrone's feature film *Gomorra* (Gomorrah), the 2008 Grand Prix winner at Cannes.

Neomelodici singers and their associates, together numbering in the hundreds, maybe even thousands, compose, record, publicize, and perform their growing repertoires within overlapping "legitimate," do-it-yourself (DIY), and clandestine fields of practice.[12] Some of the big players on the scene are powerful crime clan affiliates; they operate as talent managers and songwriters. Most of the scene's protagonists, however, are young men in their teens and twenties who have little formal education and, at best, irregular employment and limited access to resources.[13] They linger in this milieu for years, following uncertain opportunities while negotiating the risks of contact with criminal associations.

## The Art of Making Do

I began research on the neomelodica scene in 1998, at the tail end of the "Neapolitan Renaissance," the hoped-for result of Mayor Antonio Bassolino's ambitious project of urban renewal. For decades Naples had been wracked by soaring unemployment, infrastructural collapse, a cholera epidemic, a calamitous earthquake, rampant illegal rebuilding, and spiking intraclan violence.[14] This turmoil was enmeshed with local and national political upheaval. In 1992 a team of magistrates in Milan launched the *Mani pulite* investigations (Operation Clean Hands) into corruption networks entangling organized crime affiliates, public administration, all ranks of political office, and business elites throughout the country. Milan, and by extension the entire Italian state, was popularly renamed *Tangentopoli* (Bribesville), where politicians collected "a second layer of taxes" that they systematically solicited or extorted as bribes in exchange for public works contracts, public-sector employment, and business-friendly legislation.[15] In a little over a year, the magistrates, armed with the confessions of many business leaders and urged on by a disenfranchised and indignant public, convicted nearly one-third of Parliament's deputies and toppled the ruling political elite. Although the trials demonstrated that corruption was a nationwide problem, between 1992 and 1993 twenty-six Campanian regional councils were disbanded for mafia infiltration, far more than in other regions.[16]

When Bassolino became mayor of Naples in 1993, it appeared he had a cleaner slate for urban renewal. He aimed to change the city's image within Italy and in the G7 nations.[17] His primary target was the immense and densely populated *centro storico* (historic center). He focused on Neapolitans' relationship to public space by curbing the sprawl of illegal parking, clearing away trash, and reopening architectural landmarks that had long been shuttered and ignored.[18] His intention was to replace the collapsing industrial economy with a self-sustaining tourism industry that drew on the cultural resources of Naples and Campania.

One of these local cultural resources is Neapolitan-language song. Song is an allusive and alluring language of great historical significance in Naples. The city's mythological name is Parthenope, the siren who drowned herself in despair when she failed to lure Ulysses. The earliest Neapolitan-language vocal music texts date back to the thirteenth century. In the fifteenth and sixteenth centuries, Naples was home to a proliferation of single-voice and polyphonic villanelle, ironic and lurid songs from which "gentlemen" collectors gathered the inspiration for the comparatively formal madrigals that they diffused in cities of the north such as Florence and Venice. At the end of the eighteenth century, Naples was considered throughout Europe to be Italy's music capital, and Neapolitans were believed to have an "innate" capacity for artful song. At the end of the nineteenth century, Naples was the center of an international popular song industry commanded by bourgeois lyricists. For nearly half a century, they composed a massive repertoire of romantic and picturesque poems, later named *la canzone classica*, or "classic song." These songs circulated transnationally with the mass migrations of Italians from all over Italy to Europe, the Americas, and Australia.

By the 1950s the Neapolitan song culture industry had declined. Television connected the dominant pop music scenes of Italy, the United Kingdom, and the United States and inspired new musical forms, lyrical content, and types of composition in Naples. In the 1970s many new musical styles emerged from Naples, but one genre in particular has had an enduring afterlife among the popular classes: *canzoni 'e mala*, or "songs of the underworld." Although many were composed decades earlier by the very same bourgeois poets of the *canzone classica*, the *canzoni 'e mala* resonated, perhaps for some listeners too much, with the tumultuous day-to-day realities of the 1970s. In the 1980s neomelodica song, a genre described as "erotic-sentimental," emerged from this same milieu. Strikingly, these songs were composed not in the poetic language of the middle classes but in the everyday vernaculars of the popular classes. In fact, the composers, performers, producers, distributors, and fans all, on the whole, came from the same milieu. Through the availability of private and pirated television and affordable recording technologies, the protagonists of interconnected DIY music scenes began to make themselves more audible and visible. Their audiences grew to the hundreds of thousands across southern Italy and among southern Italian "emigrants" in the north and transnationally.[19] By the mid-1990s hundreds of independent singers, songwriters, and technicians crowded into these scenes, hoping to make a living or even make it big in what looks like an alternative culture industry. Today, for hundreds, maybe thousands, of people, song is a prime cultural resource for making do.

Neomelodici protagonists say that maneuvering in the scene is a precarious business that requires artfulness and artifice. For them, this means being on alert for the resources and tools that might enhance their ever-emerging plans for a better life. It means speculating on the future even as the Camorra colonizes or kills it. They adapt to events and relations as they emerge, prepared to leverage multiple forms of value—publicity, favors, and varieties of social capital. Shaking off encumbrances like rigid ethical codes, they apply instrumental reason to ethical practice.[20] People in the neomelodica music scene call their creative pragmatics *l'arte di arrangiarsi*, or "the art of making do." Making do means more to them than simply "getting by." Many people in the scene want more than to merely live with chronic indeterminacy. They seek self-determination and a life that escapes precarity altogether.

In the melodramas of making do in the neomelodica scene, peoples' desires for self-determination crystallize in the figure of the personal sovereign. The personal sovereign (in this scene typically male) makes for himself and his (actual or potential) family a life of security and a path to something even better. He transforms chronic indeterminacy into unqualified potential. He enacts a "sovereign decision" that "springs out of a normative nothingness and from a concrete disorder."[21] This figure is a fantasy that is not necessarily mimed in everyday practice, but it lures people into its shoes from where it stands, just beyond the limits of speculation. It activates "the perception of one's own vitality, one's sense of aliveness, of changeability (often signified as 'freedom')."[22] The personal sovereign fully exploits his field of potential.

## Contact Zones

The neomelodica music scene is one of many instances where the so-called formal, informal, and illicit economies overlap in Campania and beyond.[23] The scene is a contact zone where the art of making do brushes up against organized crime. In a contact zone, where heterogeneous epistemologies, sensibilities, and practices comingle, it is not readily apparent who or what dominates.[24] Everyone and everything is potentially deterritorialized in this transient space of encounter.[25]

A contact zone is a field of potential where the rules of engagement are suspended. People enter the scene in search of self-determination while avoiding ensnaring debts and obligations to criminal associations. To do so, they must attune themselves to the occulted dimension of the market and to the very real possibility that things are often *more than* what they seem. For them, this surplus, rather than being the "hidden" or "real truth," is the unregulated and undocumented vitality—and the death throes—of things. Its potency is registered in volatile events and shapeless suspicions.

Attuned to the pulsions and tensions of this contact zone, people communicate, interact, and create in ways that extend its rhythms. They harness or deflect this potency with melodramatic flamboyance and seductiveness, ironic playfulness and dissimulation, suspicion and secrecy, and overdrawn hopes—the aesthetic qualities of the art of making do. These qualities resonate in musical performances and in day-to-day engagements. They form a "porous, affective scene of identification among strangers," or an "intimate public."[26]

The art of making do is a speculative performance, the staging of a better life. Enacting it requires creative tactics for seizing opportunities and negotiating risk. Excessive speculation, however, can lead to violent determinations: the ad hoc art of making do has the potential to transmogrify into organized crime. Under these conditions the figure of the self-realized sovereign incarnates as a *camorrista* (crime clan affiliate). This is because organized crime in Campania works through contact, forever roping in new associates and affiliates. While in Sicily the mafia *padrino* (godfather) is the embodiment of a single hermetic and enduring center of power, the Campanian role of *capoclan* (clan boss) shifts or is shared among members of a family generation.[27] Clans can also splinter into autonomous, even rival, groups, inciting extraordinary levels of violence. In Naples dozens of clans have carved out and then parsed numerous territories of control as they forge federations, undergo scissions, and form new alliances. Organized crime in Naples is shape-shifting and volatile, rendering "organized" a tenuous attribution.

More important, crime clan affiliates extend association to thousands of residents in their territories in the form of flexible employment opportunities. While association with a crime clan through part-time and temporary employment does not entail the same commitments as affiliation, it constitutes an ambiguous relationship that can easily shift into deeper entanglements such as indenture. One major source of nonaffiliate employment is pirated music and video sales. Another source of employment—the focus of this story—is singing neomelodica music at weddings, baptisms, and piazza festivals.

## The Camorra Is Not a Thing

It's a unique challenge to write about organized crime in southern Italy because it has a potent affective allure. In Naples criminal organizations cloak themselves in mystery while engaging in spectacular acts of self-exposure. Organized crime affiliates cultivate fearful secrecy by making their faces and their uncapped potential for violence known among the residents of their territories.[28] While "captive" publics are gripped with fear, broader publics are captivated, at best, by the spectacle. Indeed, journalists, artists, scholars, and their publics contribute, unwittingly and willfully, to the affective allure of "Italian" organized crime by rendering it an object of fetishizing, even eroticizing attention.[29]

As an object of fear, fascination, and fantasy, organized crime in Naples has acquired thinglike qualities.[30] It has been depicted as a determinate organization that honors a precise code of silence and controls a circumscribable "shadow" economy through ritualized violence. It has been described as an illegitimate entity, an alternative state that attacks the nation-state like a predator or a parasite, or a cancer to be cut out of the life of the nation.[31] While some of these qualities can sometimes be attributed to crime clans in Naples, they do not capture a *thing*. Neapolitan crime clans engage in illicit economic practices and compete with the state's legitimated monopoly on violence, but they are not exactly distinguishable from the nation-state. Crime clans operate antagonistically *and* collaboratively with legitimated authorities as extortionists and as partners in the private exchange of public resources. It is difficult, if not impossible, to clearly discriminate between formal, informal, and illicit economic activities or, for that matter, between crime clans and big business. The blurriness of the borders is, in fact, the binding material of these groups' interdependence.

Another, related reason why it is challenging to write about organized crime in Italy is because, particularly among Italophiles and Italianists, it always already constitutes a discourse. Inevitably, references to "southern Italy and organized crime" conjure the criminal anthropologist Cesare Lombroso's racialized figure, the "violent criminal type."[32] They also summon the political scientist Edward Banfield's "amoral familism," distilled in the figure of the amoral Family, or the crime clan. In the master melodrama of modernization, amoral familism is supposed to be defeated by the "Western" figure of "civil society."[33]

Writing about southern Italy and organized crime also conjures the "Italian South," the original figuration that grounds all the others. In 1875, fifteen years after Italian unification, the historian Pasquale Villari (a liberal revolutionary who was exiled from Naples and settled in the northern city of Florence) and his intellectual contemporaries raised what he called the "Southern Question," the problem of the socially and economically underdeveloped south. Amid his searing depictions of poverty and ignorance in the former Kingdom of Naples, Villari argued that liberal intellectuals had shirked their national responsibility to lead southern Italians out of their backwardness and misery. In this way, he helped ground the figure of "the South" in a broader Italian nationalist program.[34] Since Villari and his contemporaries, southern Italy has been consistently impugned by northern Italians and Europeans as the exception to the laws of modernization and to the rule of law itself.[35]

In contemporary political, popular, and scholarly discourses on organized crime in Italy, the north-south distinction often surfaces more or less in its denigrating mid–nineteenth-century figuration. This "moral geography"[36] is reproduced across an array of binaries: in law (legal vs. illegal), economics (free markets vs. rackets), civics (associations vs. clans), and ethics (right vs. wrong). This binary thinking continues to affect how the South is imagined and how its people figure themselves.

### Affective-Aesthetic Effects

Binary thinking cannot draw the line between the camorra and the non-camorra. A crime clan holds together through forms of social organization and has determinate material effects in its territories, but it also activates potently indeterminate relations and affects. A crime clan has an atmospheric presence. An atmosphere is an object of perception, but one that is elusive and illusory, particularly when localized, identifiable *things* are a person's primary objects of attention.[37] An atmosphere is apprehended through other forms of perception, through situatedness and sensitivity in a "qualitative, quasi-energetic and affective field of forces."[38]

In turn, a crime clan is animated by the affective-aesthetic relations it activates with its territorialized residents and their relations with one another. People "find themselves" in a state and communicate and act in highly aestheticized ways.[39] They are attuned to the occulted potency of things, and they harness it in melodramatic, ironic, and seductive performances. In doing so, they also generate and reproduce the atmosphere.

Like Mercato, the broader *centro storico* immediately hit me like a welter of aesthetically and affectively charged activity. Outside 'Ncopp' 'e Mmura, the market of narcotic, gustatory, olfactory, and sensual desires, a tumult of visual stimuli also becomes noticeable. Foremost is the disarray of architectural splendor and atrocity: from the unearthed ancient Greek ruins to the aboveground palazzi revealing Byzantine, Gothic, and Angevin strata; from the upward-sprawling and chipped pale-pink baroque churches, marred by black graffiti and the gray of loitering seagulls, to the crumbling Renaissance villas with faded ceiling frescoes that peek through sooty windows and decades-old scaffolding; from the cavelike medieval arcades to the illegal steel-roofed shacks, overgrown with antennae, erected atop buildings everywhere, regardless of their historical significance. Here the Italian North and the camorra continue to produce the South through ongoing ruination.[40]

Outside the market, the aural density and kinetic vitality of Naples also attracts attention. Foremost are the vociferously performed life-scenes that seem to overinhabit the porous spaces throughout the *centro storico*:[41] from the unseen singing that accompanies, or overwhelms, the latest recording of a neomelodica song to the clanking of dinner dishes and cheering-in-unison during Sunday TV soccer matches; from the long, exaggerated horn-honking of eternal traffic jams at intersecting vicoli to the whizzing and weaving of *motorini* (scooters) stacked with man, woman, and child, and sometimes only the latter, chatting at maximum volume over the roar of engines on a cell phone or with another *centauro* (half-person, half-motorino), whose hand she holds while riding beside her; from the hyperbolic threats and tragic or indignant wailing that accompany scuffles, slaps, stabbings, and occasional shootings to the elaborate gestural contact among pedestrians who engage in exuberant, loving reunions and disengage again in the narrow cobblestone streets and across the unseen barriers of windows, balconies, the traffic, and other people doing the same along their own vectors.

Walter Benjamin and Asja Lacis noted something similar in 1927, when they wrote of Neapolitans, "In everything they preserve the scope to become a theater of new, unforeseen constellations. The stamp of the definitive is avoided. No situation appears intended forever, no figure asserts its 'thus and not otherwise.'"[42] Although everyday life is never mere theater and *no* life, for that matter, is "definitive," I could not simply dispel my initial impressions or the stereotypes composed by the many northern European and American travelers who have been taken by the atmospheres of Naples. Instead I attended to some of the affective-aesthetic events that animate these impressions and stereotypes.

Take, for instance, the bullet holes that appeared on the outside walls and steel barriers of some of the neighborhood shops on New Year's Eve of 2008. Every year, San Silvestre invokes a cataclysmic celebration in Naples, where people throughout the area launch heavy fireworks, set off explosives, and fire guns. That is why residents in the area of Mercato might have interpreted the damage on some of the storefronts in the morning as the work of errant bullets—but they knew better. The bullet holes, a resident who works for a social policy initiative told reporters under the condition of anonymity, were likely warning messages issued by clan affiliates to shop owners who had resisted paying *tangenti*. When a bomb exploded in front of a *pescheria* on the same street two days later, the message was less ambiguous. New Year's celebrations last for days, but the police believe that clan affiliates used the continuing clamor as their cover. As is often the case, the shop owner, the person perhaps in the "best" position to interpret the explosion, knew nothing.[43]

Take, for example, how commonplace sounds and ordinary speech acts can assume added significance. For five minutes every Friday at around midnight, fireworks explode from the rooftop of an apartment building in the historic center. Some of the neighbors say clan affiliates are signaling the arrival of a drug shipment and beckoning local *spacciatori* to fetch their shares. Relatedly, every day and at any hour, residents call out for their kin from apartment windows and balconies. Some of them are employed by drug handlers as their lookouts. They are beckoning *Maria!* and *Pascà!* to signal the approach of intruders.[44]

Crime clans are determinate political economic forces that reproduce themselves in indeterminacy. Crime clans do not simply impose their rule on everyday political economic life; they also insinuate themselves as affective-aesthetic effects. On the one hand, they exact violence to extort from residents their personal resources while interpellating them in tyrannical systems of deprivation and reward. They seize control of the distribution of public resources and broker dependent relationships that ensnare the resourceless. On the other hand, crime clans accomplish a great deal without doing any*thing*. An important part of their work is affective and aesthetic—composed in patterns of bullet holes and names called from balconies. Ephemeral, polysemous, and unreliable gestures and performances capture affect to generate an atmosphere. The atmosphere has a particular affective register that in turn registers itself in the sensory experience of its territorialized residents.

The radial effects of clan affiliates' violence traverse residents' lives in overdetermined and unsettlingly indeterminate ways. Crime clans create the atmosphere that they dominate, territorializing residents in an affective-aesthetic world suffused with fear, seduction, and "epistemic murk."[45] In this sense, the camorra is not a circumscribable thing but a part of everything, the atmospheric state of things.[46] In fact, crime clan affiliates and associates do not use the term "camorra." Instead, they refer to *sistemi* (systems).[47] People who find themselves in the atmosphere of a system are alert to its indeterminacies and unruly forces.

## The Art of Making Do in the Field

When I first made contact with the neomelodica music scene, I sensed atmospheres charged with fear and seduction. This had a direct impact on how people interacted with me. Interviews were out of the question; they inspired only the shellacked performances of endearing *napoletanità*, or "Neapolitanness," that, evidently, outsiders affectionately expect when they go to Naples. Casual conversation while hanging out was rarely a straightforward communication practice. Communication was often saturated with irony, flirting, warnings, and histrionics, and often all of these at once. If speculations and affirmations were not preposterously exaggerated or categorically dismissed, as they often were, they were lodged in metaphorical, allegorical, and proverbial language that resisted most of my attempts at disambiguation. My efforts to clear things up, in fact, only solicited less subtle forms of evasion, from omissions by ellipsis to dissimulation and bald-faced lies.

If talking was problematic, so was silence. When I was silent, people regarded me with suspicion. When they were silent, even if I asked them direct questions, their refusal to answer meant that I had crossed a line. I was not an investigative reporter or an infiltrator, but I felt that I was becoming one by default. And if that was how I also appeared to the people I met, then I demonstrated laughable ineptitude.

The people I met on the neomelodica scene expected me to study classic Neapolitan songs such as "Torna a Surriento" (Come Back to Sorrento) and "'O sole mio" (My Sun)—or much older music forms such as the villanella, the tarantella, and the tamurriata.[48] Folklore is abundant in Naples, and self-folklorizing tactics are part of the poetic repertoire some people use to gracefully keep strangers at a distance. This is one reason many people were vexed—and some notably unnerved—when I explained that my interest was contemporary Neapolitan music, *their* scene.

It did not help matters that I carried a video camera with me, but how could I resist? There was so much to register. But to many people, "an American with a video camera" meant opportunity. They heaped on me their hopes that I would connect them to a better future while anxiously wondering when I would go back to the future, the America of their dreams. They puffed up and self-dramatized, both courting and evading my video camera in a singular performance. They created distracting scenes to capture my attention while they made me the medium for their clichéd and self-aggrandizing autobiopics.

I was dumbfounded by how little control I had over my lens and stunned by the hours of "colorful" and "melodious" footage it accumulated. For months I frequented recording studios and TV stations, attended festivals, weddings, and baptisms, and visited the homes of composers, songwriters, managers, singers, and their fans, but it seemed I learned virtually nothing. How was that possible? Seduced by my mere presence, people opened their homes and studios to me. At the same time they feared I might get too close. The reason was in part that I, despite my better judgment, wanted to know more about the role of the camorra in the scene. I was not interested in unveiling the dirty truth about neomelodica music, but I could not help wondering whether the scene really was dominated by crime boss-impresari. If so, what did that mean for the hundreds of people who transacted with them on a regular basis?

It was clear that no one was going to talk straight with me, so I began to instigate conversation through indirection. I made music videos and TV commercials for broadcast on pirated television. I developed a portfolio with which to launch a business. I partnered with a recording studio, and through it I met a boss-impresario. Before long, I became the boss-impresario's in-house "American music video director," stepping quite effortlessly into the ad hoc performances that awaited me. These included writing my own songs and preparing, before I was interrupted, my debut as a neomelodico singer. Like others on the scene, I gave myself over to surges of becoming-sovereign. Like my associates, I was alert to the scene's uncertainties, duplicities, and potentialities, oscillating between the rush of affect and paranoiac entrenchment.

Between vitality and fear in the contact zone, the camorra resonates across multiple relations. These include ambivalent tolerance, wary forgiveness, mutual recognition, ironic playfulness, homosocial excess, erotic allure, creeping obligation, ensnaring indebtedness, burning resentment, competition, subjugation, paralyzed passivity, willful unknowing, and adamant disavowal. My participation in these relations fired up the "attentional activities" that "traverse" cognitive processes, entraining me to the neomelodica scene's atmospheres.[49]

## The Melodramatic Mode of Attention

This project stages a melodrama of contact. Contact is an affective-aesthetic happening, a commotion. It is the crossing of wires and short-circuiting of "perspective." Rather than privilege sight, contact summons multiple senses, including kinesthesia, intuition, and the sympathetic sense, opening you up to being affected. It also encompasses states of inattention such as deferred knowing or unknowing.

Contact is what happens in the zone where the rules are suspended and moral uncertainty can reign—and where play, threat, seduction, and histrionics are often the only resources for acting your way through scenes of intensity.[50] In the milieu where I lingered, contact describes how people interact in an atmosphere of fear, titillation, opportunity, and risk, drawing each other into performative entanglements. It is a modality through which meaning effects are communicated, negotiations wrought from indeterminacy, and self-determination and prepotency, at least momentarily, achieved.[51] Contact happens when people reach for the figure of the personal sovereign but instead brush up against an excessive limit: the camorrista. In the neomelodica scene, contact describes what happens during the musical performances of an intimate public that has contact with the camorra.

Contact necessarily also describes the entanglements of fieldwork and of meeting things proximally, laterally, and through indirection. It is a "contaminated critique" that unfolds in the affective-aesthetic time and space of complicity.[52] When contact happens, identifications and representations give way to the qualities and qualia of relation.[53]

In this story, I dispose myself to affective-aesthetic atmospheres. I yield to events of the senses that flare up like "profane illuminations," as Benjamin describes the productive disorientations that puncture the seamless sameness of bourgeois ("formal") capitalist experience.[54] By performing these dis-positions in writing, I want to conjure a contact zone charged with seductive vitalities and uncertain threats, leaving you to make your way among camorristi, people who behave like camorristi, and people (including me) who perform the art of making do.[55]

How do neomelodica music and organized crime make contact and spark an "underground" culture industry? This question has led many people to read in the neomelodica scene a melodrama of cultural hegemony and consent, a.k.a. complicity. However, the assertion that organized criminals use neomelodica music for the amoral education of hundreds of thousands of fans presumes a clear etiology of contact. It is the denouement of the didactive melodrama that defeats ambiguity.[56] Instead, the questions I pursue in my melodrama are as follows: What modes of attention let organized crime and neomelodica music become entangled? What worlds form through these shared experiences? What economies take effect and how do they feel to inhabit? What modes of attention let crime clan affiliates, crime clan associates, and people who simply live in the same milieu share affective-aesthetic experiences?

Like any other Italophile or Italianist focusing their attentions on Italy, I came into contact with the neomelodica music scene through affective, aesthetic, and interested entanglements. My understanding of crime clan affiliates, associates, and nonassociates is modulated by paranoid fear, anger, revulsion, intense curiosity, erotic allure, the desire to belong, the injury of being exploited, and the determination to carry out and "complete" my research, just as many of these forces have modulated others' understanding of me. Rather than look "before" or "beyond" these modulations for "narratives of origin and telos," I struggled to train, and not without lapses, my attention on atmospheres.[57] Instead of telling sovereign truths from the outside, I gathered stories that perform truths in the transient affective-aesthetic time and space between speculation and unknowing.

## NOTES

1. A *vicolo* is an alleylike street flanked by four- or five-story buildings with *bassi* (ground-floor dwellings), where sunlight can be blocked for much of the day. In the *vicoli* (pl.), domestic spaces overlap with the semipublic domain of the street, conjuring an affective-aesthetic space and a particular social geography of the popular classes.

2. *Basso* literally means "low."

3. Sal Da Vinci, "La forza di decidere" (The Strength to Decide) (EMI, 1998).

4. Mikhail M. Bakhtin, *Rabelais and His World* (Cambridge, Mass.: MIT Press, 1968), 184.

5. Matilde Serao, *Ventre di Napoli* (Cava de' Tirreni: Avagliano, 2002). Serao founded the most important Neapolitan daily newspaper, *Il Mattino*.

6. Peter Stallybrass and Allon White, *The Politics and Poetics of Transgression* (Ithaca, N.Y.: Cornell University Press, 1986).

7. Albert O. Hirschman, *The Passions and the Interests: Political Arguments for Capitalism before Its Triumph* (Princeton, N.J.: Princeton University Press, 1977), shows how liberal intellectuals during the Enlightenment argued that taming all the passions but avarice would yield a productive capitalist economy.

8. Gabriella Gribaudi, "Clan camorristi a Napoli: Radicamento locale e traffici internazionali," in *Traffici criminali: Camorra, mafie e reti internazionali dell'illegalità*, 187–240 (Turin: Bollati Boringhieri, 2009).

9. Two nonprofits, Legambiente and La Rete Salute & Gusto del Movimento Difesa del Cittadino, reported these findings, citing Campania for the highest number of incidents of incomplete or false labeling in 2004, although incidents are widespread in many regions in Italy. Legambiente, "Pesce fresco . . . Forse . . . Quasi: Primo rapporto di S&G sui prodotti ittici," *Alimentazione News*, December 21, 2004; Carolyn Nordstrom, *Global Outlaws: Crime, Money, and Power in the Contemporary World* (Berkeley: University of California Press, 2007).

10. In 2009 police raided warehouses containing 100,000 pirated copies of CDs and DVDs and duplication equipment. Marisa La Penna, "Porta Nolana, scoperti i depositi del falso, 100mila DVD," *Il Mattino*, May 22, 2009; "Centrale dei cd falsi: Oggi l'interrogatorio," *Cronaca di Napoli*, March 15, 2009, 93.63.239.228/archivio/2009/Marzo/15/Giornale_di . . . /15-03-pag.pdf. Pirated software also circulates among them.

11. Newer urban areas built in the 1960s through 1980s are called the *periferia*. Neomelodica music and performers also circulate in Switzerland, France, Spain, and, to a lesser extent, the United States, Canada, Argentina, and Australia.

12. *Neomelodici* is the plural form of *neomelodico*; both are used as adjectives and substantives.

13. There are far fewer female singers and, to my knowledge, no female composers or songwriters, and only two female talent managers. There is an old guard of male (and some female) singers (at the time of writing, in their thirties, forties, and fifties) and a number of "baby neomelodici" as young as eight.

14. In 1994 Naples had 42.7 percent "official" unemployment, and Scampia (of the periphery), 61.7 percent. In 1992, complying with European Union policies protecting fair competition, Prime Minister Giuliano Amato dismantled state-capitalist protectionist institutions, including the Southern Development

Fund, created in 1950 to stimulate economic growth. In the 1990s Naples deindustrialized with increasing speed, losing about one-third of its manufacturing industries and employment with the closings of the Italsider steel mill and Alfa Sud car factory. The service economy has not filled the gap. The Agency for Southern Promotion and Development, subsidizing agricultural and fishing development, the artisanal sector, small and medium businesses, large industry, and infrastructural development, was dissolved in 1993. Matteo Scaramella, "The Case of Naples Italy," In *Understanding Slums: Case Studies for the Global Report on Human Settlements*. (London: Earthscan, 2003), www.ucl.ac.uk/dpu-projects/Global_Report/pdfs/Naple.pdf.

15. Alexander Stille, *The Sack of Rome: How a Beautiful European Country with a Fabled History and a Storied Culture Was Taken Over by a Man Named Silvio Berlusconi* (New York: Penguin, 2006), 121.

16. Commissione Parlamentare Antimafia, *Commissione parlamentare d'inchiesta sul fenomeno della mafia e sulle altre associazioni criminali similari*, Doc. 23, no. 3 (Rome: Camera dei Deputati, Legislatura XIV, 2003). Between 1991 and mid-2007, seventy-five councils were disbanded in Campania, again significantly more than in other regions. Commissione Parlamentare Antimafia, *Consigli comunali sciolti*, Legislatura 15, 2007, http://www.camera.it/_bicamerali/leg15/commbicantimafia/documentazionetematica/23/schedabase.asp.

17. Nicholas Dines, "Urban Renewal, Immigration, and Contested Claims to Public Space: The Case of Piazza Garibaldi in Naples," *GeoJournal* 58, nos. 2–3 (2002): 177–88; Eleonora Pasotti, *Political Branding in Cities: The Decline of Machine Politics in Bogotà, Naples, and Chicago* (Cambridge: Cambridge University Press, 2010).

18. Antonio Bassolino, *Repubblica delle città* (Rome: Donzelli, 1996).

19. People in the milieu I frequented often described moving to northern Italy as "emigration."

20. For ethical practice, see Giorgio Agamben, *Homo Sacer: Sovereign Power and Bare Life* (Stanford, Calif.: Stanford University Press, 1998). See Italo Pardo, *Managing Existence in Naples: Morality, Action, and Structure* (Cambridge: Cambridge University Press, 1996), who includes religious ethics in his analysis of everyday economic and social life among some segments of the popular classes in Naples.

21. Carl Schmitt, *Uber die drei Arten des Rechtswissenschaftlichen* (Berlin: Duncker and Humbolt, 1993), 23–24, cited in Andreas Kalyvas, "Hegemonic Sovereignty: Carl Schmitt, Antonio Gramsci, and the Constituent Prince," *Journal of Political Ideologies* 5, no. 3 (2000): 348.

22. Brian Massumi, "The Autonomy of Affect," *Cultural Critique* 31 (1995): 83–110. "Capture" describes the confinement or closure of vitality (potential

or virtuality): "Affect is autonomous to the degree to which it escapes confinement in the particular body whose vitality or potential for interaction, it is. Formed, qualified, situated perceptions and cognitions fulfilling functions of actual connection or blockage, are the capture and closure of affect. Emotion is the most intense (most contracted) expression of that capture—and of the fact that something has always and again escaped" (96).

23. Roberto Saviano, *Gomorra: Viaggio nell'impero economico e nel sogno di dominio della camorra* (Milan: Mondadori, 2006), tracks the comingling of Milan-based haute couture fashion houses, undocumented and unregulated factories in Campania, and internationally organized crime networks that manage the circulation and sale of counterfeit goods.

24. Mary Louise Pratt, "Arts of the Contact Zone," *Profession* 91 (1991): 33–40, uses the term to describe "the social spaces where cultures meet and clash in often highly asymmetrical relations of power" (34).

25. Anna Lowenhaupt Tsing, *Friction: An Ethnography of Global Connection* (Princeton, N.J.: Princeton University Press, 2005).

26. Lauren Gail Berlant. *The Female Complaint: The Unfinished Business of Sentimentality in American Culture* (Durham, N.C.: Duke University Press, 2008), writes that intimate publics shape conventions of belonging and "provide a better experience of belonging partly through participation in the relevant commodity culture, and partly because of its revelations about how people can live" (viii).

27. Gribaudi, "Clan camorristi a Napoli."

28. See Renate Siebert, *Secrets of Life and Death: Women and the Mafia* (London: Verso, 1996), and Maria Pia Di Bella, *Dire ou taire en Sicile* (Paris: Félin, 2008).

29. In an episode of the MTV series *The Vice Guide to Everything*, produced by Alvi Hunter and Ciel Suroosh, the hosts visit Naples, "a city known for pizza, trash and the mob," to follow "the mafia's own music industry" and Alessio, a singer "owned by the mafia." Relatedly, New York City's Little Italy was an early-twentieth-century risqué tourist attraction for middle-class flânerie (Donna Gabaccia, "A Global Geography of 'Little Italy': Italian Neighbourhoods in Comparative Perspective," *Modern Italy* 11 (2006): 9–24.

30. Amato Lamberti, "Così governa la camorra," in *Osservatorio Sulla Camorra, 8, XII*. (Naples: Fondazione Colasanto, 1990).

31. Italian president Carlo Ciampi, quoted in John Phillips, "Fifth Mafia Boss Is Killed as Gang War Grips Italian South," *Independent*, January 7, 2005, https://www.independent.co.uk/news/world/europe/fifth-mafia-boss-is-killed-as-gang-war-grips-italian-south-26739.html.

32. Positivist social hygienists identified two distinct "races": the "Mediterranean" in the South and "European" in the North, the former predisposed to

committing violent crimes and the latter, property crimes (Gina Lombroso-Ferrero and Cesare Lombroso, *Criminal Man, according to the Classification of Cesare Lombroso* (Montclair, N.J.: Patterson Smith, 1972).

33. Edward C. Banfield, *The Moral Basis of a Backward Society* (Glencoe, Ill.: Free Press, 1958), writes that the "backward" society, an excessively inward-looking, kin-structured society (and the predominance of distrust of "strangers") is the binary opposite of "modern civil society."

34. Villari's writings, particularly *Lettere meridionali* (1875), influenced many intellectuals and politicians, including Pasquale Turiello and Matilde Serao.

35. Nelson Moe, *The View from Vesuvius: Italian Culture and the Southern Question* (Berkeley: University of California Press, 2002), shows that in the northern European imagination the south of Italy was depicted through both picturesque and denigrating terms.

36. Ibid.

37. Gernot Böhme, *Aisthetik: Vorlesungen über Ästhetik als allgemeine Wahrnehmungslehre* (Munich: Fink, 2001), 45, cited in Matthew Pritchard, "Directions in Contemporary German Aesthetics," *Journal of Aesthetic Education* 43, no. 3 (2009): 122. Pritchard summarizes Böhme's idea that atmospheres precede objects, signs, symbols, "physiognomies," and "scenes."

38. Mădălina Diaconu, "Patina—Atmosphere—Aroma," in *Logos of Phenomenology and Phenomenology of the Logos*, book 5, ed. Anna-Teresa Tymieniecka, 131–48 (Dordrecht: Springer Netherlands, 2006), 136. See also Mikel Dufrenne, *The Phenomenology of Aesthetic Experience* (Evanston, Ill.: Northwestern University Press, 1973); Gernot Böhme, "Atmosphere as the Fundamental Concept of a New Aesthetics," *Thesis Eleven* 36 (1993): 113–26; Ben Anderson, "Affective Atmospheres," *Emotion, Space, and Society* 2, no. 2 (2009): 77–81.

39. I draw on the notion of *Befindlichkeit* in Martin Heidegger, *Being and Time*, rev. ed., trans. Joseph Stambaugh (Albany: State University of New York Press, 2010).

40. Ann Laura Stoler, "Imperial Debris: Reflections on Ruins and Ruination," *Cultural Anthropology* 23, no. 2 (2008): 191–219, describes ruination as the aftershocks of empire: "Imperial formations persist in their material debris, in ruined landscapes and through the social ruination of people's lives" (194). Naples was capital of the Kingdom of Two Sicilies before it was annexed to the northern Italian Kingdom of Piedmont-Sardinia in 1860. Political economic developments accompanying Italian unification contributed to a decline in southern Italy's economy and the rise of organized crime.

41. Walter Benjamin and Asja Lacis described the city as "porous." "Naples," in *Reflections: Essays, Aphorisms, Autobiographical Writings*, ed. Peter Demetz, 163–73 (New York: Harcourt Brace Jovanovich, 1978).

42. Ibid., 166.

43. Mariano Rotondo, "Pallottole per chi non paga il pizzo," *Giornale di Napoli*, May 1, 2009; Rotondo, "Un'altra pescheria nel mirino del racket," *Giornale di Napoli*, May 1, 2009; Rotondo, "Raid incendiario contro pescheria," *Giornale di Napoli*, January 3, 2009.

44. Roberto Saviano, *Gomorra: Viaggio nell'impero economico e nel sogno di dominio della camorra* (Milan: Mondadori, 2006). Many of these voices are women's, indicative of their role in the domestic labors of organized crime. Women assist as *vedette* ("lookouts"), cut and package drugs, harbor fugitives, and protect affiliates. Women sometimes take leadership roles in crime clans, issuing orders and exacting violence. See Felia Allum, *Camorristi, Politicians, Businessmen: The Transformation of Organized Crime in Post-War Naples* (Leeds: Northern Universities Press, 2006); Gabriella Gribaudi, *Donne, uomini, famiglie: Napoli nel novecento* (Rome: L'ancora, 1999); Clare Longrigg, *Mafia Women* (London: Chatto and Windus, 1997); Renate Siebert, *Donne, la mafia* (Milan: Il Saggiatore, 1994).

45. Michael T. Taussig, *Shamanism, Colonialism, and the Wild Man: A Study in Terror and Healing* (Chicago: University of Chicago Press, 1986).

46. Anton Blok, *The Mafia of a Sicilian Village, 1860–1960: A Study of Violent Peasant Entrepreneurs* (New York: Harper and Row, 1975).

47. Saviano, *Gomorra*.

48. De Curtis, "Torna a Surriento" (Bideri, 1904); Di Capua, "O sole mio."

49. Natalie Depraz, "Where Is the Phenomenology of Attention that Husserl Intended to Perform? A Transcendental Pragmatic-Oriented Description of Attention," *Continental Philosophy Review* 37, no. 1 (2004): 5–20, calls attention to an embodied modulator of cognition. Attention has been a focus in philosophy, psychology, neurology, geography, and anthropology. See Edmund Husserl, *The Idea of Phenomenology* (The Hague: Martinus Nijhoff, 1964), and *The Phenomenology of Internal Time-Consciousness* (Bloomington: Indiana University Press, 1964); and Maurice Merleau-Ponty, *Phenomenology of Perception* (New York: Humanities Press, 1962). For psychology, see William James, *The Varieties of Religious Experience* (New York: Library of America, 2010. On neurology, see Antonio R. Damasio, *Descartes' Error: Emotion, Reason, and the Human Brain* (New York: Putnam, 1994), *The Feeling of What Happens: Body and Emotion in the Making of Consciousness* (New York: Harcourt Brace, 1999), and *Looking for Spinoza: Joy, Sorrow, and the Feeling Brain* (Boston: Houghton Mifflin Harcourt, 2003). On geography, see Ben Anderson, "Affective Atmospheres," *Emotion, Space, and Society* 2, no. 2 (2009): 77–81; and for anthropology, Thomas J. Csordas, "Embodiment as a Paradigm for Anthropology," *Ethos* 18, no. 1 (1990): 5–47, "Somatic Modes of Attention," *Cultural Anthropology* 8, no. 2 (1993): 135–56, and *Embodiment and*

*Experience: The Existential Ground of Culture and Self.* Cambridge: Cambridge University Press, 1994; Robert R. Desjarlais, *Body and Emotion: The Aesthetics of Illness and Healing in the Nepal Himalayas* (Philadelphia: University of Pennsylvania Press, 1992), *Counterplay: An Anthropologist at the Chessboard* (Berkeley: University of California Press, 2011), *Sensory Biographies: Lives and Deaths among Nepal's Yolmo Buddhists* (Berkeley: University of California Press, 2003); Michael Jackson, *At Home in the World* (Durham, N.C.: Duke University Press, 1995), *Excursions* (Durham, N.C.: Duke University Press, 2007), and *The Palm at the End of the Mind: Relatedness, Religiosity, and the Real* (Durham, N.C.: Duke University Press, 2009); Jack Katz and Thomas J. Csordas, eds., *Phenomenology in Ethnography* (London: Sage, 2003); Kathryn Linn Geurts, *Culture and the Senses: Bodily Ways of Knowing in an African Community* (Berkeley: University of California Press, 2002); Alan Klima, *The Funeral Casino: Meditation, Massacre, and Exchange with the Dead in Thailand* (Princeton, N.J.: Princeton University Press, 2002); William M. Reddy, "Against Constructionism: The Historical Ethnography of Emotions," *Current Anthropology* 38, no. 3 (1997): 327–51, "Emotional Liberty: Politics and History in the Anthropology of Emotions," *Cultural Anthropology* 14, no. 2 (1999): 256–88, and *The Navigation of Feeling: A Framework for the History of Emotions* (Cambridge: Cambridge University Press, 2001); Kathleen Stewart, "On the Politics of Cultural Theory: A Case for 'Contaminated' Cultural Critique," *Social Research* (1991): 395–412, *A Space on the Side of the Road: Cultural Poetics in an "Other" America* (Princeton, N.J.: Princeton University Press, 1996), "Arresting Images," in *Aesthetic Subjects: Pleasures, Ideologies, and Ethics*, ed. Pamela R. Matthews and David Bruce McWhirter, 431–48 (Minneapolis: University of Minnesota Press, 2003), and "Cultural Poeisis: The Generativity of Emergent Things," in *The SAGE Handbook of Qualitative Research*, ed. Norman K. Denzin and Yvonna S. Lincoln, 1015–30 (Thousand Oaks, Calif.: Sage, 2005); and Unni Wikan, "Beyond the Words: The Power of Resonance," *American Ethnologist* 19, no. 3 (1992): 460–82, and "Towards an Experience-Near Anthropology," *Cultural Anthropology* 6, no. 3 (1991): 285–305. See also works by Matei Candea, "Anonymous Introductions: Identity and Belonging in Corsica," *Journal of the Royal Anthropological Institute* 16, no. 1 (2010): 119–37, and *Corsican Fragments: Difference, Knowledge, and Fieldwork* (Bloomington: Indiana University Press, 2010); Bruno Latour, "How to Talk about the Body? The Normative Dimension of Science Studies," *Body and Society* 10, nos. 2–3 (2004): 205–29, and *Reassembling the Social: An Introduction to Actor-Network-Theory* (Oxford: Oxford University Press, 2005); and Bruno Latour and Vincent Antonin Lépinay, *The Science of Passionate Interests: An Introduction to Gabriel Tarde's Economic Anthropology* (Chicago: University of Chicago Press, 2009), for forms of social attention.

50. James W. Fernandez, "Dark at the Bottom of the Stairs: The Inchoate in Symbolic Inquiry and Some Strategies for Coping with It," in *Persuasions and Performances: The Play of Tropes in Culture*, ed. James W. Fernandez, 214–38 (Bloomington: Indiana University Press, 1986), calls this zone the "inchoate"; Gregory Bateson, "Play and Fantasy," in *The Game Design Reader: A Rules of Play Anthology*, ed. Katie Salen and Eric Zimmerman, 314–28 (Cambridge, Mass.: MIT Press, 2006).

51. For "meaning effects," see Mikhail M. Bakhtin and Caryl Emerson, *Problems of Dostoevsky's Poetics* (Minneapolis: University of Minnesota Press, 1984).

52. Stewart, "Politics of Cultural Theory." Brian Massumi, *Parables for the Virtual: Movement, Affect, Sensation* (Durham, N.C.: Duke University Press, 2002), 12–13, offers the term "productivism" to describe an alternative to critique that does not disavow its own "inventiveness."

53. Related notions: Michael Herzfeld's "local social theory" in *Poetics of Manhood: Contest and Identity in a Cretan Mountain Village* (Princeton, N.J.: Princeton University Press, 1988), and Klima's "philosophical ethnography" in *Funeral Casino*.

54. Stewart, "Arresting Images"; Walter Benjamin, "Surrealism," in *Reflections: Essays, Aphorisms, Autobiographical Writings*, ed. Peter Demetz, 177–92 (New York: Harcourt Brace Jovanovich, 1978).

55. This work resonates with performance-based and/or embodied ethnographies—see Lorne Dwight Conquergood, *Homeboys and Hoods: Gang Communication and Cultural Space* (Evanston, Ill.: Center for Urban Affairs and Policy Research, Northwestern University, 1993), and "Performing as a Moral Act: Ethical Dimensions of the Ethnography of Performance," *Literature in Performance* 5, no. 2 (1985); Norman K. Denzin, *Performance Ethnography: Critical Pedagogy and the Politics of Culture* (Thousand Oaks, Calif.: Sage, 2003); Fletcher Linder, "Life as Art, and Seeing the Promise of Big Bodies," *American Ethnologist* 34, no. 3 (2007): 451–72; Jaida Kim Samudra, "Memory in Our Body: Thick Participation and the Translation of Kinesthetic Experience," *American Ethnologist* 35, no. 4 (2008): 665–81; Julie Taylor, *Paper Tangos* (Durham, N.C.: Duke University Press, 1998); and Loïc J. D. Wacquant, *Body and Soul: Notebooks of an Apprentice Boxer* (New York: Oxford University Press, 2004)—and dialogical ethnographies; see Steven C. Caton, *Yemen Chronicle: An Anthropology of War and Mediation* (New York: Hill and Wang, 2005); Kathleen Stewart, "Politics of Cultural Theory," *Space on the Side*, and "Arresting Images"; and Dennis Tedlock, *The Spoken Word and the Work of Interpretation* (Philadelphia: University of Pennsylvania Press, 1983). It also dwells in contexts of uncertainty and ethical ambiguity—see Philippe I. Bourgois, *In Search of Respect: Selling Crack in El Barrio* (Cambridge:

Cambridge University Press, 1996); Nordsrom, *Global Outlaws*; Sudhir Alladi Venkatesh, *American Project: The Rise and Fall of a Modern Ghetto* (Cambridge, Mass.: Harvard University Press, 2000), *Gang Leader for a Day: A Rogue Sociologist Takes to the Streets* (New York: Penguin, 2008), and *Off the Books: The Underground Economy of the Urban Poor* (Cambridge, Mass.: Harvard University Press, 2006); On grappling with empathic contagions and entanglements in the field, see Ruth Behar, *The Vulnerable Observer: Anthropology that Breaks Your Heart* (Boston: Beacon, 1996); Steven C. Caton, *Yemen Chronicle*; Jeanne Favret-Saada, *Deadly Words: Witchcraft in the Bocage* (Cambridge: Cambridge University Press, 1980); and Renato Rosaldo, "Grief and a Headhunter's Rage: On the Cultural Force of the Emotions," in *Text Play and Story: The Construction and Reconstruction of Self and Society*, ed. Edward M. Bruner (Washington, D.C.: American Ethnological Society, 1984), including those centered on gender and sexuality (e.g., the contributors of Ellen Lewin and William Leap, *Out in the Field: Reflections of Lesbian and Gay Anthropologists* (Urbana: University of Illinois Press, 1996).

56. Fernandez, "Dark at the Bottom of the Stairs," 221.

57. Eve Kosofsky Sedgwick and Adam Frank, *Touching Feeling: Affect, Pedagogy, Performativity* (Durham, N.C.: Duke University Press, 2003), 8.

SIXTEEN

# Gomorrah: The Rest of the Story

*Valerio Caprara*

It is both curious and instructive to observe how the success of *Gomorra* (Gomorrah, 2008), a film based on Roberto Saviano's true-crime novel, with its ensuing and rather resounding trail of awards and controversies, has been able to collapse the plauditory house of cards built around the phenomenon of "new Neapolitan cinema." A cinema that, as one may recall, was supposed to have embodied—according to many pundits—a sudden and invigorating counterpoint, on an artistic level, to the city's "Renaissance," which is, in many ways, linked to the political ebb and flow surrounding the figure of Antonio Bassolino.[1] In a number of in-depth essays, we had already pointed out the strangeness of the equation, according to which, for example, we ought to conclude that the brightest periods of Neapolitan history could be located, in the middle of the "dark" 1950s, at precisely the time when the best films by and starring Vittorio De Sica, Totò, and the De Filippo brothers (Eduardo and Peppino), were surfacing. Having said this, it is easy to understand how a great portion of what is praiseworthy in this masterpiece by

Matteo Garrone (a Roman director, if we want to split hairs) is attributable to the director's ability to free his subject matter from the abovementioned constraints, which have more to do with petty politics than with historicity.

Garrone transposes Saviano's descent into the abyss of an underworld entity with a nonformalist's devotion and, instead, has the strength and courage to confer on the writer a renewed expressive register with a particularly cinematic design. The difference is obvious, for example, if we take the excellent *Biútiful cauntri* (Beautiful Country, 2008) by Esmeralda Calabria, Andrea D'Ambrosio, and Peppe Ruggiero, where the harsh images of the facts are channeled back to their documentary roots with the sole objective of stirring up a surge of related indignation. *Gomorra* cannot be classified based on its content, as many erroneous admirers as well as detractors have presumed, for the film plots a powerful and painful itinerary into the heart of twisted cultures, vitalistic plights, and brutal violence; a mosaic of stories that, on the entire surface of the big screen, offer a self-assessment—one minute playing out smoothly, as if hypnotized by the characters' fatalism, the next minute juxtaposing fragments of anguish and of suspense. The tireless approach can easily call to mind neorealism, but only in a Rossellinian way; that is, in a way that speaks of experiences that have not been forged from on high by the moral superiority of an artist but forged along with him. Garrone does not capture the snippets of an aberrant world for rhetorical or fiction-telling purposes, and at the same time he frees that world from documentary captions while preventing it from disintegrating into mass-media chaos. In order to achieve such an intense result he needs to blend, within this grim symphony, actors with great expertise and stature together with utter novices, who are able to hold their own against the challenges of complex and detailed sequences, adjusting the nuances of a bloodthirsty and schizophrenic slang according to the trajectories of each shoot. In this way, then, viewers won't be moved, horrified, or disoriented by the extraordinary portrayals of Toni Servillo as the toxic-waste laundering boss, Gianfelice Imparato as the bagman for the mob, Salvatore Cantalupo as a humble and disenchanted tailor, and Gigio Morra as the shady garment contractor, any more than they would be by the portrayals entrusted to such nonprofessional actors as Salvatore Abruzzese, Salvatore Striano, Carmine Paternoster, Marco Macor, Ciro Petrone, Giovanni Venosa, Vittorio Russo and many others: faces, bodies, derisive sneers, and movements that are animalistic and monstrous yet somehow recognized and recognizable, and which sink their claws into the viewers' imagination just like the leading men in Martin Scorsese's *Goodfellas* or Brian De Palma's *Scarface*. In this way, there is truly nothing in common with the luster of a color lithograph that, as far as Naples is concerned, tends to expand into the most unexpected genres: lucid and never complacent, *Gomorra* has no desire to privilege the "narrated" episodes over the "photographic" ones, and it is consequently supported by a strategically coherent soundtrack, in which the neomelodic pieces alternate with Nino D'Angelo's repertoire; then they are intermingled with the unintelligible echoes of the hellish environment around them; and finally they vanish into the obsessive cadence of trip hop band Massive Attack. The most significant element, from a moral and linguistic point of view, is revealed by the fact that the most chilling sequences are those that are filmed in long and extreme long shots to establish a postapocalyptic setting: deserted shipyards and abandoned houses, cement labyrinths and contaminated countrysides, where human beings prove to be completely secondary and can be crushed like cockroaches or rats. It would not be futile to remember, at this point, how Garrone began his association with frighteningly realistic representations by completely reinventing himself with *L'imbalsamatore* (The Embalmer, 2002), a deranged and "unpalatable" film noir that transforms some of the very locations (Villaggio Coppola and the sprawling seaside of Castelvolturno) into a narrative element intrinsic to the unsavory story of sexual subjugation.

This extremely sophisticated method, which consists of a transition from an "anti-narrative regime" to that of *conventional* narrative, is not at all a given in this phase of cinema inspired by this Gotham City in the shadow of Mt. Vesuvius. We have seen and critically praised, for example, fairly solid works like *Pater familias* (2003) by Francesco Patierno or *Certi bambini* (A Children's Story, 2004) by Andrea and Antonio Frazzi, who exude a certain something both assertive and didactic that negates their dramaturgical premise and reduces it to the recesses of good intentions, which is the greatest cliché of those artists who want to be applauded even before the show begins. Much more interesting and, among other things, innovative on the *cattivista* [i.e., radical, provocative pulp artists] side of corporate reckoning, there is *Luna rossa* (Red Moon, 2001) by the eternal outsider Antonio Capuano, who, at a time during which no one could have conceived of it, overturns the cinematic emphasis on exposés in his tragicomedy about a self-cannibalizing criminal power. In the dreamlike sequence of tableauxs, somewhere between Neapolitan *sceneggiata* [i.e., a variety of melodrama] and avant-garde theater, as the film tells the story of repentant member of a Camorra clan, it not only recalls a symphonic representation of a massacre but it also allows this symphony to reverberate in the clothes, bodies, houses, property, voices, and gestures, signs, and symbols of protagonists who are as completely wicked and low-class as they are gratified by the their own cult of personality. Capuano is, after all, a top-rate director, and militant with his camera, as we witness in his successive, and incredibly unique, experiment with his unresolved yet sincere—even to the point of wrenching—*La guerra di Mario* (Mario's War, 2006). In fact, in this case the war against the law on the part of the criminals leaves room for the all but metaphoric struggle between two Neapolitan souls—that of the well-to-do neighborhoods with their respectable citizens and that of the degraded outskirts with their aggressive and thuggish *mau-maus*. Though it seems evident that the film becomes a victim of the play between thesis and antithesis and though the film accords a whiff of age-old Manichaeism on the frustrated female protagonist's attempt to eradicate the Camorra DNA from the bad boy she has taken into custody, one cannot help but admire Valeria Golino's performance in the role of a middle-class woman filled with love and altruism that verge on other-wordly lunacy—perhaps a nod to Ingrid Bergman's similar performance in Roberto Rossellini's *Europa 51*.

Even though it was hindered by a deficient distribution, insufficient marketing, and a sort of populist rhetoric, *L'avvocato De Gregorio* (De Gregorio, Esquire, 2003), by Pasquale Squitieri, can be useful in positively elucidating the gap between leisurely acceptance of natural-law revivalism and a rash impulse of pure fiction. The trajectory of the dodgy disbarred lawyer who redeems himself by revealing the unpunished parties responsible for a workplace death is, in fact, undertaken powerfully by Giorgio Albertazzi to maintain his grasp on a life so consumed and scorned as to logically become extreme, grotesque, and the stuff of tabloid journalism. Not unlike Squitieri's overlooked film we find, among others, Marco Risi's much more well-promoted *Fortapàsc* (Fort Apache, 2008), which is a reconstruction of the murder of Giancarlo Siani, an aspiring reporter for the daily paper, *Il Mattino*, and in which the weaknesses are offset by the strengths. The last four months in the life of the twenty-seven-year-old—a victim of gunfire by the Camorra's assassins in September 1985—are reconstructed diligently based on a strategy dear to Francesco Rosi and quite often replicated by the various Elio Petris, the Damiano Damianis, and, of course, Squitieri: in terms of quality and credibility, the acting is airtight, also because Risi (contrary to what he offered us two years earlier in the no-frills biopic *Maradona—La mano de Dios* [Maradona: The Hand of God]) knows how deal with a story's "flesh and blood" (with formidable nonstandard actors like Antonio Buonomo and Massimiliano Gallo, whom he employs to lead an abominable crew of lost souls from the local pantheon of organized crime). The film's negative aspects, again, pertain to his resorting to demagogic monologues and to pedantic sketches, the temptation against which *Gomorra* is able to resist and, thus, turn around 180 degrees to form a grandiose metaphor. So gifted in the actions (and reactions) of his negative heroes, Risi is overly trusting of his clever scriptwriters when he has to note the slippery and ever-recurring connection between the mob clans and civil society: the delicate rapport, which we have found to be crucial, between representation and invention is thus shattered in the rigid lines and in the good conscience or in the politically correct considerations aimed at an assortment of traditional and easy targets.

Vincenzo Marra surely possesses just the right vision to experiment with the notable possibilities of the so-called *docufiction* and, in fact, *Tornando a casa* (*Sailing Home*, 2001)—a rather coarse and modest re-reading of the neorealist masterpiece, *La terra trema* (The Earth Trembles)—is a powerful and one-of-a-kind film. It's a shame that—first, in his dignified *Vento di terra* (Land Breeze, 2004), and, later, in his disastrous 2007 film *L'ora di punta* (The Trial Begins)—this young director has neglected the risky stylistic choices and the joy of linguistic retribution to end up settling for retracing current-event controversies that it may have been better to leave to television talk show venues like *Ballarò* or *Porta a porta*. In reality it appears that Marra's vocation is quite the opposite—that is, he has the courage to depict the contemporary bestiary by employing modalities of the classic epic. It is not by chance that his best work is the documentary *L'udienza è aperta* (The Court Is in Session, 2006), in which three professionals up to their necks in the torment of daily judicial chaos (an appeals court chief justice, an associate judge, and a criminal attorney) are shadowed by the camera with such passion and constancy as to be transformed, right before the viewers' eyes, into towering and riveting mytho-symbolic characters. In this category, which we could decidedly maintain is of a pervasive order—that is, replete with directors antithetical to the canon (and by no means do we intend to ascribe any sort of marks of distinction or excellence to this trend)—it is rather logical to aim the spotlight at a figure like Paolo Sorrentino. In fact, this director and screenwriter, born in 1970, from the Vomero section of Naples, is truly an artist, in the less rhetorical and more pragmatic sense of the word: incensed and brooding, nonconformist and capricious, bohemian and upmarket, Sorrentino—thanks also to his exploits in *Il divo* (2008)—by now is in the vanguard of the national cinema elite, but it is clearly not possible to isolate him from his peculiar roots. We just need to consider, after all, his debut film, which is, so far, the only one that takes place completely in Naples, to expound his power, his tension, his originality: *L'uomo in più* (One Man Up, 2001), one of the best Italian films of the last decade, recounts the parallel rise and fall of both a successful soccer star and a cursed crooner—each born on the same day of the same year—and, at the same time, the film develops the cathartic itinerary within the labyrinths of destiny that these postmodern antiheroes face. Thanks, in particular, to the sublime acting of Tony Servillo (but also to the dusky portrayal by Andrea Renzi), *L'uomo in più*, without any forced self-referentiality, finds a place in the leading edge of the most lucid contemporary cinema; a cinema that, with bold methods, continues to probe the most obsessive issue of all: the rapport between the gaze and the subject, the distance, or the difference, separating vision, emotion, and awareness. Quite dissimilar in the race to the top position, both among critics and at the box office, Lamberto Lambertini, Nina Di Majo, and Antonietta De Lillo contribute, nonetheless, to maintaining the relevance of auteur cinema and carefully preserving its DNA without, in the process, selling it out to stereotypes and patriotic consensus. While Di Majo, with her *L'inverno* (Winter, 2002) shows that even in the city of lights (often melodramatic and almost consciously plebian) it is possible to immerse oneself in the enigmatic shadows of middle-class alienation that bears the typical imprint of Antonioni's work, De Lillo's 2004 *Il resto di niente* (Remnants of Nothing) and Lambertini's 2006 *Fuoco su di me* (Fire at My Heart) reconstruct fundamental episodes from the city's history with limited means, but with a tireless ingenuity that translates

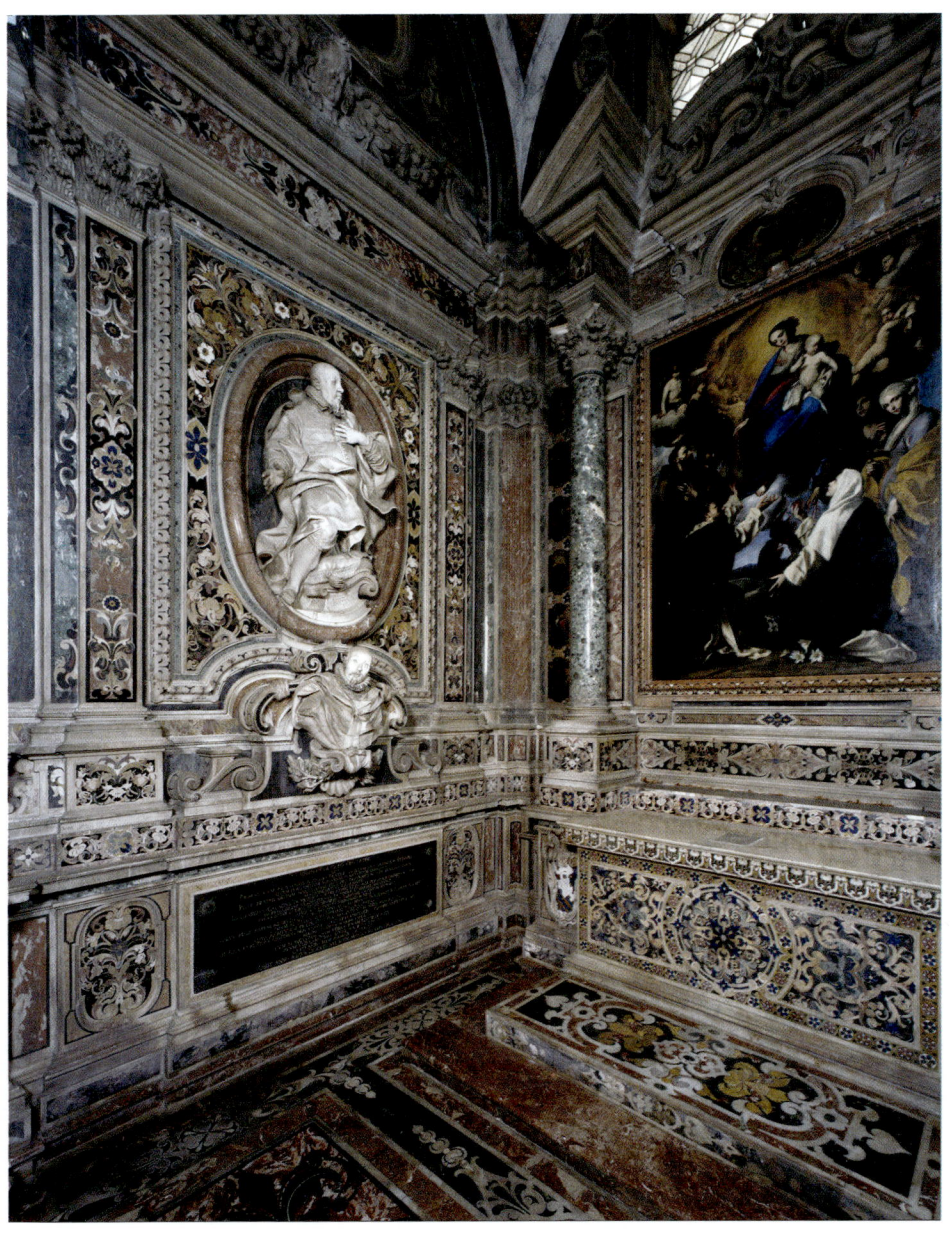

Plate 12-1. Cosimo Fanzago (with Andrea Bolgi and Massimo Stanzione), Basilica of San Lorenzo Maggiore, Cacace Chapel, 1638–50
Archivio Luciano Pedicini

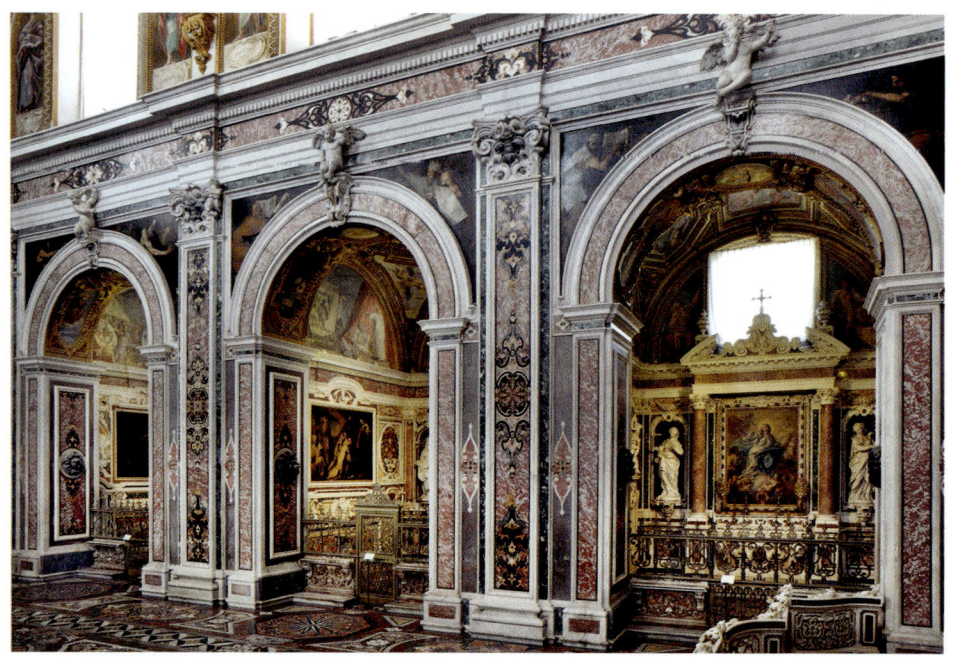

Plate 12-2. Certosa di San Martino, south wall of nave, revetment by Cosimo Fanzago, spandrel paintings by Jusepe de Ribera ("Lo Spagnoletto"), 1623–56
Photo by Fabio Speranza

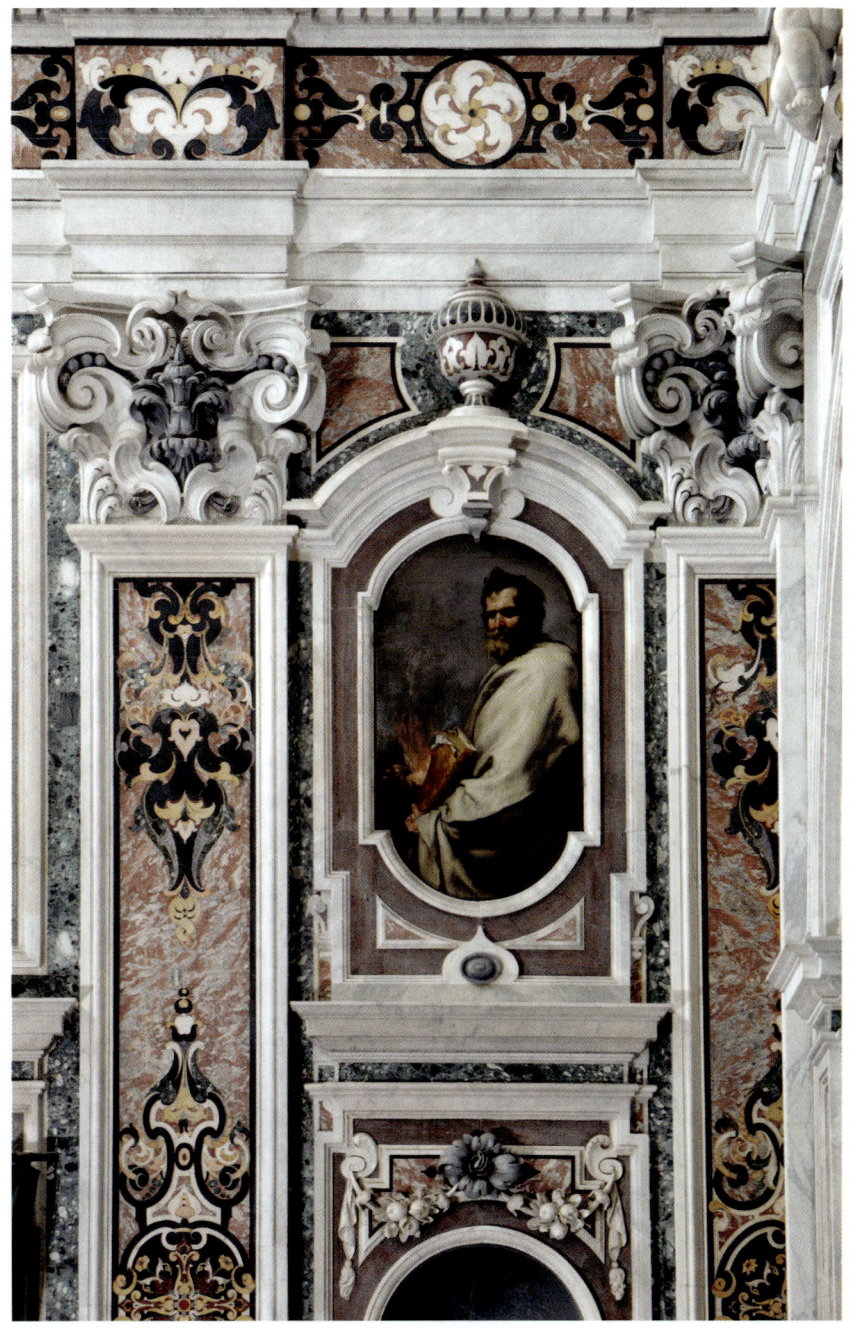

Plate 12-3. Certosa di San Martino, Cosimo Fanzago and workshop, marble revetment framing Jusepe de Ribera's painting, *Elias* (revetment 1631–56; *Elias*, 1638–43)

Photo by Fabio Speranza

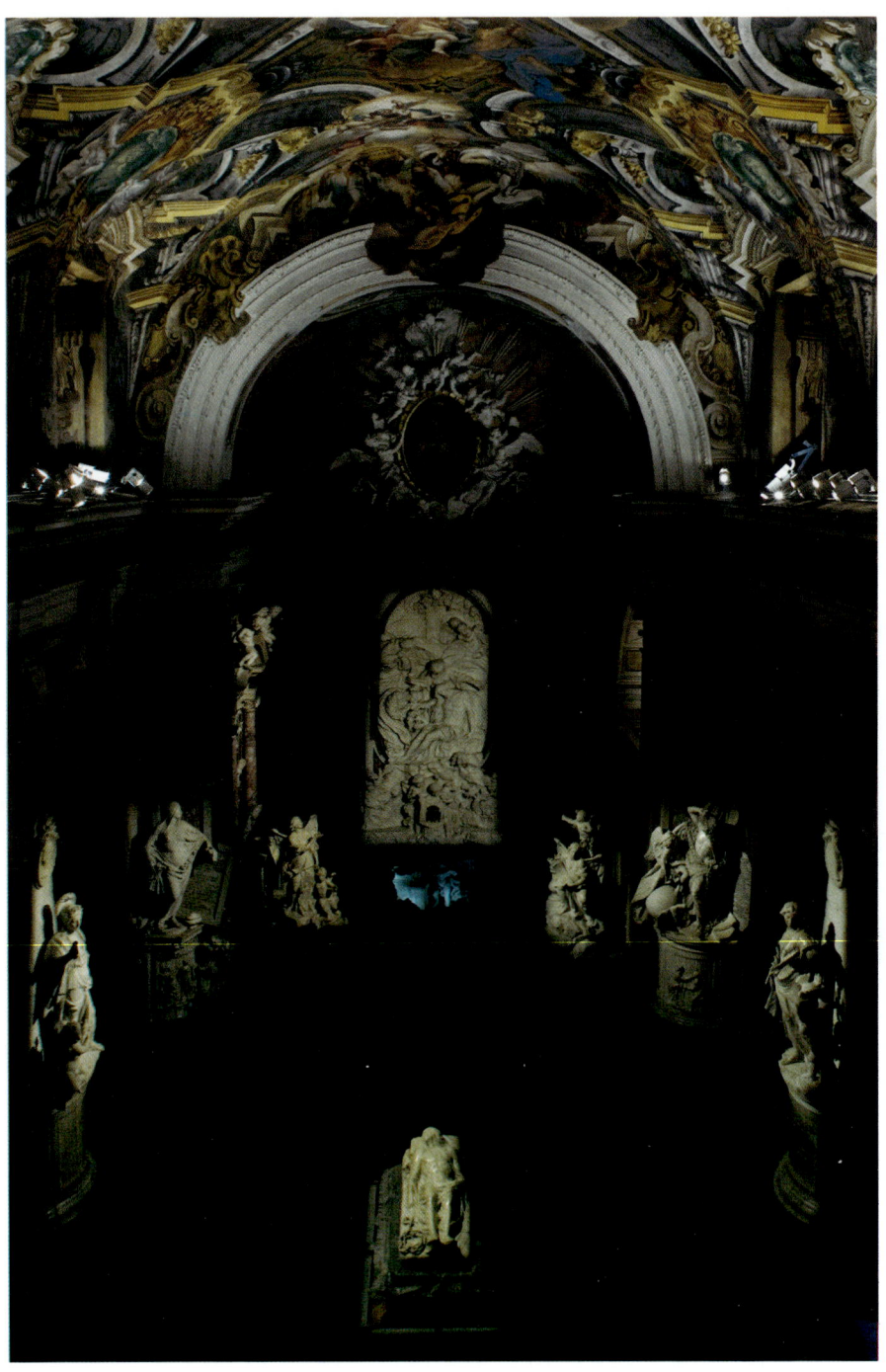

Plate 13-1. Sansevero Chapel, overview

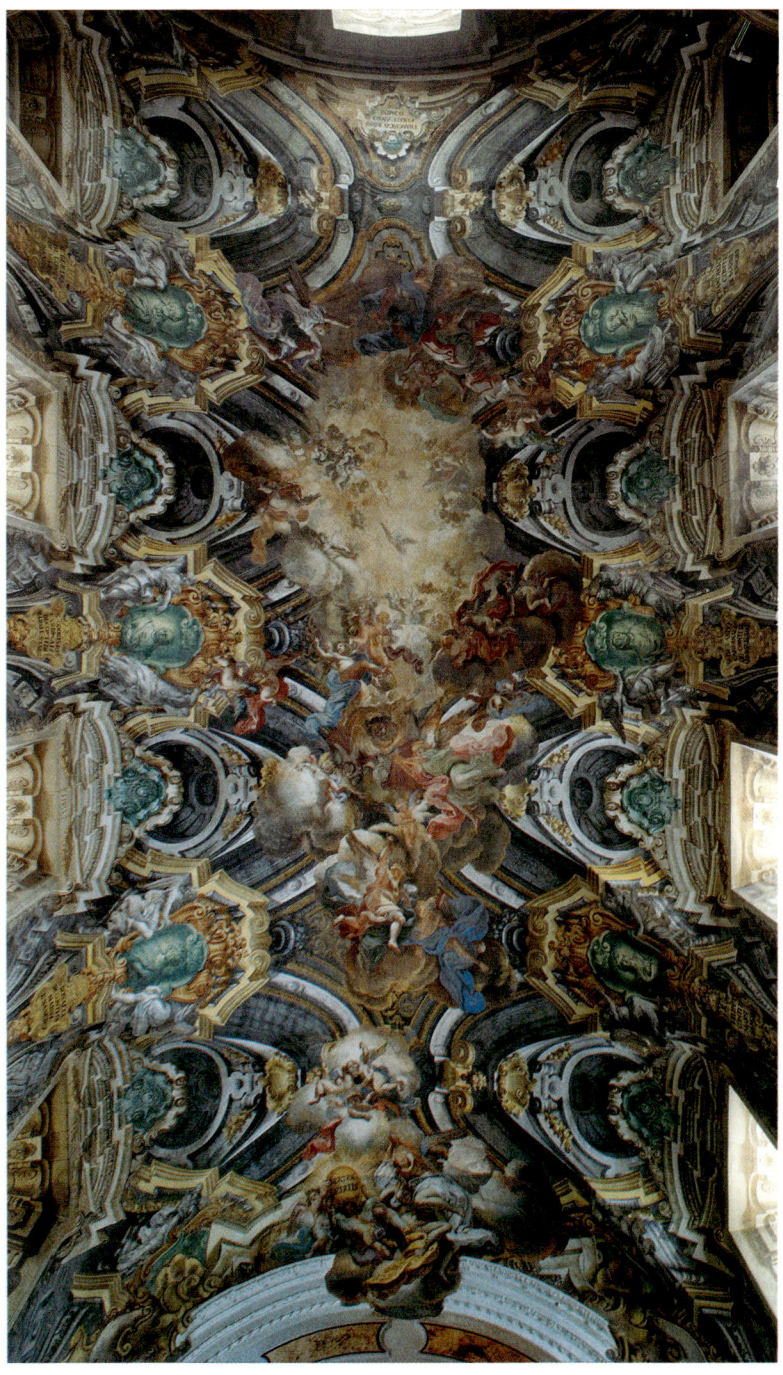

Plate 13-2. Francesco Maria Russo, vault with the *Glory of Heaven*, 1749

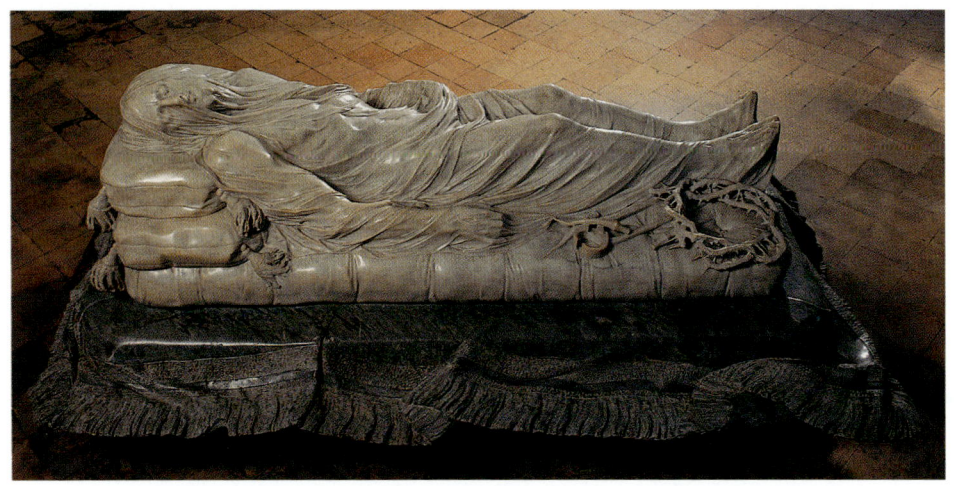

Plate 13-3. Giuseppe Sanmartino, *Veiled Christ*, 1753

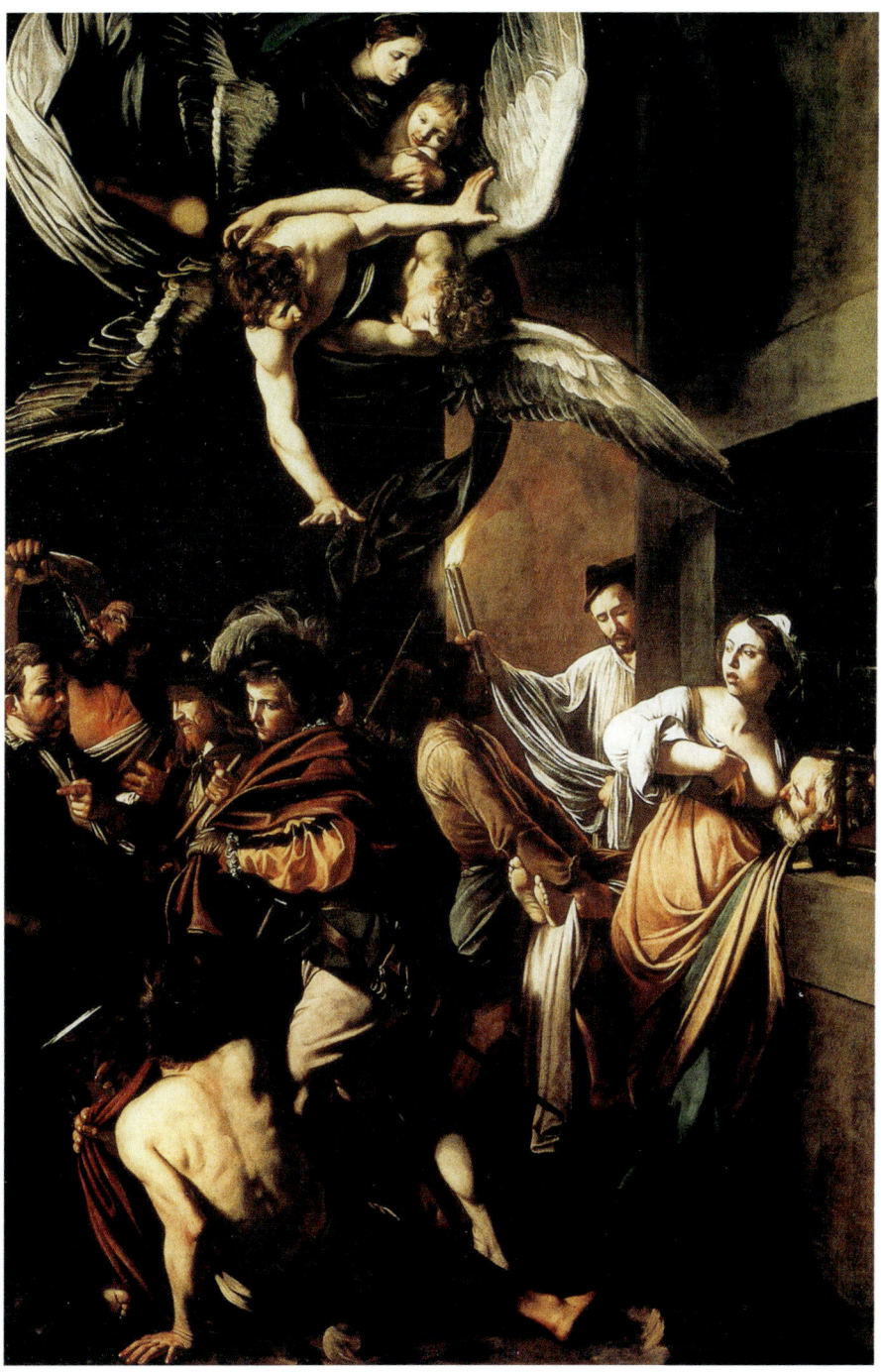

Plate 14-1. Michelangelo Merisi (1571–1610), Caravaggio, *The Seven Acts of Mercy*, ca. 1607, Pio Monte della Misericordia, Naples.

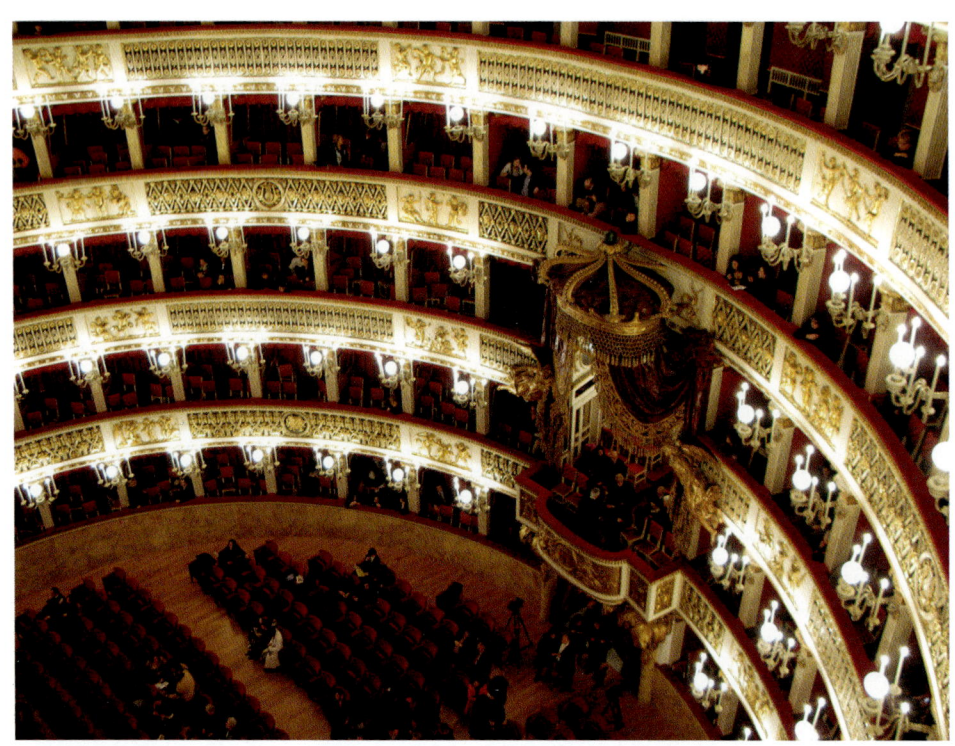

Plate 20-1. Teatro di San Carlo, 1737, Naples
Pasquale Matrisciano/Wikimedia Commons

into a series of portraits—in the former's case, high-voltage and spasmodic; in the latter's case, unhinged yet charming—that reveal an unforeseeable eloquence. The fact that a group of filmmakers, completely unsupported, from a production standpoint, were able to, albeit sporadically, express themselves at such a level, testifies to how paramount the links to cultural origins and indigenous instincts can be. This factor explains, on the contrary, the distortion of a setting on the part of an outsider like Francesca Comencini in *Lo spazio bianco* (The White Space, 2009), based on the book by Valeria Parrella. With great feminine sensitivity, this film addresses the theme of maternity, but the theme is rendered clumsily by her attempt to embellish the female protagonist's painful journey by employing a genuine diorama of political correctness.

The outsiders, as one might imagine, within the Neapolitan context, inevitably tend to subscribe to the notion of normalcy, unless, as in the case of Papi Corsicato, they happen to stay true to an occasional idiosyncratic and fickle streak that stems more from their nature than as a result of necessity. If *Chimera* (2000) marks an overall loss because extreme kitsch comes across like a Baudelairean albatross (which, like the poet, becomes ungainly and grotesque when taken out of the air and forced to succumb to land), *Il seme della discordia* (The Seed of Discord, 2008) reworks the unmistakable mix of dark humor, pop icons, foreign gadgets, and behaviors that stand out against the metaphysical backgrounds inhabited by carnal characters. Based on Heinrich von Kleist's famous story—previously adapted by Éric Rohmer—the film addresses the experiences of its characters without wallowing in armchair sociology, although it does become a latticework of images in the form of disoriented flashes, cartoon animation, aberrant details, and surges of pure surreal bliss. Corsicato certainly does not aspire to get involved in investigative journalism or talk shows dedicated to the dynamics of dysfunctional couples and to the state of the institution of marriage; what interests and jazzes him, in the context of utopian communities of the Centro Direzionale [Naples's business and service center], is the most paradoxical contrast ever between matter and the mind. In this sense, the characters' looks, the sublime substance of their intentions, and the reproachless alienation of their destinies all choreograph a ballet that seems to be frivolous and easygoing, but on a second look, it is full of moral rifts and emotional vacuums. Within the category of storytellers who are most inclined to go in for asides and pauses rather than for final pronouncements, we can add—almost in order to reward ourselves with the certainty of a restoration that is cyclic, if not eternal—a newcomer and a veteran. . . . There is clearly no similarity between the Jarmuschesque *Una notte* (One Night, 2007) directed by showbiz scion Tony D'Angelo (and to think that his father, Nino, had stopped seven years earlier with the cinematic parody, *Aitanic*[2]) and the scintillating *Napoli, Napoli, Napoli* (2009), by New Yorker Abel Ferrara; nor could we say that we are in the presence of momentous results. However, it is useful to underline how, in both cases, the motivation of redeeming a city fallen into the lowest echelon of civil coexistence comes with an renewed sense of theater and a sensibility that has departed from institutional bonds.

If there is a formula that is supported by the facts, it is the union of Neapolitan ethos and comedy, the reason for which it is not particularly surprising that the gold mine of this mega-genre will not risk exhaustion, even at this turn of the century. It might prove monotonous to list the various personalities and the more or less seasoned productions that continue to speak to audiences in the register that belonged to Totò and Peppino [De Filippo]. The luckiest and most popular is without a doubt Vincenzo Salemme, who, from *L'amico del cuore* (My Best Friend's Wife, 1998) and thereafter, released roughly one film per year—*Amore a prima vista* (Love at First Sight), *A ruota libera* (Freewheeling), *Volesse il cielo!* (God Willing!), *Ho visto le stelle* (I Saw Stars), *Cose da pazzi* (Crazy Business)—without ever even remotely reaffirming the hilarious wit of his debut. Proof that this is not a mere question of snide prejudice on our part is Salemme's output for the two-year period of 2007–8 (*Sms-Sotto mentite spoglie* [Text Message: Under False Pretenses[3]] and *No Problem*) already seem just a bit more pleasant and refined, without, however, being able to come to terms with the idea that the director-actor, who trained with Eduardo De Filippo's troupe, might be more genetically suited to playing live farce on the stage, without any obstruction on the part of the cold transference of the camera lens. It's only fair to recall Eduardo Tartaglia's *Il mare non c'è paragone* (Nothing Like the Sea) and *Ci sta un francese, un inglese e un napoletano* (There's a Frenchman, an Englishman, and a Neapolitan); *Incantesimo napoletano* (A Neapolitan Spell) and *Nessun messaggio in segreteria* (You Have Zero Messages) by the duo Paolo Genovese and Luca Miniero; Bruno De Paola's *Il sogno nel casello*

(Tollbooth Dreams); or the "foreigner," Francesco Ranieri Martinotti, who employs the sketch comedian, Alessandro Siani, to follow in the delicate and graceful steps of Massimo Troisi in *Ti lascio perché ti amo troppo* (I'm Leaving You Because I Love You Too Much, 2006) and *La seconda volta non si scorda mai* (You Never Forget the Second Time, 2008). But there is still the distinct feeling that narcissism rears its head and wastes time "running out the clock" on faces, gestures, and one-liners without paying necessary attention to the "counteroffensives" of storyline and script.

Anyone interested in this sort of thrill—that is, finding that sense of being at home at the end of an obstacle course of signposts, which are less useful for providing us with the usual information or for identification purposes than, if anything, for burning energy—ought to look to hybridized films that are able, let's say, to pass from one extreme of our imprinting to the other, just like Giuseppe Rocca's provincial *Lontano in fondo agli occhi* (Distant, and Deep in One's Eyes, 2000), Fabrizio Bentivoglio's 2007 *Lascia perdere, Johnny!* (Don't Waste Your Time, Johnny!), and Silvia Maja's metropolitan *Ossidiana* (Obsidian, 2007), which is a heart-wrenching and visionary invocation of the unhappy existential journey of the painter Maria Palliggiano in the 1950s and 1960s. Or, maybe one could get a copy of Massimo Andrei's rhapsodic and resplendent 2006 film *Mater Natura* (Mother Nature), which is a work as vivid as it is imperfect: it absorbs unprecedented, as well as conventional, allusions in the same stylistic maneuvers, as he extracts numerous pearls from the magma of a script that purposefully (and dangerously) hovers at the margins of *camp*. Albeit with a contemporary gaze, this film revisits the distressing and emotional theme of the "trans-gender with a heart of gold" who is wrapped in the trappings of luxury. Here, the actor, writer, and director (born in 1967) devotes himself, ultimately, to making over, on his own terms, the most basic method that runs from Elvira Notari to Mario Merola.

The final concern of a scholar or an aficionado ought to be, then, that of dreading the "end of history," even in this mythopoetic vector. Meanwhile, cinema about, on, and for Naples is entrusted to the qualitative leap of not-so-newcomers like Francesco Patierno and Stefano Incerti (whose 2010 *Gorbaciof—Il cassiere col vizio del gioco* [Gorbaciof—The Accountant Addicted to Gambling] was custom-fit for Toni Servillo, whose impressive talent will be able to survive the risk of authorial overexposure) and to the desirable return of outsiders like Carlo Luglio (who resurged resourcefully after the crude *Capo Nord* [North Cape] to give us the substantial and blunt *Sotto la stessa luna* [Under the Same Moon]) or Diego Olivares (creator of the small epic, *I cinghiali di Portici* [Wild Boars of Portici]). And we should not ignore the growth of Vincenzo Terracciano, who was already impressive in *Ribelli per caso* (Accidental Rebels, 2001), a brilliant libertarian parable that takes place in a gastroenterology ward of a hospital. His more recent *Tris di donne & abiti nuziali* (Bets and Wedding Dresses, 2009) that glides lithely from the classic theme of a self-destructive passion for gambling to the more innovative theme of a southern Italian familism that, in solidarity, however irregular and amoral the behavior of its members, seems to function. Not coincidentally, alongside the well-established team of Terracciano and Laura Sabatino, the script boasts the name of Giuseppe (Bepi) Improta, a brilliant intellectual, writer, and film lover who lived through and defined an epoch of transgressive youth from the Vomero district. The key to reading this slightly dark *neo-commedia italiana* lies right in that Neapolitan hillside neighborhood where middle- and working-class "normalcy" is about to be shattered by the "other" city, infamous for its widespread subjugation to crime: the gaming table, the betting halls, the illegal gambling dens or the racetrack, foreshadow, as such, the misdeeds of the soccer betting scandals—these locations are like miniature stadiums in which vitalistic gambling and anticonformism become, in their own way, a work of resistance. The escalators of Via Morghen, illuminated by the almost nostalgic tones of cameraman Fabio Cianchetti, embody, as such, a useful allegory for the pendulous narrative movement that causes the De Filippian deus ex machina (Sergio Castellitto) and the other characters to come to terms with their obsessions, but also to invest themselves with the ambiguous masks of a looming Neapolitan "Renaissance." All in all, we are left with an additional sense of optimism in that the media has begun to embrace, in their dilapidated but ever hallowed halls, such names as Angelo Curti, from Teatri Uniti,[4] and Nicola Giuliano, along with Francesca Cima, of Indigo Film[5]—names that, in other times, would have been buried in the obscurity of logbooks to which only authorized personnel would have had access.

*Translated by Gregory Pell*

TRANSLATOR'S NOTES

1. The mayor of Naples from 1993 to 2000.
2. The almost untranslatable title is a complete play on words. On a phonetic and titular level, "Aitanic," (pronounced "eye-tanic") sounds like "Titanic," the eponymous 1997 film (directed by James Cameron) that D'Angelo aims to parody here. However, it also refers to, in the greater context of the central plot, a character named Gaetano, who is nicknamed "Aitano" (ex. 'aetano).
3. Clearly, in the translation, we lose the play on acronyms: "Sms" both as "short-message-system," better known as text messaging, and the subtitle played out as an abbreviation in the original Italian title.
4. "United Theaters," a Naples-based theater and film production company, founded in 1987 by Toni Servillo, Mario Martone, and the late Antonio Neiwiller. Angelo Curti is its current president; Servillo still serves as the creative director.
5. Indigo Film is a film production house that was founded in 1994 by Giuliano and Cima, along with Carlotta Calori, all graduates of the Experimental Film Center in Rome, and has produced, for example, all of Paolo Sorrentino's films, including *La grande bellezza* (2014).

**Writing and Singing Naples**

SEVENTEEN

## Anna Maria Ortese: Breaking the Spell of Naples?

*Andrea Baldi*

> Napoli is used to following its citizens everywhere, like a shadow, if they move away.
>
> —FABRIZIA RAMONDINO

Anna Maria Ortese entertained a deeply ambivalent relationship with Naples, where, between 1928 and 1948, she spent her youth and most of her early adulthood, falling prey to the allure of the place and, at the same time, resisting and denouncing its dangerous fascination. This backdrop and its dwellers occupy center stage in the author's oeuvre, despite her temporary relocations, starting in 1939, and her definitive "flight" from the city in 1952, to return there only very few times and for brief periods, because of the controversies stirred by *Il mare non bagna Napoli* (The Bay Is Not Naples, 1953).[1] Ortese's writings tenaciously harbor and transfigure the impressions and recollections of her Parthenopean experiences. This insistence marks the long trajectory that extends through some of the narratives collected in *L'infanta sepolta* (The Buried Infanta, 1950), her second book, where at times she refashions her urban encounters in visionary terms, culminating with *Il cardillo addolorato* (The Lament of the Linnet, 1993), set in the capital of the Bourbon kingdom at the twilight of the eighteenth century and shrouded in melancholy light, drawing on folkloric and fantastic motifs (an image that counters the contemporary city, filled with "Spanish and natural horrors").[2] In the four decades between these two works, two other landmarks stand out in regard to her Neapolitan attachments. *Il mare non bagna Napoli*,[3] a collection of powerful exposés and short stories, scrutinizes the city's postwar devastation, with an eye prone to seize hallucinatory images and incidents. In *Il porto di Toledo* (The Port of Toledo, 1975)[4] Naples metamorphoses in the eponymous Spanish town, becoming the stage of a dizzying, idiosyncratic memoir that disrupts narrative and linguistic conventions, revealing Ortese's initiation to life and writing as a "theology of loss."[5]

Looking at the southern city through the "dark lenses" of her hypersensitivity and ethical rigor, Ortese cannot celebrate the "piece of sky fallen to the earth" (pezzo di cielo caduto in terra),[6] the land of enchantment consecrated across a long literary and popular tradition. Even when she lowers her guard, catching a glimpse of its splendor and letting it tempt her, she immediately rejects its lure as a spell cast over its destitute citizens, making them vulnerable to self-destructive illusions. While fascinated by Naples's sky and coastline, Ortese is dismayed by the sight of its dejected humanity. At times she describes the city as a cemetery, which threatens to enchain and annihilate her, suppressing her literary vocation. In a letter to writer Paola Masino, she confesses: "I have written other things, perhaps fine things, and I want to write more, but here in Naples I have the impression that I am laying in a beautiful grave covered with grass. Everyone is dead, I breathe in the odor of putrefaction."[7] Surrounded by these specters, Ortese feels the need to flee from social and cultural marginality and to resist the entropy of a city in constant struggle to survive. In the aftermath of World War II, she depicts "the capital of the South" as a phantasmagoric and bewitching spectacle. Even though the city is filled with the promises of a lavish nature, in her eyes it shows the ruins of a decaying civilization.[8]

Ortese's reading of Naples reworks stereoptypes associated with its traditional culture. She resents its "idleness" and "its popular tunes" as "lethal," and stigmatizes the alleged radiant sensuality of its populace as a blind retreat from the harshness of the everyday, with dire consequences: "here the emotions were a religion, and for this very reason they collapsed into vice and madness. . . . In this darkest pit, only the fire of sex was burning, under the black sky of the supernatural."⁹ Dazed by the scores of children left alone in bleak alleys, she censures the erotic frenzy that agitates the lower classes, with the blessings of the church, in "the city presided over by Saint Gennaro."¹⁰ This furious sexual passion engenders a vicious cycle of uncontrolled procreation and further misery, where the "nature-city" (città-natura) reveals its double-edged quality of "generating and corrupting *physis*" (*physis* generatrice e corruttrice).¹¹

Ortese's critique stems from a firsthand, prolonged experience of life in the streets, gathered through tireless walks in the urban labyrinth. She tries to forget herself and her disillusions by roaming in impoverished districts, which she will later describe in her writings, and venturing in enchanting Parthenopean neighborhoods. Instead of seizing the bright palette of the city's natural setting, she envisions it shrouded in a bleak aura. To the question, "Is Naples gray or colorful?," she replies,

> In the act of donating herself, nature [during the summer] reveals the city's limits to the Neapolitans. The alleys become excessively narrow, most houses have no view of the sky, those living here who are deprived of joy, or have only a fake, secondhand joy, are countless. The hope that survived in this desolation . . . and that for a moment made some exhausted human beings quiver gives way to nature's monotonous certainties and gloomy ecstasies. Thus, the too many colors and the famous blue of Naples turn out to be changeable and false: its gray, and light gray, which sometimes exudes blood, turn out to be authentic, eternal.¹²

The reference to blood alludes to violence ready to erupt in this scene of dreariness and dejection: the body of the city is always on the brink of hemorrhaging. In this sketch Ortese's description recalls Walter Benjamin's sharp verdict on Naples: "Fantastic reports by travellers have touched up the city. In reality it is grey: a grey-red or ochre, a grey-white. And entirely grey against sky and sea. It is this, not least, that disheartens the tourist."¹³ However, whereas Benjamin's eye is that of a riveted, diffident onlooker, espousing the perspective of an inquisitive visitor, the gloomy atmosphere of the place has left indelible traces in Ortese, who shares a profound connection with its inhabitants.

The contrasts that afflict Neapolitan life appear especially grim when Ortese and her family return to the city in 1945, after having fled the bombing of Campania, barely escaping the ravages of the war. Amid the rubble, Ortese finds her former neighborhood devastated and "transformed beyond recognition," and she endures a "whole year of despair." She cannot identify the city of her youth—already afflicted by disturbing contradictions—in the present state of moral dissolution, where physical destruction and material need are exacerbated by a ruthless will to survive. This fever has infected the Neapolitan lumpenproletariat, which is consumed by the veneration of money, to be garnered at all costs, including the sexual exploitation of vulnerable subjects: "The whole city was one diabolical marketplace, where everything was for sale: cigarettes, bread, women, and saddest of all, even children's innocence."[14]

What made Ortese's portraits of Naples particularly scorching at this time was the tragic experience of the war, still fresh in her mind, which she could not reconcile with the quest for pleasure and the gross inequalities she observed: "I was coming from the war time, when I had traveled throughout Italy: in the midst of fire, iron, and terror. And when I went back [to Naples] I felt how tenuous human life was; and it was folly to see this, all that southern sorrow, the people reduced to nothing, and the euphoria of the well-off who were enjoying themselves."[15]

In the attempt to exorcise images of degradation and grief, the narrator escapes a direct, unsettling contact with life in the streets and temporarily renounces the flânerie that she had cherished in the prewar years,[16] taking the vantage point of her window. In a dream of immobility and amnesia, she retreats within her four walls and searches for relief in fleeting images from her past (as Adorno has claimed in regard to Kierkegaard, "Thus the *flâneur* promenades in his room; the world only appears to him reflected by pure inwardness").[17]

To be an outcast (or to feel like one)[18] in Naples, where there is no spark of hope, is lethal. When Ortese steps outside her interiority, she witnesses a population split between brutal mercantilism and a religious formalism that condones the quasi-pagan worshipping of idols. As a spectator of Catholic celebrations that carry almost orgiastic overtones,[19] she dissects the unholy alliance of the sacred and the profane that had puzzled so many foreign visitors since the eighteenth century. These traces of "primitivism" appear particularly shocking as they clash with the dramatic shift to modernity in Italy's northern regions.

Ortese finds this condition unbearable, also because it hinders her ambitions as a writer. Confronted with this devastation and lack of prospects, she takes the painful decision to leave Naples on her way to the North, in search of a professional career. With her centrifugal move, she opposes the centripetal forces of the "capital of the South," which she fears could lead to her demise. Alternatively, she undertakes a journey up the peninsula, similar to that of southern blue-collar workers in search of jobs in the "industrial triangle" of Genoa, Milan, and Turin. Once a wanderer through Naples, she becomes a migrant ready to confront an unknown environment and a new, challenging lifestyle.

In "Dodici ore straordinarie prima di salutare Napoli" (Twelve Extraordinary Hours before Bidding Farewell to Naples), Ortese records her departure from home as a rite of separation, which heralds, along with "childish pleasures," "a harrowing melancholy" (piaceri fanciulleschi e malinconie strazianti). Leaving her putative motherland, the narrator is aware of breaking her vital bond with its popular culture and renouncing the comradeship of her intellectual friends, the contributors to the journal *Sud*. When she boards the bus that will carry her to the "land of riches," she immediately finds companions who embody the excess and the inauthentic that will surround her in the North: "Here are the fat man, who already speaks the Roman dialect, and the lady from the Emilia region whose hair is dried out with dye."[20]

When she settles in Milan, despite the excitement of the metropolis, Ortese faces a difficult adjustment[21] and experiences conflicting reactions, expressing an ambivalence that constantly marks the frequent relocations throughout her life. While she initially seems to admire the energy and entrepreneurial spirit of the Milanese—in contrast to the hopeless passivity that she attributed to traditional Neapolitan customs—she soon becomes aware of the dangerous side effect of that same spirit, an insensitivity to the plight of the outcasts.

In "La strada per Tipperery" (The Road to Tipperery) Ortese fictionalizes the uninspiring qualities of her new living circumstances.[22] The quiet of her solitary room at night in Milan cannot nourish her writing unless she can connect with vital memories. These impressions are indelibly imprinted in her psyche, but she struggles to restore them in her present condition of isolation and marginality, engulfed by silence: "It is two o'clock on a

November morning... and I am sitting at my desk, in my room, on the last floor of an old house in the oldest part of the city, with the vague purpose to write a short story. One cannot hear the faintest noise, not even the creaking of a woodworm, the city sleeps." This surreal suspension and separation from communal life causes Ortese's ability to create stories to stall. Often drawn from autobiographical fragments, her writing is hindered by the absence of auditory and visual stimuli: "There is fog. Not even heavy, just a veil, but enough to give one the impression of being even more closed in... but where?" Her Faustian pact with the metropolis compelled her to renounce her affective bonds and subdue her emotional life. In the "capital of Italian labor," the bustle of everyday activities derailed her from her vocation, as the speed of productivity gives no pause for contemplation and reflection:

> I had a few ideas before sitting at my desk, but, as soon as I sat here, they went away. The ear and the eye are extremely sensitive to everything and nothing... because there is nothing here: what could there possibly be? After all, I believe it is for this reason that I am unable to write. Around me there is nothing that allows me to be calm, and, even worse, in my memory there is nothing either. To survive in this city I have devoted myself to things that, little by little, have made me forget the others, all the others. I would give anything to remember them.

Staring into the void of the industrial city, where all traces of nature have vanished, the narrator slowly recaptures the time of her childhood in the South, when "she, too, saw... the countryside, with long, undulating hills." The recollections of her family's arrival in Naples, years later, after a disastrous experience in Libya,[23] rekindle a state of deprivation, made worse by the squalid environment: "Poverty was also ugliness, chain, limit, and it was clear that it was necessary to break it. But it was in the city, in the salty air itself of the city, in its people expanding terrifyingly and, one would have said without reason, to the point of nausea. Therefore, the only way to defeat it was to leave again."

In the maritime city, which instills a "transitory sense of habitation,"[24] the injunction "to leave again" that falls upon Ortese's brothers means life at sea. In the memorial prose "Un giorno lontano" (A Faraway Day)[25] one of them alludes ironically to the Plutarchean and Dannunzian motto, "navigare necesse est." Rather than implying heroic destiny, however, this imperative stresses a desperate need for a paying job and foreshadows tragic consequences: two of Ortese's siblings died on foreign shores, leaving behind a grief-stricken family. Distraught by this loss, Ortese sought relief in memorializing her family's sorrow with a compulsive need to revisit the scene of mourning. Her initiation to literature is prompted by this wound and unfolds as a form of commemoration, which becomes for her also a catharsis.

In "La strada per Tipperery" the narrator is enclosed within a "wall of fog and stillness." Through a voyage "à rebours" she dispels the specters of anomie that haunt her and expresses a longing to reconnect with her past: "I will return to the world of men, where the sun rises." With regard to Milan, by contrast, the metaphor of voyage implies a loss of identity. The narrator's cultural and psychological displacement is equated to having reached an unknown destination: "Clearly, I ended up here by chance, by mistake, I took the wrong train."[26]

Ortese's Parthenopean memories, however, do not offer easy relief, as they are enmeshed with her family's adversities and her impoverished upbringing. Joining the world of culture and change, she strives to free herself from a future of dejection and alienation, a purely physical existence: "Soon I would have been lost, either killing myself, or mutating in a young, white-skinned woman from Toledo [i.e., Naples], aspiring only to nourishment and material survival."[27] In order to attain self-realization in the promised land of modernity, she must become estranged from her geographical and familial roots ("I keep moving further away from you, because whoever has started off cannot stop").[28] Breaking apart from her constricting yet protective southern milieu, she is forced to confront the loneliness and anonymity looming within mass culture. The memories of her family revive in her values of simplicity and purity of heart, in contrast to the toughness she has learned as a defense mechanism against the harshness of metropolitan life.[29] The daily struggles and traumas of her childhood, seen from the perspective of impassive, modern Milan, are evoked in the light of repentance.

Her reminiscences of her life in the Neapolitan streets are thus marked by a double alterity. Like Walter Benjamin's recollections of his Berlin childhood, Ortese's journalistic pieces written in Milan in the early 1950s recount a "journey into the past, which is likewise a journey into the distance."[30]

Szondi's analysis of how time perspectives work in Benjamin is useful for understanding Ortese's narrative strategy: "The portrait of one's own city . . . [is marked by] the painful separation from the scenes of his childhood. The city is still there, but that early period lies irrecoverably within it; this is a paradox, which sharpens not only our pain, but also our perception. Gone, therefore, is our familiarity with streets and houses, though they may still surround us; we see them with a doubly alien view: with the view of the child we no longer are and with the view of the child to whom the city was not yet familiar."[31] The similiarities with Benjamin's existential and literary path are complicated, however, by Ortese's inborn "foreignness" and her vocation to isolation ("I abhor the everyday; I belong to a different race, which is now on the brink of extinction.")[32] The descriptions of her walks through the Neapolitan cityscape reconstruct an environment that elicits her passionate involvement but ultimately remains unfamiliar to her. In the labyrinth of the streets she searches for a flight from her domestic enclosure and enjoys the thrill of continuous visual discoveries. Through her wanderings she articulates her own reading of the city, resisting its obsolete master narrative,[33] which praises singing as the quintessential form of expression of the Neapolitan populace and the veneration of sentiments as its "paradise."[34]

In "Un giorno lontano" Ortese seeks to dispel her anxieties by contemplating the wonders of the everyday ("The elation of that wandering in such an impalpable and hallucinatory air made me forget about everything else"), but cannot avoid confrontations with anguish and despair. While meandering in the "old district of the city," for instance, she catches ordinary gestures: "on doorsteps . . . women chatted as usual," and glimpses of seclusion and desolation: "Behind the small dirty glasspanes of some hovels . . . dark-haired young women, turned pale because of the unhealthy air . . . were giving a fleeting and pensive glance at the street." The itinerant narrator also notices distraught survivors with no expectation for the future: "At crossroads, a seller of chestnuts, bound in a faded military coat or wrapped in a large red woman's shawl, was sitting in front of his stove, with the look of having been abandoned by God. . . . His face expressed fatigue and melancholy."[35] In reporting the "interpenetration of day and night, noise and peace, outer light and inner darkness, street and home"[36] in this neighborhood, Ortese emphasizes again the bleakness of the place and the sorrow of its people.

In other texts these encounters with life on the fringes clash with the lavishness of the surrounding landscape. With its gentle slopes and luminous shoreline, Naples is a "magic amphitheatre," a spectacle untarnished by history. As the writer remarks in "Veduta di Napoli" (A View of Naples), this intimacy with nature elicits, at its best, a form of ecstatic enjoyment:

> I have visited all Italy . . . and I take Italy as a term of comparison, because I know that there isn't any other country where imagination and grace coalesce in a more enchanting and pure line: but nowhere I have had the impression to be outside the world and, at the same time, in closer contact to the world, I have never felt a higher joy than walking on a morning in May along those trails steeped in the sky, amid those gardens and orchards smelling of oranges, in front of that calm, infinitely luminous sky, which shines between Posillipo and Capri, Sorrento and Vesuvius . . . Youth. Morning. Eternal morning. This is the revelation that Naples presents to you.[37]

Ortese's account is no escapist dream, however, for her sensitivity to a primeval world of beauty leads to a more nuanced and comprehensive understanding of conflicts and contradictions hidden behind Naples's colorful surface. This allows her to dismantle the stereotypes that flourish on its alleged fervent and naïve celebration of life. Its luxuriant landscape is an alluring, yet troubling, façade, as it entraps its dwellers, weakening their defenses and condemning them to a state of inertia. In this paragraph she evokes a human dimension found pristine among the underprivileged:

> The streets of the old town, especially of the sailor neighborhoods, are swarming with a common people, different from others, yelling, colorful, extraordinarily vivid and cheerful. These streets are lined with fish markets and fruit stalls, and others with the most varied merchandise; they are gloomy and amusing, shabby and joyful, they can make you think of an oriental city, such is the wave and confusion of sounds, the splendor and the obscurity, the mystery and the grace of each alleyway, even the most miserable, the most unadorned one. But this is not the Orient: it is Naples, that is humanity, and you realize that when you notice that even the last one of these men, the most uncouth, the one, to be clear, who does not expect anything else from life, is capable to smile at you, all of a sudden. You can be a true gentleman, a prince, but a poor Neapolitan is always something more than you are: he is a child and an angel.[38]

Benjamin pictured Naples in a similar way, emphasizing the excitement of its streets, the intertwining of private and public spaces. The "porosity" that he detects in the city's architecture is the corollary to the theatricality pervading the everyday: "Building and action interpenetrate in the courtyards, arcades, and stairways. In everything they preserve the scope to become a theatre of new, unforeseen constellations. The stamp of the definitive is avoided. No situation appears intended forever, no figure asserts its "thus and not otherwise." This is how architecture, the most binding part of the communal rhythm, comes into being here: . . . anarchical, embroiled, village-like in the centre, into which large networks of streets were hacked only forty years ago."[39] Benjamin reveals a patronizing attitude in front of these interactions, which unfold in the open, in a constant state of flux. In these practices he sees primitive customs marked by "rich barbarism": his is an aesthetic response to their picturesque qualities.

Ortese's imagery comes through a different lens, as she focuses on the permanence of this people's hardships and dejection. The vibrant performance of Parthenopean rituals does not blind her to the harsh realities behind them. Rather than writing a detached cultural critique, she exposes "the suffering and the immobility of the old Bourbon capital"[40] and she empathizes with a malaise spreading beneath all extravagance and display.

Ortese's article furthermore calls into question fixed notions about Naples, commonplaces that have portrayed the city as the "quintessential seat of backwardness, alterity, and inferiority in comparison to the rest of Italy and Europe."[41] Her passage presents a sequence of opposites, which could liken the Parthenopean lifestyle to stereotypical "Oriental" practices. This interpretive key would underscore the liminal quality of this land, defined as the border between the modern North and the antiquated, even "barbarian," South.[42] At first, Ortese's reading would seem to emphasize Naples's attachment to an archaic culture, impervious to change and carrying with it the charm of exoticism, however ambiguous this might be. Her analysis, though, subverts any simplistic interpretation of this setting and its atmosphere, focusing instead on the unexpected gentleness of its lower-class dwellers. Her claims lean toward another cliché, the one that posits the naïveté of the natives of this "virgin land." However, her sympathy for the victims of this lavish nature significantly alters this paradigm.

Although associating the Neapolitan pariah with a child might appear reductive if not condescending, Ortese's praise of childhood must be read in terms of her overall vision. Throughout her work she cherishes youth as purity of spirit and innocence: children are receptive to wonder, uncontaminated by adulthood and social relations.[43] In this context, tinged with lyrical nuances, the demons that, according to an age-old imagery, populate the city ("a paradise inhabited by devils")[44] are converted into blessed creatures: "a poor Neapolitan . . . is a child and an angel." This candor has a troubling drawback, however: "These men's goodness and innocence, which are the result of a mysterious grace of their blood, of a constant contact and conversation with the *Mothers*, their excessive tenderness and dreamlike condition, have precipitated them into the ditch of obedience and passivity. . . . The privations of some of the Neapolitan people . . . are linked to this initial generosity, to this magnificent inability to have expectations, to calculate, to assert oneself."[45]

In *Il mare non bagna Napoli* Ortese lucidly explores how this vulnerability has profound social and political implications, as the lower-class Neapolitans are unable to challenge oppression. Here, instead, she glosses over these consequences: according to a utopian vision that aims to reconcile Naples's extremes in light of its "familiarity with eternal things," the city provides evidence of the "liberty and sweetness of human life." Despite its tribulations (and implicit disparities, as the hardships afflict only "some of the Neapolitan people"), the writer construes this humanity into a bulwark against the devastating forces of modernization: "I confess to having lived for some time the nightmare that Naples could disappear in the cellophane of a modern city. With modern, I mean all that is beneath the most tragic poverty: the warrens made with dismal reinforced concrete, the machine shops and factories that blacken the air, the frenzy of vehicles."[46] In this view, the evils of standardization and industrial production appear more terrifying than the scourge of misery, which preserves some degree of individual dignity. Even though Naples's folly seems to reverse in a form of mysterious wisdom, its culture cannot propose solutions, only its inertia and refusal to change.

In other autobiographical writings, Ortese recovers her origins or summons ghosts from her adolescence, renovating—and at times assuaging—the drama of her family. In "La casa del padre"[47] (The Father's Home), for instance, the narrator's visit to her family in their new residence on the outskirts of Naples prompts a dreamlike projection of memories, conjuring a sphere of shared emotions and ethical sensitivity, of tranquility and symbiosis with nature. Returning home, she discovers that her parents enjoy humble pleasures, with sincerity of heart, almost wrapped in a sacred aura (to the point that she feels that she should kneel down in front of them). Her father's "peaceful expression" in staring at "the blue and the earth" astounds her, as it reveals a serenity that her life, "filled with obscurity and tears," desperately lacks. In their modest existence, her relatives are in touch with the little creatures of their orchard, "a superior society," in opposition to the "places" and "people" where the protagonist "is compelled to go back." In this "land of humility" Ortese discovers a splendid dignity, which she had blindly underestimated in her rebellion against social inequality and yearning to improve her station in life.

Ortese's experience of modernity and her struggle to secure a position in intellectual circles have exposed her to a frantic world of fragmentation and disillusionment. The images of her parents and siblings, frozen in time, offer her a safe haven. Among them, the stillness of habit and the repetition of ordinary gestures provide her with an antidote to restlessness and anxiety: "I immediately fell asleep, with the wonderful feeling of erasing, with that short rest, twenty years, all the gloomiest years of my life, horrendous and useless years."

Far from her family and southern culture, Ortese's quest has defied her expectations, eliciting nostalgia: "Forced to seek things that I do not desire, to smile at beauties I do not love, in the end I cannot but dream of the day when, completely frightened and tired, I will come back to sit silently among you." By now, she realizes that her "search for justice," for professional and social recognition, is fraught with humiliation and suffering, as those endowed with riches and privileges are absorbed in self-preoccupation and insensitive to the pain of others. A subtle indifference shelters the wealthy, insulating them from the plight of the disenfranchised through mechanisms of spatial separation and control.[48] This dynamic is especially evident in Milan, the cradle of Italy's "reconstruction,"[49] whose middle class relishes forms of charity but ostracizes any newcomers not grateful enough for its generosity (a rejection that Ortese herself suffered).

Even within the sphere of affluence, productive vitality, and consumerism, Ortese's aspiration to serenity and well-being fails her. The elegance and tranquility of those settings remain forbidden to her, as she cannot evade her condition of outsider, living at the margins of the "economic miracle" without benefitting from its luster. She cannot participate in its opulence, as she is always confined in poor neighborhoods or at least in unadorned rooms, facing the difficulty of making ends meet: "I would always remain—for one reason or another—in the district of my economic level, which was that of people looking for a job . . . who cannot find it, or find modest employment, and have little money."[50] Voicing the awareness she has gained through direct experience, her critique stigmatizes a power structure that relegates the disadvantaged to the limbo of "non-existence." Ortese's assessment of this disparity is often structured along geographic and spatial patterns. In her view, the most flourishing and charming northern cities either create dreamlands in their downtown areas, pushing southern immigrants and lesser citizens to their outskirts, or nurture the illusion of being shielded from the plague of suffering (as happens in Venice). Milan is the emblem of the industrial metropolis engaged in the pursuit of economic success at the price of dehumanization. Its self-defeating project of modernity has no "use" for ethics.[51]

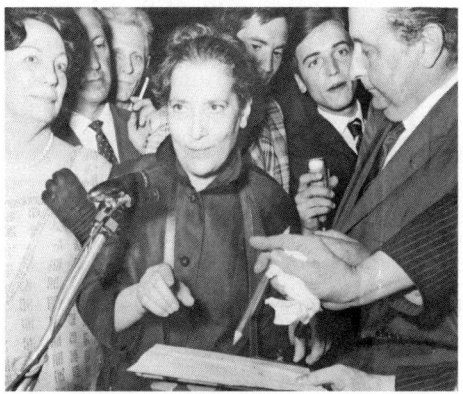

Figure 17-1. Anna Maria Ortese wins the Premio Strega for *Poveri e semplici*, 1967. (Wikimedia Commons)

Thus, despite Ortese's uneasy negotiations with her Parthenopean past, its ambivalent fascination often resurfaces as a term of comparison in her accounts of northern cities, in a dialogue between contrasting urban images. While describing her stay in Venice, she wonders, "Where is Naples now? Where are its loud noises, its dust clouds, its light?"[52] She discards the "mythology of modernity" and the seductions of prosperity, in the name of a more inclusive vision of humanity, as well as a closer connection with nature. Her troubled adjustment to new sourroudings compels her to recover her origins and the backdrop of her youth, an endeavor that will haunt her until old age. Naples's voices inhabit her. "Things foreign do not lure" her "into self-forgetfulness." Resisting "progress" and the intoxication of commodities (mostly beyond her reach), she sees herself "with an estranged vision."[53]

The mental journey back to her southern past seeks a way out of anonymity and alienation, but it does not lead to any reconciliation. In a similar fashion to what can be detected in Benjamin's memories, Ortese's "backward glance is on the shattered utopia that can kindle 'the spark of hope' only 'in the past'": she can "neither close her eyes to reality nor give up the promise of a time worthy of humanity," welding "a paradoxical bond of hope and despair."[54] Knowing the pitfalls of industrial society, predicated on the survival of the fittest,[55] she seeks refuge in the reassurances of utopian commonality. Her Neapolitan recollections are mostly drawn from evidence of personal and collective anguish as well as instances of humanity and compassion, rather than the lush landscape and the spectacular views of the city and its mythology. Being attuned to a special form of estrangement, in her narratives she often conjures images of misery, coupled with faith in the virtues of empathy and the compensatory power of writing. She opposes the *damnatio memoriae* and anaesthetization of modernity by recovering her affective and cognitive responses to the shocks of her first, harrowing experiences of sorrow and loss. Ortese cannot erase the disturbing yet vital discoveries that shaped her life and writing. Her retrospective "glance ... is directed toward those moments when the future first announced itself"[56] to her as an adolescent. Thus, the frequent imaginary visits she later pays to Naples in her fiction are returns to the realm of the "*Mothers*": the city's imprint forecasts her destiny of grief and strengthens her fraternal bonds with the underprivileged.

Having learned that "to exist . . . is . . . a collective matter,"[57] Ortese is unable to resist the call of Neapolitan culture or silence the echoes of its people. She cannot avert her eyes and the visionary power of her memory from those scenes of destitution and neglect, nor also from those glimpses of familiarity and humane understanding. Ultimately, she looks at the city as the cradle and the epitome of a "lacerated human condition" that, no matter how tragic, she, as a writer, must explore to honor her literary vocation and duty of ethical responsibility.

## NOTES

1. See Luca Clerici, *Apparizione e visione: Vita e opere di Anna Maria Ortese* (Milan: Mondadori, 2002), 240–61, and Raffaele La Capria, "*Il mare non bagna Napoli* 40 anni dopo," *Nuovi Argomenti* 4, 4th ser. (July–September 1995): 73–78. Anna Maria Ortese, "Il mare di Napoli" (1946–47), in Ortese, *L'infanta sepolta*, ed. Monica Farnetti (Milan: Adelphi, 2000), 122–38.

2. Oreste Pivetta, "'Con Elmina e Albert per fuggire l'orrore,'" interview given by Anna Maria Ortese, *L'Unità*, June 18, 1993.

3. Anna Maria Ortese, *Il mare non bagna Napoli* (1953; repr., Milan: Adelphi, 1994). Now translated into English as *Neapolitan Chronicles*, translated by Ann Goldstein and Jenny McPhee (New York: New Vessel Press, 2018). Unless otherwise noted, all citations to this work are to this edition.

4. Anna Maria Ortese, *Il porto di Toledo* (1975), in Ortese, *Romanzi*, vol. 1, ed. Monica Farnetti (Milan: Adelphi, 2002), 353–1001.

5. Cf. Marcello Bonfante, "Il puma redentore," *Linea d'ombra* 14, no. 118 (September 1996): 50–52.

6. This definition, dating back to the Renaissance, is quoted as a proverb in Cesare Cantú, *Storia universale*, 7th ed., Tomo I (Turin: Giuseppe Pomba e Comp. Editori, 1848), 768.

7. The passage belongs to a letter quoted in Mirella Serri, "Ortese. Ti scrivo le mie ossessioni," *La Stampa*, June 19, 1998. On the fluctuating relationship between the two authors, see also Maria Vittoria Vittori, "Storia di un'amicizia," *Leggendaria* 2, no. 9 (May–June 1998): 10–11.

8. In "Dove il tempo è un altro" (1980), Ortese recounts the shock of her return to Naples in 1945. In Ortese, *Corpo celeste* (Milan: Adelphi, 1997), 75–77. On the city's decay in the postwar era, cf. Antonio Ghirelli, *Napoli italiana: La storia della città dopo il 1860* (Turin: Einaudi, 1977), 255–73.

9. Anna Maria Ortese, "Oro a Forcella," *Il mare non bagna Napoli*, 67.

10. Anna Maria Ortese, "S'inteneriscono le marchese," *Omnibus* 3, no. 32 (August 5, 1948): 9.

11. Stefano De Matteis, *Lo specchio della vita: Napoli: Antropologia della città del teatro* (Bologna: Il Mulino, 1991), 17. On "phallic pride" as an anthropological feature of the lower classes in Naples, see Thomas Belmonte, *The Broken Fountain*, 2nd expanded ed. (New York: Columbia University Press, 1989), 93–94.

12. Anna Maria Ortese, "Il grigio: Autentico eterno," *Epoca* 3, no. 112 (November 29, 1952): 4.

13. Walter Benjamin and Asja Lacis, "Naples" (1924), in Benjamin, *One-Way Street and Other Writings*, trans. Edmund Jephcott and Kingsley Shorter, 163–73 (London: NLB, 1979), 169.

14. Ortese, "Il mare di Napoli," 123–24.

15. Luca Clerici, "Il dolore bagna Napoli," *L'Unità*, May 16, 1994, 7.

16. Cf. Flora M. Ghezzo, "Chiaroscuro napoletano: Transfigurazioni fantastiche di una città," *Narrativa* 24 (2003): 85–104, and Andrea Baldi, *La meraviglia e il disincanto: Studi sulla narrativa breve di Anna Maria Ortese* (Naples: Loffredo Editore, 2010), 45–58.

17. Theodor W. Adorno, *Kierkegaard: Construction of the Aesthetic*, trans. and ed. Robert Hullot-Kentor (Minneapolis: Minnesota University Press, 1989), 42.

18. According to Clerici, the economic circumstances of the Orteses were not as dire as she claimed: see Clerici, "Il dolore bagna Napoli," and *Apparizione e visione*.

19. Cf. Ortese, "Il mare di Napoli."

20. Anna Maria Ortese, "Dodici ore straordinarie prima di salutare Napoli," *Milano-sera*, June 4–5, 1951, 3.

21. See Anna Maria Ortese, *Alla luce del Sud: Lettere a Pasquale Prunas*, ed. Renata Prunas and Giuseppe di Costanzo (Milan: Archinto, 2006). On Ortese's years in Milan, cf. also Monica Farnetti, *Anna Maria Ortese* (Milan: Bruno Mondadori, 1998), 94–95, and Clerici, *Apparizione e visione*, 279–348.

22. Anna Maria Ortese, "La strada per Tipperery," *Il Mondo*, December 16, 1958, 11–12. With the title "Fantasticherie," the text can now be read in Ortese, *Angelici dolori e altri racconti*, ed. Luca Clerici (Milan: Adelphi, 2006), 246–57.

23. Ortese's father moved the family to Tripoli, following the dream of prosperity, only to see that hope dashed. He was left devastated by what he perceived as a personal failure: see Dacia Maraini, "Anna Maria Ortese" (interview), *E tu chi eri? Interviste sull'infanzia* (Milan: Bompiani, 1979), 26–27; Farnetti, *Anna Maria Ortese*, 2–3; and Clerici, *Apparizione e visione*, 44–51.

24. Iain Chambers, "Naples: A Porous Modernity," *Mediterranean Crossings: The Politics of an Interrupted Modernity* (Durham, N.C.: Duke University Press, 2008), 78.

25. Anna Maria Ortese, "Un giorno lontano," *Il Gazzettino*, December 9, 1939, 3.

26. Ortese, "La strada per Tipperery," 12.
27. Ortese, *Il porto di Toledo*, 411.
28. Ortese "La strada per Tipperery," 12.
29. On the clashes of individuals with urban modernity, cf. Georg Simmel, "The Metropolis and Mental Life" (1903), in *The Sociology of Georg Simmel*, ed. H. K. Wolff, 409–24 (New York: Free Press, 1950).
30. Peter Szondi, "Walter Benjamin's 'City Portraits'" (1962), in *On Textual Understanding and Other Essays*, trans. Harvey Mendelsohn, foreword by Michael Hays (Manchester: Manchester University Press, 1986), 135.
31. Ibid., 134.
32. Dario Bellezza, "Sono una zingara: Odio gli scrittori" (interview given by Anna Maria Ortese), *Il Mondo*, May 15, 1979, 64.
33. On the practice of street walking as a strategy of resistance, see Michel de Certeau, "Walking in the City," *The Practice of Everyday Life*, trans. Steven Rendall (Berkeley: University of California Press, 1984), 102–19.
34. See Anna Maria Ortese, "Presentazione," *Il mare non bagna Napoli*, ed. Anna Nozzoli (Florence: La Nuova Italia, 1979), v.
35. Ortese, "Un giorno lontano," 3.
36. Benjamin and Lacis, "Naples," 172.
37. Anna Maria Ortese, "Veduta di Napoli," *Corriere di Napoli*, July 9–10, 1951, 3.
38. Ibid.
39. Benjamin and Lacis, "Naples," 169–70.
40. Ortese, "Presentazione," vii.
41. Piero Bevilacqua, "Prefazione," in Nelson Moe, *Un paradiso abitato da diavoli: Identità nazionale e immagini del Mezzogiorno*, trans. Milena Zemira Ciccimarra (Naples: L'Ancora del Mediterraneo, 2004), 6.
42. Along these lines Benjamin argues, "What distinguishes Naples from other large cities is something it has in common with the African kraal; each private attitude or act is permeated by streams of communal life" (Benjamin and Lacis, "Naples," 174). On the cultural construction of Naples as a city on the periphery of Europe, cf. Nelson Moe, *The View from Vesuvius: Italian Culture and the Southern Question* (Berkeley: University of California Press, 2002); Marino Niola, "The Invention of the Mediterranean," in *Sites of Exchange: European Crossroads and Faultlines*, ed. Maurizio Ascari and Adriana Corrado (Amsterdam: Rodopi, 2006), 75–85; and Paola Paumgardhen, "Goethe and Von Archenholz in Naples in 1787: Views of the City between Myth and Reality," in Ascari and Corrado, *Sites of Exchange*, 97–104.
43. Cf. Ortese, "Dove il tempo è un altro," 58–62.
44. See Benedetto Croce, "Il 'paradiso abitato da diavoli'" (1923), in Croce, *Un paradiso abitato da diavoli*, ed. Giuseppe Galasso (Milan: Adelphi, 2006), 11–27.

45. Ortese, "Veduta di Napoli."
46. Ibid., 3.
47. Anna Maria Ortese, "La casa del padre," *Corriere di Napoli*, September 11–12, 1951, 3.
48. Cf. Baldi, *La meraviglia e il disincanto*, 73–94.
49. See Gianfranco Petrillo, *La capitale del miracolo: Sviluppo lavoro potere a Milano, 1953–1962* (Milan: Franco Angeli, 1992); and John Foot, *Milan Since the Miracle: City, Culture and Identity* (Oxford: Berg, 2001).
50. Anna Maria Ortese, "La virtú del nulla," *Corpo celeste*, 96.
51. Cf. Ortese's letter quoted in Enzo Golino, "Anna Maria Ortese: Quella vita vissuta tra il dolore e il successo," *Repubblica*, January 17, 2003, 43.
52. Anna Maria Ortese, "Città inimmaginabile," *Belvedere* [Napoli] 1, no. 18 (July16, 1939): 3.
53. Szondi, "Benjamin's 'City Portraits,'" 135.
54. Ibid., 135.
55. See Anna Maria Ortese, "Una notte nella stazione," *Silenzio a Milano* (1958; repr., Milan: La Tartaruga, 1986), 5–44.
56. Szondi, "Benjamin's 'City Portraits,'" 135.
57. Benjamin and Lacis, "Naples," 174.

EIGHTEEN

## Filumena Marturano: Eduardo De Filippo's Beloved Whore

*Rose De Angelis*

Eduardo De Filippo's 1946 play *Filumena Marturano*, situated in the war-ravaged city of Naples, begins with a heated discussion between Domenico Soriano, a middle-aged businessman, and Filumena Marturano, his mistress, a woman who, after spending twenty-five years as his de facto wife, has finally tricked him into marriage. Convinced that Filumena is dying, Domenico marries her, legitimizing her position in his home and outside it; but upon discovering her deception, he immediately redefines her as criminal "other," shouting, "Prostitute! . . . Whore! You were a whore when I met you and, in your heart, you are still a whore!"[1] Filumena has crossed the border between bad woman and good woman and blurred the boundaries between the two even though she has been marginalized once again as a whore, but she is a woman whose agency and power to transform her surroundings has only been temporarily stifled.[2]

Filumena will eventually transform what society has designated as aberrant sexuality to traditional morality and rewrite herself as wife and mother to the three sons she has had out of wedlock. In true neorealist tradition, De Filippo "portray[s] the prostitute as an ordinary human being, who faces the same problems related to alienation, economic hardship and despair" as other men and women, and suggests, to some extent, that Filumena's plight is one that any woman may face when a "hostile environment does not present her with other choices."[3] De Filippo takes a panoramic view of that "hostile environment," devastated by war and still divided by class distinctions, in which the family becomes the vehicle to and the reason for survival.

"The family is the only institution which [Italians] heed and acknowledge, the only buffer between the individual and a social power which has systematically destroyed all those institutions which in other countries have become instruments of mediation."[4] Filumena, the play's central character, has an understanding of and nostalgia for the family, the church-sanctioned marriage, and legitimacy; and she, like Naples itself, rises from the ruins of the past and confronts the many problems of "material and moral reconstruction" to emerge triumphant not in the idealism of happily-ever-after but in neorealist fashion—with a renewed consciousness, collective action, and the belief in the "inevitability of historical progress—all supported by a somewhat mystical notion of Christian brotherhood."[5]

## Naples and Eduardo De Filippo

*Filumena Marturano* unfolds in Naples, a city that was once the capital of southern Italy and under Bourbon rule a politically and economically flourishing metropolis, but by 1946 that Naples was merely a memory of its past. The struggle for an Italian nation free of foreign rule had brought about a unified Italy in 1860, but *il Risorgimento* had little mass appeal or consequence in the South, especially since most of its people had little to no education or government representation and no voting rights; these were people who worked and lived without ever realizing the promises of Giuseppe Garibaldi's democratic principles.[6] In the late nineteenth and early twentieth century, Naples characterized the political, social, and economic malaise of rural southern Italy, a region abandoned by a government that did not understand, at times disregarded, and sometimes feared the integration and participation of the South in a unified Italy.[7]

The arrival of Benito Mussolini and the National Fascist Party in October 1922 did not serve southern Italians any better than the king and the parliamentary government had. One oppressor was exchanged for another who, using the mantra of national unity and his admonition "andare verso il popolo" (reach out to the common people),[8] brought a nation already divided to war. Mussolini's declaration of war against the Allies brought more devastation and economic hardship to southern Italy. Naples, with its strategic position as a port city, became the primary target of the Allied campaign against the Italian war machinery in the South. The *New York Times* headlines told the story of destruction: "British in Africa Hail Naples Raids," "Naples Area Torn," "Italy Is Being Wrecked by Strategic Bombing."[9] In the late summer of 1943, the same newspaper reported that "several hundred medium and heavy bombers . . . set a daylight bombing record by dropping 845 tons of bombs on Naples." By the end of the war, all that remained of Naples were the stories of its glorious past and the ruins of its present. It is in this city that Eduardo De Filippo sets the stage for a theatrical *Risorgimento* via his play *Filumena Marturano*.

As Eric Bentley notes, Naples is De Filippo's stage. Here, in his native city, he focuses on the *urbanità* of the poor, whose dignity survives the

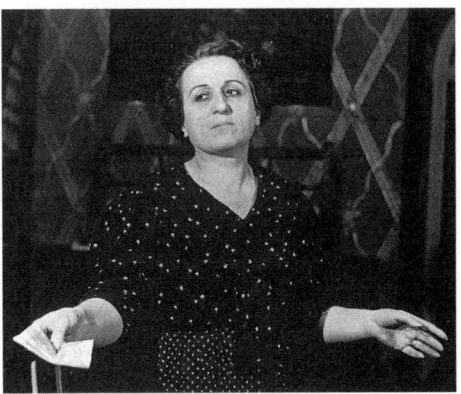

Figure 18-1. Titina De Filippo as Filumena Marturano, 1947. (Wikimedia Commons)

darkness of their Fascist past and the bleakness of their war-torn present,[10] and *Filumena Marturano* is a fusion of place and person. The eponymous "Filumena is the heartbeat of Naples; that is, there is total identification between the female protagonist and her city. Naples as protagonist is both subject and privileged geographical locus,"[11] and De Filippo had a profound understanding of the city and the plight of his protagonist, art and its imitation of life.

Born in Naples on May 24, 1900, Eduardo De Filippo, along with his older sister Titina and his younger brother Peppino, lived Neapolitan life and the issues of social alienation and illegitimacy. As the illegitimate child of Eduardo Scarpetta, the well-known stage actor, and Luisa De Filippo, his *costumier* and the niece of his legitimate spouse, he longed for a traditional family.[12] Speaking to the angst of illegitimacy, the same that will plague Filumena's sons and motivate her actions in the play, De Filippo confessed, "Se da una parte ero orgoglioso di mio padre . . . d'altra parte la fitta rete di pettegolezzi, chiacchiere e malignità mi opprimeva dolorosamente. Mi sentivo respinto, oppure tollerato, e messo in ridicolo solo perché 'diverso'" (On the one hand, I was proud of my father . . . while on the other, the extreme pettiness, the gossip, and the maliciousness brought me great pain. I felt rejected, simply tolerated, and ridiculed only because I was different).[13] De Filippo was different; he was "figlio di padre ignoto" (father unknown), and he lived that difference on a daily basis as a child. That he was "figlio di NN" (literally, no one's child) was, ironically, everyone's business.[14] De Filippo, his mother, and his siblings lived across the street from Eduardo Scarpetta's magnificent abode, where Scarpetta and his legitimate wife raised their family; and the De Filippo family vacationed a short distance away from Villa Santarella, where the "first family" enjoyed their summer.[15] Scarpetta provided financially for both his legitimate family and for his "second family," but he never left his wife. For thirty-five years he lived a dual existence on the city's stage while the Neapolitans looked on, and De Filippo's life unfolded on both Scarpetta's social and theatrical stage.[16]

As Scarpetta's illegitimate son, De Filippo and his siblings were the object of constant gossip, even though Scarpetta insisted that they call him *zio* (uncle) and referred to them as his *nipoti* (niece and nephews) as a way perhaps of dealing with the rumors; but as his theatrical heir, starting his career at age four in one of his father's comedies, De Filippo's legitimacy would never be questioned, outclassing his father personally and professionally.[17] On stage De Filippo could "translate into scenes the world which he was beginning to know,"[18] and this world was one of constant paradox. As Robert G. Bander writes, "If the word 'paradox' did not exist, it would be necessary to invent it to describe Naples. . . . It is a city of people who venerate the innocent charm of children, and where children lose their innocence early"[19] and De Filippo's protagonist, Filumena, is a paradox. She is a former prostitute who steals from her lover to raise her illegitimate children, all the while hoping that they will eventually become a family, as she makes clear when in desperation she screams, "A family—a family—I have been thinking of it for twenty-five years" (*Filumena* 2.42). In 1973, speaking about his work, De Filippo said, "At the basis of my theatre is always the conflict between man and society. . . . This conflict is based upon a reaction to injustice, anger over hypocrisy, solidarity and sympathy with a person or group, rebellion against anachronism of the world today."[20] As Donatella Fischer notes, giving too much importance to De Filippo's illegitimacy would "restrict the scope of his work";[21] however, in his play *Filumena Marturano*, there is conflict, injustice, anger, and hypocrisy, and who better to write and stage a family drama about broken promises, illegitimate children, and the lack of paternal responsibility than the man who had lived the experience?

## Filumena Marturano

De Filippo's play *Filumena Marturano* was performed for the first time on November 9, 1946, at the Politeama Theater in Naples to rave reviews: "Dal trionfo di Napoli 'Filumena Marturano' trae sicuro auspicio ed avvio ad una durevole fortunata carriera sui palcosceni di tutta Italia" (The triumph of Filumena Marturano in Naples bodes well for a long and fortunate career on stages throughout Italy) (*Roma*); "Il successo è stato pieno" (The play was a complete success) (*Il Giornale*).[22]

In the play, De Filippo posits the reconstitution of family, for he "intuitively perceived" that the family established a "'protected regimen of existence'" that was the source of survival for southern Italians, especially since other institutions had failed them; but war had placed the family in jeopardy: "the war . . . dislocated [the] social structure so extremely that, between 1943 and 1946, it seemed that the very institution of family was threatened."[23] The year before, De Filippo's play *Napoli Milionaria!* presented the Neapolitan audience with a family decentered by World War II and its aftermath.[24] In *Filumena Marturano*, premiering a year after the end of World War II, De Filippo creates a character whose maternal selflessness and unyielding resolve wills the restoration of the family, frayed and tattered by the socioeconomic conditions of the disenfranchised Neapolitans. Most postwar Italian audiences, but especially the Neapolitan audience, would understand Filumena, whom Eric Bentley called "a heroic plebian, a tigress of a mother," because, like the protagonist, most of them had had to extricate themselves from the rubble of war that had compromised the family structure and had increased the gap between them and the privileged classes, of which Domenico is a member.[25] As Bander notes, De Filippo "peoples his stage with eminently recognizable human beings; . . . Italian audiences respond to the many qualities in his characters which they also recognize in themselves. . . . They become Neapolitan portraits."[26] Besides seeing themselves, Neapolitans heard themselves, for De Filippo remained true to the Neapolitan vernacular, serving as the custodian of the Neapolitan dialect even when Fascists were banning any form of "cultural *campanilismo*." "Beginning in the late 1920s, local periodicals were prohibited from publishing stories, poetry, or songs in dialect, and aspects of folk culture such as dialect theatre were discouraged. As late as 1941 the fascists considered withdrawing from circulation all literary works in dialect, while actors were forbidden to speak even a few lines of dialect in film."[27] In its original form, the play's Neapolitan dialect underscores Filumena's prowess and pathos, for the "portrait [of Filumena] derives half its life from the language—which, in translation, can scarcely be shown."[28] Moreover, in 1946, the Neapolitan dialect made palpable the link between the actor on stage and the ordinary southern man and woman on the street—and in the audience.

Although the play in English may lose the idiomatic nuances of the dialect and the layered complexities of its meaning, as it begins, the connection is still immediate because De Filippo does not introduce the main characters to his readers and audience through unfolding exposition; rather, he confronts them with characters fully developed and battling, beginning his play *in media res*. Having made a miraculous recovery from the brink of death, Filumena Marturano positions herself in the doorway of the bedroom, her arms defiantly folded, ready for combat. She has finally gained her lawful place in society as Signora Domenico Soriano, even though she has had to feign death to do so. In the opposite corner, as if preparing for the next round, stands Domenico Soriano, her adversary on multiple levels.[29] Domenico is the man who, until now, has refused to make an honest woman of her; he is a representative of that privileged class that disregarded her poverty and then cast her aside when she capitalized on the only commodity she had—her body. Ranting, he says, "I have given you myself for twenty-five years—my brain, my body, my youth" (*Filumena* 1.2). In reality, Domenico has given her a roof over her head, and in return, Filumena has managed his businesses, his home, and him. She responds to his accusations, saying, "I was not good enough to be [your] wife, but I was good enough to be left here in charge of everything. . . . I have never had respect in this house. What have I been here, for twenty-five years? Never anything except a maid, a servant, a slave" (1.5).

While Filumena is speaking about her marginalized position in Domenico's household, the definition of herself as "a maid, a servant, a slave" could very well be ascribed to many married Italian women. The female's subordinate role was regulated by Italian law and reinforced by the Catholic Church; and, under Fascism, women did not fare any better. "As 'reproducers of the race,' women were to embody traditional values, being stoic, silent, and fervid."[30] There was a "genuine difference of the position of the man and woman in marriage and in social life,"[31] and that difference subordinated the female to the legitimate authority of the male. Moreover, the woman's agency was politically limited. Only in 1946, after a reform passed on February 7, 1945, did women get the right to vote, giving them access to the legislative process for the first time.[32]

Rosalia Solimene and Alfredo Amoroso, Filumena's and Domenico's faithful servants and confidantes, respectively, complete the quadrille, waiting anxiously for the next step, for who will take control. The shift in power, albeit temporary, is made clear when Filumena appropriates an equestrian analogy, something she knows Domenico will understand since he races horses, saying, "I have been your workhorse for twenty-five years, . . . but now it's my turn in the saddle. I hold the reins in my hand and I'm going to make you gallop" (*Filumena* 1.5). Domenico, a businessman, who has treated Filumena as little more than a low-cost investment that has more than paid for itself, cannot believe the situation in which he finds himself. He, the son of "one of the richest and most respected confectioners in Naples," has been tricked by a "woman of [her] reputation," but his anger goes beyond her attack on his male ego (1.8, 1.5). Domenico is angry that Filumena has never "shown [him] any appreciation of what [he] had done for" her, that she has "worn a mask" and, in particular, that she has never cried (1.5–6). Domenico resents the dignity and pride that have made her fight against institutionalized poverty and resist subordination to his willful male self-importance. In refusing to cry in his presence, Filumena repudiates the arrogance of patriarchal privilege, and even in her marginalized position as a former prostitute, she becomes an index for all Italian women who seek greater emancipation from the ingrained machismo of Italian men. As the play unfolds, she "rises to become a symbol of enforced degradation and the will to persevere, to fight, and to sacrifice; in turn, through her resistance, [Domenico] and society [are] put on trial."[33] Filumena sets the stage, literally and figuratively, for the societal changes, slow and gradual, in Italian society, which would redefine the roles for men and women.

Bentley writes that De Filippo "likes to bring the curtain down . . . on a terrific moment, . . . a moment when two lines of narrative suddenly intersect by amazing coincidence."[34] In *Filumena Marturano*, there are many such moments when the world of the unexpected merges with reality, and one occurs in act 1 just as Domenico thinks he has discovered the reason behind Filumena's precipitous actions: she must want money. Smugly, he says, "Ah! Money. Why? Did you think I wouldn't have looked after you?" (*Filumena* 1.8). Money, however, is not Filumena's objective. Her goal is rescripting marriage, motherhood, and identity, her own and that of her three sons. She has successfully run Domenico's house and business for many years, functioning as his de facto wife and business associate; and, during this time, she has had three sons. Filumena has amassed the component parts of the family she so desires; however, she and her children lack a name, and, without it, they have no legal recourse or social status in Italian society. She is nothing, and her children are less than nothing; they are what Domenico callously calls "the three bastards" (1.11).

The "terrific moment" of act 1 is Filumena's surprise revelation that she, *in fact*, has three sons, that she has stealthily stolen money, clothes, and jewelry from Domenico in order to raise them properly, and that now she wants to give them a name, Domenico's name, Soriano, a name that will not only give them legitimacy but will constitute them as a family. As she makes clear to Domenico, "They must know who their mother is. They must know how much I love them—how much I need them to love me. It is not right that they should feel shame if someone asks to see their birth certificates. They should be part of one family. There should be someone there they can turn to for help. They must have the same name as me" (*Filumena* 1.17). She reveals the motivation for her actions, part deception and part rebellion at being used and then discarded. Her past characterizes her as "immoral, a danger, a threat to 'normal' femininity and, as a consequence, [Filumena] suffers social exclusion, marginalization and 'whore stigma,'"[35] but Filumena exposes the immorality of a social order and hierarchy that allows state-run brothels to exploit poor young women and characterizes them as dishonorable while the men who frequent those brothels suffer no affront to their honor and take little or no responsibility for fathering a child outside of marriage.[36] Filumena, like her city, rises from the ruins of the past to a new physical morality, one that makes allowances for past mistakes and acknowledges the triumphant morality of the spirit, which Filumena has always embodied.

According to critics Bander and Bentley, "There is little politics and less religion in the plays of De Filippo," but "in play after play he [puts] his finger on the black moral spot."[37] While there might not be political pandering or posturing in De Filippo's plays, there is the palpable presence of the social critic, and it is certainly visible in *Filumena Marturano* where "the black moral spot" is the plight of illegitimate children, who, through no fault of their own, were, at the time of this play and well afterward, branded for life as outcasts.[38] Italian laws regarding illegitimacy were shameful, victimizing the innocent children. *Figlio d'ignoto* or *figlio di NN* was stamped on birth certificates, school records, and legal documents, including military service cards.[39] It was a constant embarrassment for young men and women whose only crime was to have been born out of wedlock, and it was often the cause for personal and professional discrimination.[40] The unwed mother without the support of family, church, and state often neglected or abandoned the child who was a permanent symbol of her "fallen" state. "Illegitimate children ran a significantly greater chance of dying . . . in infancy than did legitimate children."[41] These children risked physical peril as youngsters, and, as they became adults, their emotional and personal welfare was threatened by the disclosure of their illegitimacy. Having lived the experience of the illegitimate child, De Filippo had a vested interest in having his audience, past and present, take inventory of Filumena's fight for her sons' lives and livelihood and later of Domenico's acknowledgment of paternity.[42] However, as a playwright, his interest went beyond the personal. In a public address in 1973, De Filippo stated, "If an idea is not of significance and usefulness to society, then I am not usually interested in working on it."[43] In his 1946 play, De Filippo attacks the Italian social order for the injustices suffered by illegitimate children, and his protagonist, a marked woman herself, is the voice for those who suffer unjustly. As Mignone notes, "De Filippo makes it clear that the law is wrong and in urgent need of reevaluation and alteration."[44] For De Filippo, it was more than just a personal matter; it was a matter of public policy and politics.

In her former life, Filumena did not succumb to the social pressure of her workplace, the brothel, the place that allowed her to capitalize on the only commodity she had at her disposal—her body. For many women, prostitution was and still is about work and economic need; while for most men, it was and still is "a leisure pursuit" if they can afford to pay.[45] Certainly this was the case for the two protagonists in the play. When Filumena discovers she is pregnant, the women in the brothel counsel her to "'get rid of it. . . . It's so easy—so simple'" (*Filumena* 1.11). A child will impede her earning ability and complicate her life; moreover, she lacks family support or a social network on which to rely. Nonetheless, Filumena places the life of the unborn child above her own. While Filumena forfeits her honor as it was constituted by church and state, she clings to the honor of motherhood and turns to her spiritual mother—the Madonna of the Roses—for guidance. In his plays, De Filippo's "morally-aroused sensibility" is more socially oriented than religiously motivated.[46] Therefore, it is not surprising that Filumena's religious encounter with the Madonna of the Roses comes across as more consultation than prayer; nonetheless, the disembodied voice that tells her "'A child is a child'" gives her the fortitude that so many women in her condition lacked (1.12).⁴⁷ She has not one but three children. However, neither Filumena's recounting of her mystical encounter nor her maternal passion moves Domenico into discharging his spousal duties to Filumena and assuming paternal responsibilities for her—their—sons. He is unwilling to sacrifice his soon-to-be May/December marriage to Diana. Act 1 ends with the expulsion of Diana, the interloper, who hopes to become Mrs. Soriano and with Domenico storming out of the house to find a lawyer to do what he has failed to do: extricate himself from Filumena.

Act 2 begins with the lively banter between Alfredo and Rosalia in which the reader discovers that Rosalia, whose own tragic circumstances left her a widow with three children to raise and who, in middle age, found herself alone and without financial resources, has delivered three letters on behalf of her patron. Filumena has looked after Rosalia for the last twenty-five years. Playing on the age-old cliché of the "whore with the heart of gold," De Filippo underscores, as Mignone points out, Filumena's "noble" spirit, which has stayed noble "even under the most degrading conditions."⁴⁸

Filumena's identity as noble benefactor is weighed against Domenico's identity as a vain and carefree womanizer whose past gives him the identity he desires and wishes to maintain and whose machismo is sanctioned by Italian cultural codes of honor. Reminding Alfredo about their past escapades and his many conquests, Domenico says, "I slept with so many women, eh, I don't believe that I ever slept at all! . . . Paris. London. How we traveled. Travel and horses. I *was* a God, Alfredo. I owned the world. No man ever gave me an order. I was Don Domenico Soriano" (*Filumena* 2.24). Now, he finds himself taking orders from a woman, Filumena, who is preparing her house, so she thinks, for the arrival of her sons. Ironically, it is through the intervention of Diana that Domenico finds a way to re-establish his control over himself and his home. Diana brings Nocella, a lawyer who resides at the same hotel as she. He informs Domenico—and then Filumena—that their marriage is null and void, that the law says so. During the exchange, the reader learns that Filumena cannot read, which is not surprising. At the beginning of the twentieth century, 48.7 percent of Italians were illiterate, with women more illiterate than men; in 1951, five years after the publication of the play, 12.9 percent of Italians over six years of age were still officially classified as illiterate.⁴⁹

What follows the discussion is another of those "terrific moments," in reality two of them. Having realized that she has failed in her efforts to guarantee a place for her and her sons in a society in which there is a clear distinction between law and justice, especially for the poor, Filumena first calls forth the three young men who had been summoned earlier and tells them who she is—their mother—and what she was—a whore at seventeen. She then proceeds to explain the circumstances of her poverty in the slums of San Liborio, and the implications of her father's smile when, after one more evening of sitting at a table of hungry and angry faces, he said to her, "You've grown into a fine-looking girl, Filumena, and there's not a thing to eat in the house" (*Filumena* 2.41). Standing inviolate, her dignity intact, Filumena tells them about the brothel which, to her, seemed a palace and of her mother's tears when she went back to her childhood home, thinking naïvely that she could return but realizing she could not. Defiantly, she tells the three young men that she "brought them up" and "made men of" them (2.42). Barbara d'Ajeta De Miro writes, "Forse mai l'importanza della maternità rispetto alla paternità è stata evidenziata come qui, tanto da scardinare il valore della famiglia patriarcale.... Se tutti gli uomini si equivalgono..., non ha importanza il padre, ma solo la madre, come accadeva nelle società in cui vigeva il matriarcato" (Perhaps nowhere is maternity more important than paternity as it is here, so much so as to undermine the value of the patriarchal family. If all men are the same, then the father is not important. Only the mother is important, as it was in matriarchal societies).[50]

At the end of her heartrending monologue, Michele, one of her sons, says, "Come with me. Come home.... All these years the kids have asked me about a grandmother!... When we walk through the door, that will be the first thing I'll shout 'Hey, kids—here's Grandma!'" (*Filumena* 2.42–43). After twenty-five years, she has not secured her place as Domenico's legal wife or legitimacy for her sons, but her son gives her a home of her own and a respectable identity: she is a grandmother. Morality overrides legality. Justice takes precedent over law. Michele does what is morally right, what is morally just. The law serves the privileged like Domenico Soriano; the underprivileged are responsible for themselves. Michele understands the "deceit of which they are victims" and assumes his responsibility for all of his family, including his mother.[51]

As Filumena prepares to leave the Soriano household, the reader encounters the second "terrific moment" of act 2: the revelation that one of her sons is Domenico's son. Domenico, who first accuses her of lying, listens as she reminds him of the one night when he had said to her, "'Let's love each other tonight, Filumena. Let's make love because we really love each other'" (*Filumena* 2.44). But Domenico has always dealt with Filumena as if she were a business transaction, and even that night, he had left her the usual payment—a one hundred lire note. Feverishly, he demands to know which one is his son, but Filumena refuses to tell him, saying that "they must all be equal—all three" (2.45). Her primal instinct tells her that she must maintain the illusion of paternity for all three if he is to treat them equally. In so doing, she maximizes the position of her offspring.[52] Before she leaves a swearing and threatening Domenico, she tears the corner of that one hundred lire note on which she had written the date of that memorable night and returns the money to him, saying, "Here. Take it. It belongs to you. It can buy many things. It can't buy a son" (2.46).

The opening of act 3, ten months after the unraveling of a lifetime of deception on both the part of Domenico and Filumena, finds the Soriano household preparing for a wedding. In the interim, Domenico has come to understand that "a child is a child," but he has still not given up on the idea of finding out which one of the three young men is his son. Upon their entrance, he begins a question and answer session that he hopes may give him some indication as to which one is his biological son; but his efforts are fruitless, and he makes one last attempt at discovering which one is his son by asking Filumena, who enters the room dressed for her upcoming bridal role. Domenico tells her that his pride has kept him from admitting what is in his heart, that they need each other, and that "it is right" that they marry (*Filumena* 3.58). He then asks her to demonstrate her love to him by telling him "which one of those three boys is my son" (3.59). Filumena refuses him one final time, not with anger or defiance but with the pathos and passion of a mother who not only wishes to secure her sons' financial stability and legal status but also their love for one another. She wants the family unit she was denied as a child and as an adult, and family demands a collectivity based on mutual love, respect, and understanding, which cannot happen if the young men do not have equal standing. Filumena asks Domenico to think of what would happen if she told him which one was his son: "They are three brothers and you would set them at each other's throats.... Don't think of yourself, Dummi'. Don't think of me. Think of them.... Either they are all equal or they are enemies. There is still time, Domenico. Either that or let us finish, you and I" (3.60). Filumena asks that Domenico see fatherhood as something more than blood ties and future name recognition, that he see fatherhood through the eyes of the child who depends on the selflessness of his parents. Filumena understands that family, fatherhood, and motherhood are not abstract terms but rather the concrete consequences of an interdependence and reliance upon one another. Family, fatherhood, and motherhood take priority over the desires of any one individual. Filumena has not acted on her own behalf but on behalf of the family unit, and she wants Domenico to do the same. If he cannot, she will put an end to the exploitative situation that has existed between them, in part a situation of mutual connivance.[53]

De Filippo forces the reader to consider the reality of the relationship between Filumena and Domenico. The play does not have a tidy resolution or a traditional happy ending. The Italian sociocultural environment limits Filumena's educational and economic opportunities and thrusts her into a world where she becomes a commodity of exchange between men, and her lack of authority, as an unmarried woman with three children and no financial recourse, leads her to lie and deceive to achieve her objectives. Yet, when early on in their relationship she has the opportunity to end her affair with Domenico and marry a young man who had fallen in love with her, she succumbs to Domenico's tears, whether out of blind confidence that he would eventually realize the "sacrifices [she had] made for him" or simply the romantic illusion that Domenico really loved her and would eventually do the right thing (*Filumena* 1.12). Domenico, on his part, has the Italian legal system, his class, and the cultural environment that hearten his position as a male and ease his conscience. He has nothing to lose and all to gain from his relationship with Filumena. As a member of the privileged class, he represents those in authority who prosper at the expense of the underclass. As Mignone writes, "Domenico is the State,"[54] and Filumena, like the Naples she represents, has finally said no to the years of exploitation at the hands of selfishness and hypocrisy. Filumena negotiates the ideologies compartmentalizing Italian society and subverts the rigidity of social caste and gender roles. She destabilizes the artificial boundaries between a good woman and a bad woman and takes control of and conducts the "business" transactions that had once commodified her. "Filumena si pone come soggetto e in ciò è la portata rivoluzionaria di questo personaggio" (Filumena positions herself as subject, which is the revolutionary stance of her character).[55] Whatever Domenico decides, Filumena will rise from the ruins somewhat broken but with her dignity intact and finally ready to rebuild.

Frustrated, Domenico rises ready to act on the ultimatum and addresses the three young men, who answer, "Yes, Father?" (*Filumena* 3.1). The expression, declared in unison, identifies them as his sons and constitutes them as a family. As such, Domenico assumes his role as *paterfamilias*, a role, refashioned by Filumena, that no longer mandates blood sanction. While Domenico orders them to escort their mother up the aisle, Filumena checks to see if Rosalia has given the caretaker at the shrine of the Madonna of the Roses the money for flowers and the lamp and if she has arranged for fifty candles to be lit at the time of her wedding. Filumena does not forget her spiritual mother to whom she went for counsel. De Filippo's "characters are Christian-pagans for whom God, Christ, the Madonna, and all the saints are little more than agencies on hand for the purpose of healing and punishing";[56] and Filumena, like many of her compatriots, "never expected something for nothing, in neither [her] worldly dealings, nor [her] other worldly dealings."[57] Therefore, she believes that giving thanks must come in a form of a payment of some kind; and, of course, it must be accompanied by public recognition and tribute. One only has to visit *la camera dei tesori* (the room of treasures) in any church, especially in southern Italy, to understand the Christian-pagan relationship and the Italian obsession with remuneration. Jewelry, hearts and limbs in silver and gold, and other worldly possessions cover every inch of space on the walls of these rooms, sometimes accompanied by artistic depictions of the favors received.[58] Filumena is a woman who keeps her vows to church and family, and her self-styled negotiations with the Madonna and the public recognition of the Madonna's intercession on her behalf reinforce the way in which she reconciles the many paradoxes of who and what she is: she is mystical and practical, Madonna and whore, wife and mistress, subject and object, idealistic and cynical at the same time. Assured that Rosalia has done her bidding in recognizing the Madonna's intervention, Filumena and the intimate wedding party head to the study, where a priest awaits to perform the marriage.

Amid the congratulations, Domenico dispenses the wine for a toast. He says, "A child is a child. A son is a son. They come from God. When there is more than one child in a family, it's not unusual for the father to have a favorite. . . . This could never happen to us, because our family got together too late. And that's good, because this privilege I have of being allowed to love one particular son will be shared between all three" (*Filumena* 3.63). He finally concurs that family, however it is constituted, outweighs the individual and his desires. Promising to return for dinner the following evening, the three young men leave, saying, "Good-night, Mama. . . . Good-night, Father. . . . Until tomorrow, Father. . . . Good-night, Papa" (3.63). All three sons reinforce the state of their newly scripted family. All three acknowledge and take ownership of mother and father. Filumena has reached her objective: she has rescripted marriage, motherhood, and identity for herself and secured legitimacy for her sons. She has found the supposed happiness that has eluded her for so long. She has the traditional family she has always wanted. Alone at last as husband and wife, Filumena says, "I'm crying, Dummi'—I'm crying. I'm crying" (3.64). While the reader rejoices at Filumena's supposed tears of joy, he or she remembers her earlier comment about not crying: "No, you're right. I don't cry. Do you know what makes a woman cry? When she knows what happiness is, but it's beyond her reach. Filumena Marturano has never known happiness. What she hasn't missed, she is unable to cry for" (1.6). As a neorealist, De Filippo leaves his audience with a bittersweet ending, with yet another Neapolitan paradox, with tears of joy that are also tears of sadness for what Filumena has missed all these years.

NOTES

This essay first appeared as "Beloved Whore: Rescripting Marriage, Motherhood, and Identity in Eduardo De Filippo's *Filumena Marturano*," in *La Revista de Antropología Social* 17 (2008): 119–40. Reprinted with permission.

1. Eduardo De Filippo, *Filumena* (1946), trans. Keith Waterhouse and Willis Hall (New York: Samuel French, 1978), 1.3. All citations are from this English edition, which shortens the title of the play to *Filumena*. As Maggie

O'Neill writes in "Imagining Women: Prostitution, the Aestheticization of the Whore and the Social Organization of Desire," in her *Prostitution and Feminism: Towards a Politics of Feeling*, 124–53 (Cambridge: Polity Press, 2001), "Whores became bad-girls with the growth of Christianity and later of Protestantism, contrasting the ideal of good wife and mother with bad-girl and sinner" (128). Certainly religious themes of sin, redemption, and salvation are omnipresent in the play. Carlo Filosa writes, "dietro la rappresentazione immediate e la rievocazione amara . . . vibra, non solo un fremito di sociale protesta, ma sporattutto una profonda rivendicazione cristiana del sacro valore della vita umana e del dovere della praternità tra gli uomini" (Beneath the surface plot, there is not only the tremor of social protest but also the sacred understanding of the value of human life and of the male's duty to recognize his paternal responsibility). Carlo Filosa, *Eduardo De Filippo: Poeta comico del "tragico quotidiano"* (Naples: La Nuova Cultura Editrice, 1978), 203.

2. Filumena's rebellion, albeit in the private sphere of the home, serves as a prototype of feminist resistance that will emerge two decades later.

3. E. Garbolevsky, "Voices from the Edge: Caught between the Madonna and the Whore—The Representation of the Prostitute in Modern Italian Cinema," in *Turning at the Crossroads: Women, Women Studies, and the State*, 1–29 (Towson, Md.: Institute for Teaching and Research on Women, Towson University, 2005), 9.

4. Luciano Codignola, "Reading De Filippo," *Tulane Drama Review* 8, no. 3 (1964): 110.

5. Mario B. Mignone, *Italy Today* (New York: Peter Lang, 1995), 9–10.

6. *Il Risorgimento*, which was supposed to bring about Italian independence and unification so as to normalize conditions, social and political, for *all* of Italy, succeeded only in underscoring and exacerbating the differences between the North and South (ibid., 4–5).

7. The unification of Italy in 1860 ended the two-hundred-year Bourbon rule of the South, but it also initiated the exodus of disillusioned and disenfranchised southerners. Within fifty years, Italy's population was reduced by one-third; and by 1930, more than 4.5 million Italians had emigrated to the United States, most of whom were southerners. Jerre Mangione and Ben Morreale, *La Storia: Five Centuries of the Italian American Experience* (New York: Harper Collins, 1992), 31–33.

8. The translations from Italian to English throughout the essay are mine. Philip V. Cannistraro, "Mussolini's Cultural Revolution: Fascist or Nationalist?," *Journal of Contemporary History* 7, no. 3/4 (1972): 135.

9. The *New York Times* headlines are from these dates respectively: October 27, 1941, August 28, 1943, and September 5, 1943.

10. Eric Bentley, "Eduardo De Filippo and the Neapolitan Theater," *Kenyon Review* 13 (1951): 7.

11. See Robert G. Bander, "The Neapolitan Scene in De Filippo's Theater," *Italian Quarterly* 51 (1970): 3–18, for a fuller discussion of the attitudes, ideas, and values of Naples. Cf. Giuseppe Faustini, "Filumena Marturano: From Play to Film," in *Transformations: From Literature to Film*, ed. Douglas Radcliff-Umstead, 55–62 (Kent, Ohio: Kent State University, 1987), 59.

12. Eduardo Scarpetta died without acknowledging his three illegitimate children but bequeathed a lifelong annuity to their mother.

13. Nevia Buommino, "Eduardo De Filippo, ovvero una persona di famiglia," Portanapoli.com, http://www.portanapoli.com/Ita/Cultura/body_eduardo_de_filippo.html, 2 (accessed February 11, 2007).

14. At the time *Filumena Marturano* was written, "figlio di NN" still appeared on birth certificates, legal documents, and identity cards. Illegitimate children were thus "marked" for life. In his interview with the playwright, Antonio Lubrano discusses the play's anticipation of legislation eliminating this practice.

15. It is interesting to note that "Villa Santarella" means the house of the little saint.

16. This personal information comes from Mario B. Mignone's *Eduardo De Filippo* (Boston: Twayne, 1984), and Damiano Camarda's biographical essay on the author, "Eduardo De Filippo," *Una finestra sul teatro Napoletano: Il teatro Napoletano*, www.teatro.unisa.it/autori.html (accessed March 5, 2007).

17. Eduardo De Filippo's relationship with Thea Prandi produced two children, but, unlike his own father, De Filippo married Prandi in 1956 and legitimized his two children. On stage, De Filippo, as Buommino writes, transformed "le farse di Scarpetta in moderni drammi borghesi" (Scarpetta's farces into middle-class modern dramas) "Eduardo De Filippo," 2.

18. Mignone, *Eduardo*, 7.

19. Bander, "Neapolitan Scene," 8.

20. Cited in Mimi D'Aponte, "Eduardo De Filippo Moralist and Social Critic," *NEMLA Italian Studies* 13–14 (1989–90): 82.

21. Donatella Fischer, "Strong Women and Nontraditional Mothers: The Female Figures in *Napoli Milionaria!* and *Filumena Marturano* by Eduardo de Filippo," in *Women in Italy, 1945–1960: An Interdisciplinary Study*, ed. Penelope Morris, 211–23 (New York: Palgrave Macmillan, 2006), 214.

22. Eduardo and his sister Titina originated the roles of Filumena and Domenico both in Naples and in Rome at the Eliseo Theatre in January 1947. Amedeo Mazzucco, reviewing the Rome premiere, wrote, "Eduardo De Filippo ha vinto con Filumena Marturano, la sua ultima (in ordine di tempo) importantissima ed appassionante battaglia artistica" (With Filumena Marturano, Eduardo De Filippo has won an important and passionate artistic

battle in his current body of work) (*Libero Orizzonte* 16 [January 1947]). I am indebted to Claudio Novelli from La Società Napolctana di Storia Patria for his help in securing the reviews from the Archivi di Teatro Napoli in Naples, Italy. Since 1946, the play has been the "most often produced postwar Italian play both in and out of Italy." Mira Friedlander, "Reviews of *Filumena Marturano*," Archivio Eduardo De Filippo, Archivi di Teatro Napoli, www.archiviteatro.napolibeniculturali.it/adf.html (accessed November 2, 2007). There have also been two film versions of the play: a 1951 version, filmed with the play's original title, starring Eduardo and his sister Titina, and the popular 1964 version directed by Vittorio De Sica with Sophia Loren and Marcello Mastroianni in the lead roles. *Marriage Italian Style*, as the later version was called, garnered an Academy Award nomination for Best Foreign Film in 1964. Jerry Vermilye, "Matrimonio all'Italiana," in *Great Italian Films* (New York: Citadel, 1994), 166–69.

23. Codignola, "Reading De Filippo," 111.

24. *Napoli Milionaria!* revolves around an Italian family involved in the Neapolitan black market during World War II. The play positions the wife as breadwinner and the husband as the voice of traditional morality, which becomes a casualty of war.

25. Bentley, "Eduardo De Filippo," 124.

26. Bander, "Critical Estimate," 7–8.

27. Cannistraro, "Mussolini's Cultural Revolution," 130.

28. In his monograph on Eduardo De Filippo, Mignone attributes the play's first fiasco on Broadway to be a problem of translation, something with which De Filippo himself agreed. In 1978, the current translation brought the play to the St. James Theatre in London with Laurence Olivier and Joan Plowright in the leading roles; it won the Best Play of the Year award and ran successfully for two years (*Eduardo*, 85–89). Cf. Bentley, "Eduardo De Filippo," 124.

29. Donatella Fischer describes this scene as a "'boxing match' between the female and the male universes" that occurs in "the domestic space of Domenico's house where Filumena . . . takes control" ("Strong Women," 218). Unfortunately, Filumena's dominance remains in the private sphere. If she is to have true power, her dominance must extend to the public sphere, where it is recognized as such.

30. Victoria De Grazia, *How Fascism Ruled Women: Italy, 1922–1945* (Berkeley: University of California Press, 1992), 147.

31. Corrado Gini and Elio Caranti, "The Family in Italy," *Marriage and Family Living* 16, no. 4 (1954): 350.

32. Female prostitutes would have to wait one more year to get their voting rights. John Foot, *Modern Italy* (New York: Palgrave Macmillan, 2003), 205.

33. Mignone, *Eduardo*, 85.
34. Bentley, "Eduardo De Filippo," 124.
35. O'Neill, "Imagining Women," 129.
36. In 1958, Italy finally passed a law that reformed prostitution legislation and closed the state-sanctioned brothels. The Merlin Law, named for Lina Merlin, the Socialist senator who sponsored the legislation, changed the policy on prostitution that had been in place since unification. Mary Gibson, *Prostitution and the State in Italy* (New Brunswick, N.J.: Rutgers University Press, 1986), 223.
37. Bander, "Critical Estimate," 10; Bentley, "Eduardo De Filippo," 115.
38. Only in 1956 did Italian law pass legislation that prohibited asking children for their parents' surname in public (D'Aponte, "Eduardo De Filippo Moralist," 84); and only in the 1970s would there be any change to the legal status of illegitimate children.
39. De Grazia, *How Fascism Ruled Women*, 63.
40. Legislation passed in 1928 rendered illegal the practice of assigning surnames to children who were either illegitimate or foundlings that would indicate their illegitimacy or abandonment. Surnames such as Esposito and Proietti would immediately call attention to the unfortunate circumstances of their birth. "Tracing Italian Lineages of Adoptees and Ancestors Born Outside Marriage," *Italian Genealogy*, https://www.italiangenealogy.com/articles/italian-genealogy/tracing-italian-lineages-of-adoptees-and-ancestors-born-outside-marriage (accessed December 19, 2017).
41. De Grazia, *How Fascism Ruled Women*, 62.
42. For a fuller discussion of the history of Italian family law, both before and after World War II, see Lesley Caldwell's *Italian Family Matters: Women, Politics and Legal Reform* (London: Macmillan, 1991).
43. Cited in D'Aponte, "Eduardo De Filippo Moralist," 86.
44. Mignone, *Eduardo*, 83.
45. O'Neill, "Imagining Women," 148.
46. Bander, "Critical Estimate," 11.
47. Titina De Filippo recited the celebrated monologue to Pope Pius XII in a special audience with His Holiness. Barbara De Miro d'Ajeta, *La figura della donna nel teatro di Eduardo De Filippo* (Naples: Liguori, 2002), 49.
48. Mignone, *Eduardo*, 83.
49. In 1936, 21 percent of married women in southern Italy could not sign the marriage register. Martin Clark, *Modern Italy 1871–1982* (New York: Longman, 1984), 36, 278, 364. In the cinematic version of the play, Filumena's act of writing serves as comic relief.
50. De Miro d'Ajeta, *Figura della donna*, 49.
51. Mignone, *Eduardo*, 85.

52. Sarah Hrdy in *The Woman That Never Evolved* (Cambridge, Mass.: Harvard University Press, 1999) talks about the sexual counterstrategy of female chimpanzees. Hrdy theorizes that, by mating with as many males as possible, female chimpanzees are able to successfully protect their young from the violence of older male chimpanzees who will not attack if there is even the slightest chance that they might have fathered the chimp. This strategy confuses paternity and safeguards the offspring. Filumena has the same primal instincts.

53. Maurizio Grande calls this play "la 'commedia della castrazione'" (the comedy of castration). Cited in De Miro d'Ajeta, *Figura della donna*, 48.

54. Mignone, *Eduardo*, 85.

55. De Miro d' Ajeta, *Figura della donna*, 53.

56. Mignone, *Eduardo*, 23.

57. Salvatore Primeggia, "The Social Contexts of Religious Devotion: How Saint Worship Expresses Popular Religiosity," in *The Saints in the Lives of Italian-Americans*, ed. Joseph A. Varacalli et al., 68–92 (Stony Brook, N.Y.: Filibrary (*Forum Italicum*), 1999), 73.

58. As Primeggia notes, "Another cult practice, more common in Italy than in any other Catholic country, is the use of the *ex voto*. An *ex voto* is an object that is brought to the church—most often into its sanctuary—which is symbolic of a vow made to a saint or the Madonna. . . . It might be displayed in a special room adjacent to the main body of the church'" (ibid., 75).

NINETEEN

## Matilde Serao's Art of Numbers: Naples and the Game of Lotto

*Gabriella Romani*

Matilde Serao famously defined Lotto as the "acquavite di Napoli" (opium of Naples), a demonic game that intoxicated the people of Naples, vividly described by the author as they wait, indeed live for, the weekly drawings of the winning numbers.[1] Servants, shoeshiners, glove makers, clerks, porters, as well as shop owners, lawyers, judges, and even members of the aristocracy, all fall victim to the illusion of quick financial gains as they delude themselves into thinking they will guess the lucky combinations of numbers (*ambo* or *terno*) extracted on Saturday afternoons. They are portrayed as doomed daydreamers, seeking a sudden turn of events in life, a better and prosperous future, which inevitably fails to materialize and which leaves them on a cliff of desperation from which they witness the fatal dilapidation of their family's economic resources.

Serao's overall condemnation of Lotto reflected nineteenth-century antivice rhetoric, which viewed games of chance as an expression of the negative effects produced by new capitalist consumer trends, threatening social order and moral public life. Produced during the 1880s and early 1890s, Serao's writings on gambling were a response to the social and economic transformation of Italy during those years as well as to the prevailing numerical and positivistic approaches, adopted in national policies of reformation and aimed at accelerating the process of Italy's modernization.[2] Responding, for instance, to Minister Depretis's infamous comment in 1884 about the need of "sventrare Napoli" (gutting Naples), Serao challenged official policies of reformation and denounced the government's limited knowledge of reality based on statistical information.[3] A numerical narrative of nationhood, Serao claimed, could not fully account for the complexity of the realities in which people lived:

> Efficacious the phrase. You, Honorable Depretis, did not know the bowels of Naples. You were wrong, because you are the government, and the government must know everything. The colorful little descriptions written by journalists with literary intentions are not of interest to the government . . . the government should have known the other side; the government which receives the statistics of mortality and crime, and the reports from prefects and police commissioners and inspectors, the government that knows everything: how much meat is consumed in a day . . . how many beggars cannot enter charitable institutions and how many vagrants sleep on the street at night, how many destitute people and merchants there are . . . this other side, the bowels of Naples, if the government does not know it, who should know it?[4]

It is well known that Serao did not endorse the idea of progress as a panacea to the ills of nineteenth-century Italy and, later in her career, openly rejected naturalism for its lack of interest in the spiritual dimension of life.[5] Reason, she claimed, "è insufficiente a spiegare la vita" (it is not sufficient to explain life).[6] Writing at the height of positivistic enthusiasm among Italian intellectuals who believed in a teleological process of progress and observing that, in spite of scientific advancements and legislative reforms, people continued to suffer, Serao dismissed the relevance of such a rationalist approach, depicting life as a common struggle whereby people fought an endless existential war against superior forces.

> It is the voice of reason, which speaks to you too often and perhaps only to your ear. It tells you coldly how inferior you are to your adversary in the long existential fight for life. Cold reason invites you to look within yourself, to

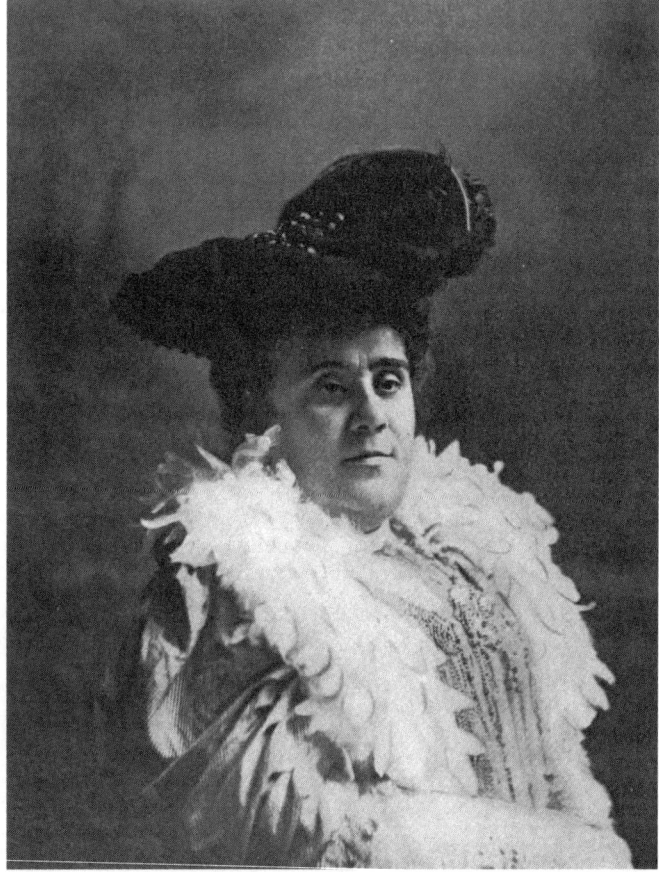

Figure 19-1. Matilde Serao. (Wikimedia Commons)

measure, weigh, calculate yourself. And you feel the scarcity of your vigor, the inevitable weaknesses inherited from the species, the misery of your blood and fiber, the implacable limitations given by nature and by God. You feel the fatal fall of your will, facing instincts that cannot be tamed, the impasse for which people agitate and that reason, cold reason, describes to you like the chain that a criminal will carry until death.[7]

Serao's objection to the positivistic method must be understood, within the context of this essay on Serao's art of numbers, as an opposition to what Silvana Patriarca defined as a "literature of facts," the vast production of nineteenth-century books, pamphlets, and articles aimed at creating "an authoritative image of Italy based on a positive, that is numerical, knowledge."[8] As Patriarca showed in her study, beginning in the late eighteenth century Italy experienced a widespread circulation of publications devoted to numerical narratives of nationhood that were supposed to express awareness of Italy's backwardness and provide scientific support for the creation of solutions to the country's atavistic problems.[9] Such publications were not addressed solely to the attention of specialists but, rather, engaged the national intellectual debate focused on creating economic and social policies as well as cultural initiatives aimed at accelerating the process of modernization of the Italian nation. Depretis's statement in 1884, about gutting the slums of Naples, constituted in practical terms a numerical solution, an attempt at zeroing in on what was perceived as the insoluble problem of southern poverty.

Depretis's visit to Naples marked the beginning of Serao's writings on the game of Lotto and her attempt to provide a narrative interpretation of facts as part of her lifelong commitment to produce cultural awareness of Italy's social realities (poverty, political corruption, women and their role in society, etc.). Like many writers of the postunification period, Serao fully embraced the educational mission and functional purpose of art and sought with both her journalistic and fictional production to educate, and therefore advance, the nation. In literary terms, the debate over Italy's modernization influenced the development of a naturalistic production in Italian literature, known as *verismo*; and while Serao has often been included among the *veristi* authors of Italy, she never completely abided by the tenets of the movement.[10] Starting with her essay "Lotto" and later more explicitly in her fiction, Serao developed an argument, thematically centered on gambling, that defied the logic of numbers and affirmed the value of art, that is, "fantasy" (*fantasticheria*), the imaginative dimension of life, as a main cultural instrument for educating people and therefore bringing progress to society. "Per levare la corruzione materiale e quella morale," as Serao argued in favor of cultural and educational interventions, "per rifare la salute e la coscienza a quella povera gente . . . non basta sventrare Napoli: bisogna in gran parte rifarla" (to erase both material and moral corruption, to recreate the health and conscience of poor people . . . it is not sufficient to gut Naples: it must be rebuilt).[11]

While endorsing a vision of cultural and social progress, Serao expressed ambivalence, however, toward modernization and the changes that modernity brought to society. As a social conservative, Serao endorsed a moderate and gradual transformation of society, mainly based on cultural rather than legal changes for a harmonic resolution of class conflict. Serao's condemnation of Lotto is to be connected to her critical view of modern consumer society and her uncomfortable relationship, similar to that of other late-nineteenth-century Italian writers (Verga's, for instance), with the notion of progress and modernization, as a solution to all of Italy's ills—a slow but pressing transformation that provoked anxieties and fears about the future of a country, Italy, still intrinsically steeped in rural and traditional lifestyle. To gamble meant to assign value to money as the only effective instrument for changing meaningfully one's life and for diverting the frustrations produced by the impossibility of making those changes in real life.[12] "Il lotto prende possesso, domina," Serao stated, "dove la durezza della vita più si fa sentire e dove solo il danaro può esser rimedio" (The lottery possesses, dominates you, where the harshness of life is most felt and where only money can be a remedy for it).[13] While hardships of life were hardly new to Neapolitans, gambling in the postunification period acquired wider appeal among the population, giving voice to what some critics named the "ontological insecurity" of the nineteenth century.[14] Above all, the game of Lotto constituted a recent but widely alluring expression of the chance—remote as it might have been—to escape social or economic constraints dictated by one's family origin or adverse life circumstances. A program, reflecting a vision of modernized Italy as a less rural, illiterate, and poor society, was widely endorsed by cultural and political institutions in the postunification era, but also feared for its potential to destabilize traditional social relations and hierarchies.

As gambling began to lure a wider than ever portion of society—indeed the whole society, for Serao—with the promise of quick financial gains, people's uncontrolled tendency toward daydreaming displayed the formation of a new hedonism and desire for commodities—markers of modern consumer culture—which for some intellectuals and writers constituted a real threat to society.[15] Serao's Lotto narratives are populated with characters who are consumed with desire for things, often food items, they simply cannot afford: "una spanciata di pranzi grassi e ricchi, divorati in immaginazione" (a binge of fat and rich lunches, devoured with the imagination).[16] In *Il paese di Cuccagna*, the shoeshiner Michele asks Gaetano, the glove maker, what he would do with the money won with the Lotto, and he answers: "Lo so io che ne fo! . . . Col vestito nuovo, con la penna di fagiano al cappelletto, nella carrozza coi sonagli, andiamo tutti a scialare ai Bue Pulcinelli, al Campo di Marte. . . . Carne e maccheroni—E vino del Monte di Procida. . . . —Tanto, una volta sola si campa" (I know what I'd do with it! With a new suit, and a hat with a pheasant's feather, in a coach with bells, we all merrily go to the Bue Pulcinelli in Campo di Marte. . . . Meat and macaroni, wine from the Mount of Procida. . . . In the end you only live once).[17] And the Marquis Cavalcanti, oppressed by debts and poverty, announces to his daughter: "Avrai di nuovo, Bianca Maria, cavalli e carrozze, la Victoria per le passeggiate alla Riviera di Chiaia, dove riprenderai il tuo posto, la elegante vettura chiusa, per la sera, per andare a San Carlo. . . . vedrai, figlia, vedrai. Ti voglio comperare una collana di perle, otto file di perle legate da un solo zaffiro e un diadema di brillanti, come lo hanno avuto tutte le donne di casa Cavalcanti" (You'll have again, Bianca Maria, horses and coaches, the Victoria for strolling along the Riviera di Chiaia, you'll see, my dear, you'll see. I want to buy you a pearl necklace, eight strings of them connected by a sapphire, and a tiara of diamonds, as all women in the Cavalcanti household have always had).[18] In Serao's fiction devoted to Lotto, no one is immune to what the author defines as a "malattia dello spirito: un contagio sottile e infallibile, inevitabile, la cui forza di diffusione non si può calcolare" [a sickness of the spirit: a subtle, infallible, and inevitable contagion, whose force of contamination cannot be measured].[19] And Serao here is not only talking about gambling but refers, more broadly, to what she perceives as an intrinsic problem with modernity: the emergence of a consumer capitalist culture that erodes social harmony by encouraging individualistic desire for desire's sake—a process that inevitably leaves the individual, as Benjamin poignantly synthesizes in the figure of the flâneur, in a state of alienation. And it was the alienation of the modern subject, literally squeezed into a phantasmagoric representation of desire, that Serao describes in her Lotto narratives.[20]

Lotto has been played in Naples since 1682 and even in earlier times games of chance had been popular there. "La beneficiata" (also called "la bonafficiata"), for instance, a game based on the drawing of numbers through which people won luxury items (gold, silver, fine textiles, etc.), predated the game of Lotto and eventually was overshadowed by it. As the Lotto became increasingly popular among the population of Naples—and was also known as "gioco delle zitelle," "gioco delle donzelle" (game of the spinsters, games of the young ladies), and "la beneficiata di Napoli" (a term still used today)—it generally received support from governments, for obvious revenue purposes, but also attracted public criticism.[21] It was banned in Naples after an earthquake in 1688 (blamed on the "sinful" game), and beginning in the eighteenth century a public campaign of condemnation gained momentum, culminating in the nineteenth century in a public campaign that pathologized gambling, presented in public discourse as a deviant practice.[22] Emblematic of the transformation of the Lotto in the public perception was the semantic shift in the expression "dare i numeri" (give numbers/go crazy), which in seventeenth-century parlance still had a positive connotation (for its clairvoyant attributes), while in the following century it connoted irrational behavior and mental instability.[23] Nineteenth-century positivistic thinkers, writers of self-help manuals, and, more generally, promoters of the belief that social advancement was the outcome of individual self-improvement and work ethics condemned the game of Lotto for depriving the subject of agency and for assigning to blind fortune a main role in determining human destiny. If, during the Enlightenment, gambling was attacked for being "a sign of human ignorance which the rational individual had a duty to resolve," with the positivistic fervor of the second part of the nineteenth century it became synonymous with vice, understood as the antithesis of virtuous behavior—one that refrained an individual from squandering precious modern assets, namely time and money; as Reith puts it, "The industrializing west needed labor power; time became a commodity only slightly less precious than money, and gambling squandered them both."[24]

Serao wrote on the game of Lotto for the first time in *Il ventre di Napoli* (1884), a collection of essays, originally published as articles on the daily *Capitan Fracassa*, in reaction to the Minister Agostino Depretis's statement that "Naples ought to be gutted," made during a visit to Naples after the 1884 cholera outbreak. These essays have since been reprinted several times, attesting to the popularity they have enjoyed up to now among both readers and critics.[25] Serao later also wrote fiction on gambling—the short story

"Terno secco" (in *All'erta sentinella*, 1889) and what has been defined as her most ambitious novel, *Il paese di Cuccagna* (1891).[26] While her essays on Lotto in *Il ventre di Napoli* are traditionally considered more accomplished from a narrative point of view than her fiction, they share a similar set of dilemmas and interpretive approaches toward a game she viewed as innately negative but also intrinsically tied to the social and cultural life of her city.[27]

Lotto was a popular game in nineteenth-century Naples, reaching in the postunification period the highest point of popularity, when in 1884 there was an outbreak of cholera.[28] Scholars have identified this increased popularity with the widespread feeling of uncertainty and fear of that time and the consolatory effects provided by gambling.[29] Serao, a "chronicler of reality," as she liked to define herself, understood the cultural and social appeal of gambling in Naples—a city where people, eternally afflicted by economic distress, would easily be drawn to fantasizing as a way to escape the harshness of reality. For Serao, illusion rather than hope dominated Neapolitans' mechanism of survival and both in *Il ventre di Napoli* and in *Il paese di Cuccagna* she referred to Lotto as a *sogno* (dream):

> Every week the poor of Naples nevertheless renew their great dream of happiness. They live for six days with a growing, overwhelming sense of hope that becomes greater and greater, until it surpasses the limits of reality. For six days the people of Naples dream their great dream, which is about everything they do not have: a clean house with fresh and healthful air to breath, a lovely shaft of warm sunshine on the floor, a high bed with clean white sheets, and a well-polished dresser. In this same dream there are pasta and meat every day, along with a liter of wine, as well as a cradle for the baby, clean linen for the wife and a new hat for the husband.[30]

> The dream, then, that feeds your existence for seven days and on the eighth one gives you a burning disappointment, ends up poisoning your blood. And to raise the chance of winning, to win at any cost, betting increases enormously, fantastically, and the desire to win becomes fury and the soul sickens.[31]

Lotto is presented here as a social practice fueled by the human impulse to fantasize (as "oppio della miseria," [opium of the poor] on which both Gramsci and Croce will later comment)[32]—a faculty, which, according to Serao, when coupled with gambling had devastating effects on society and, in particular, on the family.

Serao's Lotto stories are thematically centered as much on gambling as on the family. Their protagonists are all fathers or husbands, who fail in their responsibility to take care of their families. Only the shoeshiner Michele, who is not married, can afford to think of gambling as part of a rational system of personal accountability: "Tre soldi per dormire, otto o dieci soldi per mangiare,—continuò il lustrino,—e chi mi dice niente? Ah io non l'ho voluta prendere, la moglie, io! Avevo la passione della giuocata, io, e mi basta per tutto!" (Three soldos to sleep, eight or ten to eat—continued the shoeshiner—and I don't have to answer to anyone! As for myself, I didn't want to marry! I had a passion for gambling, and that covers it all!).[33] All other male characters of this novel have children and wives who become in their desperation the living example of the destructive effects of gambling: Gaetano, a glove maker and the father of three children, ends up killing his pregnant wife; the Marquis Cavalcanti, an impoverished aristocrat, depletes the family's patrimony and drives his innocent daughter into madness and eventually death; Cesare Fragalà, an affluent shopowner, loses a family business that had thrived for three generations, but unlike the other male characters, with the help of his wife, who takes control of the family's financial life, he is given a chance of salvation (a narrative choice reflecting Serao's view of the bourgeoisie as a main agent in Italy's advancement).

Women loom large in this scenario of desperation, not only as victims of male reckless behavior but also as carriers of hope. "Terno secco," a brilliant short story recounting the lucky drawing of three numbers—three, forty-two, and eighty-four—focuses on a female protagonist, a mother and a teacher who can barely make it to the end of the month, but who unlike her male counterparts remains immune to the lure of gambling. Struggling to pay for daily necessities, she decides to give the little money she has left to her daughter to buy something she needs for school. Meanwhile, Tommasina, her servant, finds fortuitously three numbers written on a piece of paper laying on the mother's bedroom floor, gambles them, and wins along with several other neighbors with whom she had shared the numbers. The mother, who had written the numbers in the first place, is the only person left out of this sudden stroke of luck. To the general jubilation of a crowd exalted by the unexpected win, Serao juxtaposes the mother's sad realization of a lost opportunity to gain much-needed financial help. But the sadness of this apparent defeat evaporates at the end of the story when we realize that the mother hasn't forgotten to play the numbers but consciously chose not to gamble the little money she had so that she could help her daughter. Infusing her maternal character with an aura of moral superiority, Serao elevates the figure of the mother to a level of sanctity for her role as the main protector of an institution, the family, which she considered the only place individuals would find a haven against the unexpected blows of life.

Propelled by her artistic interest in the uncontrollable forces of life, Serao intended her writings on Lotto to be consolatory and provide a narrative response to what she considered a main problem of her era: a sense of general disorientation, which she blamed on the effects produced by an increasingly rationalist society that excessively valued reason as a main instrument for identifying and eventually resolving current social problems:

> Who can be carefree today? While all scientific inventions, political laws, and artistic manifestations are meant to erase existential hardships, every day our existence seems more and more a Gordian knot that nobody is able to untie or brave enough to cut off . . . How come the art of living is no longer familiar to us? Who dried out the spring of our energy? Cold reasoning did it . . . which speaks to us and shows us the spectacle of life without any veils, without any halos, in all its naked truth. But it also reveals all the prickly thorns, the painful bitterness, the unspeakable privations and shows this long path without any poetry, without attraction or fascination. It is intoxicating to the mouth and the heart like the absinthe, without any further consolation or compensation.[34]

To the negative effects of gambling, Serao offered the consolation of human imagination, with stories turned into parables, which were supposed to warn the readers about the pitfalls of a vision—sudden change of fortune or circumstances—which brought individuals toward personal desperation and social devastation. To say it with Johan Huizinga, for Serao the *homo ludens* represented "the supra-logical nature of the human situation," that is, the sphere of life that extends the human experience beyond the realm of reasoning.[35] And this is precisely what she intended to reveal with her writings on Lotto: the pain, joy, hopes, and disappointments that fill the daily life of her characters, almost all of them unredeemable gamblers, consumed by a passion that burns not only their own life but that of an entire city. Her interest in Lotto was therefore neither inspired by the "picturesque" element of Neapolitan life nor by the moral implications of a state-sanctioned gambling system, but was, rather, the result of her belief in the transformative role of art and the liberating effects, in the form of imaginative consolation, provided by literature.

If Serao understood the role of passions in life, "Quale uomo potrebbe continuare a vivere, se la sua immaginazione non rifacesse intorno a sè la vita?" (Who could keep living if the imagination would not recreate life for us?),[36] she didn't condone them and warned that passions, when in excess (as in gambling), promoted a distorted understanding of reality that encouraged vice: "But like all dreams that are too pronounced, the lottery leads to inaction and idleness. Like all visions, it leads to falsehood and lies. Like all hallucinations, it leads to cruelty and ferocity. Like all sham remedies born from poverty, it produces poverty, degradation and crime."[37]

Serao's condemnation of Lotto, as a leisure practice leading to idleness and corruption, is not too dissimilar in tone and substance from what other contemporary authors expressed in popular literary works of the same time (Collodi's "Il paese dei Balocchi" in his *Le avventure di Pinocchio: Storia di un burattino* of 1883, comes immediately to mind, and certainly De Amicis's *Cuore* of 1886 conforms to a similar set of moral and ethical values), which subscribed to a notion of *homo faber*, based on a bourgeois work ethic and belief in the individual's virtuous behavior that translated into social progress. Starting with the popularization in Italy of Samuel Smiles's self-help manual and Michele Lessona's *Volere è potere*, a vast array of books targeting a middle-class readership circulated nationally. Major publishers like Emilio Treves (with whom Serao published several of her books, including *Il ventre di Napoli* and *Il paese di Cuccagna*) and Ditta Gianni Agnelli, both located in Milan, created new book series, named "Biblioteca utile" or "Biblioteca amena," which were supposed not only to capitalize on the growing number of readers produced by the recently enacted school reforms and relatively wider access to education, but also to realize what was understood to represent, both in rhetorical and practical terms, the main mission of cultural institutions: the creation of a civil and national consciousness that would improve the moral fabric of Italian society.[38] As Michele Lessona put it: "To those who justify their laziness by invoking fortune, we say that fortune exists. Yes, it does exist, but it doesn't show itself. It only lets itself be grabbed by those who have earned the right to see her and take advantage of her. And these are people who are industrious, intelligent, moderate, lovers of work and good savers. Without all this, you will not achieve anything, regardless of how big the earnings might be."[39]

Hard work and not fortune were presented as the main ingredients for a recipe of personal success and ultimately national advancement. In Serao's *Il paese di Cuccagna*, fortune is necessarily bad (malafortuna) because it obscures with its promise of easy earnings the true value of money based on hard work for which "si mette il soldo sopra il soldo, la lira sopra la lira, e infine, dopo due o tre generazioni, si arriva ad avere una fortuna" (you put one soldo on top of the other, one lira on top of another lira, and after two or three generations, you start doing well).[40] However, in spite of this trust in a work ethic, expressed also in the many articles Serao wrote on self-help, and regardless of the fact that her own professional career was the very narration of a story of hard work turned into personal success, she knew all too well that many of the government reforms had yet to deliver on the promise of economic development and that many people though working hard continued to live in dire poverty. The words of Carmela, a factory worker in *Il paese di Cuccagna*, express well the sense of frustration felt by those who simply cannot escape poverty by way of work:

> It wasn't enough that she worked in that nauseating job at the tobacco factory for seven days a week; it wasn't enough that she didn't have to wear a decent dress nor a good pair of shoes, to the point that at the factory they judged her badly; it wasn't enough that she fasted, four days a week, in order to give a lira to her mother, a couple of liras to Raffaele, half of a lira to her sister Annarella and all the rest, when there was any left, for the lottery. It was useless, just useless, she could never do anything for those she loved. Nothing helped, neither her effort, nor her poverty, nor her hunger. Nothing would help.[41]

And in "Trenta per cento," a short story thematically focused on financial greed and banking scandals, the pious donna Concettina says, "Ah signora mia, com'è duro, com'è difficile vivere onestamente!" (Oh my dear lady, it is so hard! How difficult it is to live honestly!),[42] giving voice to the many (indeed uncountable) people who, unable to improve their lot by honest work, welcome the possibility of quick financial gains through an improbable but all the more alluring banking scheme that promises unrealistic return profits. Like in *Il paese della Cuccagna*, here too the financial gain is nothing but a dream—a remote and mythical place, "l'isola della Cuccagna," that can only be reached by way of imagination:

> a dream about a fairy land of abundance with mountains of macaroni, sautéed broccoli, enormous plates of eel, fricassee style, marinated, fried, roasted, with vinegar, with egg, with laurel, cauliflower salads, with anchovies and mixed with hard-boiled eggs, with tuna in olive oil, roasted chickens, chickens guazzetto style, with tomatoes sauce or cooked in the oven. It was a fairy land of abundance that year, because bank money ran with fat interest everywhere. From the pockets of princes to those of butlers, from those of the rich bourgeoisie to those of the servants, and from those of merciful and generous people to the pockets of the poor. Money ran all over, and it was money coming from everywhere, especially from the province, money that came from anywhere, anywhere circulated widely and for the largesse of the abundant Neapolitan Christmas.[43]

Expressing ambivalence for a game that was enormously popular in her city, Serao considered Lotto to be an evil of contemporary society—exacerbated by the increasing appeal of consumerism and social mobility—but also as an imaginative and, for some, irresistible escape from the misery of everyday life. Like all flights of fantasy, Serao warned her readers, gambling brought the risk of a fatal fall—one that exposed in all its tragedy the frailty of the human condition. But it would be a mistake to think of Serao's writings on the game of Lotto as simple tales with a cautionary message, for they were meant to provide an artistic liberating effect from what the author considered the tyranny of numbers. To the numerical knowledge offered by statistical and positivistic publications, Serao responded with her artistic intuition and her observation of life, portrayed in all its contradictions and truthfulness.

## NOTES

1. Matilde Serao, *Il ventre di Napoli* (Pisa: ETS, 1995), 37. Unless otherwise noted, all translations are mine.

2. On Italy's financial crisis, see Stefano Fenoaltea, *The Reinterpretation of Italian Economic History: From Unification to the Great War* (Cambridge: Cambridge University Press, 2011); in particular, see "The Consumption Cycle and the 'Crisis' of the 1880s" (109–34); and Vera Zamagni, *The Economic History of Italy: 1860–1990* (Oxford: Clarendon Press, 1993).

3. Serao, *Il ventre di Napoli*, 9.

4. Ibid.

5. Her endorsement of the literary movement called "Cavalieri dello spirito" (the knights of spirit)—which never turned into a real movement and remained more of a current or vision—is a case in point. Imbued with idealism, Serao assigned great artistic value to spiritualism as a way to explore and eventually reach truths of life. See her "I Cavalieri dello Spirito," in Antonio Fogazzaro, *Sonatine bizzarre: scritti dispersi* (Rome: Ripostes, 1992), 53–59.

6. Matilde Serao, *Nel sogno* (Florence: Paggi, 1897), 15. In 1884 Serao published two articles in *Domenica letteraria* proclaiming the failure of an art founded on scientific criteria, rejecting the positivistic principle of causality, and later in the year she wrote in the *Fanfulla* an article that promoted the creation of an experimental art, able to express the irrational aspect of life. She wrote: "A malgrado dell'atavismo, del temperamento, dell'ambiente, spesso chi doveva perire, vive; e tale che logicamente doveva trionfare, cade. Questo bisogna studiare, e dirci come succede e perché succede. . . . Ancora l'arte sperimentale deve assurgere a questa interpretazione più larga e più complessiva della vita. La storia della coscienza alle prese coi desideri incomposti, con le condizioni fisiologiche, col natural bisogno di felicità e di amore, col temperamento e coi i bizzarri fatti umani—ecco quello che dovrà fare l'arte" (Despite atavism, temperament, and environment, often who is supposed to die, lives, and, logically, who is supposed to triumph, dies. This is what we must study and explain how and why it happens. . . . Experimental art, too, must be elevated to shift toward a more extensive and comprehensive interpretation of life. The history of our conscience as it deals with our fragmented desires, our physiological conditions, our natural need of happiness and love, and our temperament or bizarre facts of life—here is what art ought to be doing). Quoted in Tommaso Scappaticci, *Introduzione a Serao* (Rome: Laterza, 1995), 61.

7. Serao, *Nel sogno*, 16–17.

8. Silvana Patriarca, *Numbers and Nationhood: Writing Statistics in Nineteenth-Century Italy* (Cambridge: Cambridge University Press, 1996), 6

9. Patriarca assigns to the practice of statistical writing an important pedagogical value, and while her study is focused on the first part of the nineteenth century, the pedagogy of numbers is certainly relevant to the latter part of the century as well, when Serao, among other writers, envisioned literature (in addition to scientific interventions) as a main instrument of the cultural and social development of Italy.

10. Scappaticci speaks of a "verismo aproblematico" (unproblematized realism) when describing Serao's tendency to accept "la lezione naturalistica, ma sganciandola da presupposti scientifici . . . un verismo aproblematico, che

non ha ambizioni di scientificità e di rigore metodologico e non condivide l'entusiasmo positivistico per una scienza capace di risolvere i problemi della società e di operare radicali trasformazioni del sistema letterario" (the naturalistic lesson, liberated, however, of its scientific premise . . . an unproblematized realism without scientific ambitions or methodological rigor, which does not share positivist enthusiasm for a science capable to solve society's problems and implement radical transformations in the literary system). *Introduzione a Serao*, 58.

11. Serao, *Il ventre di Napoli*, 13.

12. Giuseppe Imbucci writes about the emergence of an existential and compensating function of gambling in time of crisis, as a result of games' ability to extend the temporal and spatial limits of reality. He explains the "funzione compensativa o esistenziale, vero e proprio ammortizzatore delle crisi sociali" (compensating or existential function, a true safety cushion in moments of social crisis) in "La cicala e la formica," where he states that "a nostro parere la risposta è nell'essenza stessa del gioco, nella sua capacità cioè di torcere la dimensione del tempo ed aprire attraverso la ripetizione ludica gli orizzonti del futuro. . . . In tempo di crisi il futuro non promette alcuna speranza, soprattutto se queste crisi sembrano croniche o di sistema. Il gioco invece apre al futuro perché promette speranze" (in our opinion the answer is in the essence of gambling, in its capacity, that is, to twist the temporal dimension and widen the horizon of the future through the repetition of the game. . . . During a time of crisis, the future does not promise hope, especially when these crises are chronic or systemic. Gambling, instead, opens up the future because it provides hope). Giuseppe Imbucci, "La cicala e la formica: Comportamenti e funzioni sociali del gioco," *Il gioco pubblico in Italia: Storia, cultura e mercato*, ed. Giuseppe Imbucci (Venice: Marsilio, 1999), 7–31, 26, 27.

13. Serao, *Il ventre di Napoli*, 35.

14. Gerda Reith, *The Age of Chance: Gambling in Western Culture* (London: Routledge, 1999), 41, identified in the nineteenth century a significant shift in the perception and usage of the notion of probability, which resulted in an "ontological insecurity," understood as a "breakdown of a sense of order, of wholeness and meaning." Such insecurity produced, according to the critic, an avalanche of numerical data and statistics.

15. Roberta Sassatelli, *Consumer Culture: History, Theory and Politics* (London: Sage, 2007), 17.

16. Matilde Serao, *Il paese di Cuccagna* (Milan: Treves, 1925), 16.

17. Ibid., 5.

18. Ibid., 62–63.

19. Serao, *Il ventre di Napoli*, 34.

20. Emblematic of Serao's criticism toward modernity is an article, published on December 1, 1886, in *Corriere di Roma* and titled "La donna réclame," in which she denounces the commodification of women by consumer society. Horrified by the scene of young women walking outside of Parisian department stores with signs advertising fashionable clothes, Serao demystified the lure of consumer seduction by revealing the alienation produced by public exposure. Her concerns were not related exclusively to those women who carried commercial signs, but more generally addressed the rise in contemporary life of cultural and social practices that assigned economic capital to women's bodies and turned them into visual sites of seduction for consumer desire.

21. The game of Lotto had, since its inception, a charitable function as it provided a dowry to young orphan women at the age of marriage. Each number drawn was connected to the name of a woman, who received 25 "ducati" as a dowry—a practice that was terminated in 1865 when, with the reforms to the family laws, women were no longer required by law to bring a dowry into their marriage. See Franco Schiattarella, *La beneficiata* (Naples: Editrice EDART, 1968), in particular the chapter on "Maritaggi" (135–52).

22. For a history of the Lotto, see Paola De Sanctis Ricciardone, *Il tipografo celeste: Il gioco del Lotto tra la letteratura e la demologia nell'Italia dell'Ottocento e oltre* (Bari: Edizioni Dedalo, 1987); Paolo Macry, *Giocare la vita: Storia del lotto a Napoli tra Sette e Ottocento* (Rome: Donzelli, 1997); Schiattarella, *La beneficiata*; Franco Strazzullo, *I giochi d'azzardo e il lotto a Napoli: Divagazioni storiche* (Rome: Liguori Editore, 1987).

23. Macry, *Giocare la vita*, 46.

24. Reith, 29 and 85.

25. See Quinto Marini's afterward to Matilde Serao, *Il ventre di Napoli* (Pisa: Edizioni ETS, 1995), 65–83; and Jon Snyder, "A 'study of truth and suffering': Matilde Serao's Early Writings on Naples," *California Italian Studies* 3, no. 1 (2012), which is followed by a translation in English of the two essays devoted to the game of Lotto in Serao's *Il ventre di Napoli* (https://escholarship.org/uc/item/7492w5hs).

26. Initially published by Treves as a volume in 1884, *Il ventre di Napoli* has had several new editions during the author's lifetime and after her death: in 1905 by Editore Perrella, in 1973 by Edizioni del Delfino, in 1988 by Adriano Gallina Editore, in 1995 by ETS, in 2002 by Avagliano, in 2005 by Guerra Edizioni, in 2010 by Imagaenaria, in 2012 by BUR Rizzoli, and in 2014 by Biblos.

27. Croce, for instance, considered them more spontaneous and original than her novel: "l'opera è danneggiata e sacrificata a un fine didascalico . . . e io confesso di preferire i bozzetti e le novelle." "Matilde Serao," in *La letteratura*

*della Nuova Italia* (Bari: Laterza, 1929), 53; see also Tommaso Scappaticci, who praised the essays as "un'opera di grande organicità" (a work of great cohesion) over her novel, whose value "si riscontra nelle single parti più che nell'insieme" (may be found in the single parts more than in its whole composition). *Introduzione a Serao* (Bari: Laterza, 1995), 81 and 103.

28. Giuseppe Imbucci, *Il gioco pubblico in Italia: Storia, cultura e mercato* (Venice: Marsilio, 1999), 64.

29. See Paolo Paolo, *Giocare la vita: Storia del lotto a Napoli tra Sette e Ottocento* (Rome: Donzelli, 1997), 50, and Domenico Scafoglio, *La vita in gioco: Antropologia, letteratura, filosofia dell'azzardo* (Salerno: Marlin Editore, 2006), 6.

30. Matilde Serao, "The Lottery," in *On Naples, 1878–1884: Six Translations*, trans. Jon Snyder, *California Italian Studies* 3, no. 1 (2012): 5, https://escholarship.org/uc/item/7492w5hs (accessed December 19, 2017).

31. Serao, *Il paese di Cuccagna*, 254.

32. Antonio Gramsci, quoting Croce's analysis of Serao's lottery narratives, identifies Hegel and Pascal (via Balzac) as possible sources for the notion of lottery as "opium of misery." The lottery, like religion, according to Gramsci's reading of Pascal's *Pensées* (1670), is consolatory because it is juxtaposed against the impossibility of reason to explain life with certainty. Given such a margin of uncertainty in life, and according to the principle of probability calculation, it is more advantageous for people to believe in gambling as well as religion than not. See Antonio Gramsci, *Quaderni dal carcere*, vol. 8 (Turin: Einaudi, 1977), 1837–39. See also Benedetto Croce, *Conversazioni critiche*, 4th ed. (Bari: Laterza, 1950), 300–301.

33. Serao, *Il paese di Cuccagna*, 6.

34. Matilde Serao, *Nel sogno* (Florence: Paggi, 1897), 15–18.

35. Johan Huizinga, *Homo Ludens: A Study of the Play-Element in Culture* (London: Routledge and Kegan Paul, 1949), 3–4.

36. Serao, *Nel sogno*, 28–29.

37. Serao, "The Lottery," 7.

38. Adriana Chemello, *La biblioteca del buon operaio: Romanzi e precetti per il popolo nell'Italia Unita* (Milan: Edizioni Unicopli, 1991), 16.

39. Michele Lessona, *Volere è potere* (Florence: Barbèra, 1869), 38.

40. Serao, *Il paese di Cuccagna*, 52.

41. Ibid., 22.

42. Serao, *All'erta sentinella* (Milan: Treves, 1889), 238.

43. Ibid., 259–60.

TWENTY

## Opera and the Classical Tradition in Naples

*Joseph Rescigno*

My roots are Neapolitan (on my father's side). My grandfather, who was my first teacher when I was literally a year and a half old, was a graduate of San Pietro a Majella, the conservatory of Naples. He played trumpet with the Metropolitan Opera for thirty-six years, getting the second chair position when he was very young. He was seventeen years old and had just finished a tour of North America with an Italian opera company. The second trumpet chair had opened just as he was going back to Italy, and he auditioned and got it. He stayed in the United States but had to retire prematurely because he became hard of hearing. He was only in his early fifties. As fate would have it, I was born at just that time. I was the first of his grandchildren and he talked music to me when I was still in the crib.

Given this history I was, naturally, favorably disposed toward speaking on music in Napoli. What I had not systematically studied was the monumental importance that Naples has to music. When one thinks of music in

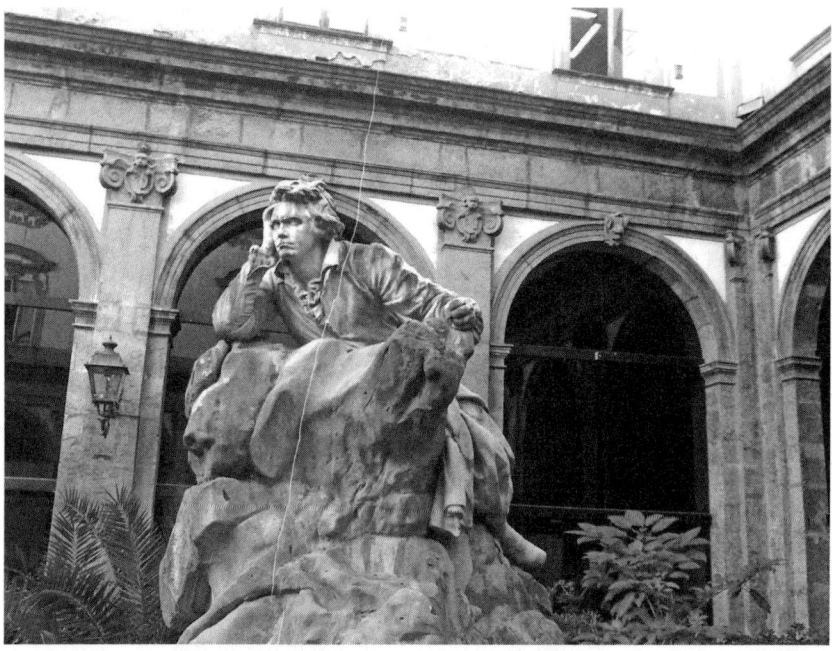

Figure 20-1. Statue of Ludwig van Beethoven (1895) by Francesco Jerace, in the cloister of the Conservatorio di San Pietro a Majella, Naples. (©IlSistemone/Wikimedia Commons/CC BY-SA 3.0)

Italy, obviously, La Scala in Milan comes to mind. Its position has been dominant, one might say predominant, since the 1880s.

However, for 120 years, the two centers of music in Italy were Venice and Naples. Naples is important for two reasons. The first is its theater, Teatro San Carlo, which to me is the most beautiful theater in Italy (see plate 20-1). It is the oldest continuously operating theater in Italy, founded in 1737 by Carlo di Borbone, the monarch of Spain. (Naples and Sicily were under Spain at that time.) Unlike so many important theaters, it has never been lost to a fire or changed its name. It remains the Teatro San Carlo in honor of its founder. The other important musical institution of Naples is its conservatory, San Pietro a Majella, which was founded in 1808. It was a merger of four conservatories with roots going back several hundred years.

In addition to supporting these two very important institutions, Naples was a center of lute making as long ago as the 1300s. The city's instrument makers even invented what might reasonably be characterized as the official instrument of Neapolitan songs: *il mandolino* (the mandolin). In the fourteenth, fifteenth, and sixteenth centuries, an instrument called the *mandola* evolved in Naples becoming, in time, *il mandolino*. Legend has it that the instrument got its name from the Italian word *mandorla* (almond) because of the almondlike shape of its body. It is a story that has its charm, but Webster's traces the name of this stringed instrument, along with others, to a Greek word for "lute": *pandoura*.

Before San Pietro a Majella was formed early in the nineteenth century, there were four conservatories. The first one was Santa Maria di Loreto and another was Sant'Onofrio a Capuana. Two others had more colorful names. One was called La Pietá dei Turchini (named, in part, for the turquoise-colored shirts its students wore), and the other is perfect for musicians, I Poveri di Gesù Cristo (Paupers of Christ). This last reminds me of an exchange in Rossini's *Il barbiere di Siviglia*, where the Count asks Figaro, "Chi è questo Don Basilio?" (Who is this Don Basilio?). Figaro answers, "Un imbroglione sempre senza un quattrino. Già è maestro di musica" (A con man who never has a dime. Of course, he's a music teacher).

The students of these conservatories at this time included a "Who's Who" of Italian composers: Alessandro Scarlatti and his son Domenico, Niccolò Jommelli, Giovanni Battista Pergolesi, Domenico Cimarosa, Giovanni Paisiello and Niccolò Piccinni. Cimarosa, Paisiello, and Jommelli were born in Naples. Pergolesi, one of the great composers, tragically died in his twenties but still left a little jewel called *La serva padrona* (The Servant Turned Mistress) as well as a fantastic Stabat Mater. He was born in Jesi but studied in Naples. Alessandro Scarlatti was born in Palermo but studied in Naples and remained there for the rest of his life. He wrote many operas, although not too many are performed today. I did one while I was still a student at the Manhattan School of Music, conducting from the keyboard. It was called *Il trionfo dell'onore* (The Triumph of Honor), a comedy. Alessandro's son, Domenico Scarlatti, was born in Naples. His music is well known to pianists and their audiences. Vladimir Horowitz and Arturo Benedetti Michelangeli often played a sonata or two to start a concert. Famously, Igor Stravinsky said that Antonio Vivaldi did not write two hundred *concerti grossi* but, rather, wrote one *concerto grosso* two hundred times. This, however, cannot be said of the slightly younger Domenico Scarlatti; all of his sonatas are quite different, wonderfully varied.

Another thing that happened by about the eighteenth century was the invention of comic opera. It arose out of something called *l'intermezzo Napolitano*. In the 1700s, there was no television; there was no radio. When one went to the theater one could spend five or six hours there, and in the intermissions between the serious works, a half hour comedy would be presented. And that is exactly what Pergolesi's *La serva padrona* was—*un' intermezzo*, written while the composer was a student at the Conservatory. But, to be fair, comic opera was created both in Naples and simultaneously in Venice. Venice's contribution arose out of the improvisational school of the *commedia dell'arte* with its masques and stock characters. Such writers as Carlo Goldoni and Carlo Gozzi incorporated this style into plays and opera librettos during the eighteenth century, preserving it for us.

After the four conservatories were combined in 1808, among the students of the Conservatory of San Pietro a Majella were Vincenzo Bellini and Saverio Mercadante. In subsequent generations, the Conservatory produced a number of the verismo composers; Ruggero Leoncavallo, Umberto Giordano, Francesco Cilea, and Franco Alfano were all students there. In addition, composers in other genres emerged from this school, including Giuseppe Martucci (known mostly for songs and instrumental music) and Paolo Tosti (known for songs). Conductor Riccardo Muti is just one of the more prominent graduates in recent years. So it has remained a very important institution of musical education.

What I did not know until I began my research was that from 1815 to 1822, the *direttore artistico* of the San Carlo Opera was Gioachino Rossini. Among the operas that he wrote for San Carlo were: *Elisabetta, regina d'Inghilterra* (Elizabeth, Queen of England); *Otello*; *Bianca e Falliero*; *La donna del lago* (The Lady of the Lake); *Maometto Secondo*; *Ermione*; and *Zelmira*. Notice that here we have a master of comic opera directing the theater that created the idea of small comic operas, and yet most of this *direttore*'s output at this theater was "serious."

We are all familiar with Giuseppe Verdi's *Otello*, of course, but Rossini's treatment of the subject, which I heard some years ago, is wonderful. *Elisabetta, regina d'Inghilterra* may nowadays be best known for sharing its overture with that of *Il barbiere di Siviglia*. The only difference is that it has more instruments (most importantly, piccolo, timpani, and three trombones). This is characteristic of Rossini, who seemed to work effortlessly and would have been baffled by later concepts of the tortured Romantic artist. Recycling was just good business. Similarly, Rossini recycled a tenor aria cut from *Barbiere* (sometimes restored in scholarly productions) to become the final tour de force for *La Cenerentola*'s heroine. In any case, I mention the double life of *Elisabetta*'s overture to illustrate a point. Sometimes, young singers or young musicians tell me, "Oh, the music tells me this . . ." But, in opera, what does the text that you are singing say? That is what is important. If this is not blindingly obvious enough, I remind them that Rossini wrote the same overture for a tragedy and a comedy. So how can the answer lie in the notes? You can make the notes funny, or you can make the notes not funny.

Rossini left the Teatro San Carlo in 1822, apparently because he became involved romantically with the girlfriend of the *sovraintendente*, or general director. (He married her.) Giovanni Pacini became the artistic director for six months, but he was replaced by another eminent musician named Donizetti. During the period 1822 to 1838, Gaetano Donizetti became the artistic director of San Carlo, and during part of that time he was also the head of the Conservatory. (Bear in mind that he was also writing for a lot of other theaters during this same period and for France, where he had always had a connection.) Donizetti wrote four of his greatest works for San Carlo—*Maria Stuarda*, *Roberto Devereux*, *Poliuto*, and *Lucia di Lammermoor*—but none of his wonderful comedies. His reputation for fecundity is well deserved, as is Rossini's, of course. Like Rossini, Donizetti wrote both comedies and tragedies but, also like Rossini, his comic genius was on display almost exclusively outside Naples.

After Donizetti left, Naples continued to be important, but it receded from prominence a little because it did not have the same kind of connection with the most important Italian composer, Giuseppe Verdi. Only one really important opera of Verdi's was premiered at San Carlo, *Luisa Miller*. The opera that we know as *Un ballo in maschera* (at first titled *Gustavo III*) was to have premiered in Naples, but the censors would not permit this because it showed the murder of a king. The political atmosphere was explosive, including bombings and assassination attempts both successful and unsuccessful. Because of the censors, Verdi withdrew the opera and negotiated a premiere in Rome where the papal censors turned out to be more flexible. (Their only major requirement was that the opera be set outside Europe. Hence, the anomaly of *Ballo*'s setting in Puritan Boston. Quite a distance from Naples, that.) Still, all of Verdi's operas were not about to run afoul of the Neapolitan censors. He was passionately devoted to the cause of Italian unification, however, and therefore not a big fan of either the Catholic Church or of that whole southern portion of Italy, which was ruled by Spain. (Naturally, Spain and the Church were opposed to the unification of Italy. Both would eventually lose a lot of land as the Risorgimento succeeded.) Giuseppe Verdi centered most of his activities where he lived in Reggio Emilia. Milan boasts far more Verdi premieres than Naples or Rome.

Naples managed without Verdi, however. It continued and continues to be a very important musical city. For example, after Donizetti's tenure, the Conservatory still produced the composers of the verismo school mentioned above. Giuseppe Martucci was the head of the Conservatory when my grandfather was a student there and, after Grandpa graduated, Francesco Cilea succeeded to that post. Important composers visited and conducted the students, much as they always have visited important schools and much as we can hope that they always will. Grandpa was one of the youngest people to graduate from the Conservatory at only age fifteen. He told me that when he was fourteen, Richard Strauss visited and conducted the student orchestra in two of his pieces. I was impressed when I heard that. I still am.

But, how does it happen that Naples has contributed so much to music? I am not the first to observe that music can reflect, in part, its surroundings. The human-made beauty in cities like Venice and Florence is a joy, to be sure. But I do not think that I have ever seen any place that has the natural beauty of the coastline from Sorrento down to Salerno, and especially the two towns of Positano and Amalfi. The location, the bay—what God gave that portion of Italy—is overwhelming. It has inspired many people.

There is a less famous but incredibly beautiful town perched way up above the coast, a little town called Ravello, from which you get to see the beauty from a different view. At the end of his life, Richard Wagner visited and stayed there and was overwhelmed by the beauty of the site. Wagner is reported to have signed the hotel guestbook, "The magical garden of Klingsor is found," suggesting that this was where the composer found at least some of the inspiration for his *Parsifal*.[1] There is a festival there called the Wagner Festival held every year since 1953, and that is the connection between this little Italian town and the composer who practically defines German opera in the popular imagination.

I dare say, though, that even though my father's side of the family came from Naples, I was not entirely prepared for the Neapolitan patience and sense of irony. I don't have that patience. I remember when I was nineteen and had been living for two years in Italy, studying in Rome. I was to leave by ship because I had a lot of things to take back home, and I left via Naples on a ship called the *Michelangelo*. There was a garbage strike that year, 1966. I was walking near the port, and there were piles of garbage everywhere. I remember a very distinguished gentleman in his sixties with a nice straw hat and a cane. I was waiting at a light and my face must have revealed my disgust. He looked at me and said, in the local dialect, "Eh, signorino, e chist è o paise d'o sole!" (Ah, young man, and this is the land of the sun!).[2] That ability to see the humor in a situation—and a situation that never much changes—was something of a revelation in itself.

I have read that of all of the works of art in the world, 53 percent of those in existence were created in Italy, and I do not doubt it. Italy has been a major birthplace of the arts, and Naples absolutely holds one of the top positions within Italy. That is, Naples is much more than its culinary contributions, however great, such as *la pizza margherita* and *mozzarella di bufala* or even *spaghetti al pomodoro*, major accomplishments by any reckoning. So, much as we wish that some things that never change would change, we (and countless tourists and artists) have taken the bad with the good.

In conclusion, virtually all the great composers of Italy (except Giuseppe Verdi and Giacomo Puccini) either headed the Teatro San Carlo or the Conservatory, sometimes both, and many were students of the Conservatory. Of course, we cannot fail to mention the whole tradition, from the late 1800s to the 1940s and 1950s, of the songs of Naples. I would say that 95 percent of all the Italian songs that have become popular worldwide are Neapolitan songs. But time does not permit me to discuss this aspect of Neapolitan music or do it justice.

I will leave you with an anecdote about something that you may have never read about, and the time is probably now past when anyone will have the good fortune to hear it from the proverbial horse's mouth as I did. My grandpa told me that when he was a student, it was expected that music students would serenade their girlfriends. And I said, "Grandpa, with a trumpet?" Well, he one-upped me, admitting that some instruments were more obviously "naturals," but the strangest of all was the tuba player. Yes, out in front of the window of his girlfriend, his serenade was, "Buona sera, Terè" followed by a solo tuba's boom, boom, boom. So, I took from this a moral: Whether or not you are a guitarist or mandolinist—even if you are a tuba player—you are expected to serenade your sweetheart. At least in Naples. Now there's something that should never change.

NOTES

1. The Ravellian tourist website http://www.ravellotime.it even supplies the date, lending some credibility to the story.
2. He was, of course, making ironic reference to the song that no one in Naples could fail to recognize, "The Land of the Sun." At this writing, several performances by amateurs and professionals, including Luciano Pavarotti and Claudio Villa, may be heard on youtube.com.

TWENTY-ONE

## Poetry

*Charles Sant'Elia*

*Lásseto*

Na jurnata nfucata
Te voglio lassà,
Na sciusciata int"e fronne,
Feneste 'e primmavera arapute,
Nu cielo senza fine
Manco nguacchiato
Cu na chélleta 'e núvola,
Nu mare annanze
Futo e sbrénneto,
Ca t'hadda nchiuvà a riva
A sunnà
Addò nisciuna varca
T'hadda maje purtà
Luntano.

*Bequest*

A fiery day
I want to leave you,
A blowing in the leaves,
Spring windows open,
A sky without end
Not even marred
By the hint of a cloud,
A sea before you
Deep and splendid,
So that it will have you fixed by the shore
Dreaming
Where no boat
Will ever take you
Far away.

Sulo chesto te voglio lassà,
Quanno nun t'arrecuorde chiù
Manco 'o nomme mio
E nun nce pienze
Ca nce sò passat'i'
Na vota.

Only this I want to leave you,
When you don't even
Remember my name anymore
And you think about it,
That I passed by there
Once.

### Nce Susimmo 'A Matina
(Nápule–New York)

### We Get Up in the Morning
(Naples–New York)

Nce susimmo 'a matina,
Nu poco 'e ghielo 'a dinto
L'aucielle già mmuolo,
Penziere luntane,
'E tralicce 'e ll'elettricità,
'A Duana d''e Piécore,
Tiempe belle 'e na vota,
Nfunne 'o pane int''o pignato,
Spíerdele sti suonne,
Taglia 'a pizza 'e grano,
Fa ca nun more
'O mumento,
E purzì 'o taluorno salato
'E st'aria 'a copp'a l'onne,
Ucchiuzzulle ncuollo,
Quanno nisciuno vede,
Struscianno p''e vie,
'A Zì Matalena sta ancora
Mmocc''a porta,
Na canzuncella sbota vico,
Int'a qua' léttera
'A putéssemo maje scrívere
Ca nce rummanesse—
'On Michele tene 'a cóppola mmano,
'E trene stanno partenno,
Acrisante e mármolo,
L'ore ca cuntammo nziemme
Aprriess''e juorne nuoste,

We get up in the morning,
A little frost inside
The birds are already in flight,
Distant thoughts,
The electric power lines,
The Dogana delle Pecore,
Beautiful times of yesteryear,
Wet the bread in the pot,
Spread these dreams,
Cut the sweet grain pie,
Don't let the moment
Die,
And even the salty drone
Of this air from atop the waves,
Little eyes on you,
When no one sees,
Strolling through the avenues,
Aunt Maddalena is still
In the doorway,
A little song changes course,
In what letter
Could we ever write it
So that it would stay—
Don Michele has his hat in his hand,

The trains are leaving,
Chrysanthemums and marble,
The hours we count together
After our days,

| | |
|---|---|
| Guardammo asfardo e prete spaccate, | We watch asphalt and split stones, |
| Cavalle arranfecanno | Horses climbing |
| 'O princípio 'e n'ata primmavera, | The beginning of another spring, |
| Zì Donato sta purtanno 'o cane | Uncle Donato is taking the dog |
| A passià 'o' campusanto, | For a walk by the cemetery, |
| Téneno nu poco 'e russo | The little cheeks of a baby |
| 'E faccelle 'e na criatura, | Have a bit of red in them, |
| Nónneta torna a rírere, | Your grandmother starts to smile again, |
| Piglia 'o vino e adduórmete | Take the wine and fall asleep |
| Int"a potrona, | In the armchair, |
| 'O prufummo d"o suppigno | The fragrance of the attic |
| Sott"o naso | Under your nose, |
| 'E máchene jéttano fummo, | The cars spew smoke, |
| Camminammo c"o sole nfronte | We walk with the sun on our brow |
| Pe despietto 'o viento | For spite the wind |
| Nce arrefredda 'e mane senza guante, | Makes our gloveless hands cold, |
| Salutammo a Don Francisco | We greet Don Francesco |

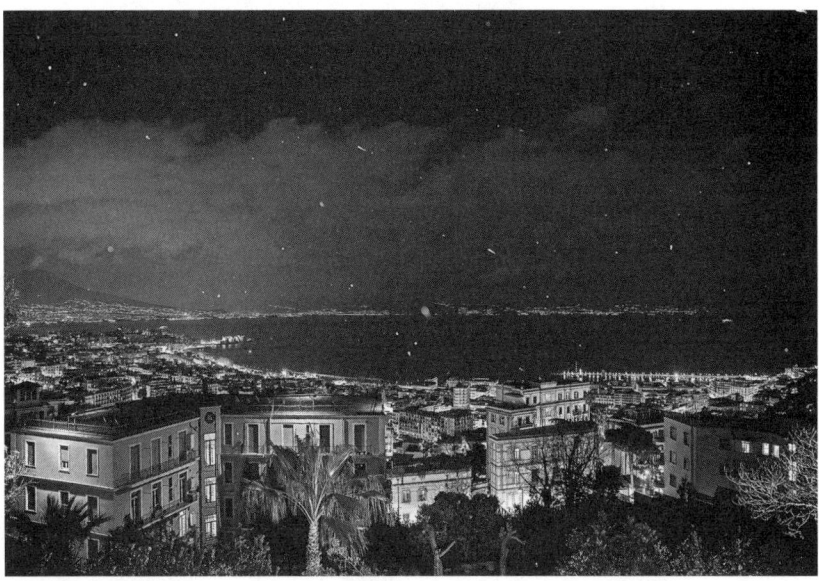

Figure 21-1. Starry night over Naples. (Luca Di Martino)

E tenimmo mmocca  
L'acqua d''e funtanelle,  
L'évera sott''e piede,  
Na libbertà  
Ca nun avimm''a scuntà chiù.

And we have in our mouths  
The water of little fountains,  
The grass under our feet,  
A freedom  
That we no longer have to pay.

*Tutt''E Sere*

*Every Evening*

Tutt''e sere te veco int''o becchiere mio,  
Comm''a santa 'e Mugnano,  
Accussì piccerenella e fina,  
Na guagliuncella senza aità,  
N'auciello venuto 'a luntano  
Fatto pe tenè a mente  
L'uorte scanusciute 'e ll'ate,  
Primm''e partì n'ata vota.

Every evening I see you in my glass,  
Like the saint of Mugnano,  
So tiny and fine,  
A young girl without age,  
A bird come from afar  
Made to look at  
The unknown gardens of others,  
Before departing again.

TWENTY-TWO

## Evoking Naples in a Story and a Story about Stories

*Gioia Timpanelli*

*Bedda Matri della Cava*
*Dat' aiuta a chi Vi chiama*
(Blessed Mother of the Cave
Give help to those who call on Thee)

There are many ways to show the heart and soul of a place and its people, many ways to feel its volatile spirit. Certainly the old folktales told from memory are based on careful living in a specific place. Like the old tales, Naples is known to be beyond words or description and insists on being lived and expressed. And perhaps because Naples is an old Greek polis, *Neapolis* in the sixth century B.C.E., *Parthenope* in the eighth century B.C.E., or maybe because it was already in the place and people from Rhodes, who in the ninth century B.C.E. settled the Island of Megaride in the Gulf of Naples, that we can track the story of Naples to ancient theater. It is this old drama in dance and song that gives us back the living rites of myths, calling forth a *delirious Dionysian spirit* as it moves through the actors in this play of life and art. There is a loosening here, a letting go of the rigid parts of the self so if the spirit comes, its spontaneity will be apparent. If Dionysus is present in any performance there is a freedom, an abandon in song and dance, a measured ecstasy; where the thyrsus meets the ground, flowers appear spontaneously, instantly, and joyously from below. For this kind of *playing* one must be truly present to participate. And this inspired, improvisational participation, in turn, inspires a natural excitement that shows creation from places beyond technique. In this improvisational theater, a tragedy or a comedy, the spontaneous part of life exhibits a *showing*, a *playing out* where the body meets its soul, its old mate, its partner and lover, where passion may possibly show spirit.

This participation, this recognition that life does not only come from what we see and imagine we know, allows an unusual depth of soul to appear. Now there is the courage to dare and to see what will happen; here is the possibility that we will meet uncharted places. The old maps are marked: *hic sunt leones* (here there be lions). In this case, even if we are small and frail, there is nothing to do but use all that is inside and out and depend on it. As Antonio Porchia said, "Even the smallest of creatures carries a sun in its eyes."[1] If there is consciousness here, there is truly expansive living that can be streetwise, know misery, recognize cunning, and also love reason, thought, feeling, and imagination, but above all, as Giambattista Vico showed, it is not reductive.

We know that history is a story or stories retold by different people and heard by different ears, but we can agree that in the long history of music, love songs about the place still inspire total strangers. Naples, one of the oldest cities continuously inhabited, has one of the world's great ports, which encourages trade, tourists, exchanges of all kinds. It is to Neapolis, this ancient city of *Magna Grecia*, that Romans came to experience the extraordinary beauty of nature and forget their worldly troubles; it is where they come to learn Greek language and culture. Noted for art and music, festivals and religious feasts, Neapolis has a theater, an Odeon and a temple dedicated to the heavenly twins, Castor and Pollux, one mortal and the other immortal, horseman and sailor, profane and sacred, effable and ineffable; restriction and freedom struggle in their stories, allowing devotees to see the twins individually and yet united, learning paradox from the stories. Now, the patron saint of Naples, San Gennaro, continues to bring the news of other worlds to this one.

The Neapolitan Giambattista Basile (1575–1632), *poeta e novelliere*, Conte di Torrone and Conte Palatino, was a scholar and man of letters who wrote the first European collection of folktales. *Il Pentamerone* (1634, The Tale of

# IL PENTAMERONE

*DEL CAVALIER*

GIOVAN BATTISTA BASILE

OVERO

LO CUNTO DE LI CUNTE

Trattenemiento de li Peccerille

DI GIAN ALESIO ABBATTUTIS.

*TOMO II.*

NAPOLI MDCCLXXXVIII.

Presso Giuseppe-Maria Porcelli

*Con Licenza de' Superiori.*

Figure 22-1. *Il Pentamerone del Cavalier Giovan Battista Basile, overo Lo Cunto de li Cunte, Trattenemiento de li Peccerille*, Napoli, 1788.

Tales), written in sixteenth-century Neapolitan, is a baroque collection of tales, including the first European examples of famous folk motifs like Cinderella, Cinder Lad, and Puss-in-Boots. The oral tradition uses metaphors and gathers examples from ordinary life to talk of the profane with the possibility of the sacred. Although Basile's literary retelling uses ornate epithets and elaborate—very elaborate—metaphors, his images do not obscure the simple force of the original folk stories. While grounded in place and the vivid Neapolitan language, spoken by all classes of Neapolitans, its genius rests in the verbal brilliance of a forceful, personal, and original writer's voice (with moral metaphors on the cultural and political life), showing the eternal struggle of all human life. In this respect it is a brilliant book of literary folktales, a reflection of the medieval "matter" and "sense," where story was always the matter, the deep fund of plots wherein communal tales of life were told, and sense was the author's ability to bring this matter to life.

In 1995 I was inspired by Benedetto Croce's translation of Basile's seventeenth-century Neapolitan into Italian to write the libretto for a one-act opera with the composer Peter Wetzler based on "The Dove," one of the stories in *Il Pentamerone*. Reading the Italian made me intrigued with the Neapolitan original. The story had a mythic quality to it and a motif I had found in a long Tibetan tale. When I met Nancy Canepa, professor of Italian at Dartmouth, who had brilliantly and faithfully translated *Il Pentamerone* from Basile's seventeenth-century Neapolitan and published *Giambattista Basile's The Tale of Tales, or Entertainment for the Little Ones*, I developed a new interest in Basile. Canepa's new translation has copious notes (including Croce's) that finally bring to light the cultural meanings gathered from many sources for Basile's Neapolitan metaphors and epithets. Now I could read the tales closer to Basile's original intent and because of this the English reader finally can understand and appreciate what Basile had accomplished. I begin with Canepa's translation and then retell the story, keeping a different eye on the inner possible Neapolitan/human journey. While praising Basile's original complexity, humor (often bawdy and scatological), social and moral swipes at the unfair conditions of human life (which sound quite contemporary), and Canepa's lively translation and extraordinary scholarship, in the main I begin with her translation and then retell the story as a straightforward folktale in order to keep an eye on the basic tale from the oral tradition that Basile himself is retelling.

What can a catenation of images, stories, and experiences evoke about delirious Naples? A story can hold us among the many things of the world. It does this while nurturing the imagination, which is not a superfluous gift but a necessity for seeing with the material into the structure of our real lives. Since the old folktales especially have a sneaky logic found in poetry, metaphor, and dreams they are uncommon treasure boxes of the human mind and mirrors of its soulful life.

Depending on the events and their actions the story can be joyous or frightening, beneficial or harmful. It is at the place of the realized heart, *il gentil cor*, the place of unity expressed by love and empathy where the action and outcome of the story benefit all life. Not all stories find this place of the heart, but it is on the same road, maybe around the bend a little, and when it is found, everything changes. Most stories are journeys to find and restore balance so the group and the individual can go on (what was missing at the beginning is found at the end). What seems both outside and inside are experienced in the same place; what seems hidden and small is an entire world. Everything has a story and often it begins in the middle of trouble.

To give you the flavor of Giambattista Basile's language, here is the beginning of a humorous story with a lovely set of arty characters in the form of a cockroach, a mouse, and a cricket from Canepa's translation.

### *The Cockroach, the Mouse, and the Cricket*
Fifth Entertainment of the Third Day

"There once was, on the Vomero[2] hill, a very rich farmer named Miccone, who had a son named Nardiello, the most wretched blockhead you could ever find on any ship of fools.[3] The poor father was embittered and miserable, for he knew of no way or means of inducing his son to lead a level-headed and useful life. If Nardiello went to the tavern to guzzle with his buddies he was cheated by crooks; if he associated with women of ill repute he was given the worst for the top price; if he played in gambling dens they kneaded him like a pizza and took him out when he was nice and hot. And so, in one way or another, he had dissipated his father's wealth.

"For this reason Miccone was always armed and ready to defend his castle and would shout and threaten, saying, 'What do you think you are doing spendthrift? Can't you see that my wealth is trickling away like water at low tide? Leave, leave those damned taverns,[4] which start with the name of the enemy and end up signifying evil! Leave them, for they are migraines to your head, dropsy to your throat, and diarrhea to your wallet! Leave, leave that godless gambling, which puts your life at risk and gnaws away at my fortune, which repels happiness and eats up cash, where the dice reduce you to zero and the words whittle you down to a peg![5] Leave, leave your bordello commerce with that evil race of daughters of ugly skin, where you squander and spend!"[6]

(And so on and so on . . . said the father to his son.)

"'Listen, Son, here are a hundred ducats; go to the Salerno Fair,' said the Father earnestly to his son.[7] 'Buy for us as many oxen as you are able to get with the money and in a few years we will have so many oxen we will plow huge fields and then we can deal in wheat and if we meet up with a good famine we'll weigh our coins by the bushel and at the very least, I'll buy the title on some friend's land and then you'll be titled too,[8] like so many others.'"[9]

(So this is the way a father teaches his son, telling him to take advantage of a good famine to become rich? Where is the teaching of compassion or empathy? The father has shown what stuff he's made of.)

Here is my retelling of

**The Cockroach, the Mouse, and the Cricket**
Fifth Entertainment of the Third Day

"Ok, Father, I can do it."

His father forked out the money and Nardiello was off to the fair but he didn't get very far, for as he entered an elm wood he saw a tiny fairy dancing on a rock and a cockroach, not just your common, everyday cockroach; ahhh, this cockroach was playing a tiny guitar so beautifully that Nardiello was entranced with the scene. The cockroach sat straight and closing its eyes played from a place where the angels were teaching. The rhythm changed and they were now off on a road to the stars.

"I'd give my eyes for such a creature."

"Oh," said the fairy, "that's not necessary. If you have a hundred ducats you can have him."

"Great!" said Nardiello, "this is a bargain. Here's the money." And she put the cockroach and his tiny guitar in a little box.

In no time the boy was back to his father.

*Evoking Naples in a Story*   357

"How come you are back so soon?"

"Look here and you will see what a great jewel I have found, bought and brought back to you, dear Father, in no time without even having to go all the way to the fair." Now the father thought there must be some great emerald or the like in the little box so he grabbed it and opened it slowly. Well, you can imagine his shock and anger when he saw it was a cockroach. "Don't be angry; look at what this fellow can do," and Nardiello waited until the cockroach took his tiny violin and began to play a piece by Giovanni de Macque and had barely begun playing when the ambitious father was so furious that he bellowed at the boy, making the music of a croaking frog instead of hearing the divine violin Nardiello heard, "Shut up, say not a word, you ass. Take this cockroach back and with these added hundred ducats, fulfill your commission. Go now!"

Without another word Nardiello closed the little box, put it in his satchel, and went off to the Tower of Sarno, but as luck would have it he came to the same stone in the elm wood and there was another fairy, this one playing with a little mouse that was dancing so gracefully that Nardiello's eyes stared in awe at the intricate steps the mouse was executing. Now we all know when a dancer comes into the room our hearts stop out of pure joy to see the body's grace change the feeling in the room. The mouse made a leap and Nardiello understood that here before him was a small force of nature he could not live without. "Oh please, Madame," he says to the fairy, "I must have this lovely being." They bargained for a hundred ducats and the exchange was made and she gave him the little mouse in a little box and once again he hurried home to tell his father of his great treasure. And once again Miccone opening the box could not believe his eyes and began throwing himself around like a beaten octopus, a great *purpo*, first throwing himself against the wall and then on the floor and then that wall and again this floor and then he stopped and looked at Nardiello with such vengeance in his eyes that he would have done himself and Nardiello harm if a neighbor hadn't just chanced by and saved them both.

"Now that is that! No more of your tricks. Go to the fair and buy the oxen with these hundred ducats and woe to you if you do not come back with your commission, woe to you and the mother who bore you. There will be great lamentations and no one will be able to stop me." Nardiello said not a word, understood his position, dangling as it were between life and the other state, when he sheepishly put the bag of ducats in his pocket and made straight away to Salerno.

But, Friends, would you believe it? While passing that very same elm wood and on that very same rock—yes, he saw another fairy. Was she with a cockroach who could play the violin or a mouse dancing its heart out? No, but she was there with a cricket who was singing madrigals one minute and when she finished began to sing great Neapolitan love songs, beautiful Canzoni Villanesche. He had heard the songs before; hadn't he tried to sing one himself to a beautiful maiden on a balcony just last week? But, Friends, he had been a crow croaking while the delicate cricket sang the strong music of the spheres and the love song she had just finished brought tears to his eyes. And when she sang again she reached a point that the magic of the *duende* showed and he touched his heart and said quietly, "Yes, yes, yes. I understand my life has now begun." The fairy accepted the bag with the hundred ducats (what could he do?), and he put the cricket in a small cage made out of a long hollowed *cucuzzella*. Nardiello was so pleased with his fortune that he hurried home, and only when he entered the room where his father was sitting did he realize something might go wrong. But still he waited for the cricket to start its love song when the father, not even able to speak, took a great cudgel and dealt the boy a blow that would have done him real harm if luck had not intervened and the father slipped, preventing the second blow. He understood it was time to leave his father's house and he left with little except the clothes on his back and his satchel full of magic beings: the cockroach that played the violin, the mouse that danced, and the cricket that sang so sweetly that it could lull people into a sweet and peaceful sleep or sang in full voice like a nightingale in love. What ecstasy!

Nardiello with his creatures set off for the road to Lombardy and there he heard of a great lord named Cenzone, who had an only daughter, named Milla, whom he loved more than the sun and the moon, but because of an unexplained illness she suffered from melancholy, a kind of lack of hope, and because of this sadness no one had seen her laugh in seven years. Her father had tried remedy after remedy and finally said that whoever could make Milla laugh would have the honor of marrying her. But then who might want to marry a young woman who was so sad? Whoever might help her be rid of this terrible wan hope would certainly catch her attention and, well, she thought to herself, that might make me happy enough to want to marry him. Her father issued the proclamation and Nardiello went right to the great lord and said, "Lord Cenzone, I am sure I can make your dear daughter laugh." When the lord saw this man of humble means he wasn't sure he wanted to encourage him. *"Be mindful, my friend, if you do not succeed, your hood will lose its shape." "My hood and my shoes can lose their shape, for all I care, for I want to try my luck, and whatever happens will happen."* The lord and his sad daughter sat under an elegant silken tent and waited to see what this poor fellow would do. Nardiello took his three creatures out of their boxes and the cockroach played his guitar with such passion and the mouse danced with elegance and the darling cricket sang so beautifully the owls came from the forest to see what was happening, and Milla . . . laughed and laughed and laughed. She had never seen or even imagined such a sight. Nardiello was triumphant just hearing her laugh, the animals were satisfied, and the Lord disgruntled. Why should he give his beautiful girl to this fool of a man? He had made a promise and everyone knew it, so he said, "I will give you my daughter and her fine dowry, but if by chance you do not consummate the marriage in three days, I will throw you to the lions."

The wedding went well and evening came—*when the sun like a thief was taken off to the prison of the West with a cape over its head*—the bride and bridegroom went to bed. But the great lord had played his hand sneakily and had a sleeping potion put into a nightcap and poor Nardiello did nothing but snore all night long. And when he consumed another draft the next night and the next it looked as though Lady Fortune was turning her wheel and leaving poor Nardiello high and dry and out of luck.

"Dear animals of mine, since we have lived so much together and you have been my darling treasures, and since you have changed my life for the better and I have nothing else to leave you, I will set you free and give you my gratitude."

"Dear Master Nardiello, we have talked among ourselves and decided we will not leave your side. We still have a few trumps up our sleeves. Wait up in the shack at the end of these steps and have no doubt he who does good, gets good in return. We are enchanted creatures and we plan a way to help you." And indeed when the poor bridegroom was sent to the lions, the creatures showed him the way up some secret staircase to a shack where he was to wait for them. Sure enough, when they showed themselves to the lions whether it was the fast dancing steps of the mouse or the wild and beautiful playing by the cockroach or finally the sleepy lullaby the cricket sang in her best and softest voice, there was not much fight left in the lions, and the little creatures escaped up the stairs and were reunited with their dear Nardiello. Rejoicing was all around, but the Bridegroom said, "I have fear that Cenzone will give my Bride to a foreign Prince who has come to claim her. There was a wedding this very day and I heard this groom has the same constraints on him as I did. I wish with all my heart that we could stop this wedding being consummated and I might have my own dear Milla again, for I truly love her and can not think of my life without her."

The three went into a conference and came out confident that all would be well. "Stay here," said the cricket sweetly, "and wait for us to return. We will succeed. In three days, Lady Milla and you will have the sugar almonds to give out, have no fear."

Now when the three little beings crept into the bridal chamber they were pleased at what they saw: the Prince had celebrated in his usual fashion and was snoring in bed with his schnapps breath wafting through the scented air. They went to work, having brought with them a sleeping draft that the cockroach deftly administered. When the Prince sat up in the night he could barely move and quickly fell back to sleep, but in the morning the beautiful bride was surrounded by a most disturbing liquid all over her wedding sheets. She absented herself and told her disgust to her parents. "Hmm most strange they all thought. Not a fortuitous night." In the morning, the Prince's men went into fighting mode and were determined this would not happen again. But, friends, the little ones were tenacious and on the second night when the Prince's men wound cloth upon cloth around their handsome lord, feeling secure that if the Prince's stomach troubled him again this mummies' cloth would prevent any untoward display. In the night the Cockroach was stopped for only a minute, for when the Mouse found the barricades up, he chewed the best and finest mouse hole (as his ancestor had famously done to unburden himself from a debt to a lion in another story) and the Cockroach found safe passage and was able to administer the second draft. And in the night the Prince awoke with a worse mess around him than the night before. He hoped he was dreaming but it was all too real. There was no possibility of any consummation except for consuming a cup of herbaceous tea to quiet his troubled and stormy bowels. But on the third night the Prince reassured his bride that he was over whatever bad food he'd eaten, and his men defended their lord with barricades upon barricades so that nothing could get through, but the Mouse counter-rallied by going to the pantry, dipping his tail into a pot of the hottest mustard he ever smelled, and going back to the unfortunate bridal chamber wafted his tail under the Groom's nose, which caused the loudest and most explosive sneeze, and the ramparts all around the Prince became the last scene in the most famous imperial fireworks display that the Imperial court in the Hidden City had ever seen. Missals went flying and firecrackers exploded, making great noises. Instead of a bridal bower the place was a battlefield and the Bride said, "Enough!" and ran in fear to her mother's chamber and would not stir again. "Enough is enough! I have seen the war and as an innocent bystander I have raised the white flag." Her mother was frightened for her daughter, the father furious. The poor Prince went home with his tail between his legs.

The Bride cried and said to her father, "Look what you have done. Where is my dear husband Nardiello?" The Lord beat his chest and said, "It is too late, too late! He has gone to the lion's feast." But just then, when doom seemed to conquer the story, the little creatures rejoiced, saying to Cenzone, "Nardiello is alive and safe right nearby." The cricket went to get him, and before Nardiello entered the room they each did some fine civilizing magic for the bumpkin. Music, dance, and beautiful singing have their own effects on the human heart but in addition, to tell another truth, all these terrible, dangerous, and sad experiences had opened the young man's eyes. Milla had already made her preference known for her Nardiello. Nardiello with his new joy called for his parents from Vomero. Milla and Nardiello were married.

The Famous Three performed at the wedding and their work was so beautiful that no one could doubt that future greedy plans, hopes for friends' failures to get their land and titles, spending much time imagining the counting of ducats in an unsound bucket . . . were all changed through love, the cooperation of invention, imagination, gratitude, and, yes, at times, enchantment.

And they lived happily ever after.

(Remember: *they* lived happily ever after; no one ever said that *we* would live happily ever after).

People who give themselves over to natural awe, who, with the same heart, see love and loss, plenty and scarcity, suffering and joy, life and theater, strangers and family, Castor and Pollux, are found culturally, artistically, socially, psychologically, statistically, physically, spiritually, naturally, in great abundance in Naples.

NOTES

Epigraph: *Bedda Madre* is an invocation in Sicilian to the Blessed Mother of the Cave from my family home in Pietraperzia, Sicily. (There are other couplets asking for help in natural disasters.)

1. Antonio Porchia, *Voices*, trans. W. S. Merwin (Port Townsend, Wash.: Copper Canyon Press, 2003), 107.
2. From *Giambattista Basile's The Tale of Tales, or Entertainment for Little Ones*, trans. Nancy L. Canepa, illus. Carmelo Lettere, foreword by Jack Zipes (Detroit: Wayne State University Press, 2007): "A hilly area near Naples, in which at this time villas and country houses were beginning to appear." Benedetto Croce, ed., *Giambattista Basile e il cunto de li cunti* (Naples: Biblioteca Napoletana di Storia e Letteratura, 1891), 574.
3. *Permonara* (Neap.): "an old ship (kept at wet dock) that was used as a hospital" (ibid., 282).
4. *Ostarie* (Neap.) One of the many burlesque etymologies that we find in Basile. The origin of *oste* is posed as *ostis* (Latin, enemy) and that of *rie*, *rio* (wicked) (Canepa, *Tale of Tales*, 247n4).
5. *Pirolo* (Neap.): "the peg on a violin for screwing up the strings" (Croce, *Giambattista Basile*, 283).
6. This Basile collection, praised two hundred years later in the Grimm Brothers' preface to their household tales, and praised by others who could read the stories in the sixteenth-century Neapolitan dialect, has suffered further wider distribution because of its raunchy, bawdy, scatological telling and fallen into bowdlerizing its very vivid telling. To read the texts closely to what was written, I urge you to read Canepa's translation with important introductions and forewords. She is still working on Basile and other baroque period writers who wrote in Neapolitan. I look forward to her continuing work on this extremely significant work in folklore.
7. The note from Canepa: "The Salerno Fair was one of the most important fairs of the time. It lasted eight days, beginning on the eve of St. Matthew's Day, people came to it 'from very far away,' and animals and every sort of goods were exhibited" (Croce, *Giambattista Basile*, 574; who cites the 1703 work by Pacichelli, *Il regno di Napoli in prospettiva*.)

8. *Sarrai tu puro tritolato* (Neap.): a play on words between *titolato* (titled) and *tritolato* (ruined, destroyed, torn to shreds) (Canepa, *Tale of Tales*).

9. "The Venetian ambassador Lippomano noted, in 1575, the ease with which merchants of the kingdom of Naples bought, from one day to the next, fiefs, estates, and houses" (Croce, *Giambattista Basile*, 574). "The buying and selling of noble titles was, in the first half of the seventeenth century, a thriving business" (Canepa, *Tale of Tales*).

**Omaggi, or Parole d'Ammore**

TWENTY-THREE

**Tributes to Shirley Hazzard**

*Joseph Connors and Jonathan Galassi*

Shirley Hazzard was born January 30, 1931, to a Welsh father and Scottish mother in Australia. At age sixteen she began working for British Intelligence Services and in 1956 was posted to Naples. She was an essayist, novelist, and short story writer. Her books on Naples include *The Bay of Noon* (1970), *Greene on Capri* (2000), and her last work of nonfiction, *The Ancient Shore: Dispatches from Naples* (2008), co-written with her husband Frances Steegmuller. Hazzard died on December 12, 2016.

*Shirley Hazzard and Naples*

JOSEPH CONNORS

Naples has had its lovers in America, but few more knowledgeable and none more passionate than Shirley Hazzard, or Mrs. Shirley Steegmuller, as it says on the doorbell. She has been the companion par excellence for Anglophone visitors to Naples—the connoisseur who knows every church, every crypt, every *vicolo*, every inscription—for over half a century. Porte Aperte drew visitors of my generation to Naples spring after spring in the 1980s and 1990s, but no door was more open than the great villa gate of Via Ferdinando Russo 27, where, over lunch on that marvelous terrace overlooking the gulf and Vesuvio, one learned all the news of Naples. She is also a connoisseur of Capri and a proud honorary citizen. The welcome there was always just as warm. No matter that it was a late-night ferry under driving rain, Shirley would be waiting on the piazza for dinner and stories of English, American, and Russian men of letters whose spirited conversations echoed in the restaurant at the Arco Naturale. *Greene on Capri*, that wonderful short book, is the story of two tall men of letters on the island, one celebrated in the title, the other her beloved Francis, who shared her Parthenopean passions and, as readers of the *New Yorker* remember, knew the

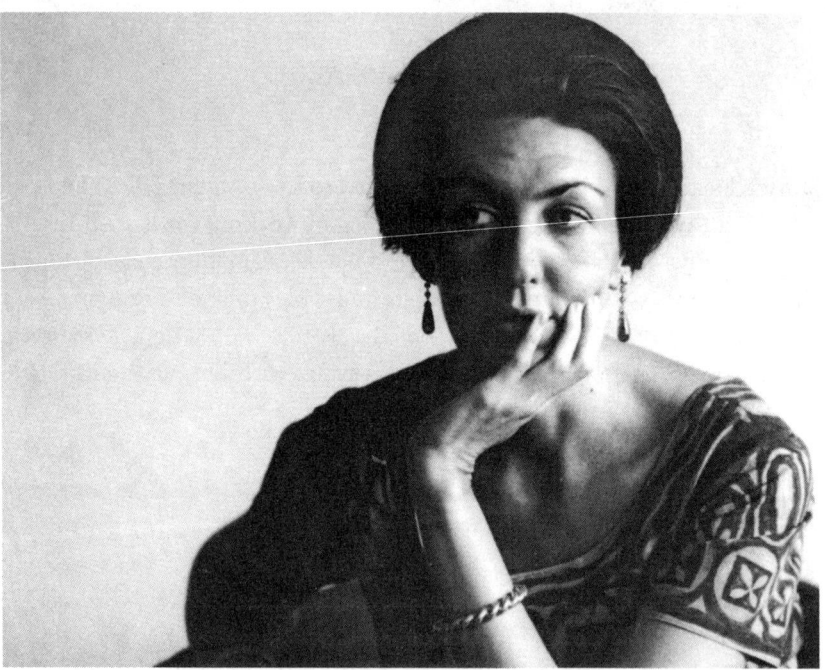

Figure 23-1. Shirley Hazzard. (Jon Naar)

hospital scene so well. Now we have, in her and Francis's *Dispatches*, the companion volume that I like to call "Hazzard in Naples," about a difficult, beautiful city and the tall, supremely eloquent woman who has shared her love of it with so many of us since 1956.

## Shirley Hazzard in Naples

### Jonathan Galassi

Walking in Naples with Shirley was an unforgettable experience. Not only did she know every stone of the city, ancient and modern. She also knew everyone as well, every portiere, every guardian, every waiter, and what was unquestionably the best *caffè*, Scaturchio, as well as what the name meant (repel the Turks).

She had the greatest respect for the ancientness of the city and shared its denizens' contempt for mere modernity. Along with them, she was partaking of something ongoing, something far bigger and more meaningful than the mere sublunary present. With Shirley one always felt continuities—with a larger community across time and space, the community of letters, of awareness, of empathy, of what used to be called civilization.

Shirley herself had clearly experienced the great time-honored meeting of northern and southern sensibilities that she immortalized in her incandescent novel, *The Bay of Noon*. She was utterly Anglo-Saxon in her attitudes, but her understanding of what was around her, of its depths and layered multiple meanings, was always evident. Whether walking past Benedetto Croce's house in the heart of Spaccanapoli, or visiting Leopardi's and Virgil's tombs behind the train tracks at Mergellina—a place that many Neapolitans don't seem to know today, but one of the most perfectly appropriate memorial spaces in the world—one always felt in her presence that this was someone perfectly attuned to her environment, eager to share it with those who had eyes to see. No one has ever had a better cicerone, anywhere.

TWENTY-FOUR

## A Tribute to John Turturro's *Passione*

*Stanislao G. Pugliese*

Actor, writer, director John Turturro has crafted an astonishingly eclectic, thoughtful, and insightful body of work: from Spike Lee, Adam Sandler, the Coen brothers, and *Transformers* films to small, finely cut jewels such as *Mac* (1992), *The Truce* (1997) and *Passione* (2010).[1] If, in *Mac*, Turturro was a working-class Italian American struggling with the conflicting demands of Italian traditions and American capitalism (winner of the Camera d'Oro at the Cannes Film Festival); and in *The Truce* he was the sympathetic Holocaust survivor and writer Primo Levi, in *Passione* Turturro is our Virgil as he escorts us through the streets of Naples, guiding us on a tour of the city's astonishing musical legacy.

*Passione* is a film that manages to be wildly entertaining as well as a work of history and cultural anthropology, plumbing the depths of *napolitanità*. To his credit, Turturro refuses to be seduced by the tourist industry images of Naples. His film is shot in the gritty districts of the Forcella, the Sanità, and the Quartieri Spagnoli.

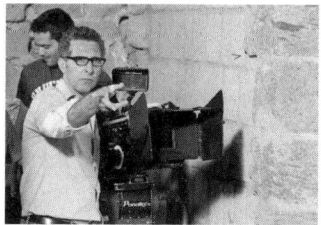

Figure 24-1. Filmmaker John Turturro on the set of *Passione* (Iole Capasso/Squeezed Heart Productions)

Turturro is no stranger to Naples. Some years ago, he performed Eduardo De Filippo's *Questi Fantasmi* in New York and Naples. Francesco Rosi (a native of Naples) was the director of *The Truce* and introduced Turturro to the theater of De Filippo and the culture of the city. For some time, Turturro has been thinking of adapting Norman Lewis's memoir *Naples '44* for the screen. With a father from Puglia and a mother from Sicily, Turturro has triangulated his familial legacy and arrived at the historical and cultural capital of the Mezzogiorno, Naples.

As the opening credits, street scenes, and historical photos roll, the hauntingly beautiful *Carmela*, written by Salvatore Palomba and Sergio Bruni, is sung by Mina. The images are both familiar and provocative: an fresco of the Christ child with fingers to his lips is immediately followed by a black-and-white photograph of a *scugnizzo con sigaretta in bocca*, emphasizing the constant mix of the sacred and profane on the streets of Naples. Like New York, Naples is a crossroads of cultures. In its dialect, the faces of its people, the architecture and music, faint (and not so faint) traces of a dozen different civilizations engage in a creative mix. Where else in the world can one find people in the streets singing songs derived from Portuguese Fado, Spanish flamenco, Andalusia, Italian opera, jazz, soul, reggae, hip-hop as well as *malouf* or *nuubaat* from north Africa? Improvisation and re-invention—so critical to contemporary music—is central to the Neapolitan character. Improvisation is the art of the poor and downtrodden, the cultural armor of the defenseless, in music as in life.

"There are places you go to and once is enough," Turturro tells us in the opening scene, "and then there's Napoli." The city is now in its third millennium, having survived not only earthquakes and volcanic eruptions but also human-made tremors, revolts, and eruptions. The question to be asked: is it in spite of this calamitous history or because of it that Naples has produced a musical tradition second to no other city in Europe? The answer, Turturro argues, lies in the contradictions, paradoxes, and irony at the heart of Neapolitan culture. As the Esposito brothers argue among themselves over the relative merits of Enrico Caruso versus Fernando De Lucia, they also point out that music is in the DNA of the Neapolitans by forging a balance between those who write music and those who listen to it. Or, as Peppe Barra, another performer notes, the very language of the city, its much-maligned dialect, is music itself.

From the small monks' cemetery of the Chiostro of the Certosa di San Miniato above the city, Monica Pinto of Spakka-Neapolis 55 sings what is both a love song and a curse to Vesuvio: the "disaster mountain" of "dancing flames." "My life," Pinto cries out, "depends on you," acknowledging the city's precarious relationship with the volcano that "trembles with death."

In Naples after having screened an advance copy of the film, this writer was struck by how the faces of statues in the city's famous *presepi* reflect the faces in the film. One of those faces belongs to singer Peppe Servillo of Avion Travel, who sings "Era di Maggio" as a smoldering duet with the Portuguese fado singer Misia before a baroque church in a decaying courtyard near Santa Chiara. A facial gesture or a graceful turn of the hand here tells a tale of love and longing. As always, the lyrics are double entendres: "the water in the fountain never dries out and the wounds of love never heal"; or, in proper Neapolitan: "Ll'acqua, llá dinto, nun se sécca maje, e ferita d'ammore nun se sana."

*Passione* presents not only professional singers but also the ordinary folk of Naples singing and dancing in the streets. Teenagers on the steps of a local church launch, a cappella, into their versions of "Dicitencello vuie" and "Maruzzella." A half dozen young women use the famed staircase of the Palazzo dello Spagnuolo designed by Ferdinando Sanfelice, as a set to dance to "Comme facette mammeta."

One aspect of the genius of Naples is the city's ability to constantly reinvent itself and its musical inheritance. Thus, Sergio Bruni's 1950s rendition of "O sole mio" blends into a version by a young Massimo Ranieri in the 1960s, followed by a contemporary interpretation by the Tunisian singer M'Barka Ben Taleb sung in Arabic.

Angela Luce is sultry in a performance of Raffaele Viviani's "Bammenella." Raiz and Almamegretta (the dialect rendition of *anima migrante*, or wandering soul) blend world music, reggae, and other traditions in "Non te scurdà," with the imperative to remember because "there is no other reason to live" while Pietra Montecorvino, in the role of the local *puttana*, tells us that she is "the mirror you never want to use." Raiz, also known as Gennaro Della Volpe, muses on how living in Naples fosters a sense of being truly cosmopolitan, a world citizen: because of its history of invasions (Greek, Roman, Norman, Arabic, French, Spanish, Piedmontese, German, and American), "belonging to this place means belonging to anywhere." A citizen of Naples is at once "everybody and nobody."

From nobody to somebody is, instead, the story of James Senese, saxophonist and jazz great. Son of a black American soldier and a Neapolitan mother, "Jamesiello," or Little James as he was nicknamed by the locals, was befriended by a neighborhood girl, Sofia. But the color of his skin was a literal marker and he was taunted with shouts of "Nigger!" "I was lucky, I made something of myself . . . But how can you forget something like that?" His soulful version of "Passione," performed with a small ensemble at the Bluestone Jazz Club in the Santa Lucia district, is interspersed with a wartime film of the bombing of Naples and the March 1944 eruption of Vesuvio. Mixed-race children of African American soldiers and Neapolitan women eventually grew up and, in their twenties and thirties, opened jazz clubs in their city, cross-fertilizing two indigenous musical traditions. Those children are the subject of "Tammurriata nera," which chronicles their appearance on the streets of Naples, and carry traditional names like Ciro, Peppe, and Gennaro, but are irrevocably marked by the color of their skin and the "sins" of their mothers.

The song of the *lavandaie* (washerwomen) of the Vomero is a haunting lullaby filmed in one of the many subterranean passages of the city, the Piscina Mirabilis, while "Catarì," performed by guitarist Fausto Cigliano, is recorded in the Pio Monte della Misericordia before Caravaggio's monumental *Seven Acts of Mercy*.

Massimo Ranieri and Lina Sastri perform "Malafemmena," written by Totò (Antonio De Curtis), a figure who represents a twentieth-century version of Pulcinella, the truest incarnation of the Neapolitan psyche, while Gennaro Parlato, with streaking eyeliner, laments the whims of "Maruzzella." Exuberant and whimsical instead is the rendition of Renato Carosone's "Caravan Petrol" where Fiorello and guests, including Turturro and a wise donkey, dig for oil in the smoking and flaming Campi Flegrei, just west of the city. They may be digging for oil, but they are far more likely to find something altogether different, for the ancient Greeks thought these burning fields were the entranceway to hell and the Romans thought the place home to Vulcan, the god of fire.

There can be no singing without dancing, and the choreography by Max Casella (who joins Barra and Ben Taleb in "Tammuriata Nera") enlists the talents of professional dancers as well as folks plucked from the streets. The dancing can be joyous and sorrowful at the same time. Life in Naples is "beautiful but difficult," confesses a young woman with dark sunglasses and an air of melancholy.

In an interview, Turturro insisted he didn't want to produce a history lesson. "You've got to make sure you connect to the moment—now." Yet he pointed out how Naples was the site of the first film industry in Italy, naturally growing out of the city's musical and theatrical traditions. In Naples, "you see the problems of the past and the problems of the future." "The people of Naples are really great storytellers," he continued. "They are masters of improvisation with a deadly sense of humor. . . . It's a very unique place."[2]

The film concludes with Enzo Avitabile crying out to "Faccia Gialla" (a reference to the yellowed face of the bronze statue of San Gennaro) to liquefy his blood in the Duomo. The people of Naples don't meekly ask or pray: they engage in protracted negotiations with the city's patron saint and demand the miracle. The closing images of the music festival of Piedigrotta, together with photographs and film from the immediate postwar period as well as contemporary shots of Neapolitans singing and dancing in the streets, is accompanied by Pino Daniele's "Napule è":

| | |
|---|---|
| Napule è mille culure | Naples is a thousand colors |
| Napule è mille paure | Naples is a thousand fears |
| Napule è a voce de' criature | Naples is the voice of a child |
| che saglie chianu chianu | who silently returns home |
| e tu sai ca' nun si sulo | and you know you are not alone |
| Napule è nu sole amaro | Naples is a bitter sun |

| | |
|---|---|
| Napule è addore e' mare | Naples is the scent of the sea |
| Napule è na' carta sporca | Naples is litter in the street |
| e nisciuno se ne importa | but no one is concerned |
| e ognuno aspetta a' sciorta | and everyone awaits his fate |
| Napule è na' camminata | Naples is a walk |
| Int' e viche miezo all'ate | among the alleys with others |
| Napule è tutto nu suonno | Naples is all a dream |
| e a' sape tutto o' munno | as the entire world knows |
| ma nun sanno a' verità. | but they don't know the truth |
| Napule è mille culure . . . | Naples is a thousand colors . . . |

Naples is a tricky subject for any artist. How is one to balance the two competing and contradictory images of the city? "See Naples and die!" was the cultural imperative of the Grand Tour and the age of Romanticism. Chaos, Camorra, and trash are the flip image. Seductive, exasperating, bewildering. A death-haunted city that flaunts its vitality; a melancholy city that revels in its celebrations; a city beloved and hated by its own inhabitants who left by the millions, scattered to the four corners of the world. A city marked by longing, loss, and nostalgia. *Passione* captures these characteristics with verve. Naples is a "city painted in sound," Turturro notes, and, like many poor places in the world, "music is a form of emotional and spiritual transportation . . . a form of prayer."

NOTES

1. "Passione," written and directed by John Turturro. Screenplay by John Turturro and Federico Vacalebre; based on an idea by Carlo Macchitella; sound by Antonio Barba (AITS); editing by Simona Paggi (AMC); costume design by Alessandra Gaudioso; cinematography by Marco Pontecorvo (AIC); produced by Alessandra Acciai, Carlo Macchitella, and Giorgio Magliulo. "Passione" was presented at the Venice Film Festival and at the Toronto Film Festival. It opened June 22, 2010, at the Film Forum on West Houston Street in New York City.

2. See "Turturro's Passion between Naples and New York," YouTube, June 27, 2011, www.i-italy.org at https://www.youtube.com/watch?v=1LeBFDFMoQk (accessed November 25, 2017).

TWENTY-FIVE

## A Celluloid Tribute to Thomas Belmonte

*Pellegrino D'Acierno*

Stanislao Pugliese and I have written tributes to the late Thomas Belmonte, our esteemed and brilliant colleague and beloved friend, that appear in the twenty-fifth anniversary edition of *The Broken Fountain* (2005), a classic in urban anthropology in the form of an anthropological "novel" that stages a powerful and immersive encounter with Naples and the everyday existence of the underclass inhabitants of Fontana del Re, an imaginary place name for an impoverished neighborhood in Naples. As a way of honoring his memory, Pugliese is in the process of overseeing the construction of a "broken fountain"—an art installation in the form of a functioning fountain—on the campus of Hofstra University. My memorial to Tom, I hope, will take the more tenuous form of celluloid for I am now in the process of writing a screenplay based on *The Broken Fountain* at the behest of Maurizio Grimaldi, the co-producer of Martin Scorsese's *Gangs of New York* and the son of the celebrated Neapolitan film producer Alberto Grimaldi, who graced Italian and world cinema with countless masterpieces.

My attempt to turn *The Broken Fountain* into a screenplay involves the following basic premise: the film must stage an encounter not only with the Neapolitan slum, fictitiously titled Fontana del Re, but also with Naples and its culture at large, as did Roberto Rossellini's 1954 film *Viaggio in Italia*. This will involve the representation of the Belmonte character as a young man who leads a double and somewhat conflicted life during his sojourn in Naples: (1) an anthropologist who must infiltrate the slum as a "professional stranger" and come to comprehend its complexities and enter its life by becoming an insider—a "family member" of sorts; (2) a kind of intellectual and cultural and even amorous "tourist" in search of a larger comprehension of Italian and Neapolitan life, including its *per bene* dimension, as part of his attempt to Italianize himself and to come to grips with his identity as both a political activist and an Italian American.

Since this book begins with a tender tribute to Belmonte by Theresa Aiello, why not end it with another tribute to him? Such a strange loop will make the book "cyclological" and thus pay a tribute—albeit indirectly—to Giambattista Vico as well. My tribute to Belmonte will take the improbable form of a voice-over excerpted from the screenplay in which I try to get inside Belmonte's head by representing his conflicted self as he prepares to encounter Naples for the first time.

Opening shot: the titles and credits superimposed upon a long shot of a dilapidated and nonfunctioning fountain in Fontana del Re.

1. FIRST SEQUENCE: TRAIN FROM ROME TO NAPLES— CONVERSATION ON THE TRAIN WITH A BEAUTIFUL PASSENGER—ARRIVAL AT THE STAZIONE CENTRALE— FINDING A HOTEL

Belmonte finds himself in a compartment on the Rome-Naples express with a typically noisy Neapolitan family—husband and wife and three little children, two crammed into the same seat, and a baby in her mother's arms. The mother is unabashedly breastfeeding her baby while singing a lullaby. Opposite Belmonte, a reserved seat remains empty but will soon be occupied by an elegant and mysterious young woman.

INT: Belmonte is shown writing an entry in his diary, something that he will do throughout the film.

BELMONTE (VOICE-OVER—we hear what he is writing):

> O Delirious Naples, city of the scorching southern sun, capital of chaos, and kingdom of the tremors and flashes of Vesuvio and the whispers and caresses of the bay, what do you have in store for me? O Inscrutable Naples, paese of Pulcinella where even the saints are tricksters, will you grant me access to the mysteries hidden in your solar labyrinth? O Seductive Naples, city of desire, will you provide me with an Ariadne—be she a Madonna or a whore—whose thread will guide me through your great labyrinth of palaces and slums, of splendid vistas and squalid back street alleyways? O Teeming Naples, people's city, city of the lazzaroni and the lumpenproletariat, will you allow me to tell the story of your poor and downtrodden? Will you enable me to encounter the subjugated lives of your slum-dwellers without betraying them and without betraying my vocation as an anthropologist? O Violent Naples,

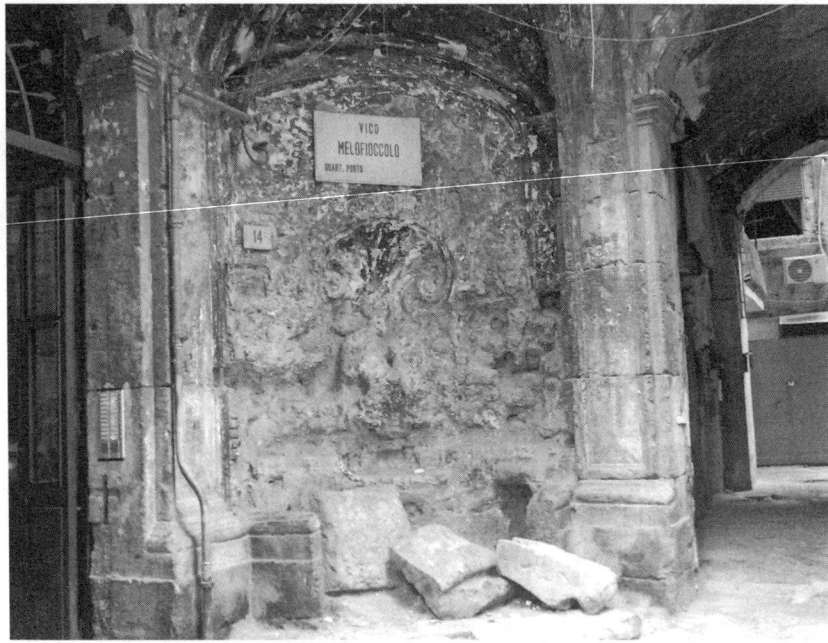

Figure 25-1. Tom Belmonte's *Broken Fountain*. (Stanislao G. Pugliese)

city of convulsive feasts and convulsive beauty, they have called you since the sixteenth century the "Paradise inhabited by Devils." How am I to study and to befriend these Devils of yours and to enter their point of view, their conception of the world, to experience their solitude their alienation, their joy? Will I, too, become one of your Devils? Will I lose myself or find myself in the drunkenness of your labyrinth? O Enigmatic Naples—Ancient and Immutable—will you give me a narrative? Will you give me a book?

Breaking off his writing and turning toward the train's window, Belmonte speaks out loud to himself:

This WON'T DO! The first entry is much too personal, much too literary. My mentors at the university will make mincemeat of such rhapsodic writing. I shall have to learn how to write Naples in a different way.

I must resist the temptation to use the persona of the anthropologist to write a novel. I must refuse to become a dilettante of chaos. I am an anthropologist not a mythologist. So much for writing on trains.

Belmonte tears the page out of the diary and crumbles it up. He then starts reading a paperback copy of Hemingway's *The Sun Also Rises*.

ACKNOWLEDGMENTS

The editors gratefully acknowledge the support of Hofstra University President Stuart Rabinowitz; the former provost and vice president of Hofstra University, Herman A. Berliner; the current provost, Gail Simmons; and the dean of the Hofstra College of Liberal Arts and Sciences, Bernard J. Firestone, for their intellectual and financial support of this project. The conference was co-hosted with infinite grace and unbound generosity by our dear friend and colleague Stefano Albertini, director of the Casa Italiana at New York University.

Many of these essays were first presented at an academic conference at Hofstra University, hosted by the Hofstra Cultural Center. We thank the director emerita, Natalie Datlof, and the current director, Athelene A. Collins, and Jeannine Rinaldi, Carol Mallison, and Amy Trotta for their dedicated professionalism. At Fordham University Press, the editors were fortunate to work with director Fredric Nachbaur, editor Will Cerbone, managing editor Eric Newman, and copyeditor Kathleen Meyer. We raise a celebratory glass of Falanghina to extraordinary chefs Antonio Bove of Uva Rossa (Malverne, New York) and Gianfranco Sorrentino of Il Gattopardo in New York City for their epicurean support. Queensboro UNICO—an Italian American philanthropic organization—and Sal Mendolia financially supported the academic conference and the late Tina Piscop (1922–2016) was an early benefactor. We thank our colleague and *napoletanissimo* friend Gregory Pell of Hofstra University for his translations and hope to celebrate the publication of this book together in delirious fashion in Naples.

We also wish to express our wild gratitude to those musicians whose exquisite performances brought the rhythms of Naples to New York and imparted an acoustical dimension to the conference that obliged our audience to pass from hearing to listening. Above all, we wish to thank the supreme conductor Stefania Rinaldi, direttrice laboratorio "Coro di Voci Bianche" del Teatro di San Carlo di Napoli, for her *virtuosità* and muse function in leading our Hofstra music students to perform as the Delirious Naples Chorus in two astonishing concerts that bore witness to the musical development of their voices under the tutelage of Maestra Rinaldi and to the "Neapolitanization" of their rhythm and timbre through passion. Also grazie infinite to guitarist John La Barbera and guitarist and singer Enrico Granafei for their exquisite homage to Roberto Murolo (1912–2003), which celebrated Murolo's inimitable singing of the canonic Neapolitan songs with his soul and in a way that combined the passion and exacerbated melancholy that define Neapolitan musical expression.

We thank William Papaleo for permission to reproduce his paintings; B. Amore for permission to reproduce her artwork; Mimmo Jodice for his photo from Pompeii; Luca Di Martino for his photos; Luciano Pedicini for his photo of the Cacace Chapel in the Basilica of San Lorenzo Maggiore; Fabio Speranza for his photo of Jusepe de Ribera's paintings in the Certosa di San Martino; the Marquand Library of Art and Archeology at Princeton University; Lucio De Matteis of the Biblioteca Molajoli at the Castel Sant'Elmo; Rita Pastorellia and Anna Imponente of the Ministero dei Beni e delle Attività Culturali e del Turismo, Polo Museale della Campania; bookseller Raimondo Di Maio and Laura Grandi for assistance with permissions; and the Fondazione Museo Cappella Sansevero for permission to use images from the Sansevero Chapel in Naples. The editors wish to extend a most Neapolitan embrace to Gennaro Guarino from Pozzuoli for his exuberant photo that graces the back cover, Iole Capasso in Naples for the photo of John Turturro on the set of *Passione*, and Christina Belmonte Wexler for the poignant portrait of her father, Tom Belmonte.

The editors acknowledge and thank the following for permission to reprint.

John Domini's essay first appeared in *Ninth Letter* 2, no. 1 (Spring–Summer 2005): 49–59.
Jason Pine's essay first appeared in his book *The Art of Making Do in Naples* (Minneapolis: University of Minnesota Press, 2012), 1–18.

Francesco Durante's essay first appeared in his book *Scuorno (Vergogna)* (Milan: Mondadori, 2008), 9–28.

Erri De Luca's essay first appeared in his book *Napòlide* (Naples: Dante and Descartes, 2006), 5–34.

Robert Zweig's essay first appeared in his book *Return to Naples* (New York: Bordighera Press, 2011), 45–62.

Valerio Caprara's essay first appeared in *Napoli, una città nel cinema*, edited by Maria Cristina De Crescenzo, Antonio Lucadamo, Chiara Masiello, and Adriana Muti (Naples: Dante and Descartes, 2010), 153–59.

Rose De Angelis's essay first appeared as "Beloved Whore: Rescripting Marriage, Motherhood, and Identity in Eduardo De Filippo's *Filumena Marturano*," *Revista de Antropología Social* 17 (2008): 119–40.

"One of These Days," by Ilaria Marchesi and Simone Marchesi, is translated by Erin Brady from their book *Live in Pompei* (Rome: Laterza, 2016), 31–51.

Terence Ward's essay is excerpted from his book, *The Guardian of Mercy: How an Extraordinary Painting by Caravaggio Changed an Ordinary Life Today* (New York: Arcade, 2016), 3–11, 23–31.

CONTRIBUTORS

THERESA AIELLO is Associate Professor at the New York University Silver School of Social Work. She is Director of the Advanced Practice Certificate Program and codirects the Advanced Certificate in Child and Family Treatment. Dr. Aiello is also a psychoanalyst and has written extensively on psychoanalysis, oral history, and narrativist approaches. She won the New York University Distinguished Teacher Award and was elected to the National Academy of Social Work as Distinguished Scholar and Practitioner. She is in private practice in New York City.

B. AMORE is an artist, educator, and writer. She studied at Boston University, University of Rome, Accademia di Belle Arti di Carrara, and is the recipient of Massachusetts Cultural grants, a Fulbright Grant, a Mellon Fellowship, as well as a Citation of Merit Award presented by the Vermont Arts Council. She is founder of the Carving Studio and Sculpture Center in Vermont. Amore taught for many years at the Boston Museum School and has won numerous public art commissions in both the United States and Japan and is represented by SOHO 20 Gallery, New York, and Boston Sculptors Gallery. *Life line—filo della vita*, her multimedia exhibit, which premiered at the Ellis Island Museum, has recently been published as *An Italian American Odyssey, Life line—filo della vita: Through Ellis Island and Beyond*. Her art and literary reviews appear in *International Sculpture Magazine* and *Art New England*, and her creative writing and art in *VIA, Italian Americana, Biancheria*, and *Speaking Memory*, among others. *Rondini di Passaggio* is on view at the Museo dell'Emigrazione, Sant'Angelo dei Lombardi, Province of Avellino, Italy, and is a re-evocation of her *Naples/New York* exhibit created for the Delirious Naples Conference at the Hofstra University Museum.

ANDREA BALDI is Professor of Italian at Rutgers University. He has published articles on sixteenth-century conduct books, a monograph on Alessandro Piccolomini (2001), and is the coeditor of *Essays in Honor of Marga Cottino-Jones* (2003). He has also devoted his critical attention to contemporary Italian literature, publishing articles on the relationship between literature and cinema (Luigi Pirandello, the Tavianis and Italo Calvino, Monicelli) and on women's writing (Anna Banti and Elsa Morante). He has worked extensively on Anna Maria Ortese, editing and prefacing *The Iguana* (2005) and publishing a monograph on her short fiction entitled *La meraviglia e il disincanto* (2010). He is currently completing a manuscript on the representation of urban spaces in Ortese's works.

ANGELO CANNAVACCIUOLO was born in Naples in 1956 and earned his degree in Arabic from the prestigious Instituto degli Studi Orientali in Naples. He has worked as an actor and director and has written for the theater, movies, and television. He wrote the libretto for the opera *Il soffio delle fate* (based upon his novel by the same name) that world premiered in May 2009 and the *Oratorio di speranza, cantata drammatica*, for theaters in Stralsund and Grünsfeld, Germany. In February 2009 he was awarded the prestigious *Archita* by the Istituto Italiano per gli Studi Filosofici for the complexity of his literary achievements. He is currently writing his second opera with Maestro Filippo Zigante. He is the author of *Guardiani delle nuvole, Acque basse, Le cose accadono, Parole in viaggio / Words in Journey*, and, most recently, *SacrAmerica*. He created the annual international literary event Words in Journey—Parole in Viaggio, held in Campania.

VALERIO CAPRARA has been professor of film history and criticism in the faculty of Lettere e Filosofia at the Università Degli Studi di Napoli "L'Orientale" since 2011 and currently teaches at the Università Degli Studi di Napoli "Suor Orsola Benincasa." He has been film critic of the Neapolitan daily newspaper *Il Mattino* since 1979. From 1983 until 2000 he was the artistic director of "Incontri Internazionali del Cinema" in Sorrento, and since

2010 has been President of the Film Commission for the Campania Region. In 2011, Caprara was named to the commission for cinematography in the Ministero per i Beni e le Attività Culturali.

JOSEPH CONNORS has taught at the Boston Latin School and in the art history departments of Chicago, Columbia, and Harvard, and was Slade Professor at Oxford in 1999. He was elected to the Accademia Nazionale di San Luca in Rome in 1993 and the American Philosophical Society in 2006. He served as director of the American Academy in Rome from 1988 to 1992 and of Villa I Tatti in Florence from 2002 to 2010. He has published on Roman urban planning and architecture; his long-term research centers on the genial Swiss-born architect of baroque Rome, Francesco Borromini (1599–1667).

PELLEGRINO D'ACIERNO is Professor Emeritus of Comparative Literature at Hofstra University, where he has been honored to serve as the inaugural Queensboro UNICO Distinguished Professor of Italian and Italian American Studies. The chair marks the culmination of his career-long attempt to render Italian texts central to the curriculum of the American university. He has taught and been a visiting professor at Columbia University, Cornell University, and New York University, and a visiting critic in the graduate schools of architecture at Yale, Rice, and the Southern California Institute of Architecture. He served at NYU as the first Tiro a Segno Visiting Professor in Italian American Studies. He has been awarded fellowships from the Guggenheim Memorial Foundation; the Rockefeller Center at Bellagio; the Italian Academy for Advanced Studies in America at Columbia University; Villa I Tatti, the Harvard Center for Italian Renaissance Studies; the Fulbright Program; and a Prix de Rome in Post-Classical Humanistic Studies from the American Academy in Rome. His publications in prose include *F. T. Marinetti and the Freedom of Poetry* (1988); *The Itinerary of the Sign: Scenes of Seeing in Giotto's Frescoes in the Scrovegni Chapel* (1995); *The Italian American Heritage: A Companion to Literature and Arts* (1999); and *Thirteen Ways of Crossing the Piazza: Rome as a Cinematic City* (forthcoming). He is coeditor of *C. G. Jung and the Humanities* (1990). His first book of poetry, *The Fat Man Arpeggios*, was published in 2014, and he is now preparing for publication a collection of his earlier poems written over three decades.

ROSE DE ANGELIS is Professor of English at Marist College. She has published articles on American and Italian-American authors and has edited a volume of essays entitled *Between Anthropology and Literature: Interdisciplinary Discourse* (2014). She recently published an article on *The Rose Tattoo* in *The Tennessee Williams Annual Review* and edited a special issue of *Italian Americana* in which her article on Louisa Ermelino's novels appeared.

ERRI DE LUCA, Italy's most widely read living author, was born in Naples in 1950. In 1968, he left Naples for Rome where he became a member of Lotta Continua until 1976. He worked as a laborer in Turin, Naples, France, Milan, Catania, and Rome. He was a volunteer worker in Tanzania and ran humanitarian aide convoys during the Yugoslav wars of the 1990s. In the spring of 1999, he was in Belgrade to protest NATO bombing of the city. He considers aerial bombing of cities an act of terrorism. He is the author of many books, which have won numerous awards abroad, but not in Italy, where he refuses to submit his books for literary prizes. He is a mountain climber and self-taught linguist, translating the Hebrew Bible and works of Yiddish. Among his books published in English are *Sea of Memory* (1999), *God's Mountain* (2002), *Three Horses* (2005), *The Day before Happiness* (2011), *Me, You* (2011), *The Night Shift Belongs to the Stars* (2012), *The Crime of a Soldier* (2013), *The Story of Irene* (2015), and *A Dissenting Word* (2015). He is the screenwriter of two films, *Di là dal vetro* (2011, in which he also stars) and *Il turno di notte lo fanno le stelle*, which was nominated for an Oscar and won an award at the Tribeca Film Festival in 2013.

JOHN DOMINI often gets to Naples, where his father was born and raised, and where he still has family. He has taught, published, and served on symposia in the city. In the United States, his writing has won awards in all genres, with fiction in the *Paris Review* and elsewhere, nonfiction in the *New York Times* and elsewhere, including Italian journals. Grants include a fellowship from the National Endowment for the Arts. He has three books of stories, the latest *MOVIEOLA!*, and three novels, two of them set in Naples. One more such story is coming in 2019, completing a trilogy. In 2009, his novel *Earthquake I.D.*, in Italian translation, was runner-up for the Domenico Rea Prize. Other books include a selection of reviews and criticism. He has taught at Harvard, Northwestern, and elsewhere.

FRANCESCO DURANTE, born in Anacapri, teaches the Culture and Literature of Italian Americans at the Università Suor Orsola Benincasa in Naples. As one of Italy's foremost journalists and literary critics, he has written for various Italian newspapers and journals. He is the author and editor of numerous books, including the groundbreaking *Italoamericana. Storia e letteratura degli italiani negli Stati Uniti, 1776–1943*, in two volumes (the second was published with the same title by Fordham University Press in 2014); *Figli di due mondi. Fante, DiDonato & C: narratori italoamericani degli anni Trenta e Quaranta*; *Scuorno (vergogna)*; *I napoletani*; and, together with the late Rudolph J. Vecoli, *Oh Capitano! La vita favolosa di Celso Cesare Moreno in quattro continenti*. He has edited two volumes of Mondadori's prestigious Meridiani series on John Fante and Domenico Rea. In addition to various editions of mannerist and baroque poets and American writers, he has translated seven volumes of John Fante, two by Bret Easton Ellis, and other writers such as William Somerset Maugham, George Arnold, and William Dean Howells. Durante is the artistic director of the annual Salerno Literary Festival. His latest book is *La letteratura italoamericana* (2017).

SIMONA FRASCA earned a doctor's degree in History and Analysis of Musical Cultures at La Sapienza University, Rome. Her field of research is the social history of music, free jazz, the early sound reproduction era in relation to popular production and the Italian migration to the United States. She was a Fulbright Researcher at the Calandra Institute in New York City as well as a freelance music critic. Frasca is the author of *Norah Jones, Piano Girl*; *Birds of Passage: La diaspora dei musicisti napoletani a New York*, which has been translated into English. She is currently working on issues of piracy and the illegal music market in Italy.

JONATHAN GALASSI has translated the poetry of Eugenio Montale, Giacomo Leopardi, and Primo Levi, and is the author of three books of poems, *Morning Run* (1989), *North Street and Other Poems* (2001), and *Left-Handed*

(2013), as well as a novel, *Muse* (2015). He is president and publisher of the publishing house Farrar, Straus & Giroux, in New York City.

FRED GARDAPHÉ is Distinguished Professor of English and Italian American Studies at Queens College/CUNY and the John D. Calandra Italian American Institute. He is the former director of Stony Brook University's American and Italian/American Studies programs. His books include *Italian Signs, American Streets: The Evolution of Italian American Narrative*; *Dagoes Read: Tradition and the Italian/American Writer*; *Moustache Pete Is Dead!*; *Leaving Little Italy*; *From Wiseguys to Wise Men: Masculinities and the Italian American Gangster*; and *The Art of Reading Italian Americana*. He is cofounder/coeditor of *VIA: Voices in Italian Americana* and editor of the Italian American Culture Series of SUNY Press. He is also an editor of i-Italy.org.

PATRIZIA LA TRECCHIA is Associate Professor at the University of South Florida where she directs the Italian Program and Associated Faculty at the USF Patel College of Global Sustainability. Her research includes film, media, literature, globalization, migration, citizenship, the Italian South, food and identity, culture of food, sustainability of diets and food consumption, and food waste. She is the author of one monograph, two textbooks, and over two dozen peer-reviewed articles. Her book *Uno sguardo a Sud* deals with the representation of the Italian South in a global perspective, focusing on the city of Naples in media discourse, literature, film, and music. Her articles have appeared internationally in scholarly peer reviewed journals. She is one of the faculty of the Food Studies Certificate and of the Film Studies Certificate at USF.

ILARIA MARCHESI is Professor of Classics and Comparative Literature at Hofstra University, where she directs the Classics Program. In 2008, she published *The Art of Pliny's Letters: A Poetics of Allusion in the Private Correspondence*, a monograph on intertextuality in the letters of Pliny the Younger for which she won an NEH grant. She also edited and contributed to the book *Pliny the Book-Maker: Betting on Posterity in the Epistles* (2015). Besides epistolography, her research interests include Latin satirical poetry and the ancient novel; she has published articles on Horace, Petronius, and the reception of classical authors in Petrarch. Most recently, she has published *Live in Pompei*

(2016), an essay in narrative form on the cultural value of the archeological past for the young generation, written with her husband, Simone Marchesi.

SIMONE MARCHESI is Associate Professor of Italian Literature at Princeton University. His main research interest is the dialogue established with Latin classics by Italian writers from the medieval period, in particular Dante, Petrarch, and Boccaccio. He has published two monographs in this field: *Stratigrafie decameroniane* (2004) and *Dante and Augustine: Linguistics, Poetics, Hermeneutics* (2011). He has translated into Italian Robert Hollander's monumental commentary on Dante's *Comedy* (2011) and has recently edited the school version of the same commentary (Dante, *La Commedia*, 2016). His current research concerns medieval ideas about translation, as they are reflected in twelfth- to fifteenth-century vernacular fictions, a study provisionally entitled *The Tower and the Garden*.

J. NICHOLAS NAPOLI earned his Ph.D. at Princeton and specializes in baroque art and architecture in Europe and the Americas. He has taught art history and expository writing at Pratt University, Rutgers University, the University of York (UK), the University of Virginia, and Bard College. Napoli has contributed articles to *Napoli Nobilissima*, *Art History*, and *Memoirs of the American Academy in Rome*. He is currently writing a book on the Carthusian monastery in Naples, the Certosa di San Martino.

SALVATORE NAPOLITANO was educated in Naples and Paris and has been Research Fellow and Lecturer at the Warburg Institute, London; the Institut National d'Histoire de l'Art, Paris; the Andrew W. Mellon Foundation, Washington; the Bayeriche Akademie der Wissenschaften, Munich; the Kunst Historische Institut, Florence; Université de Paris-Sorbonne IV, France; University of Malta, Malta; University of Warsaw, Poland; Scuola Normale Superiore, Pisa; Italian Institute of Historical Studies "Benedetto Croce," Naples; and the CNR-Italian Research Council, Rome. He is currently full professor of Humanities (Classics and Italian) at La Scuola d'Italia "Guglielmo Marconi," New York City, while lecturing at New York University as Visiting Scholar in the Classics Department. His interests are focused on the relationship between visual evidence and written texts; the role of monuments in the transmission of cultural memory and identity; and the reception of the classical past in European modern scholarship. He is the author of the forthcoming *"Cold Genius": Luigi Lanzi's "History of Painting in Italy." Art Historiography, Antiquarian Studies, and Philosophy of History in the European Enlightenment*.

GREGORY PELL is a Professor in the Department of Romance Languages and Literatures at Hofstra University, where he teaches courses on language, cinema, literature, and translation theory. His critical articles examine such poets as Dante, Paolo Ruffilli, Mario Luzi, Davide Rondoni, Tommaso Lisa, Mario Tobino, and Eugenio Montale, the latter of which is the subject of his full-length monograph, *Memorial Space, Poetic Time: Memory in Eugenio Montale* (2005). On cinema he has published pieces on Mihaileanu, Kore-Eda, Sergio Rubini, Vicenzo Marra, Mohsen Melliti, and Matteo Garrone. He is coeditor of *At Whom Are We Laughing? Humor in Romance Language Literatures* (2013). His ongoing research projects focus on Vitaliano Trevisan and the Northeast, the prose and poetry of Goffredo Parise, and the narrative works of Angelo Cannavacciuolo, whose latest unpublished novel he is in the process of translating. His newest book is *Davide Rondoni: Art in the Movement of Creation*.

JASON PINE is Associate Professor of Anthropology and Media Studies at SUNY Purchase. His research focuses on people's everyday pursuits of personal sovereignty in alternative economies and alternative ecologies. In his first book, *The Art of Making Do in Naples* (2012), he examined how underemployed aspiring singers become entangled with the Camorra, the region's powerful and volatile organized crime networks. His current book project, *A Decomposition: Meth Labs and the Matter of Life*, is on small-scale methamphetamine manufacture in rural Missouri and the decompositioning of people, objects, and late industrial landscapes. Pine's research has been supported by the Wenner-Gren Foundation, Chemical Heritage Foundation, and the American Academy in Berlin.

STANISLAO G. PUGLIESE is Professor of History and Queensboro UNICO Distinguished Professor of Italian and Italian Studies at Hofstra University. A former research fellow at the Italian Academy for Advanced Studies at Columbia University, the United States Holocaust Memorial Museum,

Oxford University, and Harvard University, he is a specialist on the Italian antifascist Resistance and Italian Jews. He is the author, editor, or translator of fifteen books, including *Bitter Spring: A Life of Ignazio Silone* (2009), winner of the Fraenkel Prize (London), the Premio Flaiano (Pescara), and the Marraro Book Prize in Italian History (American Historical Association). Pugliese is editor of the Italian and Italian American Studies Series with Palgrave Macmillan. He is coeditor, with Brenda Elsey, of *Football and the Boundaries of History: Critical Studies in Soccer* (2017), and, with William J. Connell, of *The Routledge History of Italian Americans* (2018). He is currently working on a new book, *Dancing on a Volcano in Naples: Scenes from the Siren City.*

JOSEPH RESCIGNO has served as Artistic Advisor and Principal Conductor of the Florentine Opera Company (Milwaukee) since 1981 and became Music Director of La Musica Lirica festival in Italy in 2005. In these and other positions as well as guest engagements, he has conducted music from across the repertory for such companies as the Montreal Symphony and the New York City Opera. From 1996 to 2000, he also served as music director of L'Orchestre Métropolitain in Montreal, where he made five studio recordings: *Beethoven, Brahms, Mendelssohn, Mozart,* and *Verismo*. In addition, he conducts the live recordings of *Jōruri* and *Río de Sangre*, two operatic world premieres. Rescigno comes from a long line of musicians on both sides of his family and holds a Master of Music (piano) from the Manhattan School of Music. His home is New York City where he is also working on his first book.

GABRIELLA ROMANI is Professor of Italian at Seton Hall University. Her research is mainly focused on nineteenth-century cultural history and literature: women's participation in the rhetoric of the Risorgimento political and cultural movements, the pedagogical and educational developments of Italy during the pre- and postunification era, popular culture of the late 1800s, gender and cultural studies. She is the coeditor of *Writing to Delight: Italian Short Stories by Nineteenth-Century Women Writers* (2006); has edited and introduced Edith Bruck's *Letter to My Mother* (2007). She is the coeditor two volumes of essays, *The Formation of a National Audience in Italy (1750–1890): Readers and Spectators of Italian Culture* (2017) and *The Printed*

*Media in Fin-Siècle Italy* (2011). She is also editor of Edmondo De Amicis, *Impressioni di Roma* (2011). Her most recent book is *Postal Culture: Writing and Reading Italy in Post-Unification Italy*. She co-translated Enrico Castelnuovo, *The Moncalvos* (2017) and is currently working on a book project about Jewish Italian writers in late–nineteenth-century Italy. Romani is the Director of the Charles and Joan Alberto Italian Studies Institute at Seton Hall University.

CHARLES SANT'ELIA heads Enotria Translations, a boutique translations firm in Manhattan. He studied political science and Italian literature at New York University and political science at the University of Florence before studying law at Pace University. He formerly resided in Naples and Florence and is a member of the Association of the Bar of the City of New York and is a consultant for UNESCO. Sant'Elia is a knight of the Sacro Militare Ordine Costantiniano di San Giorgio. Since 2007 he has served as delegate of the Comitati Due Sicilie of the Associazione Culturale Neoborbonica in the United States and is a member of the Real Circolo delle Famiglie Nobili e Notabili delle Due Sicilie. Sant'Elia has been writing poetry in Neapolitan for twenty-five years and he has translated the scholarly works of linguist Mario Alinei, musicologist Simona Frasca, and Neapolitan poet and songwriter Luciano Somma, among others.

GIOIA TIMPANELLI is one of the founders of the worldwide revival of storytelling. She is one of the handful of artists who significantly changed the way our culture views narrative and the oral tradition. Often called the "Dean of American Storytelling," she is today considered one of the world's foremost storytellers—widely respected as both a master and scholar of the ageless art. She won two Emmy Awards (Citations of Merit) for *Tales from Viet Nam* and for her series of thirty programs on storytelling, *Stories from My House*, on educational television, where she created, wrote, produced, and appeared in eight series of literature programs shown on PBS stations throughout the United States. She has also received the prestigious Women's National Book Association Award for bringing the oral tradition to the American public and the Maharishi Award. She has performed her improvisational telling of ancient and modern stories and given talks in collaboration with respected masters of other art forms, especially in the world of poetry and letters throughout the United States and in other countries. She is one of the founding members of the New York Storytelling Center in New York City. Her most recent book is *What Makes a Child Lucky*.

TERENCE WARD is a writer, documentary producer, and cultural consultant who has worked in the Middle East and the United States. He also participated in humanitarian missions for the Open Society to Burma and the United Nations in East Timor. His first book, *Searching for Hassan: A Journey to the Heart of Iran* (2003), has become a cult classic in America, a best seller in Iran, and is being developed as the first American Iranian coproduction for a feature film to be shot in Iran since the Revolution. His book *The Guardian of Mercy* (2016), is a moving narrative that interweaves Caravaggio's life story with those of people in contemporary Naples whose lives are transformed by the power of art—and mercy. Ward and his wife, Idanna Pucci, are International Trustees of the World Conference of Religions for Peace—the world's largest interfaith organization.

ROBERT ZWEIG is a professor of English at Manhattan Community College of the City University of New York. He teaches courses in Literature, Writing, Modern Poetry, and for many years was the Intensive Writing Coordinator for the college. He has a doctorate in English Literature from the City University of New York. Zweig has numerous peer-reviewed publications in journals, encyclopedias, and books. He is also coauthor of *Literature: An Introduction to Reading and Writing*, a best-selling work. His memoir, *Return to Naples: My Italian Bar Mitzvah and other Discoveries* was translated and published in Italy under the title *Ritorno a Napoli* in 2008, when he was invited by the mayor of Naples to a reception for his book in the City Hall of Naples. He has received several scholarships and awards, including a Mellon Fellowship and the Phi Beta Kappa award for "Outstanding Teaching Skills" as one of the Top Ten Professors at Manhattan Community College.